NEW YORK UNIVERSITY SERIES IN
EDUCATION AND SOCIALIZATION IN AMERICAN HISTORY

The publication of this work has been aided by a grant
from the Andrew W. Mellon Foundation
and
The University of Texas at Austin

The
Revolutionary College

A North-West Prospect of Nassau-Hall, with a Front View of the Presidents House, in New Jersey.

The
Revolutionary College

American Presbyterian Higher Education 1707-1837

Howard Miller

New York • New York University Press • 1976

Library of Congress Catalog Card Number: 75-27053
ISBN: 0-8147-5407-4

Library of Congress Cataloging in Publication Data

Miller, Howard, 1941-
    The revolutionary college.
    Includes bibliographical references.
    1. Presbyterian Church in the U.S.A.—-Education.
I. Title.
LC580.M48   377'.8'5   75-27053
ISBN 0-8147-5407-4

Manufactured in the United States of America

For Ruth

Contents

Acknowledgments

One of the rewards of completing a long-term project is the opportunity finally to express one's appreciation publicly to those who have rendered aid and comfort along the way. In this case they are many. Gordon Wood, John Shy, John Higham, Norman Fiering, and David Potts read all or parts of the book and made incisive criticisms at crucial points of its evolution. A year at the Davis Center for Historical Studies at Princeton brought me into contact with stimulating students of education and provided the freedom to become familiar with what was to me a new field of interest. My thanks to David Allmendinger, Arthur Zilversmit, Gerald Strauss, Selwyn Troen, James McLachlan, and to the Center's Director, Lawrence Stone, for sharing their insights and good cheer with me. One of the delights of the early stages of the study was to make the acquaintance of the archivists and librarians of the colleges I study. Without exception they were unfailing in their good humor and good sense. I am particularly grateful to Mrs. Martha Slotten of Dickinson College, this researcher's dream of an archivist come true. I am also indebted to the staffs of the Departments of History of the two American Presbyterian Churches, the Presbyterian Historical Society in Philadelphia and the Historical Foundation of the Southern Church in Montreat, North Carolina.

I am glad to acknowledge the generous financial support of several institutions. The Horace H. Rackham School of Graduate Studies and the Department of History of the University of Michigan, as well as the Danforth Foundation, financed in part the early stages of research, while the University Research Institute and the Dora Bonham Fund of the Department of History of the University of Texas at Austin assisted in its completion.

Other debts are more personal. At a crucial point early in my academic career Hugh Mason Ayer of North Texas State University made the study of early American history a challenging and rewarding enterprise. More recently Susan and David Allmendinger have aided in ways they cannot fully appreciate. Finally, my greatest debt is to my wife, Ruth Humble Miller, a scholar in her own right who now knows more than she ever needed to know about colonial Presbyterians. She graciously assisted in every stage of the manuscript's preparation and the book is gratefully dedicated to her.

Introduction

This study begins with the conviction that most works of history do not dare enough and that we historians of education are among the most timid of Clio's disciples. Here I have tried to be adventurous without, I trust, being foolhardy. I have taken as my subject one of America's leading religious denominations, the Presbyterians, and for more than a century, 1707–1837, have looked at their views of the good society, politics, and religion as those views helped shape the Presbyterians' first institutions of higher learning. And I have endeavored to fashion from the investigation a central thesis about the early Presbyterian experience that relates directly to crucial changes in American culture. It has been a risky business because it is based on several assumptions that are debatable. The study assumes that it is possible and worthwhile in a monograph to deal with large periods of time and a number of important social institutions; that the articulate elite still have things to tell the historian and are worth listening to; and, most important, that the categories into which historians have divided past human experience—political, religious, economic, etc.—too often stand in the way of addressing the past on its own terms. If, as we have been told of late, the historian of education should study the way in which culture is transmitted from generation to generation, it is appropriate that he or she be among the first to challenge those rigid divisions.

These remarks are made not because they are original. On the contrary, they are all too often made by scholars who then fail to act on them. This has been particularly the case with the students of American religious and educational institutions. Frequently, their work has been preoccupied with the internal history of those institutions. More often than not, their investigations have not been directed by pointed questions at all, but by a desire to present their institutional subjects in the best possible light. Thus, the history of religion in America has too often been self-serving denominational history, rightly scorned by secular historians; while the historian of education in America characteristically has chronicled the story of individual schools and colleges with little or no reference to the social functions of those institutions. The historians of America's religious and educational institutions also have engaged in ideological struggles in which their histories play important parts. Thus, denominational histories have defended one side or another in the dreary procession of ecclesiastical schisms that have punctuated America's religious past. Historians of schools and colleges in America, too, have been arrayed on either side of contemporary pedagogical or curricular squabbles. Too often, then, their histories have been characterized by stultifying antiquarianism, on the one hand, and a stubborn present-mindedness, on the other.*

The present study attempts to overcome some of the limitations of past institutional histories. The work itself, though, began traditionally enough. It was originally planned as a straightforward history of seven colleges and academies established by American Presbyterians before 1800. The first and of course most important of them was Princeton, established in 1746. Within a half-century, sons of Princeton established in the middle states and in the upper south a Presbyterian educational empire consisting of six struggling academies that survived to be numbered among the nation's better liberal arts colleges. They were Hampden-Sydney in the Southside of Virginia and, across the Blue Ridge, Liberty Hall Academy, which finally became Washington and Lee University; in Pennsylvania, Dickinson College in Carlisle, and in the Presbyterian-dominated western part of the state, Washington and Canonsburg academies, the forerunners of the present Washington and Jefferson College; and, finally, in the bluegrass country of Kentucky, the Presbyterians established Transylvania Seminary at Lexington.

Once the prior decisions—to study early American educational institutions and to venture outside New England—were made, the choice of institutional subjects virtually made itself. The Presbyterians obviously were the most active group in establishing schools outside New England in the late colonial period and the early republic. Their colleges were sometimes the first (and in the case of Transylvania, the only) institutions of higher learning in the middle states and the south. Moreover, the colleges that were established in that area by other Protestants, such as the Dutch Reformed Church's Queen's College in New Jersey and the German Reformed Church's Franklin and Marshall College in Penn-

* These points have been effectively made in Bernard Bailyn, *Education in the Forming of American Society* (Chapel Hill, N.C., 1960). But for a critique of Bailyn, see Laurence R. Veysey, "Towards a New Direction in Educational History: Prospect and Retrospect," *History of Education Quarterly,* 9 (Fall, 1969): 343–359; and [the present writer's] "Education in Early America: Documents and Directions," *ibid.* 14 (Fall, 1974): 379–390.

sylvania, were created at least in part to counter what was perceived as Presbyterian domination of existing schools.

For several reasons, the seven Presbyterian institutions were a functional unit that lends itself readily to historical investigation and analysis. They were, of course, all established by Presbyterians within a half-century of each other. And they not only were founded by the graduates of Princeton, but in some instances—Hampden-Sydney, Liberty Hall, and Transylvania—were established in part by the *same* Princetonians. At Princeton the aspiring Presbyterian minister-educators had imbibed the same peculiarly Presbyterian version of Scottish realism, especially after the forceful John Witherspoon took over the college in 1768. There, too, they made life-long contacts, decided to study theology under the same ministers, and married each other's cousins and sisters. By 1800 these young men constituted a unified ministerial elite, an elite that dominated—and in turn unified—the early history of the Presbyterian colleges. Young men at Harvard and Yale, of course, had similar experiences, and like their Presbyterian counterparts at Princeton, they too established colleges late in the century. But the Congregational founders of Williams, Middlebury, and the University of Vermont did not function as parts of a purposive, effective religious hierarchy. The Princeton-educated Presbyterians did, and that fact goes a long way to explain the unity of the Presbyterian colleges they founded.

In organizing the study it became obvious that its unconventional foundation would be the enormous body of records produced by the Presbyterian hierarchy in the eighteenth and early nineteenth centuries. It would rest firmly on the mountains of records produced by sessions, presbyteries, synods, and the General Assembly, and it would put to those neglected records questions never before asked of them. Of course, the records of the colleges themselves suggested all sorts of traditional questions about finances, curriculum, discipline, and pedagogy. And often these were asked. The minutes of the boards, faculties, and student organizations were used, often for the first time by a historian. But continued research indicated that the colleges, although they responded to internal dynamics of their own, were being shaped by forces outside their walls. They were in fact the institutional manifestations of crucial changes within American Presbyterianism. A decision then was made to treat at the same time two fields that historians traditionally had dealt with separately. The work would be a study of both religious and educational institutions.

The records of the colleges suggested that a basic change had been effected within the Presbyterian schools by 1820; that the frontier colleges as well as Princeton were by that date significantly different from what they had been as late as 1795. That change manifested itself in many ways. It affected the way the Presbyterian educators viewed their students—and vice versa. It produced innovations in pedagogy, in discipline, in curriculum, and even in the way the colleges were financed. The changes are clear enough from the records of the schools and are important in and of themselves. The records of the Presbyterian hierarchy, however, put those educational changes into a broader cultural context and give them added meaning and significance.

The changes in the colleges are important, finally, because they reflected, indeed because they were produced by, a basic transformation within American Presbyterianism that also was complete by 1820. The Presbyterians by that date had accepted as a legitimate mode of organized religious life the denominational competition that seemed to follow naturally the Revolutionary generation's decision to end all establishments of religion in the new republic. By 1820 the Presbyterians had created a formidable denominational machinery with which to engage in that competition. That they did so reluctantly should not obscure the more important fact that, like almost all white Americans, the Presbyterians in the early nineteenth century embraced an unexampled experiment in voluntarism.

That experiment was sometimes as strange and frightening to Americans as it was always perplexing to European visitors like Alexis de Tocqueville. Tocqueville's remarks on religion in Jacksonian America are undoubtedly the least incisive in *Democracy in America*. But if he missed the religious nuances of the revolutionary developments in the young American republic, Tocqueville caught as has no other observer, foreign or native, the central change that made possible all others. In fact, the young Frenchman coined the word that thereafter denoted the crucial change, *individualisme*. The Americans, Tocqueville announced in 1835, exulted in the equality they deemed the most significant product, the defining element, of their Revolution. They insisted that no man was by birth or nature superior to any other. Then, secure in that equality, they struggled to rise, theoretically without the aid of the state, in a society where contention and conflict seemed endemic, and competition, the natural state of man. Impetuously, the more adventurous of them cast off all that would impede their rise in the free New World and flung themselves into the wilderness in search of success. On the western frontier—and on the new urban frontier, too—they lived in isolation and sought in themselves and in their families the psychological sustenance they had drawn previously from stable and well-defined communal relationships.

Tocqueville, however, also perceived what historians have been rediscovering of late. Those same Americans were an anxious people, often deeply troubled by the freedom and equality they so stridently demanded. The same society that left them free to rise, left them free also to fall; and, in the absence of an ancient system of caste or class that arbitrarily but universally dictated social positions, failure in America uniquely was fraught with moral implications. A man failed in egalitarian America not because of externalities beyond his control but because of internal, moral weaknesses that he refused to control. That being the case, it did not surprise Tocqueville that the Americans often failed to find within themselves the stabilizing forces that had once flowed from traditional community arrangements. Troubled Americans turned, then, to an insistence on conformity to certain ideals and values and sought in that conformity a secure retreat from the terrifying instabilities that attended freedom and unbridled competition. That conformity might occasionally conflict with the American desire for freedom—a man was free only to do what community standards allowed. But, Tocqueville noted, conformity was the unavoidable complement to the American demand for equality, a demand that invariably was more powerful than the American desire for freedom. Thus, Tocqueville's acute, central observation: Jacksonian Americans were at the same time an egalitarian and a conforming people.

Tocqueville's observations are directly relevant to an understanding of American Presbyterianism in the Age of Jackson and may serve as the key to understanding the fundamental change that slowly transformed the denomination and its institutions in the eighteenth century. Presbyterians in the early republic looked back nostalgically to one social ideal while they lived their lives by a very different one. Their colonial forebears, though often truculent, contentious Scotch-Irishmen, had not accepted the legitimacy of social conflict and competition. Far from it. In the early eighteenth century they adhered to a view of society that was still medieval in many significant ways. In that view, social competition was abhorred as destructive of the common good and the public welfare, phrases that retained meaning for eighteenth-century man. The political, economic, and religious competition that disturbed even those Jacksonians who defended it would have been incomprehensible to early eighteenth-century Americans and only slightly less disturbing to the men who made the Revolution, in whose name competition was later defended.

In the case of the Presbyterians, it is possible to document the change from one view of society to another rather precisely. The study begins and ends with a traumatic revival of religious fervor—it commences with the colonial Great Awakening and concludes with the great frontier revival, the Second Great Awakening of the early nineteenth century. Both dramatic events convulsed American Protestantism, the Presbyterian rather more violently than other denominations. Each revival, in fact, produced a schism, a formal division, in the church. And as they divided, the Presbyterians in each instance debated the fundamentals of social unions. They inquired into their origins, argued over the nature and location of final social authority, and contended over the power and limitations of majorities and the rights and responsibilities of minorities. Most important of all, they prescribed the conditions under which social unions might be dissolved and schism tolerated. The colonial and later republican debates were explicit, far-reaching in their implications, and, for the scholar, invariably enlightening. At their best, they were sophisticated analyses of fundamental issues that historians have heretofore assumed were debated only by politicians and constitution-makers. But, well before the Presbyterians joined the patriot cause, they had debated fully during the colonial schism the perils of undivided, unchecked authority. Before they gave their allegiance to the revolutionary concepts of republicanism and federalism, the Presbyterians had fashioned—in large part out of that schism—an ecclesiastical polity that incorporated elements of both. And northern and southern Presbyterians went to war with each other in 1861 at least in part over the issue of majority and minority rights that half a century earlier had divided the denomination and given birth to not one but two new churches.

The debates attending the eighteenth- and nineteenth-century schisms, then, define the chronological limits of the present study and provide the most important documentary evidence for its central thesis. But those debates also illuminate the Presbyterian response to the American Revolution, that epochal event that stood midway between the two revivals and was itself a greater awakening than either of them. The Revolution was in significant ways the culmination of the colonial revival, the secular fulfillment of its sacred expectations. By the same token, the second Great Awakening was in large measure the work of Protestants who became convinced that the Revolution had not so much fulfilled as betrayed those expectations. It is an important and complicated story. It will suffice in these introductory remarks to make the following comments about the Presbyterians and the Revolution and about the relevance of that relation to the present study.

No single religious group was more firmly identified with the patriot cause than the Presbyterians. More than most denominations, the Presbyterians invested much of their group identity in the war for independence and in its success. The Reverend John Witherspoon, the leader of colonial Presbyterianism, was the only minister to sign the Declaration of Independence. The Presbyterian expectations of the transformation to be worked by the Revolution were as high as those of other denominations, perhaps more extravagant than most. Possibly for that reason, the Presbyterian disillusionment with the Revolution was equally intense. For, no less than the revivals that preceded and followed it, the Revolution raised issues that divided the Presbyterians, now into political rather than religious factions. In Pennsylvania some Presbyterians applauded that colony's new radical republican constitution; others opposed it vehemently. The two sides divided once again over basic issues of social authority and of majority and minority rights. And in Virginia, Presbyterians of the Revolutionary generation disagreed over the implications of the attack on established religion that was mounted by deists like Jefferson and Madison and the pietist sects, most especially the Baptists. The Presbyterian clergy in particular were much disturbed by the end of all compulsory public support for organized religion. But they quickly found themselves out of step with those Presbyterian laymen in Virginia who apparently accepted with fewer qualms than the clergy that important result of the American Revolution. Thus, controversial repercussions of the Revolution—what Bernard Bailyn has aptly called the "contagion of Liberty"—polarized Presbyterians just as they divided other Americans. And in the Presbyterian instance, the polarization produced a third set of articulate debates over the nature of social union. Now, though, the debates were over the origin and structure of secular societies, and assumptions about secular society that had been only implicit in earlier ecclesiastical debates suddenly became explicit. What emerged was a full-blown Presbyterian theory of social union and a tentative defense of the legitimacy of competition within organized societies, if not yet as a positive good, at least as a necessary evil. It was a theory and defense that grew directly out of the debates surrounding the colonial schism and that anticipated and laid the foundation for the final nineteenth-century legitimization of social competition.

As the Presbyterians gradually developed that defense of social competition, they altered fundamentally the nature and function of their institutions of higher learning. Princeton, a product of the colonial Great Awakening, had been conceived of as an integrative institution. It, of course, principally served the Presbyterians; but the college also attracted an intercolonial, interdenominational student body, was supported by a transatlantic evangelical community, and was intended to further the reformation of colonial society that would eventuate in the millennium. The Presbyterian colleges established during and after the Revolution, as well as Witherspoon's Princeton, were intended to inculcate the public and private virtue necessary to sustain the Christian Republic, the secular fulfillment of the Awakening's millennial expectations. And if some Presbyterians had already begun tentatively to defend sectarian colleges as the necessary response to disestablishment, the constrictive implications of their proposals were forced in the last decades of the eighteenth century to coexist with the expansiveness inherent in the republican ideology of the Revolution. By 1820, though, the defenders of sectarian education held the field. The Presbyterians' colleges by that date had become bastions of Presbyterian orthodoxy and important weapons in the sectarian competition of the early nineteenth century. The change was as significant as it was complete.

Beyond the fact that they created important institutions of higher learning, there are several reasons why the eighteenth-century Presbyterians especially reward historical inquiry. They were, for one thing, among the largest of the eighteenth-century denominations. The Scotch-Irish migrations of the 1720s, 1730s, and 1770s swelled the Presbyterian ranks until by 1800 the Presbyterian Ulstermen constituted the single largest non-English element of the white American population. Moreover, the Presbyterian hierarchy proved quite adept at organizing and concentrating the denomination's power, giving the Presbyterians influence even beyond their considerable numbers. And the Presbyterians were a far-flung people. They gravitated quickly to the Pennsylvania frontier and from there followed the Appalachians down to the backcountry of Virginia and the Carolinas. There they were a potent, sometimes a dominant, political and social force. Finally, because they insisted upon college-educated ministers, the Presbyterians produced a highly articulate and unusually vocal clergy, made up of men who were often the spiritual leaders and moral arbiters of numerous frontier villages. As such, they freely expressed opinions on a wide variety of issues of historical importance. Those opinions often were published, and of course they have been studied before in a variety of contexts. But that fact should not preclude the historian from looking carefully for answers to questions not before asked. Thus, while no claims are made for either the universality or the uniqueness of the Presbyterian experience, clearly there are compelling reasons for investigating certain aspects and implications of that experience.

It remains, then, only to make a few observations concerning the organization of the present work. Because of its diverse subject matter and, more important, because of its extensive chronological span, it was thought best to develop the narrative in a topical fashion within a broader chronological scheme. Thus, the work is divided into three broad chronological sections. The first begins with the original Presbyterian settlements in the early eighteenth century, treats the first Great Awakening in depth, and concludes with the reunion that healed the colonial schism. The second, dealing with the revolutionary years between 1775 and 1795, is, of course, dominated by the Presbyterian response to the war for independence and its republican ideology. The final section deals with the Presbyterian disillusionment with the Revolution and with the denomination's reaction to the altered religious landscape of the young republic.

Within each section there are three chapters which attempt to do the same thing for each part. The first of those chapters (the first *two* in the case of Part One) analyzes in depth one of the three Presbyterian debates over the nature of social union. The next chapters, then, relate those debates to the changing Presbyterian perceptions of higher education's social function. These second chapters trace the evolution of the Presbyterian defense of sectarian education within the context of the relevant debates and conclude by discussing the changing ways in which the Presbyterians financed their colleges. The final chapter in each section analyzes the internal arrangements of the Presbyterian schools. These chapters discuss pedagogy, curriculum, and discipline, and are based on the conviction that changes in any of these areas can shed as much light on broader developments in American Presbyterianism as do the articulate debates within the church.

In these last chapters, particularly, it is necessary to discuss developments that have important internal histories of their own. Thus the colonial Presbyterian emphasis on oratory at Princeton is used to illustrate a central point about the millennial expectations of the Presbyterian revivalists. This is not to deny that oratory was everywhere in the eighteenth century gaining in popularity and prestige for reasons that have nothing to do with colonial Presbyterianism, let alone with the millennium. By the same token, many of the developments discussed in the present study have an importance far beyond the Presbyterian reaction to them. The adoption of the Pennsylvania Constitution, the ratification of Virginia's declaration of religious freedom, indeed, the entire debate over the nature and implications of the American Revolution are only a few developments of that nature. All are discussed at much greater length elsewhere. But, treating them as important elements in a study of American Presbyterianism does not detract from their intrinsic importance, nor does it deny that other Americans may have reacted to them in other ways.

The present study will not attempt to go beyond the Presbyterian instance to those other Americans, as important and as imperative as that task eventually will be. That limitation is dictated by the present state of, particularly, American religious history. For all the denominational histories that have been written, for all the hagiographies, we still know very little about the social dimensions and implications of the early history of those denominations. Until that situation is corrected—until we have many more studies like the present one—ambitious works of synthesis seem premature. There will be time enough for those works when we can speak with confidence about the nature of a wide range of denominational experiences in the eighteenth century. To investigate those individual experiences in creative and enlightening ways, at present, is task enough.

List of Illustrations

PART ONE

Reformation
1707–1775

CHAPTER I

The Presbyterian Church as a Social Union

"THAT TRUE CHRISTIAN COMMUNION"

In 1704 a Scotch-Irish Presbyterian missionary sailed from Maryland for London. Francis Makemie, the "father of American Presbyterianism," had for twenty years itinerated through Maryland, Virginia, the Carolinas, and Barbados, first as a young missionary from the Irish Presbytery of Laggan and more recently as the unofficial senior minister of the embryonic Presbyterian Church in British North America. In 1704 Makemie sailed to England for several purposes. He intended to recruit young ministerial candidates for the struggling American church, and he hoped to convey to the English dissenters the colonial dissenters' mounting alarm at the aggressive intentions of the new Anglican Society for the Propagation of the Gospel in Foreign Parts. While in London, though, Makemie undertook a third and equally important task, one that grew immediately out of his experience of the conditions of life in the middle colonies.

While itinerating among the infant Presbyterian congregations in Maryland and Virginia, the Irish missionary became concerned about the failure of stable communities to coalesce and flourish in the area of the Chesapeake Bay. The rivers that fed the bay seemed to lure settlers away from tiny coastal villages and disperse them into the wilderness where no community could protect—or restrain—them. Makemie himself had succumbed to the lure of those rivers and had become a large landholder and a trader as well. But by the time that he sailed for England in 1704, Francis Makemie was convinced that the unwillingness of the Chesapeake men to settle in towns and villages threatened to preclude forever the emergence in the bay area of an ordered and prosperous society. Thus troubled, Makemie composed, presumably in London, and published in 1705 "A Plain and Friendly PERSWASIVE TO THE INHABITANTS OF VIRGINIA AND MARYLAND, For Promoting Towns and Cohabitation," in which he voiced his alarms and prescribed his remedy.

As several scholars have observed recently, the settlers in the middle colonies of British North America, by dispersing to isolated farms outside the confines of stable communities, were merely anticipating what would in the eighteenth and the nineteenth centuries become the characteristic pattern of land settlement in most of Western Europe and North America.[1] Seventeenth- and eighteenth-century observers of that dispersion, however, were much disturbed by it, even when participating in it themselves. Thus, Makemie's plan for promoting towns in the bay area was only one of many such proposals. As early as 1622 Governor Edwin Sandys had urged the necessity of "orderly villages" in a Virginia that had just escaped virtual annihilation at the hands of aroused Indians. Then, in a later, more peaceful period, Virginia appeared to one clerical observer to be as threatened by social dispersion as it had been by Indian attacks. The Reverend John Clayton complained to the Royal Society in 1688 that in Virginia "Plantations run over vast Tracts of Ground . . . whereby the Country is thinly inhabited," and then observed of the Virginians themselves that "their liveing is solitary & unsociable," their trading, "confused and dispersed." Bacon's Rebellion and the uprisings that followed the Glorious Revolution in turn heightened official concern about maintaining control over the dispersed population of the Chesapeake region. Consequently, the Virginia legislature on six different times in the seventeenth century enacted laws establishing port towns or encouraging citizens to at least gather weekly in central locations for communalizing worship services. Each act in its turn was disallowed by the Privy Council or, more often, was ignored by the populace and by the legislators who passed the stillborn acts. The last such piece of futile legislation was passed and allowed to die in 1705, the year in which Makemie appeared in print in London.[2]

Much of Makemie's "Friendly Perswasive" reflected the author's experience as a Chesapeake landowner and trader, emphasizing as it did the need to diversify the bay area's economy and especially the "absolute Necessity for falling off the excessive part of Tobacco-making, and falling upon something else . . . ." But at the center of the minister's analysis was his view of social unions and of the ways in which they should be ordered and maintained. The principal issue was immediately joined. Some way must be found, Makemie believed, "for allying the Heats, and curing the Animosities both in the Ecclesiastical and Political Body of the present Constitution of Virginia . . . ." Those conflicts originated in what was for Makemie the single most alarming fact about the societies then emerging in British North America. Certainly he was disturbed by the overproduction of tobacco in the bay area, no less than he was concerned about the failure of towns to emerge in Maryland and Virginia. But beyond those concerns was Makemie's perception that those developments, as disturbing as they doubtless were, were only manifestations of the disintegration in the New World of the venerable idea of organic social union. Men in the bay area became infatuated with the unparalleled opportunities for advancement in the tobacco colonies, and in their rush for economic aggrandizement blindly pursued their own selfish interests and ignored the claims of the social organism of which they were only a part. It was that selfishness on an appalling scale that seemed to Makemie to threaten the realization of ordered societies in the middle colonies. Thus, in the strongest language of his pamphlet, the Irish missionary urged his adopted countrymen to reverse immediately a course that could otherwise eventuate only in social catastrophe. He insisted that they at long last put on the public spirit that too long had been absent from the conduct of public affairs in the bay area. The colonists must "combine with harmonious and united Counsels, avoiding Partiality, waving Self-Interest, or causing it [to] truckle to the Common Good." Then, they must arm themselves "against all dividing Debates, and smother or stifle all Heats" in their public deliberations.[3]

The Presbyterian Church to which Makemie addressed his "friendly perswasive," though a child of the Protestant Reformation, in many ways found congenial the organicism that informed the pamphlet. As an ecclesiastical system, presbyterianism was characterized by an emphasis on hierarchy and on orderly relations among congregations, as opposed to congregationalism's insistence on congregational autonomy. Doubtless a seventeenth-century Presbyterian would have objected strenuously to any suggestion that his church was hierarchical in nature. "Hierarchy" was still associated at best with Laudian episcopalianism and at worst with the Catholic panoply of bishops, archbishops, cardinals, and pope that had been instrumental in bringing on the Reformation in the first place. A Presbyterian instead would have defined his church by the fact that local congregations chose their own pastors and then elected lay elders from among the membership to assist the minister in governing the congregation. That of course was true but was no less true of congregational polity. Clearly what distinguished presbyterianism, especially from congregationalism, was the relationship among session, presbytery, and synod. In that relationship is to be found presbyterianism's hierarchical nature and its affinity for organicism.

As an ecclesiastical system, presbyterianism was believed to be particularly capable of producing a unified society because it provided a framework for ascertaining, establishing, and protecting the "general will" and the "common good" of an ecclesiastical union. Within individual congregations the elders, who made up the session, cooperated with their minister to determine the needs and wishes of the congregation. These sometimes were determined by directly consulting with the members. At other times the minister and session decided upon the congregational general will in private convocation. In like manner the presbytery, which was composed of sessional representatives, ascertained the general will of that larger body while annually sending representatives to the synod, which legislated the common will of the entire church. To ensure that only the common will of the church was furthered and the common good served, each level of the hierarchy vigilantly checked the potential ambitions of the others. Ideally, the system permitted the lower levels to influence the decisions of the upper and thus prevent any level from becoming tyrannous. At the same time, the hierarchy gave the presbytery and then the synod the opportunity to rise above the interests of the individual sessions and presbyteries and to legislate in the best interests of the entire ecclesiastical union.[4] The hierarchy also efficiently translated ecclesiastical theory into reality. By 1700 Presbyterians in Switzerland, England, and especially in Scotland were promoting the interests of their denomination with an effectiveness that was due only in part to the devotion of the true believer. By that date the doctrines that were common to Presbyterians had been codified into the Westminster Confession of Faith, which gave verbal form to the organic unity of those who subscribed to it.[5] When, as in Scotland during the reign of William and Mary, the Presbyterian Church became the established church of a state, the church's propensity for organic unity was fully satisfied—the interests of church and state were one.

But if presbyterian ecclesiology could for these and other reasons foster church order, Presbyterian theology was potentially destructive of that organic unity. Presbyterians, like all other disciples of John Calvin, faced alone the awful God of reformed theology, the revolt against Catholicism having swept the heavens clear of all mediators between the deity and fallen man except for Jesus Christ. To be sure, the "covenant" theologians of the late sixteenth and early seventeenth centuries in effect had bound the deity and emphasized, first tentatively and then with increasing precision, the individual's role in the process of salvation. They urged fallen man to seek out and to cultivate any spark of divine favor within, always insisting, though, that his efforts finally would fail if he was not of the elect.[6] Thus the Calvinist in the seventeenth century was enjoined to seek that which he might not find, to attempt that which he might never accomplish. The resultant introspection and uncertainty fundamentally affected individual Calvinists. Their biographies reveal men and women who were intensely aware of themselves *as individuals*— sometimes tormented, sometimes ecstatic—but always individuals.[7] Most of those individuals confined their solitary struggles to their own hearts and remained within the structure and procedures of the church. But the occasional enthusiast obeyed what he perceived as a higher law. Enthusiastic or aggrieved Presbyterians in sufficient numbers could disrupt the operations of the hierarchy. Worse still, they could gain control of one of its parts—session, presbytery, or synod—and turn it against the rest of the organism. Or, most seriously, they could simply deny the claims of shared interests and renounce the jurisdiction of the hierarchy altogether.

For the first decades of its existence, the American Presbyterian Church was able to hold together the potentially antagonistic aspects of its theology and ecclesiology. That success is not really surprising because for the first half-century of its history in America the Presbyterian Church was content merely to survive. Indeed, the historian must engage in a wide-ranging "sorting out" process to untangle the "people of Presbyterian persuasion" from the Congregationalists of New England, the Anglicans of the south, and, especially, from the rich religious heterogeneity of the middle colonies. The first Presbyterian settlements were made in the mid-seventeenth century on Long Island by New Englanders who tended toward a presbyterial rather than a congregational polity.

Later in the century similar settlements were made in the Raritan River valley of New Jersey, at just about the time Makemie was establishing his Presbyterian outposts on the eastern shores of Maryland and Virginia. Small Presbyterian congregations were gathered simultaneously in both New York City and Philadelphia, while in New England a very small contingent of Scotch-Irish and French Presbyterians was laying the foundations for a peculiar New England branch of American Presbyterianism. In the seventeenth century these scattered Presbyterian gatherings were essentially autonomous congregations. They called their own ministers, maintained discipline themselves, and generally concentrated on surviving. They were anomalous institutions: Presbyterian churches without a presbytery.[8]

In the first decade of the eighteenth century the Presbyterian inclination toward hierarchy and union asserted itself to alter this extraordinary situation. Indeed, that decade produced a marked shift toward organization and centralization throughout American Christendom. The Anglicans led off in 1701 by introducing the missionaries of the Society for the Propagation of the Gospel in Foreign Parts into the British colonies. Then, in 1707, the rigorously congregational Baptists organized the Philadelphia Baptist Association to strengthen their councils. More significantly, in 1708 the Connecticut Congregationalists adopted the Saybrook Platform, setting up a system of "consociations" that would function informally as presbyteries did in arbitrating disputes between congregations. Finally, in 1706 and 1707, the scattered Presbyterian churches created the Presbytery of Philadelphia, thus instituting the fundamental requirement for a presbyterian form of ecclesiastical government. By 1716 the presbytery had grown to nineteen members representing forty congregations and about three thousand members. In that year the presbytery was divided into three new presbyteries, and when those in turn created the Synod of Philadelphia, the hierarchy was complete.[9] At its annual meeting in Philadelphia the synod gathered representatives from the middle colonies and Virginia, attempted to promote an intercolonial perspective and to resolve disputes over ministerial qualifications and presbyterial and sessional boundaries. It heard complaints against ministers by congregations—and vice versa—and it sought to mediate between the various national components of its membership. It did not always succeed in maintaining peace, but that should not obscure the larger fact that almost synonymously with its birth American Presbyterianism established a system charged with unifying and fostering the common interests of a growing segment of American society.

For the first twenty years of its existence the Presbyterian hierarchical system functioned properly. Members of a settled congregation were not allowed to separate from that congregation without the consent of their pastor. Thus, in 1728 the synod forced a renegade faction of Malachi Jones's congregation at Abington, Pennsylvania, to return to his care and to acknowledge that their action had been a "disorder and a fault for which they are very sorry . . . ." [10] Moreover, the hierarchy, through the presbyteries, controlled the placement of ministers. The presbytery super-intended the "calling" of a minister, insisted that the call be unanimous, and required that all male members of the congregation pledge a stated amount to the prospective minister's support. Duly elected, the minister arrived among his congregation clothed in the authority of the hierarchy. That authority derived not from any personal merit the minister might possess but instead followed from his having been "appointed and author-ized by God," and, in the words of the Reverend Jonathan Dickinson, acting in God's "name and stead." [11]

In his divinely appointed position the Presbyterian minister exercised the powerful, informal functions of catechizing, teaching, and preaching, each of which depended to some extent upon the skill and personality of the individual minister. The minister's authority over the church ses-sion, however, was formal and not so dependent upon personality for its efficacy. He presided, for instance, when the session sat as an ecclesiastical court and tried cases dealing with adultery, theft, assaults, breaking the sabbath, and all manner of business frauds, especially those dealing with land transactions. When the session could not satisfy both parties in a dispute, the aggrieved party was expected to take his complaint to the next level of the Presbyterian hierarchy, not to a court of law. Unfor-tunately, colonial Presbyterians apparently hauled each other into court at the slightest provocation. The extent of Presbyterian litigation became so notorious that several presbyteries felt obliged to warn against it repeatedly. Thus the Donegal Presbytery lamented the "spirit of contention & un-charitable stifness of temper" among its members and condemned their willingness to sacrifice the peace of Christ's church to "their own privat interests & humor." [12] The session had the power to censure, suspend, and expel members from church privileges, and as long as the elders were united among themselves and supported the minister in those decisions, the session as ecclesiastical arbiter of public morals in small villages was a potent force indeed.

Just as the ministers sought to preserve the unity of their churches on the local level, so the presbyteries endeavored to maintain that unity on a larger scale. Crucial to that effort was a continuing struggle to preserve the integrity and boundaries of individual congregations. Already in the early eighteenth century factions arose in local churches, and dissidents demanded the right to establish separate congregations. They were motivated sometimes by an antipathy to the pastor, less often by doctrinal disagreements, and usually by a simple desire for a more convenient meeting house. Before 1730 those demands were almost invariably denied.[13] And the presbyteries insisted that no minister preach within their bounds without permission and that no minister interfere with another's congregation. Then, after 1716, the synod and presbyteries alike were on guard against "unqualified" Irish itinerants who came from the Old World to plague the New.

For the most part, though, the Presbyterians did in fact as well as in theory "dwell in peace" for a quarter-century. The church's scattered constituency did not question the as yet unarticulated interests and doctrines that were assumed to unite the body. In a frontier environment hostile to institutions of any kind the immature hierarchy intelligently allowed what contention it could not prevent and maintained the whole. There were, of course, disturbances that led many to complain of "unhappy jarrs and contentions." But these instances are noteworthy for their isolation and amicable resolution and, rather than documenting widespread disunity and unrest, they illuminate the ways in which the hierarchy functioned to maintain unity. For as Jonathan Dickinson said, the American church was "a Garden enclosed, a Fountain sealed, . . . [and] a Vineyard given out by Parcels, to proper keepers . . . ." Around it those keepers had erected a high "Hedge of Discipline." So long as the hedge held and the workers did not quarrel among themselves, the garden would prosper.[14]

PRELUDE TO CONFLICT:
THE SUBSCRIPTION CONTROVERSY

While the organic ideal was reflected in reality as well as expounded in rhetoric, while the clergy and their constituency shared basic if unarticulated interests, the colonial Presbyterians did not analyze, discuss, much less debate the nature of their union. In the 1720s, though, several older clergymen from Ulster joined the Synod of Philadelphia. They brought with them the scars of a long, acrimonious battle within the Synod of Ulster to require subscription to the Westminster Confession of Faith as a condition for membership in that body. The Subscriptionists had prevailed in 1722, and in 1726 had excluded those who refused to subscribe.[15] Some of the men most intimately involved in that struggle found their way to America in the late 1720s. Sternly orthodox, the Scotch-Irish clerics instinctively rebelled against what they perceived as the laxity of the young American hierarchy. In the 1727 meeting of the synod they demanded that the synod require its members to subscribe to the Confession. That demand occasioned the first sustained debate over the nature of the Presbyterian union in America.

The issues in the Subscription Controversy were most thoroughly analyzed by John Thomson, a Scotch-Irish advocate of subscription, and by Jonathan Dickinson, the New England-born leader of the opposition.[16] Thomson argued, traditionally enough, that each ecclesiastical or civil society "must have some bond of union, by which the several Parts are joyned together, to make or constitute them one entire whole . . . ." That process was a mechanical one. Union did not evolve naturally and unaided from the shared interest of a society. Rather, it *followed* the rigorous codification and public adoption of those interests. Thus, a union was viable only when its true members—and enemies—were identified and its physical and intellectual boundaries demarked and defended. Subscription would flush out the "secret Bosom enemies" within the church and fortify it against "all Assaults and Invasions" from without.[17]

Jonathan Dickinson shared neither Thomson's alarm at the state of the American church nor his view of social union. The third-generation Puritan insisted that societies were unified not by externally imposed creeds but by internalized bonds that were not susceptible to codification and subscription. The church was united by certain principles of theology and ecclesiology, *not* by heavy-handed efforts to force subscription to those principles. On the contrary, attempts at enforced subscription historically had divided rather than united the church, which had been most effectively united when its external bonds were weakest. It seemed axiomatic to Dickinson that anything creating *"Disunion* and Division" could not be made a *"Bond* of *Union."* And, if union could not be established on divisive ideas, neither could it be defended by contention. The Christian must not "maintain and defend the Truths of the Gospel, by Schisms, Contentions and Confusions . . . ." Rather, Dickinson concluded, he must adhere to those unarticulated fundamentals that united the church and tolerate those who differed on nonessentials.[18]

Thomson accepted none of Dickinson's arguments. Far from causing schism, he insisted, subscription would establish a common mind within the church. And in the unlikely case that schism should follow enforced subscription, not the creed itself but those who refused to adopt it would be the source of disunion. Those few who could not subscribe in good conscience should separate, hopefully to cooperate in the future with the true—and now pure—Presbyterian church when they could. For in the final analysis, Thomson believed, it was a "Pity to deprive a whole Church of the Benefit of such an excellent Confession, for the Scruples perhaps of a few . . . ."[19]

Clearly Thomson was willing to test Dickinson's warning that subscription would divide permanently the Presbyterian union. Of course he did not enthusiastically embrace schism. Peace and unity are "sweet and beautiful," Thomson gladly admitted, "when joined with Truth and a good conscience . . . ." But when they are not, he declared, *truth* must prevail. And just as he accepted the possibility of a struggle for the truth, he articulated a martial image of Christ that strikingly contrasted with a more traditional image of the Prince of Peace. Not surprisingly, Dickinson rejected the image of Christ militant and affirmed the traditional image. But Dickinson asserted his *own* willingness to do battle for justice and truth in Christ's stead. In particular, he insisted upon his right to defend his cause in print. In fact, Dickinson and Thomson both became combatants in causes they believed righteous and took their cases directly to the members of the church—and to the public—in a series of pamphlets.[20] And as they openly debated the nature of the Presbyterian union, they inevitably weakened it by exposing in public its lack of a common will. In those pamphlets the two combatants articulated assumptions and ideas that now served as the rallying points for hostile camps rather than as the bonds of union for an entire church.

But the subscription controversy was only a prelude to more divisive debates still in the future. In a manner redolent of a more peaceful era, the controversy was settled in 1729 by compromise. Bowing to Scotch-Irish pressure, the synod agreed to require subscription. But anticipating protests from Dickinson and from younger Ulstermen, the synod also passed an "Adopting Act" that allowed candidates for the ministry to register their scruples about any part of the Confession deemed "non-essential" by the synod. Thus the hierarchy endeavored to identify, externalize, and codify the society's bonds of union without alienating those who believed those bonds to be beyond human contrivance.[21]

AN ARMY WITH BANNERS

The task proved impossible. In the 1730s martial images began to appear frequently in Presbyterian sermons and in the deliberations of the hierarchy, while a decade of contention within the churches tore the denomination apart. In 1741 the American Presbyterian Church officially split in two. It had become, in the metaphor most frequently used to describe its alarming state, "an army with banners."

In the face of increasing demands for congregational divisions, the hierarchy at first vacillated. Very few such requests had been granted in the 1720s. But in 1735 the Donegal Presbytery reluctantly allowed some of the members of the Forks of the Brandywine Church in Pennsylvania to establish a separate congregation. The presbytery, however, took extraordinary measures to protect the established congregation. A list of all those planning to separate had to be presented to the minister, who could prevent anyone from leaving if he chose. The settled congregation was given a veto over the site of the new building, all arrears were to be paid the settled minister before anyone left his care, and the dissidents were forbidden to bury anyone in their cemetery until the settled congregation was completely satisfied with all new arrangements.[22] The presbytery instructed each session to keep a record of its proceedings for annual inspection, and it agreed to rotate its annual meetings among its churches to facilitate direct contact with each session and pastor.[23]

In the latter half of the 1730s the presbyteries grew very reluctant to allow separations. Dissidents were told to remain under their minister's care and to be grateful for their blessings and privileges.[24] The Presbytery of Philadelphia in 1738 even institutionalized perpetual conflict rather than allow a separation. When the congregation at Neshaminy, Pennsylvania, divided over whether the aged William Tennent should hire an assistant, the presbytery demanded that an assistant be hired and that each party remain in the church and support either the minister or his new assistant. As vacancies occurred in the church's membership, they were to be filled by equal numbers from each side.[25] The presbyteries were even more adamant about protecting a settled congregation in those few instances in which a division was allowed. If the settled part of a congregation complained, for instance, that a proposed building of a seceding faction threatened the established church, both sides were required to attend a perambulation of the contested area. At times the presbytery even notched trees to mark off the boundaries of old and new congregations. And if too many objections were raised about the new establishment, the presbytery would simply refuse to allow it.[26]

But by 1740 the presbyteries were fighting a losing battle and knew it. Their efforts to maintain unity in the churches only caused the congregations to split faster into warring factions. To an extent, the ecclesiastical machinery that was intended to reduce congregational frictions instead encouraged them. In each decision it made concerning a proposed separation, a presbytery added its authority to one of the two sides and alienated the other. And the necessity of winning the presbytery's support often intensified each faction's propagandistic efforts. Finally, the meeting of the presbytery itself ceased to be a forum for ordered and rational discussion of differences and became an arena for unrestrained combat. So long as there was a recognizable common good to be established and protected, the presbytery served an important function in furthering it. But when unanimity of interest disappeared, the presbytery became something to gain control of to further a "party" interest.

Thus, many ministers gradually lost control of their congregations while the presbyteries became the objects of heated competition for their control. After 1729 the struggle for control of the synod was even more heated. The older Scotsmen, on the one hand, and the New Englanders and younger Scotsmen, on the other, divided in the 1730s over the related issues of ministerial examinations and qualifications, the relation of piety to learning, ministerial itineration, and, most important, the origins of the revivals that began in that decade. By 1740 the lines were drawn, and the hierarchical machinery began to break down at the synodical level. Different levels of the hierarchy ceased to communicate with each other through channels and instead began to denounce each other in the public press. Disunion was inevitable.

In June of 1741, amid a heated pamphlet war and acrimonious synodical debates, the Presbyterians split into factions immediately styled the Old and the New Sides. That division was but part of the turmoil occasioned by the central event of colonial American history, the first Great Awakening. Lesser revivals had flared up in the Dutch churches of the Raritan River valley and in Jonathan Edwards's congregation in Northampton, Massachusetts, during the 1730s. But it was not until the English evangelist George Whitefield arrived in the colonies first in 1739 that the American phase of a general revival of pietistic religion began. The pulpits of virtually all churches were opened to Whitefield as he preached from Georgia to Maine, leaving in his wake a transformed religious landscape. But by 1741 the euphoria had abated. Critics arose to denounce the techniques of Whitefield and his disciples and to warn of the enthusiastic excesses which the revival had begun to produce. Church by church, Christian America divided into opponents and supporters of the revival. The schism in the Presbyterian Church was simply the most spectacular of those divisions.

Perhaps the most important fact about the Presbyterian schism is the reluctance with which the Presbyterians on both sides entered into it. In the year before the schism George Gillespie, a leading Old Side minister, preached a sermon against division within the church, using as his text Paul's rebuke to the Corinthian Christians who had split into his followers and those of Apollos and Cephas. All are of Christ, declared the apostle, and Gillespie echoed with, "In the Church of Christ triumphant in Heaven, there are no divisions; but a perfect Unity and Holy Harmony." The New Side Jonathan Dickinson agreed. The opportunity to reconcile the warring children of God was man's greatest privilege and his most solemn duty, he affirmed. Gillespie had recourse to the organic theory of society in a graphic way in denouncing social division. "We would esteem that Man mad, that would be tearing the Flesh, and eating the Members of his own Body." Why then, he asked, should the members of the body of Christ try to devour each other? [27]

One should pay a great deal of attention to the Presbyterians' assertions that they abhorred disunion. That sincere abhorrence eventually would end the schism. But while they protested that they sought only peace, both sides in 1741 were at great pains to demonstrate that the Bible sanctioned contention and even disunion in the cause of truth. In the Subscription Controversy of 1729 John Thomson had insisted that the church must "fortify itself against all Assaults and Invasions that may be made upon the Doctrine it professeth according to the Word of God." The "secret Bosom Enemies" of the church must be ferreted out and marked so they could no longer deceive. To that end enforced subscriptions and oaths were entirely appropriate. And if worse came to worse, had not Christ said that he came not to bring peace but sword, fire, and division to the earth? [28] In 1729 Jonathan Dickinson had rejected Thomson's martial arguments entirely.[29] A decade later Dickinson was still maintaining that "Nothing can be more contrary to the Spirit and Tenour of the Gospel, than divisive Principles and Practices." [30] And in 1741 the young New Side evangelist Samuel Finley warned that a divided church would "destroy itself by intestine Broils, and become an easy Prey to a foreign Enemy." But Finley in the year of the schism also noted that godly men like Paul and Elijah had contended for the truth with great vigor. And Finley quoted the scripture invoked earlier by Thomson and rejected by Dickinson: Christ had come with a sword to divide each family against itself.[31]

It remained for the controversial New Side leader, Gilbert Tennent, to put into its definitive form the argument that the Bible sanctioned conflict and schism. In a notorious sermon preached at Nottingham on the Pennsylvania-Maryland border, Tennent in 1740 warned of the dangers to religion of an "unconverted" ministry. In that diatribe he had observed that the natural enmity between good and evil in the world "will now and then be creating Jarrs," and in 1741 he granted that "Divisions are to be lamented" because they encouraged sinners to scorn the people of God. But Tennent insisted that the Bible clearly indicates that the gospel would always be attended to a greater or less degree by divisions. He quoted in full the scripture about Christ coming with a sword and made the now perfunctory qualification that contending for the truth was never the real cause of division but "the innocent Occasion only." Obviously for Tennent the primary cause of schism was the Old Side's opposition to Christ's cause. To that cause Tennent was ready to sacrifice peace and union. With Martin Luther he affirmed finally that "an honourable and necessary War was preferable to a mean and ignoble Peace."[32]

In the end, though, the Presbyterians embraced disunion not because a tortured reading of a few scriptures permitted it but because both sides became convinced that they were simply too different in fundamental ways to remain in a union that no longer served any purpose. In 1740 Gilbert Tennent had asked, "Can Light dwell with Darkness?"[33] But the Old Sides retorted, if they were as evil as the New Sides presented them, the revivalists had no choice but to separate from them.[34] The Old Side Robert Cross believed that the contentions of the 1730s had made disunion unavoidable, as indeed they probably had. "In sum, a continued Union, in our Judgment, is most absurd and Inconsistent, when it is so notorious, that our Doctrine and Principles of Church Government, in many Points, are not only diverse, but directly opposite: For, how can two walk together, except they be agreed?"[35] Once the fundamentals that were supposed to have united the Presbyterians were examined closely, it appeared that they disagreed about them in important ways. That disagreement, the Old Side argued, "dissolves the Bond of Society," and in that case an "orderly Separation" was to be preferred over "united

Schism." [36] By 1741 the Old and New Side alike agreed that "a regular
Separation, tho' the last Remedy, would be less hazardous to Truth,
Peace, and good Order, among us, than such a schismatical Union as
hath subsisted among us for some Years past. For the last Remedy is a
Remedy still, and much better than a desperate Disease, which threatens
no less than the whole Constitution." [37]

THE NATURE OF AUTHORITY

What had happened between 1729 and 1741 to lead the American
Presbyterians to believe that they disagreed with each other on the most
basic of religious issues? It is true of course that the Awakening was
enormously divisive and raised major controversies about theology and
ecclesiology. In the debates that followed, however, the Presbyterians
realized that they disagreed also about the nature of social unions and
social authority.

The immediate cause of the Great Schism of 1741 was disagreement
over the authority of the synod to dictate the requisite qualifications of
its own membership and the membership of the presbyteries under its
control. For two years before the schism the opponents of the revival
attempted to use the synod to prevent the evangelically oriented Presbytery
of New Brunswick from ordaining men whom the Old Sides deemed
uneducated. Then in June of 1741 the Old Sides in effect expelled the
supporters of the revival from the synod, arguing that the synod certainly had the authority to determine its own membership. [38]

To the Old Sides the issue of authority was simple. First, in all social
unions final power was indivisible, in the words of Thomson, "a power
invested in one Person or Party, to command, oblige, and require another
to do such a Thing, tho' it be contrary to his own Will, Judgment or
Inclination, and what he would not do, were he at his own Command."
To divide that ultimate authority among two or more bodies would "sap
and overthrow the very Fundamental Laws of all Societies in the World:
For how is it possible that any Society can stick together unless . . . all
be Subject to the Authority of one . . . ?" That indivisible power also
was absolute. Certainly the presbyteries and sessions retained all sorts
of rights, Thomson conceded. But he cautioned that "if the Synod had
no power to bind its members in all matters, then it had power to bind
them in none." [39]

To the Old Sides it was obvious that final, indivisible authority rested in the synod because all Presbyterians were represented in that body. All Presbyterians were also represented in the session and in the presbytery; indeed the representation in each was "actual," that is, the ministers and elders who served at both of those levels of the hierarchy were directly elected by other members of the local congregation for that purpose. At the synodical level, too, each minister and elder was assumed to represent his individual church and presbytery in a literal sense. But in addition they were believed to "virtually" represent all Presbyterians because all were assumed to share certain common interests. As a judicatory, Thomson believed, the synod represented "the whole collective Body" of the Presbyterian Church; therefore, when the synod made a decision, it bound the entire church because those decisions "are the Conclusions of a just Representative of that Body; and consequently are virtually the Conclusions of the Whole . . . ." The synod could make no decisions detrimental to the liberties of its churches because its members were members of those churches and, Thomson declared, men will not make laws that harm themselves. The Old Side theory of indivisible authority was based on the belief that the members of the Presbyterian churches and their representative rulers shared certain common interests and that the existence of those interests and shared goals protected the people from their rulers' becoming tyrants who heedlessly disregarded the people's rights while pursuing their own selfish and distinct interests.[40]

The Old Sides believed that the indivisible authority of the synod was based upon a written, publicly subscribed creed, a formal statement of those doctrines that at the same time unified Presbyterians and set them off from all other groups of Christians. The Old Sides thus rejected the New Side suggestion that the scriptures alone could serve as the church's creed and that men in the same denomination could agree on scriptural fundamentals while disagreeing on certain specifics. All Christians "owned the scriptures," Thomson reminded his opponents, and for the Presbyterians to do only that would in no way set them apart. For the Old Sides the Presbyterian community could never be "a mixt Communion of different Perswasions; who yet hold the Foundation . . . ."[41] It must instead agree upon the Christian "truth" as interpreted by the final authority of the synod and then codify that truth while there were still enough "friends of truth" in the synod to assure its passage. Without that creed, the Old Sides argued, corrupt men would be allowed to enter the ministry and preach error because "the Truth was never publicly received among us."[42]

Like authority, the Old Sides believed that "truth" was unitary, indivisible, and they believed that it was at all times knowable. In the scriptures, God had supplied a yardstick by which all ideas and acts could be accurately judged. With that guide, godly men could—and must—ferret out error. In all debates, the Old Side reminded the New, "one Side must be wrong." [43] That view of course made the Old Sides very reluctant to compromise any position once taken. And when they were chided for their stubbornness, they replied with impeccable logic, "If the Opinion we maintain be true and right, surely it's no Fault to be stiff in it . . . ." [44] Thus they rebuffed early attempts to heal the Great Schism. Surely, they insisted, in such a division "one of the parties at least, must be certainly and really in the fault . . . ." [45]

The New Sides challenged the Old Side views on authority at all points. They were particularly suspicious when the Old Sides asserted that certain shared interests made the members of the synod the "virtual" representatives of all American Presbyterians. The New Sides were more interested in limiting—and especially dividing—authority in the church. The young revivalist Samuel Blair insisted in 1744 that there must somewhere be a proper medium between "Tyranny and Anarchy; between unjust Oppression and lawless Confusion." [46] The New Sides believed that they were merely rejecting the extremes of both. In the decade after the Subscription Controversy of 1729, they had objected to virtually every attempt to expand the powers of the synod at the expense of the presbyteries. They had forced a modification of the Subscription Act itself and then the repeal of laws that forbade ministerial itineration and that required all ministerial candidates to be examined by a synodical committee prior to licensing and ordination. While the Old Sides sought to make acquiescence in each of those rules a prerequisite for synodical communion, the revivalists objected simply that the synod had no authority to pass such "legislation."

The New Sides at all times asserted the sufficiency of Scripture as the basis of all ecclesiastical authority and denounced any exercise of power not explicitly sanctioned in the Bible. Jonathan Dickinson could find no biblical foundation for subscription, and Gilbert Tennent later extended Dickinson's arguments in the Subscription Controversy to suggest that the continual enactment of ecclesiastical rules reflected a basic doubt about the sufficiency of the Bible and its injunctions. Both he and Samuel Blair insisted that, in the absence of one of those injunctions, the synod must only advise the lower levels of the hierarchy, not "legislate" for them. Dickinson was most emphatic on the subject. Unscriptural injunctions usurped Christ's authority over His church and therefore must be opposed even when they are "painted over, with the fair Colours of *Apostolick Tradition, Antiquity, Order and Decency, the Band of Union and Communion, the Well-Government or greater Good of the Church*, or whatever other Pretence . . . ."[47]

Like the Old Sides the revivalists believed that the broad outlines of presbyterian ecclesiology were of divine origin. For all he knew, Dickinson declared, that system was "the most conformed to the *Laws of Christ*, of any whatsoever; and does . . . as exactly quadrate with the Rule, as may be hoped for in this state of Imperfection." But Dickinson cautioned that Christ had left very few specific instructions concerning ecclesiology; consequently, mere mortals must be very careful about claiming divine authority for man-made innovations.[48] The New Sides reminded their opponents that the Protestant Reformation had opposed the Catholic assertion that all sorts of trivial religious laws were of divine ordination and necessary to salvation.[49] It behooved Protestant hierarchies, Samuel Blair believed, merely to suggest that a certain law "tended" in the "general direction" of the scriptures and that such laws were acceptable expedients for producing some good among the people of God. Those laws, it went without saying, must never become part of the church's terms of communion.[50]

Perhaps the most effective criticism the New Sides made of the Old Side emphasis on confessions, creeds, and subscriptions is that it would inevitably produce schism. Tennent reminded his opponents that men of good will would always be of "different Minds" about the great scriptural truths and that to coerce subscription to one specific version would only open the way for "a Succession of Schisms in the Church of God."[51] During the Subscription Controversy Dickinson attempted to demonstrate that allegation. Before the Council of Nice, he observed, the church had been preserved not only as a "Garden enclosed, but a Garden of Peace." After the Council imposed its creed, however, the church fell into innumerable schisms and produced heresies on an unprecedented scale. Under the papacy, he continued, confessions had been the traditional engine of tyranny, and a subscription controversy was at the moment tearing the Church of Ireland apart. Finally, Dickinson suggested that throughout history confessions and creeds had failed even on their own terms. They did *not* ensure doctrinal purity. Creeds were not needed to confirm true Christians, and a hypocrite would subscribe to anything. All Christians subscribe to the scriptures, but that had not

prevented Christianity from becoming a *"Babel Confusion* of Sectaries."
In the final analysis creeds could not produce doctrinal uniformity
because each Christian would subscribe to his own sense of the confession.
That is, of course, exactly what the Presbyterians had institutionalized
with the Adopting Act of 1729.[52]

The Old Sides answered some of the New Side charges more easily
than others. For instance, they quickly dismissed the allegation that the
synod was imposing new and unscriptural rules on unwilling members.
Far from being "legislative, supreme, or dictating," John Thomson
affirmed, the authority of the synod to make rules is "declarative" of what
is already in the Bible, is always "subordinate" to God, and is "executive"
rather than "legislative." In fact, Thomson argued that judicial decisions
never contained anything new but, rather, were "a new Application of
the old infallible standing Rule of the Word to new Cases and Emer-
gencies intended by it, and comprehended under the Regulation of it."
Nor did Thomson see how that theory could produce tyranny. Surely it
was the "Abuse and not the righteous Use of this Authority to make
Rules" that produced the unhappy effects described by the New Sides.[53]

The Old Sides were unable to answer the charge that their insistence
on absolute synodical authority made schism inevitable. John Thomson
simply believed that the members of any social union must submit to their
rulers, whether they approved of those rulers or not. If they could not
submit in good conscience, they first must endeavor to change the ruler's
mind and, if unsuccessful, separate from him in peace. The ruled could
never judge the fitness of their rulers: "the Judicatory are the first rightful
Judges of their own Conclusions and judicial Determinations." Thus the
Old Sides could uphold absolute synodical authority while satisfying themselves that they restricted no one's liberty of conscience. While a man
could not judge his rulers, he could still decide whether to obey them.
And, Thomson insisted, "it's better to separate than sin."[54] With that, the
New Sides could agree.

MAJORITY AND MINORITY

Ultimately, the controversy between New Sides and Old Sides came
down to the right of the majority of the synod to determine the fundamentals of religion and to force those fundamentals as prerequisites for
synodical communion on a reluctant minority. The volatile issue of
majority rule and minority rights was relatively new to the American

church. There was implicit in the theory of majority rule an acceptance of contending social interests that was antithetical to the organic ideal of the pre-Awakening church. And, in fact, the hierarchy's deliberations in the first decades of the eighteenth century had not been marked by recourse to majoritarian theory. To the contrary. Rulers were charged with ascertaining the "general will" of their congregations, not with determining majority opinion. Thus we find the Donegal Presbytery in 1732 ruling in favor of the minority in a congregational dispute because it appeared to the presbytery that the smaller group represented the congregation's "general will," notwithstanding the "superiority of numbers in the other part who oppose them." [55]

In the heated aftermath of the Great Schism such rulings did not go unchallenged. But the debate following the expulsion of the New Sides from the Synod in June of 1741 indicates that both sides were still reluctant to accept strict numerical majority rule as the final arbiter of disagreements within a social union. The Old Sides presented to the 1741 meeting of the synod a "protest" against the New Side itinerations and against their attacks on the Old Sides. Forty-four lay and clerical representatives attended that meeting. Twenty of them signed the protest. And because the entire evangelically oriented New York Presbytery was absent, even the Old Sides admitted that less than half the synod had actually voted to expel the New Sides.[56] Indeed, the Old Sides at first did not justify the expulsion on the basis of numbers. The Old Sides had the right to expel the revivalists not because of majority status but because they were right. Their opponents, Robert Cross insisted, "had no right to sit whether the major or minor part." The Old Sides, he asserted, were "the true *Presbyterian Church* in this Province," and that legitimacy derived not from numbers of any sort but from the Old Side adherence to Presbyterian tradition and their faithfulness to revealed truth.[57]

In the immediate aftermath of the New Side expulsion, both sides denounced the mustering of numbers to support their cases. Gilbert Tennent observed that majority decisions changed with majorities and could therefore never be made essential terms of communion. And as we have seen, the Old Sides based their protest not on numbers but on venerable rules of Presbyterianism.[58] But even though they did not represent a numerical majority of the synod, the Old Sides insisted that, because of their adherence to received truth, they did represent the "common will" of the Presbyterian union, which they now used interchangeably with the "majority will" of the church. They had always asserted that the Presbyterian union was founded on certain shared interests. Now, momentarily sure of their strength, they contended that the "majority will" was in fact the "common will" and that a "majority" invariably embodied those unifying interests. Before 1741 they had insisted that ultimate authority in any union was indivisible. Now they vested that authority in a majority that would be determined by numbers when the Old Sides were assured of superiority and by appeal to revealed truth when they were not. And in either case, the Old Sides insisted, the rights of all members of the union were protected. The majority, in truth, embodied the interests of the minority as well as the majority. John Thomson granted that a minority in a society could raise and even debate issues, but by submitting them to a vote, the minority agreed to be "determined" by the majority. Thus, a *genuine* common will arose, made possible and defensible by the mutual interests of all members of society.[59]

Since the minority's interests were subsumed by the majority, the Old Sides saw little reason to tolerate perverse and obstinate dissidents. They conceded that an occasional sensitive individual might justifiably plead for liberty of conscience in some controverted matter. It would have been difficult for any eighteenth-century Presbyterian to argue differently. But they then insisted that dissidents must not organize a "party" with which to oppose the obvious common will of society as expressed by the majority. Conscience was a completely private matter, and therefore could not "be a Rule to any Community . . . to walk by." Any individuals or groups who persisted in opposing the interests of the larger community by definition removed themselves from that union. Since they no longer shared the interests of the community, they must be expelled. With the dissidents disposed of, the synod could function as a true social union, fostering the shared interests of its now purified membership.[60]

Having expelled the dissident evangelicals, the Old Sides consistently equated the government, or the synod, with themselves and refused to acknowledge that government might exist outside themselves. To be sure, the Old Side defense of their actions was published not in the name of "the synod" but by "some of the Members" of the synod. But in that defense they referred to "the synod" as a body in which the New Sides had no further part. Then, in the immediate aftermath of the schism, the Old Sides pointedly demonstrated their inability to locate authority outside themselves. In the synod of 1742—held without the evangelical wing of the church in attendance—the moderate men of the New York Presbytery, led by Jonathan Dickinson, attempted to correct some of the damage done in the 1741 session by moving that the present synod investigate the expulsion of the New Sides and rule on its legality. The Old Sides, still securely in control of the synod, retorted that they had legally constituted the synod in 1741 and that they had "only cast out such members as they judged had rendered themselves unworthy of membership . . . ." Again, according to the Old Sides, New Side obstinacy, not Old Side tyranny, had split the union. Having purified that fellowship and reestablished it firmly on shared and articulated interests, the Old Sides refused to be judged "by any judicature on earth."[61]

As the Old Sides created a contracted and purer union and assumed authority over it, they accepted with equanimity the resulting disunion in the larger Presbyterian community. They could affirm with others the "absolute necessity of union and good agreement in a religious society" and could just as easily endorse the ancient wisdom that "a kingdom divided against itself cannot stand."[62] But in the midst of the contentions brought on by the revival, the Old Sides clearly preferred division to union with the evangelicals. They therefore insisted that civility, let alone reunion, was impossible until they had received satisfaction "for the past most public and injurious treatment" received at the revivalists' hands.[63]

By 1744 Old Side intransigence had alienated the New Yorkers and their moderate leader, Jonathan Dickinson. In that year the New Yorkers proposed the organization of a new synod to perpetuate the revival, that synod to be composed of the presbyteries of New York, New Brunswick, and New Castle. They hoped to separate peacefully from the Old Side and even sought the blessings of the Philadelphia Synod. But instead of acquiescing in the proposed separation, the Old Sides denounced the New Yorkers. In effect, they condemned in the New Yorkers the process whereby they themselves had gained control of the hierarchy. To endorse the proposed synod, the Old Sides believed, "would infer our consenting" to building up "the interest of our own respective parties or Synods respectively, in opposition to one another . . . ."[64] But in fact the Old Sides in 1744 were not disturbed by the prospect of synodical competition. Indeed, they seemed almost to welcome that competition as a reason to consolidate their own union and as an opportunity to vindicate their position before the reformed churches of an "impartial world."

From outside the Old Side contracted community, the New Sides challenged at all points their opponents' view of social union and authority. That challenge undermined a traditional organicism in at least two ways. The New Sides insisted that fundamentally divergent views and interests existed within the Presbyterian communion, and they demanded that those differences be tolerated by authority within that union. Having denied a mutuality of interests within the union, the New Sides rejected any effort to equate majority will with a common will arising from those interests. They conceded that, in the normal course of events, the union would be ruled by a numerical majority. But they denied any suggestion that the majority's legitimacy derived from the union's shared interests. Rather, the opposite was true. Precisely because the church encompassed several divergent opinions and interests, union could be maintained only by the rule of a tolerant—and changing—majority. "So long as Men are in this imperfect fallible State, subject to such Diversity of Judgments," Samuel Blair could not see "how the Peace and Order of Churches can subsist, unless the minor Part be subject to the judicial Determinations of the Major in all cases wherein they can be subject without Sin." [65] That is, the majority may not force the Christian to violate his conscience by acquiescing in decisions he considered unscriptural. And, if a group of individuals united to oppose such decisions, the majority must allow their protest and neither force them from the union nor presume to encompass their divergent opinion.

Having once again insisted that the union consisted of groups holding potentially antagonistic views on some issues, the New Sides took the crucial step of locating government outside those groups. The Old Sides clearly located indivisible authority in the synod, which they in turn equated with themselves. But Tennent archly noted that the Old Sides could not consistently claim to be the synod and at the same time present a protest to that body. By taking their case to the synod, he asserted, the Old Sides signified that the governing body was "a Number distinct from them in their own Judgment." The Old Sides ought then to commit their charges against the New Sides "to the deliberate Judgment of the Synod, exclusive of the two Parties accusers and accused," and then abide by the synod's impartial judgment. [66] The Old Sides, of course, made no such concession. The fact is that the New Side spokesmen had accepted the conclusion that the Old Sides had embraced in practice but could not concede in theory. Control of government, the New Sides believed, was the legitimate end of competition between differing parts of a social union.

REUNION

In 1745 the Synod of the Presbyterian Church in America convened in Philadelphia—and in New York City. In the City of Brotherly Love the Old Sides consulted in huffy petulance, compared notes on new revivalist affronts, and determined that the expelled brethren must repent of past sins or remain forever excluded from the councils of the righteous. To the north Jonathan Dickinson molded the Synod of New York from the men of the New York Presbytery and those of the expelled brethren who condescended to attend. For the next twelve years the two synods functioned as autonomous and competitive bodies, the result of intransigence and excess, a dramatic witness to the divisive power of the great revival, and a constant affront to every tenet of Presbyterian ecclesiology. The church was officially divided into two parts that loudly defended their divisive actions, protected their prerogatives and boundaries, and charged the other with responsibility for the schism, with "erecting altar against altar." [67] Old and New Side Synod alike supervised presbyteries, ordained ministers, appointed missionaries, established schools, in short, functioned as the head of a well-defined and purposive hierarchy. Though the two hierarchies attempted to wrench apart a body once united by tradition and belief, not all the bonds would break. Thus the body appeared to many on both sides a wounded monster with two heads that alternately ignored and snapped at each other, a grotesque perversion of a venerable ideal.

This unhappy state was the product of extraordinary circumstances, of engaged men's conviction that they did holy battle with the forces of darkness. As the revival passed, those convictions cooled. In the heat of battle men had taken, or been forced into, extreme, exposed positions that they now with varying speed and grace modified or abandoned entirely. Following the lead of New England's erratic James Davenport, Gilbert Tennent repented of some of his earlier enthusiasms, while after 1741 the zealous Moravians in the middle colonies sobered many New Sides by pushing to their extremes some of the revivalists' controversial theological positions.[68] At the same time, some of the fiercest combatants, most notably John Thomson, died soon after the New Sides were expelled. The experience of organizing and directing a hierarchy made the New Sides more appreciative of social order and regularity, while the Old Sides became more sensitive to minority rights as New Side ranks continued to swell and threaten to dominate any future union. Therefore, Old and New Sides moved to regain in the late forties and fifties the center they had earlier abandoned. They found, though, that the schism itself had shifted dramatically that middle ground.

Major concessions were made on each side between about 1749 and 1758. While they disagreed over the actual results of the Awakening, the Old Sides were finally persuaded that good as well as ill had been done, and the New Sides conceded that dangerous excesses had marred the otherwise commendable revival.[69] Likewise, some Old Sides granted the merits of itineration while the revivalists deplored its abuse. Even the fate of the congregations that had sprung up during the revival was open to bargain and compromise between Old and New Sides. Despite these crucial areas of potential agreement, Presbyterian reunion remained impossible so long as Old and New Sides disagreed on the nature of the union now proposed. On that issue, the New Sides were most emphatic. For instance, the constitution of the Synod of New York documents their commitment to tolerant majority rule and respect for minority rights. If a man could not conscientiously agree to an issue deemed an essential doctrine of faith by the synod, he could peacefully withdraw from its fellowship without causing contention within the union and without airing his grievances in the press.[70] The Old Sides, of course, had said no less. But where the Old Sides had insisted on codifying and promulgating the tenets that unified Presbyterians, the New Sides insisted on synodical restraint in enunciating essential truths. "What is plain sin and plain duty in one's account, is not so in another's," they noted. Therefore, the synod must make nothing a term of communion "which Christ has not made." And the revivalists were fairly certain that He had "not made every truth and every duty a term." [71]

In 1751 the Synod of Philadelphia made a significant concession to the New Sides by agreeing that a reunited Presbyterian Synod should legislate only in "matters that appear to the body plain duty" or that "relate to the great truths of religion." [72] It was six years later, though, before the New Sides were convinced that their opponents had truly modified their previous view. Finally, in 1758 the two synods were reunited as the Synod of Philadelphia and New York. The Plan of Union, meticulously negotiated for a decade, provided for majority rule in all cases of disagreement and directed that the synod declare as essentials only those doctrines clearly sanctioned in scripture and universally esteemed necessary to vital religion. Francis Alison, the minister-educator who inherited Thomson's position as spokesman for the Old Sides, best articulated the Old Side reversed position: "acts of uniformity in religion are of no use, but to fetter the conscience, and . . . harass Christ's subjects." Alison affirmed in 1758 what the New Sides had insisted upon for a generation. The Presbyterians "must maintain union in essentials; forebearance in lesser matters, and charity in all things." [73]

As the Old Sides moderated their view of the Presbyterian union, they also agreed to locate final synodical authority outside themselves. The location of final authority and its relation to the Old Side protesters of 1741 remained a volatile issue because in the 1750s representatives of the New Side encouraged the Synod of Philadelphia at least to put that protest and the New Side expulsion to a new vote if they could not void it outright.[74] The Old Side was intransigent on the subject for a decade. But in 1755 the Synod of New York observed that many of the present members of both the Old and New Side Synods had taken no part in the schism. The synod noted further that the Old Side representatives who were negotiating a possible reunion of the church had begun to distinguish between the 1741 synod and the individuals who had protested to it. That being the case, the New Sides wondered, why could not the Old Side synod now, in 1755, simply declare the 1741 protest void?[75] Interestingly, the Old Side reply to that query did not contain the expected retort that they would be judged by no one. Instead, they took a page out of the revivalists' book and defended the 1741 protesters' rights to "private judgment." They now argued, somewhat disingenuously in view of past positions, that acceptance of the protest and the expulsion had never been required of their members, and they insisted that to declare either void would exceed the authority of the synod.[76] By 1758, though, the Old Sides—now a minority—were ready to concede in the Plan of Union that the protest had not been an act of the synod but "the act of those only who subscribed it . . . ."[77] Somewhat belatedly the Old Sides granted that the synod in 1741 had existed outside themselves, and that concession made reunion possible.

What impelled Old and New to reunion? Passions had cooled, and difficult substantive issues of itineration, the location of authority in the synod, the relation of synodical authority to the presbyteries had been satisfactorily compromised if not completely resolved. It is also possible that reunion became a possibility when the New Sides became strong enough to force it on their own terms. That was clearly the case in 1758. And, as the most astute study of the reunion contends, it simply took a decade of hard work to construct a presbyterial system flexible enough to accommodate the repercussions of the Great Awakening.[78] Finally, the reunion surely must reflect the determination of the Presbyterian Church, like any institution, to maintain itself at any cost. For the reunion was not entirely amicable. The Old Sides had lost, and they knew it. And once in power the New Sides proved as harsh in insisting upon their points— such as the rights of a congregation to judge its minister's gracious estate—as the Old Sides had been in maintaining their own. Well might Francis Alison observe wearily to Ezra Stiles in 1767, "We are united, but it is as water and oil." [79]

But the fact remains that the Great Schism of 1741 was healed in 1758. The Presbyterians simply were not willing to accept permanently the existence of two competing Presbyterian churches in America. They could not yet repudiate completely the organic ideal that had undergirded the colonial church. Therefore they dismantled their defense of conflict and schism and replaced their martial Christ with a more traditional, pacific one. Thus Tennent in 1749 could assert that God was not the "Author of *Confusion,* but of *Peace,* and therefore of *Order,"* and Francis Alison could join him in extolling the "peaceful religion of Jesus" and in castigating hatred and strife.[80] The leaders of both sides still compared the church to an army, but that army was now a holy band happily united against common foes. It was once more a band of soldiers "in good Order, gather'd together into a close compact Body . . . ."[81] In that "compact Body," as in the human body, all "are appointed for mutual service." No part of that body could say to another part, *"I have no need of thee,"* warned Tennent. For, in Francis Alison's organic metaphor, "they are the useful and active members of the same body." [82]

It is possible, of course, that these organic metaphors were mere rhetorical flourishes to be used when the "real" issues dividing Presbyterianism were resolved. But there is no reason to dismiss as mere rhetoric the language that attended the resolution of those issues. One need only read carefully the records of the pained negotiations between Old and New Sides to appreciate the deep spiritual turmoil occasioned by the anomalous existence of two competing synods. In the final analysis, it may have been the determination to resolve that anomalous situation that produced reunion. That determination surely measures the Presbyterian commitment to the organic nature of their ecclesiastical union.

That union, however, was not in 1758 what it had been in 1740. In a sense, the communal language, the organic metaphors, demonstrate Presbyterian awareness of that fundamental change. When the union had in fact functioned as an organic whole, there had been little discussion of its organic nature. But at the moment of reunion organic metaphors abounded. They surely reflected the deepest desire of both sides to recapture an earlier communal ideal, and clearly represented the central force toward reconciliation. But the metaphors hardly reflected reality. The schism had forever altered the union. Its divided councils had been publicly advertised and institutionalized in competing hierarchies, and ultimate authority itself had been officially divided for thirteen years. Now the Plan of Union even contained the guidelines for future schisms, providing as it did for peaceful withdrawal in the event of unresolved differences. The Presbyterians hoped to reunite "upon such Scriptural and rational terms as may secure peace and good order, tend to heal our broken churches, and advance religion hereafter . . . ."[83] Reunite they did. Secure "peace and good order" they could not. For theirs would never again be a "true Christian communion."[84]

CHAPTER II

The Presbyterian Minister as Social Leader

In the year of the reunion Gilbert Tennent was asked to write an introduction to a sermon by David Bostwick, a young New Side minister. The sermon was entitled "Self disclaimed and Christ exalted," and in his introduction Tennent blasted what he believed to be the root cause of the Great Schism: selfishness. Selfishness, he declared, is "the most egregious, enormous, and blasphemous villainy!" It is "pregnant with numerous and crimson iniquities," and is "the fatal source" of the evil and calamities that have forever plagued "this lower world." In the sermon proper, the young Bostwick outdid his elder by denouncing selfishness as nothing less than original sin, "man's original Apostacy." Indeed, three-quarters of a century before Alexis de Tocqueville coined the word *individualisme*, David Bostwick with great sensitivity described and deplored the pursuit of self that the noted French commentator believed was the defining element of nineteenth-century American society. The Presbyterian revivalist castigated the man who turned from God and his fellow man and retired "into himself as his last and ultimate end." There the self-centered man fell prey to "an habitual disposition to treat himself, in the same manner that he ought to treat the God Of Heaven; i.e. to love himself supreamely, and seek himself ultimately and finally, and set up himself in one shape or another as the grand center to which all the lines of his busy thoughts, anxious cares, and subtle projects, bend and terminate." [1]

31

Historians are only beginning to appreciate the mid eighteenth-century concern with selfishness that Bostwick's portrait evinces. At all levels of colonial society men between 1740 and 1760 became convinced that their advancement in a developing economy was threatened by men actuated by boundless selfishness. Men at the upper reaches of that society were alarmed at growing restiveness in the lower levels and, simultaneously, began to suspect that entry into the very highest reaches was being limited to those with royal connections. At the same time, colonists in the lower reaches of colonial society inveighed against rulers who seemed to ignore or even to aggravate their economic hardships. At times in the late colonial period those complaints gave way to urban disturbances, rent riots, and the several backcountry rebellions that alarmed the uneasy leaders of the established order. On one level, the revival of evangelical religion may be seen as an effort to halt this alarming spread of social distrust, selfishness, and contention and to substitute for it a new order of peaceful selflessness. In part, the Great Schism was healed because its divisiveness seemed to epitomize rampant selfishness and to foredoom any Presbyterian effort to reform colonial society. That effort, it was argued, would succeed only if made by a church unified by love and forebearance. And it would succeed only if led by a new kind of social leader. The qualities of that leader of society were debated between 1740 and 1760 by the Old and New Sides as they contended over the nature of social union itself.[2]

AT EASE IN ZION

The debate over the "character of the good ruler" centered, for the colonial Presbyterians, on the nature of their spiritual leaders, the clergy. Before 1730 the Presbyterians, by and large, did not debate the nature of the ministry, just as they did not analyze the nature of their ecclesiastical union. But just as the revival of evangelical religion prompted debates over the nature of social union, it also produced fundamental disagreements between the Old and New Sides over the qualities of the godly minister and the circumstances under which he was to be obeyed—and scorned.

The two debates were intimately related. In the latter half of the 1730s the presbyteries of Donegal and Philadelphia, for instance, were beseiged with charges against ministers brought by disgruntled or enraged parishioners.[3] Those charges characteristically related to visible indiscretions, usually fornication or intemperance. And the charges became increasingly frequent as the various presbyteries made their rounds of local sessions. Those perambulations had been intended to increase the hierarchy's control over local congregations. But when the presbyteries began to inquire into the relations between congregations and their ministers, they found a growing number of parishioners eager to bear witness against their pastors. The presbyteries at first vacillated before those complaints, just as they momentarily hesitated over requests for congregational separations. In both instances, though, the hierarchy soon learned to censure rather than accept complaints.[4]

As the revival began, that task grew more difficult. Congregations rejected ministers chosen for them by the presbyteries. In 1738 the Philadelphia Presbytery was forced to allow a dissenting part of a New Jersey congregation to hear another candidate before the dissidents would agree to accept the one recommended by the hierarchy.[5] And in 1736 the Donegal Presbytery precipitated a riot by imposing a minister on a reluctant congregation. When they instructed the Reverend Alexander Craighead to supply the Paxton congregation in central Pennsylvania, the congregation refused to hear him because they disagreed with his theology. Then, when the presbytery brought Craighead to trial for failing to force himself upon the good people of Paxton, his *own* congregation interrupted his trial by "rising into a tumult, and railing at the Members in the most scurrilous . . . terms." Beseiged in their meeting place, the Presbyterian rulers were forced to flee, declaring as they went that they had seen nothing like this "since we have been capable to mark any thing on the world."[6]

This popular dissatisfaction with the clergy found forceful expression in Tennent's notorious Nottingham sermon of 1740. In his warning against the "dangers of an unconverted ministry" the New Side evangel blistered those "natural" men who could not impart to the lost a sense of saving grace they themselves had never received. Legalistic enemies to any belief in original sin, they keep "Driving, Driving, to Duty, Duty, under this Notion, That it will recommend natural Men to the Favour of God, or entitle them to the Promises of Grace and Salvation: and thus those blind Guides fix a deluded World upon the false Foundation of their own Righteousness . . . ." When the "life of piety" ventured near the churches of these "stone-blind" and "stone-dead" men, they "rise up in Arms against it, consult, contrive and combine in their Conclaves against it . . . ." They stood condemned, Tennent believed, of the ultimate sin, for their every act tended to exalt self rather than to magnify the Lord and edify His church.⁷ Tennent's evangelical colleague, Samuel Finley, agreed that the ministrations of much of the clergy were but a "dry Formality." While Christians grew "careless, unholy, unguarded," while the ordinances of the church were performed as lifeless and power-less duties, the complacent clergy did "in general seem at Ease in Zion."⁸

The clergy seemed most complacent and selfish when they insisted on their salaries. Tennent denounced them as men "whose chief desire," like Judas, was "to finger the Pence, and carry the Bag."⁹ In the 1730s some Presbyterian pastors went to court to compel their parishioners to pay their arrears. Others, more sensitive to public opinion, had to be forced by the hierarchy to be firm with delinquent congregations. Negligent parishion-ers were occasionally barred from communion until they paid up, and the presbyteries refused to receive complaints about such severity.¹⁰ It is true that some congregations ran up astonishing debts to their pastors. At one point, for instance, the Paxton congregation owed their unlucky minister more than £200 in back salaries.¹¹ But their efforts to collect those monies had by 1740 made the Old Sides in particular appear avaricious to their flocks.

In 1738 James Anderson, the Old Side minister of New York City's First Presbyterian Church, deplored the reluctance of some ministers to sue at law for fear of offending their members. Anderson noted that, without coercion, many members refused to support their ministers. He acknowledged that some Presbyterians were hard-pressed financially and that clerical support was a burden to them. He recommended, though, that those poorer church members should "study frugality & guard against prodigality and extravagance . . . ." He warned them in particular against "Profuse & needless Spending in publick houses." To the Donegal Presby-tery, Anderson recommended that persistent delinquents be declared "disorderly" by their session and denied communion until they settled their affairs with the pastor. Stringent measures would expose the incorrigible and encourage others to their duty. At all times, though, the ministers should stress that "'tis God's glory and the good of peoples' Souls, more than our private Interest, we have most at heart."¹² The rate at which Presbyterians fled Old Side churches in the 1730s and 1740s suggests that Gilbert Tennent's accusations were more believable to many Presbyterians than were the Old Side protestations of altruism.

SUCCESS AND THE GREATER GOOD

The clergy's concern about salaries was disturbing enough to the New Sides and their followers. But that concern for the things of this world symbolized for the revivalists a host of other affronts to the sacred calling, each one of which further disqualified the Old Side clergy as worthy social leaders in a revived society. And the New Sides had some very controversial ideas about what made a social leader "worthy." By 1741 they had embraced the revolutionary idea that he must be above all else successful. Even more astonishingly, they asserted the right of the people to be the judges of his success.[13]

Tennent realized the radical nature of the proposal that the people judge their minister's success. In normal times, he believed, that judgment would not be required. But in extraordinary days, the Christian must look to his own salvation. For "when Persons have their Eyes opened, and their Hearts set upon the Work of God; they are not so soon satisfied with their [ministers'] Doings, and with want of Success for a Time."[14] "Want of Success," the New Sides believed, reflected a minister's "want of grace." Success was the direct result of a minister's own experience with God. "Such as the Lord sends not . . . shall not profit the People at all," Tennent declared. The revivalist Samuel Blair was equally blunt: *"By their Fruits ye shall know them;* says our Lord; *do men gather Grapes off Thorns? or Figs off Thistles?"* [15] Of course, Tennent and his colleagues were careful to concede that a sovereign God could use any instrument, even an unconverted minister, to further His Kingdom. Admittedly, only God could change a man's heart. But surely, the revivalists urged, a greater blessing must reasonably be expected from the more godly instruments. "Otherwise, the best Gifts would not be desirable, and God *almighty* . . . by not acting according to the Nature of Things, would be carrying on a Series of unnecessary Miracles; which to suppose is unreasonable."[16]

The New Sides even suggested that the minister in American society be held to the same standards of competency demanded of leaders in other areas of life. He should be able to lead others to share the salvation he had experienced himself. And Gilbert Tennent insisted that the people demand of their ministers the same proficiency they would look for in a lawyer or doctor. "To trust the Care of our Souls to those who have little or no Care for their own, to those who are both unskilled and unfaithful, is contrary to the common Practice of considerate Mankind, relating to the

Affairs of their Bodies and Estates." [17] No one yet contended that the ministry was merely another profession, but it was obvious that the New Side emphasis on success as the crucial criterion for judging a clergyman certainly weakened the once unchallenged axiom that all ministers exercised divine authority simply by dint of their ordination.

Nor did the New Sides shrink from urging the Christian to flee an unconverted pastor. Those "who live under the Ministry of dead Men, whether they have got the Form of Religion or not," must for their own sake fly "to the Living, where they may be edified." The Christian was urged to seek out a more gracious shepherd even if his rightful pastor was a "pious Minister of lesser Gifts." [18] And, Tennent declared, the Christian was under an absolute obligation to leave unsuccessful ministers when more successful ones drew near. Judged solely by numbers, of course, the most successful ministers, especially in the early years of the revival, were the itinerant preachers. Tennent pointed with undisguised pride to the crowds that thronged after the traveling evangels, men who "find themselves spirited to uncommon Labours, and perceive those attended with uncommon Successes." [19] To Samuel Blair, the throngs that followed the itinerants clearly demonstrated God's approval of itineration just as they marked those ministers who were and were not worthy of support.[20]

The New Side support of itineration threatened the concept of boundaries that was at the bottom of presbyterian ecclesiology. Presbyterians were urged to take care, first of all, for their eternal souls. Not the comfort of the settled clergy, not even the unity of the church, but the "greater good" of the individual Christian was the revivalists' principal concern. Their emphasis on the individual's greater good was perhaps the most radical of New Side ideas, because it made each man's own wellbeing the center of his universe even as it made the individual Christian the judge of every force that touched his life. Clearly the idea carried within it the seeds of rampant selfishness. Therefore, when possible, the revivalists urged the individual always to seek the good of the whole when he could do so without endangering his soul. And the Christian was warned not to foment divisions in the body of Christ for trivial or selfish reasons.[21]

In the end, though, the New Sides accepted the radical implications of their advice and muted the implicit threat to ordered society as best they could. Tennent, for instance, defended that advice by appealing to "natural reason" and to "common sense." All creatures, he insisted, have a natural instinct for choosing the greater good. "Natural reason" dictates that "good" is desirable for its own sake; surely, then, the greatest good was manifestly the most desirable. God himself enjoined man to "covet earnestly the best Gifts" and to "prove all Things, and hold fast that which is good." If there exists a variety of means, then the best is to be chosen. If one does not choose the best, the choice is not a rational one because it does not conform to common sense. Surely, Tennent believed, no minister would object if a member sought the greater good of his own soul and thereby refused to function as a "senseless Stone, without Choice, Sense, and Taste." [22]

He was wrong. A great many clerics did object, and not all of them were of the Old Side. Jonathan Dickinson would later become a leading New Side, but in 1739 he opposed the people's right to judge their ministers. Dickinson was devoted to ecclesiastical order and in 1722 had insisted upon the people's "indispensible Obligation" to accept their preacher's words as those of God—when he preached gospel truths. But even then Dickinson reserved to the people the final right to decide if their ministers preached the gospel. [23] By 1739, after a decade of contention in the church, Dickinson was ready to limit severely that right and the consequent right of the people to leave an unsuccessful minister. In the first days of the Great Awakening he attacked, first of all, the idea that a minister's success reflected his own skills. Some preachers had "brighter Capacities, and more eminent Degrees of Learning, Knowledge, Grace, and other useful Furniture for this sacred Trust" than others. But, according to the moderate Dickinson, it made no difference that some ministers were more animated, sagacious, and eloquent than others, for all ministers were but tools used by God, each tool being as good as another. He warned against "giving the Honour to the Instrument, which belongs only to the principal Agent . . . ." And he defended those who were "decry'd as unsuccessful and therefore culpable" simply because the crowds did not throng to them, even while he castigated those who were deemed successful just because they gathered great hosts of converts, "as tho' *by their own Power and Holiness* they could convince Men to God." [24]

Since the unequal talents of God's servants were of little final significance, Dickinson insisted that Christians remain under the care of their lawful, settled ministers, even if they did not have "such superior Capacities or desirable Qualifications, as we see or imagine in some others." Therein lay the "Way of God and Duty." No duty was more explicitly enjoined upon the Christian, for if all went seeking after a favorite minister, soon there would be "no such Thing as an united Congregation left; nor any such Thing as a religious Society in the World." [25]

Dickinson could be firm because he rejected the idea that the Christian's principal task was to seek his individual greater good. Rather, he believed that minister and member alike should seek above all else the good of the whole church and the preservation of local communities of believers. He denied flatly that "we are bound to seek our greater Edification; and consequently to desert that Ministry under which we cannot find equal advantage to our Souls." Dickinson even suggested that if a Christian did not find sustenance under a respectable minister, the fault probably lay with the Christian, not his minister.[26]

But in his 1739 pronouncements on the "dangers of schisms and contentions," Dickinson made an important reservation that echoed his stand in the Subscription Controversy of 1729 and that anticipated his position in the Great Schism. Only the "faithful" minister should be obeyed and supported. When he ceased to be "faithful," separation was justified. "When our Consciences are imposed upon by sinful Terms of Communion, or what we esteem to be such; when our Minister is openly vicious or immoral; or his Doctrines heterodox and subversive of the Fundamentals of Christianity, and of vital Piety . . . I think a Man may then have a Call to peaceably withdraw from such a Ministry, and lift himself under another." And Dickinson reserved to the Christian the right to make those final judgments. He simply believed that few ministers deserved to be deserted and that in no case should a cleric's "success" be the criterion by which he was judged.[27]

The Old Sides disagreed fundamentally with both Tennent and Dickinson and, in doing so, revealed a very different attitude toward the prerequisites for social leadership in colonial America. They rejected any use of success as a criterion for judging anything or anybody. The Old Side leader John Thomson noted that, judged by the New Side standard, prophets like Jeremiah and Elijah must be judged failures since no great crowds hung on their every word and disturbed the public peace. Thomson's Old Testament history was a trifle shaky, but his meaning was clear enough. If crowds of screaming people signified success, the Old Sides in 1741 wanted none of it.[28]

Even when success was defined strictly as the simple winning of souls, the Old Sides rejected it as a criterion for judging the condition of a minister's soul or his worth to the Kingdom. George Gillespie, another leading Old Side, noted that a godly minister might be unsuccessful in winning souls for any number of reasons, some of which were ingenious, and none of which won Gillespie any friends among the revivalists. Like the New Sides, Gillespie firmly believed the doctrine of election. And he used that theological tenet to argue against judging the success of *any* Calvinist minister. Gillespie posited a situation in which a minister's congregation happened to include an unusually large percentage of the damned. Surely no fair man could condemn that minister for failing to cultivate a barren field over which he had absolutely no control. And Gillespie excelled Thomson in discovering illustrious unsuccessful ministers in the Bible. When contrasted to the throngs converted by Peter at Pentecost, did not Jesus Christ himself appear a failure by New Side standards? After identifying the Old Sides with the Son of God, Gillespie shielded them further from complaints about their lack of converts by insisting, once again, that ministers are only the secondary, not the primary, "Causes of Conversion." [29]

The Old Sides also insisted that God was the source of all ministerial success. In fact, the Synod of Philadelphia argued that the Lord sometimes gave the wicked success in order to test the godly, a not so subtle stab at the eminently successful New Sides. "Doth not God oft give wicked Men great success for the trial of better Men than themselves? And do not godly Men as oft meet with Crosses and Disappointments for their great Trials?" Thus the Old Sides assumed the role of long-suffering, holy martyrs set upon by godless persecutors.[30]

The Old Sides also rejected the contention that a minister's success reflected his spiritual state. George Gillespie conceded that no presbytery should knowingly license or ordain an unconverted man. But he also believed that an unconverted hypocrite could deceive a presbytery and be ordained. That possibility did not alarm Gillespie, though, because for him the minister was only the secondary means of conversion. If God wanted to use a hypocrite as an effective soul-winner, that was certainly within His power. In fact, Gillespie argued that an eloquent, learned hypocrite might prove a more effective soul-winner than a gracious minister who was tongue-tied and ignorant. Certainly Gillespie agreed with the New Sides that God would in the normal course of events use gracious men to advance the Kingdom. But, he concluded, had not Jesus also called Judas Iscariot to His side and used him effectively for three years? [31]

Of course the Old Sides did not easily compare themselves to Judas. In the midst of a pietistic revival, they could not ignore completely the assertion that the godly minister was usually successful. They devised an ingenious explanation for the New Side success and their own failure. Repeatedly after 1741 the Old Sides charged that the revivalists were successful only because they reaped where others had sown. The Synod of Philadelphia believed that the success of itinerants like Whitefield and Tennent could be explained in no other way. "Men should have a due Regard, to the publick Peace, the common Interest, and even the usefulness and Characters of orthodox and regular Ministers, who planted and watered Congregations, in which upstart Intruders proclaim their Success." If the truth were known, then, the laudable successes of the Great Awakening were the results of the tireless—anticipatory—efforts of the Old Side clergy.[32]

In the main, however, the Old Sides attributed their lack of success to the separations fomented by the New Sides. Gillespie condemned the tendency of Christians to "cry up one Minister, and cry down another," and to build the reputation of one man of God on the ruins of another's good name and character. For in the final analysis, to leave one's pastor was to threaten the stability of the fixed, settled gospel ministry that, for the Old Sides, was the foundation of any ordered, regular society. Like Dickinson, Gillespie insisted that after a minister was called, no one could leave his care so long as the minister remained moral, regular, and faithful. But unlike Dickinson, Gillespie and the other Old Sides could hardly conceive of a situation in which a regularly ordained minister might be found immoral and irregular.[33] Thomson, for instance, insisted that dissatisfied members could not charge a minister with anything that resulted from "human Frailty, and the sinful Infirmities that in some Measure cleave to the best of Christians . . . ."[34] And, in any case, if serious charges were appropriate, they should be handled by the duly constituted authority of the hierarchy, not by the irregular actions of a few disgruntled members of a congregation. Finally, the Old Sides rejected the idea that a Christian might separate from his pastor for the member's "greater good." George Gillespie insisted that any reason for separations must be evident and rational; the pursuit of one's greater good was most assuredly neither, he believed. In the final analysis, then, the plea for the greater good was rejected because it threatened the foundation of all social order.[35]

VISIBLE AND INVISIBLE SAINTS

The New Sides, then, urged colonial Americans to judge the performance of their ministers in the sacred office and to use as one criterion of judgment the success with which the clergy preached the gospel. Fervent evangelicals during the revival introduced another, even more controversial, way in which the people were encouraged to evaluate their spiritual leaders. Having told the people to weigh the external evidence of numbers of converts produced by a clergyman, the New Sides then instructed the Christian to delve into his minister's soul and to pass judgment on the cleric's spiritual state. And the Christian was assured that his own experience with God qualified him to perform that delicate task. Clearly one of the most important effects of the evangelical revival was to interject into the colonial understanding of social leadership this suggestion that the people had the right to use the prompting of their own hearts to judge the worthiness of their rulers.

It was the most controversial of all the revivalists' ideas. One of the central tenets of the Reformed tradition was that a person's true inner state could be known only to God. In the seventeenth century the American Puritans had grappled with the conflict between that fundamental postulate and their desire to establish "purified" churches made up only of "true" Christians. Their solution was to distinguish between a visible and an invisible church made up of visible and invisible saints. The visible saints were those men and women who by public profession and exemplary lives appeared to be among the elect. The Puritan could demand of a candidate for the "visible" church no more than the "external" evidence of his profession and daily life. The Puritans also accepted the obvious corollary of that axiom. Inevitably, the visible church would contain men and women who were not true Christians. On the other hand, the "invisible" saints were known only to God. The Puritans in America were determined to force their visible churches to approximate as closely as possible that invisible church, but they accepted their inability to do so completely.[36] In the debates preceding the Great Awakening the Presbyterian Old Sides adhered staunchly to this traditional view that only God could know finally the condition of any man's soul. The New Sides began fundamentally—if cautiously—to alter it.

At the heart of the debate in the 1730s was the revivalists' insistence that a ministerial candidate be required to give a public narration of his conversion experience. The Old Sides objected vehemently. God had given man no way of knowing "when Men's Mouths and Hearts do agree," they argued. How, then, could anyone distinguish between a real and a contrived narrative of conversion? Indeed, the Old Sides did not accept the fundamental proposition of the New Sides. They did not believe that the Christian could be assured of his *own* conversion and gracious estate, much less be able to judge others. The opponents of the revival sensed correctly that the Awakening had intensified the affective dimensions of religious life, that it had made men conscious of themselves as emotional beings. They knew that Christians could now relate their conversion experiences in graphic terms and that they were as aware of their own gracious state as they would be of a "stab or wound." Indeed, the conversion experience itself was often described by the pietist in precisely those terms. The Old Sides rejected the entire development. The practice of relating conversion experiences merely made men boast of their "Experiences of Grace, Comforts—and Visions . . . ." And it followed that if the Christian could not be assured of his own salvation, he could not judge his minister. No one, John Thomson asserted, has the right "to know the secret Intercourse between me and my God . . . ." [37]

Rather, the Old Sides insisted, men must be judged by external appearances only. All that could be required of a minister was a "Competency of Knowledge," an "unblemished Character," and a "Profession of sincere Resolution to engage in and keep Covenant with his God and Saviour." Consequently, men like Thomson and Robert Cross stressed the importance of externals such as temperance, observing the Sabbath, and engaging in frequent private prayer. They granted that these might be feigned by graceless people but then maintained that to be "constant" in those externals was surely a "good probable Sign or Symptom." Thomson noted with compelling logic that a "competent Proportion of congenial Fruits" had to indicate godly "internal marks." Thomson was reluctant, though, even to allow the Christian to judge those external "Fruits." Under no circumstances would he allow the Christian in addition to judge his pastor's "internal marks." [38] And the Synod of Philadelphia argued during the Schism that an examination of externals would more readily trap hypocrites than would an investigation of easily feigned "internal" evidence: "as we judge according to Appearance, we see just Cause to alter our Judgment and Conduct, when Men's fair Declarations are contradicted by their foul Acts." [39]

Not surprisingly, the Old Sides often censured ministers for obvious, sometimes blatant, breaches of decorum and morality. Those offenses were matters of externals and were therefore legitimate objects of official—though not unofficial—inspection and discipline. The presbyteries dominated by Old Sides, however, were notoriously reluctant to condemn ministers who were charged with the "internal" sin of being graceless or unsuccessful. Thus, the Donegal Presbytery refused to separate a minister from a congregation with which he had been openly at war for years. But at one point in that war it forced the minister to make a public apology for his chronic drunkenness.[40]

If the Old Sides were appalled at the new insistence on "internal judging," their New Side opponents were at first uncomfortable with it. Samuel Finley, for instance, asserted that the "internal" evidence the New Sides sought was, in truth, but another kind of "external" proof. The revivalists judged men only "from what appears to us, in so far as we know of their Manner of life, and Christian Experiences." But the Old Sides correctly charged the New Sides with innovation. Later in the same sermon in which he renounced "internal judging," Finley clearly stated that external evidence simply was inadequate proof of a man's gracious condition.[41] And in 1734 the evangelical Gilbert Tennent had urged the synod to "diligently examine all candidates for the ministry in the experiences of a work of sanctifying grace in their hearts" and to admit "none to the sacred trust that are not in the eye of charity serious Christians."[42]

The revivalists' insistence on a discerning judgment of a minister's spiritual condition measured their conviction that a true Christian could be assured of his own salvation. Although they might fall from it, Tennent contended, all gracious people "ordinarily have a lesser or greater Degree of comfortable Perswasion of their gracious State . . . ."[43] Intimately aware of the affective dimensions of the revival, Finley believed that after a person has himself been converted and learns "what Emotion of Heart" results from that rending experience, he will "the more readily discern, when another speaks, prays, or preaches with the same Relish of divine Things . . . ." And Tennent believed that only hypocrites would shrink from the opportunity to share their conversion experience with others. Only the "false shepherds" that appeared so frequently in New Side denunciations were "against all Knowing of others, and Judging, in order to hide their own Filthiness; like Thieves they flee a Search, because of the Stolen Goods." Tennent was ready to admit that Christians were not infallible judges, but he maintained that they could make a "near guess" as to which ministers were truly converted by observing their "Method of Praying, Preaching, and Living."[44]

Nor was it enough simply for the members of a congregation to judge their minister. They were to take action if they found him unconverted. They were to be rid of him. Tennent indicted those who remained under the charge of dead men: "such who are contented under a *dead Ministry,* have not in them the Temper of that Saviour they express."[45] Thus the

New Sides believed a congregation's judgment of its minister reflected the spiritual state of the congregation. If that society tolerated an ungodly leader, then its members must also be graceless. The implications for the larger colonial society were obvious.

It would be misleading to suggest that the Old Sides invariably opposed any examination of the clergy and the New Sides always insisted upon judging the ministry. The Old Sides were always ready to test a minister's orthodoxy and were willing to impose creeds and confessions to that end. The New Sides regularly opposed any such investigations. On the other hand, the revivalists insisted that a minister's success and his spiritual state—his conversion experience—were legitimate objects of close scrutiny. And, always, each side assured the other that it was interested only in "external" evidence. Both sides also insisted that some areas of a minister's life and character were reserved from any kind of official scrutiny. The Old Sides opposed any questioning of a man's success or the condition of his soul, while their opponents insisted that no man's orthodoxy should become the subject of an "inquisition."

Both Old and New Sides were slightly uncomfortable debating in public the qualifications for social leadership. All involved in the arguments preceding the Great Schism seem vaguely aware that debates over the prerequisites of social leadership should not be aired in the public press. Both sides, however, were highly motivated, and their concern enabled them to overcome their reservations. Thus, throughout the 1730s and 1740s, the Old Sides championed those examinations of the clergy that were designed to preserve standards, to protect orthodoxy, and to maintain social order. The New Sides, on the other hand, championed those examinations that were intended to revitalize a dead piety and to produce for colonial society a more deserving and responsive leadership.

The revivalists, in particular, were raising some highly significant questions for the first time in American history. They were suggesting that one very important element of colonial society's leadership must *earn* its right to rule and that the people themselves were uniquely equipped to force their religious leaders to do just that. A generation after the Great Awakening the American colonists fought a Revolution, in part to answer the question of who was to rule at home in America. The answer was, one who is attuned to the needs and aspirations of the American people and who has demonstrated his public "utility." Those questions were first asked and answered by the evangelical wing of American Protestantism in the Great Awakening.

From an unusually large number of important funeral sermons preached in the 1750s by the New Side clergy one can put together an idea of the revivalist ideal of social leadership, of the man who through selfless concern, experience, and skill had earned the respect of his people and the right to rule them.[46] That man's right to rule was based not on his wealth, social position, pedigree, or orthodoxy but instead flowed directly from his usefulness, success, and selfless piety.[47] Such a man was Jonathan Belcher, the late governor of New Jersey who was eulogized in 1757 by his friend, the Reverend Aaron Burr. Belcher was above all else a selfless man, Burr declared. He had disdained the opportunity to enrich himself at the expense of others while governor. And he had realized that reformation of colonial society awaited the end of the contentions that were tearing that society apart. Thus, upon arriving in New Jersey, Belcher had used "steady, wise and prudent Measures" to end the "Tumolts," "Confusions," and the "riotous Disorders" that had for so long plagued the province. Throughout his administration he had "steadfastly pursued, with unwearied Pains, and disinterested Views" the best interest of the colony. And, finally, Belcher had been a true Christian. His religion had been no "nominal, formal Thing, which he received from Tradition, or professed in bare Conformity to the Country where he lived . . . ." Instead it had been "real and genuine, such as commanded his *Heart* and governed his *Life*." To command the heart and thereby to govern all of life was the ultimate goal of the pietistic religion of the eighteenth-century revival.[48] With its stress on success, usefulness, and a pervasive heart-felt piety, Aaron Burr's eulogy of Jonathan Belcher captures the ideal of social leadership that was produced by the Awakening. The New Side Presbyterians were convinced in the late colonial period that only men who fitted that ideal could lead their reunited church in its crucial task of reviving and then reforming American society.

Jonathan Dickinson

Aaron Burr, Sr.

Jonathan Edwards

Samuel Davies

THE PRINCETON PRESIDENTS, 1746–1821

Samuel Finley

John Witherspoon

Samuel Stanhope Smith

Ashbel Green

THE PRINCETON PRESIDENTS, 1746–1821

CHAPTER III

An Expansive Vision

Revival and reformation were the principal concerns not only of the New Side Presbyterians in British North America but also of a transatlantic Protestant community that included evangelical Christians in Germany, England, Scotland, and Ireland, as well as New England. In 1715 the ever alert Cotton Mather had first sensed the emergence of that pietistic communion. He concluded some remarks on the Christian school of A. H. Francke in Halle by observing, "The World begins to feel a Warmth from the *Fire of God,* which thus flames in the Heart of *Germany,* beginning to extend into many Regions; the whole World will e're long be sensible of it." [1] The Great Awakening extended those holy flames into the far reaches of the New World. And it involved evangelical Americans in transatlantic efforts to create a Christian commonwealth that would, finally, bring in the Kingdom of God. The New Side Presbyterian determination to reform American society by ridding it of selfishness and contention was part of that effort. And as the New Sides cooperated with European evangelicals, the Atlantic, which seems to have grown wider after 1689, began to contract, and the vision of the American revivalists began to expand. The result was an evangelical community that was both energetic and purposive. The American Presbyterians' first institution of higher learning was one of the most important products of that community.

THE PROTESTANT COMMONWEALTH AS COMMUNITY

For most American evangelicals, the conviction that fundamental reformation of their society was possible had to mature slowly. For instance, when the first revival—the "little awakening"—broke out in Jonathan Edwards's contentious Northampton church in 1735, all welcomed it and were gratified when the congregation pledged to feud among themselves no more. Public excitement, however, was as restrained as the revival was temporary, and no one in 1735 saw the little awakening as a portent of basic social changes. With the beginning of the *Great* Awakening in 1739, though, expectations began to mount. In that year Jonathan Edwards made his first millennial speculation. He traced the "History of the Redemption of Mankind" and tentatively predicted the imminent culmination of God's design for mankind.[2] With each year of the revival, Edwards became bolder in his predictions.[3] In "Some Thoughts Concerning the Revival," which he published in 1743, Edwards identified the Great Awakening as "the dawning, or at least a prelude, of that glorious work of God," that in the fullness of time will "renew the world of mankind." And, in the midst of the Awakening, he took another significant step. He suggested that the New World was the only fit scene for the final chapter in God's plan for redeeming mankind. The New World, it seemed, was the only appropriate location for the second coming of the Christ and the beginning of the millennium.[4] Of course, other Americans had said no less. John Winthrop had viewed the New World as "a shelter and a hiding place" in which he and his fellow Puritans might await the outpouring upon England of God's wrath.[5] But in the 1740s Edwards expected no imminent Armageddon. His millennial speculations were "non-cataclysmic"[6] and they centered not on the dramatic convulsions envisioned by seventeenth-century chiliasts but, instead, anticipated the gradual but irresistible triumph of the church over its enemies and the consequent return of Christ.[7]

The Presbyterian evangelicals also viewed the Great Awakening as the beginning of the culmination of history. In the words of Samuel Finley in 1744, "the kingdom of Christ is come unto us this day."[8] Others—Samuel Blair, for one—described the "blessed Effusions" of grace in their midst and anticipated even further blessings.[9] Aaron Burr, Edwards's son-in-law, in 1756 captured the sense of development and process that characterized the millennialism of the Presbyterian evangelicals. In a sermon of that year Burr affirmed Edwards's earlier position that Christ would not rule personally over the thousand-year triumph of His church, that He would instead return at the *end* of the millennium. The New Side millennium would "consist in the universal *Promotion* of *true Christianity* and real Religion, the Gospel's having its *genuine Effect* on the Hearts and Lives of Men . . . ." [10]

It was squarely up to the faithful to bring in the Kingdom. Edwards assured them that God would fill His servants "with knowledge and wisdom" and would plant in them a "fervent Zeal" for promoting the "kingdom of Christ." But both he and Burr warned the godly that they must exert themselves to their "most vigorous Attempts for a thorough and general Reformation." [11] Only that exertion could sustain the "surprising" work begun by God. Without it, the hopeful flames of the revival would sputter and die and, with them, the chance to reform colonial society.

As the revivalists saw it, their task of reformation was two-fold. First, men and women had to be roused from their spiritual stupor, from the fatal inertia that had overtaken Christianity in the first decades of the eighteenth century. It seemed to the New Sides that most colonists ignored the claims of religion altogether. Those who did not seemed to satisfy "their Consciences just with a dead Formality in Religion." [12] That was deplorable, of course, and the New Sides missed no opportunity to berate smug laymen. But the evangelical Presbyterians did not stop with criticizing the laity for the sorry state of colonial religion. Equally at fault were unconverted ministers who Sunday after Sunday dulled the sensibilities of their members with learned disquisitions that did not arouse those "affective" parts of the human personality that moved men to action. Those same dead ministers encouraged in their parishioners a "fatal security" that their good works would satisfy a reasonable God who, by 1740, little resembled the arbitrary deity of original Calvinism. [13] The first task of the evangelical minister, then, was to destroy that sense of security before it was too late.

The second task before the New Sides was to end the selfishness and strife that tore at the vitals of colonial society. That selfishness seemed related to the spiritual laxity that was the evangelicals' first enemy. To assure men of the worth of their own good works and to denigrate the divine majesty inevitably was to lead men to glorify self. Doing good works became a way to curry divine favor and to court public esteem rather than a means of furthering the Kingdom of God. Of course, on one level the evangelicals were simply condemning ever present greed.

But, on another, they made an acute psychological judgment: men whose wills had been undermined by spiritual pride appeared to be incapable of choosing the greater good of society over their own selfish interests, much less of furthering that common good by selfless activity. The New Sides were convinced that, as proud men recast God in their own reasonable and benevolent image, they would invariably put self-advancement before social reformation.

The revivalist clergy faced the delicate but imperative task of arousing men from their religious apathy without encouraging a fatal self-centeredness. They had to undo many of the compromises that several generations of Calvinists had made with the rigorous doctrines of the Calvinist Reformation. They freed Calvin's God from the bonds of the covenant and stressed once again His absolute sovereignty and His power arbitrarily to save or condemn fallen man. At the same time, they insisted upon man's inability to "work his way to salvation." That view of God and man was epitomized in Edwards's celebrated description of "sinners in the hands of an angry God." The sermon was intended to set forever upon the minds of sinners a gripping impression of their hopelessness. Edwards used the psychological insights of John Locke and other Enlightenment thinkers skillfully to address "sensational" impressions to the "affections," the "passions" of his hearers. For example, his repeated reference to weight, to sinking and sliding, and to falling are intended to arrest the attention and to humble the will of his hearers.[14]

But there is more to Edwards's sermon than a pitiful spider hanging by a slender thread over the pit of hell. Edwards did not intend merely to overwhelm his audience with a sense of helplessness. Helpless men would never reform anything. The tone and language of the end of the sermon are very different from that of the beginning. Having demolished the pride of the sinner, Edwards laid before him the hope of undeserved salvation and urged him to act, to grasp at that promise. Edwards's God may be casting sinners into hell at the beginning of the sermon, but the conclusion is dominated not by God but by Jesus Christ, the sacrificed Son of God who stands at the open gate of mercy "calling and crying with a loud voice to poor sinners" to come to the Father. Now the Lord is "hastily gathering in his elect in all parts of the land"; souls are "pressing into the kingdom of God." "How awful is it to be left behind at such a day!"[15] The unrelenting emphasis is on the individual's responsibility to exert himself in the pursuit of godliness.

It was perhaps the central achievement of evangelical Christians in the pietist revival of the first half of the eighteenth century to reassert the centrality of the affectional aspects of the religious experience. In Germany and England as well as in the American colonies, they legitimated the heart as the focal point of the human personality and assigned to it the central task of interpreting and integrating the sensory impressions received by the rational faculties of the mind.[16] In doing that, though, the Presbyterian New Sides did not encourage an appeal to unrestrained emotion. The same men who defended the use of emotional and affective language also insisted, in the words of the young revivalist Samuel Davies, that the sinner come to a reasoned, intellectual conviction that "upon the testimony of God," Jesus Christ "is the only Savior of men." That conviction, not "an uncertain emotional experience," the New Sides saw "as the psychological foundation of the new life in Christ."[17]

The revivalists had to be very careful. Implicit in their emphasis on "experimental knowledge," "affective sensibility," and final recourse to the heart, there was a crucial emphasis on the individual.[18] If unchecked, that emphasis could lead to a concentration on self that was as undesirable as the Arminian insistence on doing good works. The New Sides had to face that problem in determining when the Christian might legally disrupt an ecclesiastical union for the good of his own soul. In addition, the New Sides in practice—as opposed to theory—came to stress the importance of the sinner's *trying* to come to God. They ritualistically warned him that God was not bound to respond, but they also insisted that it was the responsibility of the hopeful sinner to try to claim the promise of grace. In their drive to reform colonial society, the revivalists urged sinners to exert themselves: "It is not the portion of the negligent and slothful, but of the active and industrious. There are many duties to be performed, which are contrary to the grain of depraved nature, many enemies to be resisted, armed with polity and power; many hardships to be undergone, ungrateful to flesh and blood; which demand unwearied pains and labour, undaunted courage and resolution and constant watchfulness and diligence."[19]

The New Sides believed that only men whose hearts had been transformed and who were committed to godly exertion could mount the social reformation the revivalists intended. Only they would bring in the millennium. The evangelicals conceded that the true Christian's enthusiasm might occasionally disrupt society, but momentary convulsions were to be tolerated if social reformation followed. With that reformation would come the millennium. Then, Edwards believed, "shall all the world be united in one amiable society"; finally, all "shall then be knitt together in sweet harmony."[20] With the New Side Presbyterians, Edwards anticipated the day when "this work shall have subdued the world, and Christ's kingdom shall be everywhere established and settled in peace, which will be the lengthening of the millennium, or day of the church's peace, rejoicing and triumph on earth . . . ."[21]

The millennialism that accompanied the revival of evangelical religion was, in one sense at least, dependent upon the revival for its life. The millennium as understood by most New Side Presbyterians was to be brought in by the extension of pietistic religion. The pietistic revival, though, came to an end in 1745. However, before the evangelicals could become very worried about the future of the Kingdom in the absence of an ongoing revival, the news of the fall of Fort Louisbourg broke like a thunderclap over colonial society. Even more than the recent revival, the capture by British and colonial forces of the great hulk that glowered out over the Nova Scotia coast seemed a surprising, even an astonishing, work of God. The New Side clergy dutifully explained to their congregations the meaning of the unexpected Protestant triumph over Catholic France. Ritualistically, the clergy reminded their hearers that all divine favor was undeserved and unearned. A just God might have punished the colonists' sins rather than lead the Protestant forces to victory. But the clergy in 1745 did not dwell on those sins. Instead they gloried in a God who scattered His enemies even as He awakened His church.[22]

The capture of Louisbourg appeared as unexpected and as unmerited as the Great Awakening. The revivalists had been ambivalent in the Awakening about the importance of human effort in the process of conversion. Now they were undecided about the efficacy of human arms in physical warfare. In the pulpit and in the battlefield the Calvinist emphasis on an all-powerful God and helpless man made problematical any exhortation to human effort. God would prosper and destroy whom He chose. He would save and damn those whom He foreordained. In practice, though, the revivalists understood that the reformation of colonial society depended upon individual and communal exertion. Consequently, the New Sides very carefully gave credit to an omnipotent deity for the capture of Louisbourg. At the same time, though, they suggested that the recent revival of religion in Protestant America might partially explain the Protestant victory over papist France. There they let the matter of human exertion and divine sovereignty rest. In 1745 the revivalists were content to see in the Great Awakening and in the victory over France two glorious manifestations of divine benevolence that surely portended a new colonial order with eschatological significance.

Expectations so high could only be disappointed. By 1750 the suspicions of 1745 were confirmed. The revival was over. And by 1755 it was clear to many New Side Presbyterians that not all of its influences on colonial society had been good. Like a rising flood, the revival of evangelical religion inundated colonial society and its past. After 1745 that flood quickly ebbed to reveal institutions shattered, authority weakened, traditions challenged, a social landscape fundamentally changed. Perhaps the most basic thing that can be said of the colonial revival is that, in all areas of American life, the Great Awakening heightened the self-awareness of individuals. Whether the young, who were so often the first recipients of reviving grace; or dissenters—non-Anglicans in the south and non-Congregationalists in New England—who now demanded religious toleration and political power of reluctant political and ecclesiastical establishments; or "outlivers," who frequently combined both youth and nonconformity and who now challenged settled geographic limits and traditional settlement and economic patterns; or those colonists who at all levels and in all places strained against the less tangible limits of seventeenth-century social arrangements, many Americans in the aftermath of the Great Awakening simply were no longer willing to accept the arrangements of the past.[23]

Like all epochal events, the revival of religion released in society a great surge of physical and psychic energy. In the case of the Presbyterians, that energy split individual congregations and eventually divided the denomination. And throughout other denominations congregations also were divided. Those new ecclesiastical units quickly became the centers of new settlements that first disrupted and then extended the geographical, social, and economic boundaries of colonial society.[24] In all parts of the colonies disagreements that arose over religious questions in the revival quickly took on political overtones, especially as regarded religious taxation and the entire problem of the establishment of religion. Those political battles produced *ad hoc* coalitions that for a time functioned as recognizable political parties, an unexampled development in a culture in which organized political competition was anathema.[25] In less tangible ways, the revival also affected the development of American capitalism. The Awakening was supposed to halt the spread of selfishness. But, in a way that remains to be fully understood, the revival instead released the incipient American capitalist from that feeling of guilt that often attended his entrepreneurial activities. As it developed in the 1740s and 1750s, the conversion experience proved to be a cathartic experience. The sinner was urged to renounce his greed, to prostrate himself before God, and to be purged of sin. And if the experience did not permanently relieve anxiety, the convert could always remember that moment when sin once had been forgiven.[26]

These developments point up the fundamental irony of the Great Awakening. Not reformation but increased strife and selfishness followed the revival, and in the dark days of the 1750s many evangelicals conceded that much had gone wrong with the Great Awakening. For instance, the Christians of Northampton who had pledged in 1742 to follow Jonathan Edwards in unity and peace by 1750 had driven the great man from their midst, the victim of ugly warfare in both town and congregation. And as Jonathan Edwards retired to the Massachusetts frontier, evangelical Protestants everywhere were hard-pressed to defend a revival that had so thoroughly divided society and then failed even on its own terms. That pressure, however, did not lead the supporters of the Awakening to abandon their efforts to reform colonial society. Instead, it intensified those efforts.

In the dark days following the revival, reformation appeared more necessary than ever. For as the revival ebbed and took alarming shapes, the specter of papism reappeared, now ominously allied in the western forests with red men. The frontier skirmishes that broke out in the early 1750s quickly escalated into the Seven Years' War, the French and Indian War that was an international conflict to decide the ownership of French North America. For the Presbyterian clergy that conflict became the proving ground for the revival, the trial that would measure the success of the late reformation. In the first years of the war that reformation appeared inconsequential indeed. To the Presbyterian minister Ebenezer Prime, vital piety seemed the first casualty of the war. He denounced those who used the hostilities to "excuse their Neglect of all the Forms of Piety and Devotion, and satisfy themselves with a freedom from gross Abominations" and who were content to be merely honest neighbors rather than active crusaders against corruption and selfishness.[27] Most New Sides were more critical of Presbyterians during the war. To most of them the conflict seemed to unleash selfishness on an unprecedented scale.

In Virginia the reaction of the colonists to the French and Indian War appeared to Samuel Davies the same destructive combination of lethargy and greed that had poisoned pre-Awakening society. Situated near the center of Virginia in Hanover County, Davies was appalled at the indifference with which the eastern Tidewater viewed the Indian threat to the frontier. It seemed to him that men everywhere had sunk into "a deep sleep," and had been unmanned by a "stupid security" until they could not recognize danger a few miles away. (Interestingly enough, Davies used the same terms to describe those men who were neglectful of their physical security that he and other revivalists used to describe those who were unconcerned about the fate of their souls.) On the Tidewater colonists refused to hear the call of the defenseless west for assistance. Some of those easterners even endangered the security of their fellow Virginians by trading with the enemy. Others took up arms only to turn profiteer and enriched themselves while pretending to serve their country. Small wonder that Davies described Virginia society in pathological terms. Just as it was endangered from without, the body politic of Virginia had proven rotten within, its head sick, its heart weak, the entire organism "full of wounds, and bruises, and putrefying sores."[28]

In Virginia, Samuel Davies argued that the colonists ignored the responsibilities of social union and thereby weakened the social organism. At the same time, Presbyterians on Pennsylvania's frontier believed that government itself was ignoring the responsibilities of leadership in a social union. During the war the growing Scotch-Irish Presbyterian population on the frontier demanded with increasing fervor that the Quaker government protect the colony from the Indian allies of the French. The Quakers were caught between the pacifist doctrines of their faith and the obvious need to defend the citizens under their rule. In 1763, while the Quakers debated alternative courses of action, some frontiersmen took the law into their own hands and murdered six friendly Indians living under the protection of the Quakers. Shortly thereafter the "Paxton boys," as they were called for Paxton, a little Presbyterian community in the central part of the province, marched on Philadelphia to demand greater legislative representation for the western counties and, more urgently, a harsher Indian policy. The Paxton crisis is discussed in detail in other studies and concerns us here only insofar as it clarifies the Presbyterian view of those developments that threatened social union in the late colonial period.[29]

The Presbyterians and their Quaker rulers defended their actions in the public press, each presenting the other as a danger to the social organism. Quaker defenders asserted that the citizens of Pennsylvania and their government constituted a "body Corporate, which body composes a Society in civil Government." The members of that corporate body were "bound together by Unanimity and Concord, under the sanction of Laws," which body could be destroyed only when one or more of its members overthrew the laws that united the whole. The violent Presbyterians were doing just that, it was charged. The government's defenders advanced a theory of shared interests and virtual representation that closely resembled that put forward by the Old Sides during the Great Schism.[30] And like the New Sides in that conflict, the Presbyterian spokesmen in Pennsylvania during the Paxton crisis would have none of it. The Presbyterians denied any mutuality of interests with the Quakers. Instead they denounced the Friends as a minority, a "particular faction" that alone was responsible for "almost all the contentions and all the miseries under which we have so long struggled." Opposed to the Quaker minority, in this view, was "the majority of the province," which had been deprived of their just power in the government by malapportionment. The Quakers were a grasping minority, "possess'd of the virtue of self love in great perfection." For, while they ignored the west's pleas for help, the Quakers lavished public funds on the Indians, "his Majesty's worst of Enemies . . . ." The Presbyterians believed that the imperatives of community as well as their slain brothers had been sacrificed to Quaker ambition and greed.[31] They could agree with Samuel Davies in Virginia that if the members of a social union did not aid one another, those members "might as well have continued in a state of nature, as be united in a society . . . ."[32]

In New England in 1749 the Reverend William Balch had echoed Samuel Davies's advice that the colonial societies should "consider themselves as making but one body" and then "have the same care for one another as in the body natural . . . ." In the same year another New Englander, the Reverend Jonathan Mayhew, had described the force that alone could hold those societies together: "Love is the spirit that cements mankind together; and preserves that order and harmony amongst them which is requisite in order to the general safety and welfare."[33] To the south, Samuel Davies also identified love as the solution for the problems that plagued colonial society at the midcentury. In a sermon entitled simply, "God Is Love," the evangelical Presbyterian advanced a theory of social union that defined love as that force that held all unions together and that defined as virtuous the man who valued the interests of society more highly than his own personal desires. Love was a concern for one's fellow man evidenced in a willingness to forgo economic and social advancement for the sake of a larger whole. Davies's concept of love was not as abstract and static as was the more conservative Mayhew's. It was a force with which to counteract the destructive and divisive force of American individualism. Without love, Davies believed, "the great community of the rational universe would dissolve, and men and angels would turn savages, and roam apart in barbarous solitude." He asked, "Can a social creature be happy in eternal solitude or in a state of society, while ill-affected towards the other members of society or while they are ill-affected towards him and he to them, *hateful, and hating one another?*" The answer was obvious.[34] The same forces that made the Presbyterian reunion imperative now made it urgently necessary that Americans cease their selfish ways and establish a Christian commonwealth in which America would be reformed and prepared to receive the second coming of Christ.

But love alone was not adequate to the task of bringing in the Kingdom. After the failure of the Awakening to permanently transform colonial society, the Presbyterian clergy used the resurgence of the papist threat in the 1750s to exhort their followers to exertion in a holy war against the Antichrist. It is clear from those exhortations that the clergy used the occasion of the war to remind Americans of the responsibilities of social union. Aaron Burr sounded the theme before the assembled New Side Synod of New York in 1756 when he bewailed the colonies' *"divided Councils."* [35] In the same year Gilbert Tennent stood before a volunteer militia company in Philadelphia and thundered, *"Brethren,* we were born not merely for ourselves, but for the Publick Good!" The call to serve that public good through selfless exertion resounds through the sermons of the 1750s and reflects the same concern for individual and social reformation that characterized the exhortations of the Awakening. The evangelicals located in Catholicism the final obstacle to reformation in the colonies. And Tennent assured the militiamen that "Shedding the Blood of our Enemies in a *lawful* [defensive] *War,* is a good Work, it is the Lord's Work . . . ." And in Virginia Samuel Davies warned the women of his Hanover congregation that they must not use their "soft entreaties and flowing tears" to "unman the stronger sex, and restrain them from exerting themselves in so good a cause." [36]

In 1761 the Protestant forces prevailed in that cause, and the Presby-

terian clergy quickly gave all the credit to God. They earlier had
declared that virtuous exertion would assure victory, but they had never
bound God to reward the efforts of His people. Now, Samuel Davies
in a "Thanksgiving Sermon for National Blessings" informed his audience
that God had granted victory to the Protestants because His honor and
good name were at stake. God allowed the English and colonists to
prevail over France "not for our own sake, but for his own name's
sake . . . ." But Davies also suggested that God was bound in an un-
breakable covenant with the Americans: "the honour of God may be
so intimately concerned in the protection of a people, that he may work
deliverance for them, even when they deserve to be cut off; and when
it would be just and fit to give them up into the hands of their enemies,
were it not that he has assumed such relations, and come under such
engagements to them." [37] Davies then could consistently urge his people
to virtuous exertion while reserving to God the undisputed—but unused—
right to withhold success from them. He could encourage the colonists
to godly activity, secure in the hope that the deity would, in the normal
course of events, reward it.

THE SOCIAL FUNCTION OF HIGHER EDUCATION

The Presbyterians knew that their ideas about the importance of selflessness and virtuous exertion had to be institutionalized if they were to
have any permanent effect on colonial society. Both the Old and New
Sides understood that the Great Awakening had loosened the traditional
structures of colonial society and appreciated that, in an almost physical
sense, the revival had made society momentarily malleable. Both the
defenders and the opponents of the revival realized that institutions had
to be created to mold that ductile postrevival society into desirable forms.
In particular, each side was determined to create an institution of higher
learning to give shape to the society coming out of the revival. Both
Old and New Sides, of course, were heir to a venerable Presbyterian
tradition of support for education. John Knox's *First Book of Discipline*
in 1560 had instructed that "everie severall churche have a school maister"
and that each father in a congregation be compelled, no matter what his
"estait or conditioun," to bring up his children in "learnyng and virtue." [38]
And while on a tour of Scotland in the late seventeenth century the
English Bishop Gilbert Burnet had been much impressed by the Presbyterian regard for education. He had been surprised to find even "a

poor commonality" able to dispute fine points of secular and sacred government and was even more surprised to find knowledge "among the lowest of them, their cottagers and servants." [39] Allowing for exaggeration, it is obvious that the Presbyterians in both the Old and New Worlds had a high regard for the importance of education. They appreciated its power to mold the young and were even more aware of education's power to form societies, particularly new societies. Both Old and New Sides could have agreed with the Presbyterian layman, William Livingston, when he asserted in 1753 that "A College in a new Country" will "more or less, influence every Individual amongst us, and diffuse its Spirit thro' all Ranks, Parties and Denominations." [40]

The differences between the Old and New Sides were never clearer than when institutionalized in competing schools in the late colonial period. Those differences flowed directly from different perceptions of America's future and of the social forces threatening that future. We have seen that the Old Sides did not accept the New Side view of social union or of social leadership. It is equally important that the opponents of the revival did not share the evangelicals' millennialism. They did not see the Great Awakening as the penultimate chapter in a cosmic historical development. It is not surprising, then, that the Old Sides did not feel impelled to prepare in the colonies a suitable stage upon which the last chapter of that development could unfold.

In their own way, though, the Old Sides were as disturbed as the New Sides about the future of British North America. The Old Sides above all else were alarmed as social order was threatened, first by religious contention and turmoil and then by the flood of German immigrants into the middle colonies after 1740. The crisis of social order that was created by the revival and immigration seemed directly related to a crisis of ministerial authority. The Old Sides were determined to meet and resolve both crises. To that end they moved to stabilize society in the middle colonies and to professionalize the ministry. Education was essential to both solutions.

The Presbyterian Old Sides in the decade before the Great Awakening prescribed for the first time the process whereby men entered one of the learned professions in America.[41] In the thirties and especially in the forties the Old Sides sought to restrict entry into the profession and in particular attempted to raise the literary standards for entering the Presbyterian ministry. In the presbyteries that they controlled, the Old Sides demanded letters of recommendation of any foreign candidate for the ministry.[42] They required that each candidate familiarize every member of the presbytery with his theological views and with his reasons for wanting to enter the ministry.[43] And in the "trials" each candidate had to pass before ordination, the Old Sides emphasized literary accomplishment and competency in natural and moral philosophy as well as extensive grounding in theology.[44] As a result of this rigor, ministerial trials in one of the Old Side presbyteries took anywhere from eighteen months to almost three years.[45]

All efforts to raise ministerial standards, however, were dependent finally upon the Old Sides' creating their own college. They required a college degree or its equivalent of all candidates but in the 1730s had no way of offering that education themselves. A few could tolerate William Tennent's "Log College" at Neshaminy, Pennsylvania, when it was first established in the late twenties but withdrew that support after the school became the center of the revival in the middle colonies.[46] For a while in the late thirties the Old Sides were content to require a degree from a New England or European university and to hope that a rigorous synodical examination would "prevent unqualified men from creeping in among us . . . in these remote parts of the earth . . . ."[47] But, when the Great Schism left them free to do so, the old Sides established a school completely under their own control. In 1744 the Old Side Synod of Philadelphia set the learned and tolerant Francis Alison over an academy in New London, Maryland, where he was to teach the languages, philosophy, and divinity.[48]

Francis Alison was one of the best-read men in colonial America, and it is clear that the Old Sides sincerely intended that his school raise the intellectual level of the Presbyterian ministry. But the New London Academy—later moved to Newark, Delaware—had another important, social function. By raising and standardizing educational requirements for the ministry, the Old Sides hoped to stabilize an increasingly heterogeneous society in the middle colonies. To that end, they first sought the assistance of the Old Light Congregationalists who had just driven the Great Awakening from Yale. The Old Side Presbyterians recommended to Yale's crusty president, Thomas Clap, that he receive Alison's graduates and complete their education, thereby strengthening order and stability in both New England and the middle colonies.[49]

When Clap had to refuse, the Old Sides turned to the Calvinist ministers who served the growing number of Dutch, German, French, and Welsh immigrants in and around Philadelphia. Those immigrants

alarmed the Old Sides because they either abandoned their religion altogether in America or fell easy prey to ranting evangelists. The Old
Sides tried to persuade the Dutch and the German ministers in particular
to cooperate with the Presbyterians in supporting Alison's academy,
thereby promoting a stable population by raising ministerial standards in
all churches. But the European Calvinists were suspicious of the motives
of the Old Sides and refused to support the school. Whereupon the
Presbyterians appealed directly to the classis of Holland, which had
responsibility for the Dutch Church in America. The Old Sides urged
the classis to stabilize the chaotic situation among its charges, lest they
fall prey to the "deceitful and erring sentiments which are found
abundantly in this region." [50] To their own agents in Holland, the Old
Sides were more honest about their motives. Certainly they were concerned about unassimilated immigrants in the middle colonies, but the
Old Sides also were alarmed by the barbarism they saw encroaching
upon their own infant congregations. There "are found many vacancies
among us," the moderator of the synod observed to one of the agents,
and they "seem likely still more to increase, since the numbers of
those who confess Presbyterian sentiments in this and surrounding
Provinces over which the care of our Synod extends," yearly increases.
When coupled with the alarming influx of immigrants, this view of
encroaching barbarism on the opening frontier was a powerful impetus
for the founding of Alison's academy. [51]

Other Pennsylvanians shared the Old Side fears. The Anglican provost
of the College of Philadelphia, the Reverend William Smith, distrusted the
Germans as the foundation of Quaker rule in Pennsylvania and sus-
pected that they might rally to the French in the event of war. Smith,
then, joined with Old Side Presbyterian ministers, such as Alison and
Robert Cross, and Presbyterian laymen, such as Chief Justice William
Allen, to establish a system of charity schools that were intended in part
to eradicate German culture in the middle colonies. These Presbyterians
supported many civic improvements in Philadelphia, but they endorsed
most enthusiastically those intended to assimilate Philadelphia's immigrants and to elevate professional standards. Alison's academy would
attend to the latter; the proposed charity schools, the former.

The perceived German threat to social order was a complex one, and
the charity school scheme was carefully constructed so as to meet each
aspect of the menace. The Germans were accustomed to monarchical
rule, Smith believed, and had to be "taught to feel the meaning and exult

in the enjoyment of liberty . . . ." That accomplished, "a high and commanding sense of the great differences" between the slavery of papal monarchies and Protestant liberty could be inculcated upon the Germans. The immigrant youths would become convinced of the superiority of English culture and willingly "quit their national manners." With that, Smith indicated the true social function of the schools. Education was "the only means for incorporating these foreigners with us . . . ." Once the rising generation was educated, "no acts of our enemies will be able to divide them in their affection; and all the narrow distinctions, etc., will be forgot—forever forgot—in higher interests." [52]

The charity schools were also to inculcate hierarchical principles. Smith believed that schools should provide one kind of education for the sons of an elite, who would enter as a matter of course the "learned professions," and another kind of instruction for the "remaining people of the country," who would be content to enter "mechanical" callings. Such a division reflected unalterable social distinctions, Smith insisted, and was "absolutely necessary" if youth were to remain in their "proper sphere." [53] With the Germans in those proper spheres, the clergy could discharge their duty "to form the social temper" by inculcating right thinking upon them. That inculcation, Smith believed, was especially crucial in a free society: "Those who are in most cases *free* to speak and act as they please, had need be well instructed how to speak and act . . . ." [54]

These efforts to assimilate foreign elements in the middle colonies were prompted in part by fear and, in turn, alarmed the Germans. Some responded with initial enthusiasm to the idea of uniting in the proposed charity schools. They expressed a "just and lively sense" of the "pleasures resulting from a unity of languages," and anticipated from that unity a more fundamental "unity of sentiments." [55] More typically, though, the Germans retorted that they were neither in need of religious instruction nor did they care to learn English from the charity schools. Pique settled into firm resistance when Provost Smith, who apparently did not trust education to vanquish entirely the German culture, recommended that Parliament disfranchise those Germans who would not learn English and then suppress the flourishing German presses. Far from being silenced, those presses, especially that of Christian Saur, launched an effective counter-attack against Smith and the Old Side Presbyterians. By the early sixties the charity school movement in Pennsylvania was dead. [56]

And so was the Presbyterian–Anglican alliance. That cooperation had always been tentative. [57] It is true that Alison left the Newark Academy in the fifties to become the vice provost of the Anglican College of Philadelphia. But he was always uncomfortable there. Consequently, when Provost Smith began to alienate most Presbyterians by leading the campaign for an Anglican bishopric, Alison returned to the academy and the cooperation came to an end. Back at Newark Alison continued to instruct a number of young men, some of whom were founders of the American republic. But the Old Side academy did not flourish. That fact is due, in part, to the arrival in 1768 of the Reverend John Witherspoon from Scotland to superintend the New Side college at Princeton. In the struggle for control of American Presbyterianism, Witherspoon simply outmaneuvered Alison, and in the late colonial period the New Side college flourished while the Old Side academy struggled along. More important, though, in explaining the latter's relative lack of success was the marked contrast between the vital New Side synod and the moribund Synod of Philadelphia. In 1745 the Philadelphia Synod numbered twenty-five ministers and the new Synod of New York, twenty-one. By 1758 the Old Sides had lost three members and the New Sides had trebled in size. In a less tangible way, the Old Side academy lagged behind the New Side college because the energy behind it proved to be implosive; the motives behind it were correctly denounced as constrictive; and its impact on colonial society was, finally, negligible.[58]

The New Side educational venture, on the other hand, was impelled by the explosive energy of the revival. The evangelicals' piety, their millennialism, and their emphasis on selfless exertion in the cause of colonial reformation, when institutionalized, proved to be an expansive force in colonial society and produced in Princeton College the institutional expression of the revivalists' aspirations for colonial society as well as the principal instrument for realizing those aspirations.[59]

The New Sides were convinced that an educational reformation must precede any effort to reform society at large. That conviction was part of the eighteenth-century evangelical insistence that all mental activity, all operations of the rational faculties must be interpreted and integrated by the heart. The New Sides denied vehemently the Old Side charge that they were, for that reason, anti-intellectual. Gilbert Tennent proudly admitted to opposing the "Metaphysical Niceties and sublime critical Disquisitions" that too often displaced "the Defence of Gospel-Truth" in the sermons of the Old Sides. And Samuel Finley disdained those Old Side ministers who possessed only mere morality and "Head-Knowledge."[60] The New Sides insisted that if souls were to be saved, if society was to be reformed, a minister's education must prepare him to address all levels of intelligence, to command the respect of all social levels, not only that of an educated elite. The minister must, of course, be a cultivated man, able to "apprehend Things clearly," to "Methodize his Conceptions regularly, and Reason solidly." But he must also remember to "speak instructively" rather than learnedly, and to "suppress a Thousand flowery Expressions for the sake of one that is pertinent and level to the Capacity of His Hearers." [61] Finley was arguing for an education that accepted as legitimate the affective and emotional basis of evangelical religion. The New Side system of ministerial education was founded on that base.

That system of education was intended to vitalize rather than professionalize the ministry. New Side presbyteries, like the strongly evangelistic men of New Brunswick, continued to examine candidates in the learned languages, the arts, and the sciences. Occasionally, they even failed a man on an exam, something that the Old Sides never did.[62] But the revivalists also examined the "Work of converting Grace" in a candidate's heart. It is true that the New Sides shortened the length of candidacy—but not by reducing standards. The New Side synod after 1745 vigorously supervised a number of missionary and benevolent activities. The press of those activities forced the New Side presbyteries to increase the number of their meetings. While the Old Side Presbytery of Philadelphia met only once in 1744 and 1745, the New Brunswick men convened at least quarterly. Since candidates were examined at presbyterial meetings, the unanticipated result of the more frequent meetings was to greatly abbreviate candidacy. By the late fifties the New Sides were licensing young men within two months of beginning trials and ordaining them a year later. By 1761 the pace of candidacy had become so frantic that three harried candidates communicated to the New Brunswick Presbytery their "great Fatigue, and continued Hurry, in riding from Place to Place," supplying pulpits and preparing for exams. They begged to be excused from one small part of one examination and, after discussion, were allowed to do so.[63]

The New Sides were able to abbreviate candidacy while maintaining standards because they immediately established a vigorous school charged with the responsibility for facilitating ministerial education. The College of New Jersey, or Princeton, as it later was called, was established in 1746 by the men of the Synod of New York, who were joined in that endeavor by the Scotch-Irish supporters of the Log College after the death of William Tennent in that year. The school was founded in particular by Aaron Burr and Jonathan Dickinson, two sons of Yale who were displeased with Yale's recent expulsion of revivalistically inclined students. The New Side founders were quite open about the school's primary purpose. "The great & chief design of erecting the College," Dickinson announced, "is for the Education of pious & well qualified Candidates for the Ministry, that vital Peity [sic] may by that means be promoted in our Churches, and . . . Religion may be transmitted to Posterity." [64]

But the New Side school was to be much more than a provincial theological seminary. It was a broadly conceived intercolonial instrument of social integration and reformation. From its inception the men of New York, New Jersey, and Pennsylvania were determined that their New Jersey school would be an intercolonial and cosmopolitan institution as Harvard, William and Mary, and Yale had never been. When the Synod of New York appealed to the Scottish Presbyterians for aid for its college, it stressed that the churches of six colonies depended upon Princeton for their ministers. When the Princeton trustees appealed to the English dissenters for assistance, they reminded them that the college served not only the middle colonies but all of British America.[65] Moreover, the trustees attracted to the Princeton presidency men from New England (Jonathan Edwards), from the south (Samuel Davies), from the middle colonies (Finley, Dickinson, and Burr), and finally lured John Witherspoon from Scotland, in part by emphasizing the intercolonial and interdenominational nature of the college. And when the Scotsman arrived in America he found that the trustees had not exaggerated. In his classes were young men not only from all the colonies but from Canada and the West Indies as well.[66]

Of course it is easy to make too much of colonial Princeton's cosmopolitan nature. Certainly it was a Presbyterian school, and no one connected with the school tried to hide that fact. But in the religiously heterodox middle colonies, it would have been suicidal to announce that Princeton would welcome only Presbyterian students. Additionally, the Presbyterian school was not the only college created after the Great Awakening to attract large numbers of students from outside the province in which it was located. One study of the student populations of colonial colleges finds that, while twenty-five percent of Princeton's student body came from New England and from colonies south of the Mason–Dixon line, fully seventy percent of the College of Rhode Island's students came from outside Rhode Island. And that same study suggests that Princeton, Rhode Island, and Yale attracted the largest number of out-of-colony students simply because they were the least expensive of the colleges available.[67] Finally, it is important that Princeton was the first American college to be chartered in a colony in which no single denomination was legally established. Moreover, it was created by a charter granted by an Anglican governor to a group of Presbyterian ministers and laymen. Consequently, there was no mention in the charter of preparing a godly ministry.

In fact, Princeton in the colonial period was not simply a seminary for the production of Presbyterian clergymen. Throughout the eighteenth century the percentage of college graduates entering the ministry had constantly declined, and the creation of Princeton accelerated that trend. Of the more than two hundred young men who graduated from Princeton between 1748 and 1766, fewer than one hundred entered the ministry.[68] The imperatives of evangelical religion and social reformation dictated that all professions and "callings" be filled by pious men. Consequently, according to Samuel Blair, the college was intended to produce men of letters, lawyers, and politicians who would mold society in accordance with the dictates of evangelical religion.[69] New Side Presbyterians like Blair were convinced that American society had reached an important turning point at the mid-eighteenth century. They believed that the Awakening had unsettled society and that the social organism might settle back into undesirable new forms. Among other things, Princeton was intended to prevent that from happening.[70]

The Presbyterian belief in education's power to mold societies was most graphically illustrated in the debate over chartering King's College in New York City. That debate primarily dealt with the proposed college's relations with the Anglican Church and will be discussed in that context in the next section of the present chapter. But the debate over King's also saw three Presbyterian laymen, William Livingston, William Smith, Jr., and John M. Scott, express the New Side Presbyterian view of the social function of institutions of higher learning, most especially in new societies. As had the New Side revivalists during the French and Indian War, Livingston emphasized the malleability of youthful societies. They were inert and ductile organisms that could be manipulated and shaped almost at will. The principles learned at a college would "run thro' a Man's whole future Conduct, and affect the Society of which he is a Member, in Proportion to his Sphere of Activity . . . ." And in a new country, a college would make vast alterations in all "Affairs and Condition, civil and religious." [71]

Having established the power of educational institutions to affect social development, Livingston then concisely stated his view of the "true Use of Education," the end toward which schools should direct society and its sons: " 'Tis to improve their Hearts and Understanding, to infuse a public Spirit and Love of their Country; to inspire them with the Principles of Honour and Probity; with a fervent zeal for Liberty, and a diffusive Benevolence for Mankind; and in a Word, to make them the more extensively serviceable to the Common-Wealth." [72] No New Side minister ever phrased more aptly the Presbyterian hopes for the new college at Princeton and the confidence that those aspirations would be realized.

THE COLONIAL DEBATE OVER SECTARIAN EDUCATION

Not all colonists accepted the Presbyterian description of Princeton and instead labeled it a "party-scheme" that was intended only to advance the Presbyterian cause. [73] In the colonial period the Presbyterians did not really have to answer those charges. Just as the school was established, the colonial Anglicans began to agitate for the appointment of an American bishop and for the creation of Anglican colleges in several of the colonies. Those demands created an unprecedented uproar in the non-Anglican churches of America, and they formed the context for the first sustained debate in America over sectarian education. The Presbyterian response to the newly aroused Church of England varied from colony to colony and is relevant to the final Presbyterian participation in the debate in New York City over the chartering of King's College.

In the late colonial period Presbyterians in Virginia were most numerous in the center of the colony and on the Southside. There they were a convenient buffer between the Indians to the west and the Anglican majority to the east. Throughout the late colonial period those Presbyterians maintained that they would "chearfully submit to the usual Tests of Loyalty & orthodoxy imposed by Authority upon Protestant Dissenters . . . ." They demanded only that they be granted all the privileges guaranteed by the English Act of Toleration. The new Presbytery of Hanover in 1756 reminded the governor of the colony that they were part of the established Church of Scotland and that they fully appreciated the social benefits of uniformity and stability that accrued from established but tolerant religions.[74] When New England Congregationalists began in the 1750s to bristle over the threat of an Anglican bishopric, Samuel Davies denounced their opposition as "hardly consistent with a spirit of toleration."[75] Davies later in the colonial period led the struggle of the Virginia Presbyterians for full toleration as loyal dissenters, but he did not support the harassed Baptists' demands for complete religious freedom. Nor did the New Side synod ever instruct their missionaries to Virginia to support the Baptists in those demands.[76]

In New York the relationship between Presbyterian and Anglican was quite different. The Anglican Church, which probably numbered among its members no more than ten percent of the colony's population, claimed nonetheless to be the established church of the colony and demanded of the colony a college that would promote "religion in the way" of a national church. The proposed college was to be controlled by an Anglican board and to be presided over by a churchman. The Anglicans argued that their demand was justified because their numbers included the best and wealthiest men in the city and because they, like all established churches, encompassed and served the interests of all denominations, who were in any case protected under the benevolent Anglican establishment by the English Toleration Act.[77]

The Presbyterian William Livingston lead the attack against those Anglican claims and demands. He outlined a new vision of a cosmopolitan society in which education was controlled by the state and dedicated to the advancement of the entire society. In a series of essays Livingston buried in a deluge of evidence the Anglican claim to be established and scornfully dismissed their pretension to represent all of society.[78] He insisted that the Anglicans were only one denomination among many, that they were a "faction," and a dangerous one at that because they represented in some way the interests of the crown. And for one denomination to control education in a heterogeneous society was unacceptable to Livingston because it would create social conflict and contentions. In a homogeneous society, like that of Massachusetts, he conceded that a college might be controlled by one denomination to the "universal Satisfaction of the People," who after all did share real interests. But in a heterogeneous population like New York City's, sectarian control of the one college would be disastrous. Precisely because it would be a potent instrument for molding society, Livingston insisted that the proposed college must not be an "Engine . . . for the Purpose of a Party

. . . ." A sectarian school would immediately establish a tyrannous minority which might—or might not—tolerate dissenters. And that school also would force members of other churches to send their sons to other colonies to be educated. In either case, Livingston warned, society at large was the ultimate loser in the "general Discontent and Tumult" that would doubtless ensue.[79]

If the proposed college was to produce the selflessness necessary to social reformation, Livingston argued, it must be "constituted for general Use, for the Public Benefit . . . ."[80] It must therefore be chartered and controlled by the people's representatives in their legislature. Livingston's argument for legislative rather than sectarian control of higher education was, on the one hand, a traditional one. Only a nonsectarian school, directed by the people's representatives, could impress upon the student the crucial fact that he "was not designed for his own Happiness but also to promote the Felicity of his Fellow-Creatures." That traditional defense, though, was balanced by an innovative one. Livingston suggested that only in the legislature could the potential tyranny of one interest group be checked and balanced by the power of other groups. The "Jealousy of all Parties combating each other, would inevitably produce a perfect Freedom for each particular Party." Out of that social conflict would emerge a "public good" that, even in a heterogeneous society, would be viable because it represented the concessions and compromises of all parts of the society. The product of conflict, this public good was the only means William Livingston could see of holding together New York's increasingly contentious population.[81] In Livingston's view, legislative control would produce and then protect the "common good" of society through the controlled, legitimate conflict among the various interest groups that made up New York's population. And legislative control would encourage the student (the future citizen) always to prefer the public interest to his own.

The New York Presbyterians failed to forestall Anglican control of King's College, but the college at Princeton fulfilled in many ways Livingston's demands for a school firmly established on a catholic scheme that would attract students from all colonies and alleviate many of the ills that plagued colonial society.[82] Princeton's charter guaranteed that no person would be barred from the school "on account of any speculative principles of religion."[83] Its board was interdenominational, containing one Welsh and one Dutch Calvinist, two Anglicans, and two Quakers, and was drawn from all the middle colonies. No percentage of the board was required to be Presbyterian; the president was not legally required to be a Presbyterian; and the school's worship services did not have to be Presbyterian. Moreover, the records of the New Side synod do not mention the school until six years after its creation in 1746. Princeton's board was self-perpetuating and was independent of the synod. It alone had responsibility for hiring the school's president who, in turn, had to answer to no one for his teaching methods and ideas.[84]

The Old Side school at New London and Newark, on the other hand, was a thoroughly ecclesiastical institution dominated by the Philadelphia Synod. During the Great Schism that synod had argued that it was neither unscriptural for the church to have the means of educating its clergy under its direction nor unreasonable for the synod to inspect the school's progress.[85] Consequently, when the synod established its school in 1744, the trustees were instructed to "inspect into the master's diligence in, and method of, teaching; consider and direct what authors are chiefly to be read in the several branches of learning . . . and in sum, to order all affairs relating to said school as they see expedient, and be accountable to the Synod, making report of their proceedings and the state of the school yearly." [86] The synod also was instructed to fill any vacancies in the faculty, which they did as such arose.[87] No such intimate relationship existed between the New Side synod and the school at Princeton.

COLONIAL FINANCES

Princeton's catholic foundation, its expansive, intercolonial, even transatlantic nature can perhaps best be seen in the way it was financed. At no time in the colonial period were the presbyteries or their churches the college's principal source of income. Occasional appeals were made by the synod for gifts to support "poor and pious youth" who were studying for the ministry, but the presbyteries' response to those appeals was minimal and always unstructured. Collections had to be postponed, sometimes indefinitely.[88] Moreover, the denomination's limited resources had to be divided among the several philanthropic and missionary activities that the New Sides mounted in the years immediately following the Great Awakening. The New Side response to the revival produced many demands on the denomination's limited funds. In 1761, for instance, the demands of "several useful designs"—the needs of widows, orphans, Indians, the frontier—forced the synod regretfully to defer "to a more convenient season" the Princeton board's request for assistance in establishing a divinity professorship. That more convenient season was deferred throughout the entire colonial period.[89]

When individual philanthropists were persuaded to contribute funds to Princeton, their gifts did not make of it a sectarian theological seminary. It is true that some did leave money to train poor and pious youth for the ministry and presumably to strengthen Princeton's Presbyterian identity. But other donors left legacies that were intended to do neither. The largest gift of the colonial period, the £535 given by the Phillips brothers of Boston, was given for unspecified purposes, not for ministerial education.[90] When Governor Jonathan Belcher, who had granted Princeton's charter, left the school his library and portrait, the pious Congregationalist modestly assured the board that his benefactions were intended only to encourage learning and piety in the province. Grateful, the board responded to the man who had come to symbolize the selfless virtue that was the New Side ideal and praised his "disinterested Motives, which activate every part of your Excellency's Conduct . . . ."[91]

The intercolonial and interdenominational emphasis fostered by private and institutional philanthropy was further strengthened by the far-flung trips made by Presbyterian laymen and clerics in the college's behalf. Those men were dispatched by the board in pairs to spend up to six months traveling hundreds of miles, from New England to the West Indies.[92] And when John Witherspoon arrived in 1768, the denomination and the board of trustees "set on foot a general subscription" throughout the colonies, probably the first of its kind in British North America. Witherspoon, himself one of the most striking symbols of the school's transatlantic character, traversed virtually the entire Atlantic seaboard, acquainting thousands of Americans—not just Presbyterians either—with Princeton, and in the process raising more than £7,000 for the college.[93]

Like these fund-raising trips, efforts to raise money for Princeton by lottery emphasized the school's "public" nature. While still governor, Jonathan Belcher on several occasions attempted to arrange public aid for the school but with no success. Between 1748 and 1762 the trustees petitioned the colonial legislature in the broadest terms. They reminded the legislators of the aid rendered to other colleges by other colonial governments. And, when requesting permission to mount a lottery, they reminded the lawmakers that it would bring money into the colony from outside its borders. They stressed that the lottery was a "public" and not a "private" one. They assured the assembly that the college was founded on the most catholic of foundations and welcomed all Christians. But to no avail. (Later the failure of the colonial government to render any aid to Princeton redounded to the school's benefit by making credible the school's claim that it was independent of the state as well as the church.) [94]

When the New Jersey legislature persistently refused the board permission to hold lotteries within the colony, President Aaron Burr extended the scope of the board's fund-raising to New England. A native of Connecticut, Burr used personal contacts to persuade that colony's legislature to grant the Princeton board the right to hold a lottery in New England, whereupon the president praised the Connecticut lawmakers as "inspired with a noble greatness of Spirit, which looks down with Disdain upon those petty Jealousies which are too apt to activate publick Bodies . . . ." [95] The legislators' gesture measured the power of Burr's personal intercolonial contacts and indicates the validity of the college's claims of widespread support.

That support extended across the Atlantic as well as over colonial boundaries. The Protestant commonwealth the New Sides hoped would succeed the Great Awakening, though centered in reformed America, included also the urban centers of the British Isles. If the millennium was to begin in Philadelphia, the friends of vital piety in Edinburgh, Glasgow, Belfast, Dublin, and London would be as responsible for the glorious event as the more happily situated American evangelicals. The founders of Princeton had many contacts in those cities, often of the closest personal nature. Those friends were immediately solicited in Princeton's behalf, and their gifts invariably strengthened the college's cosmopolitan nature.[96]

In 1753 Samuel Davies and Gilbert Tennent embarked upon the most ambitious of those transatlantic efforts to raise money for Princeton. The two New Side ministers sailed for London armed with personal recommendations and introductions, a petition to the General Assembly of the Church of Scotland assuring that body of the college's dedication to the "public good," and the personal endorsement of a group of New England ministers. The trip was quite successful. The Scottish Assembly promised its aid; a Scotsman gave Tennent £300 to support an Indian student at Princeton; and several Englishmen donated a substantial fund to further ministerial education. The two ministers collected more than £3,000 dedicated to a variety of causes. The effort to put those causes into practice in the two decades after 1753 was to a large extent responsible for the scope of the New Side Presbyterians' activities and for the vigor of their young college.[97]

While on his "begging trip" to England, Samuel Davies kept a diary. On May 7, 1754, the New Side minister recorded this thought: " 'Tis but little that so useless a Creature can do for God during the short Day of life; but to be instrumental . . . [in] laying a Foundation of extensive Benefit to Mankind, not only in the present but in future Generations, is a most animating Prospect . . . ."[98] With his emphasis on extensive usefulness Davies caught the New Side Presbyterians' determination in the late colonial period to rid American society of the selfishness and lethargy that seemed to threaten its vitals. And he was in Great Britain gathering far-flung support for an institution he believed was indeed a foundation "of extensive Benefit to Mankind." Founded at the height of the Great Schism, Princeton was intended by its founders not to acerbate the divisions created by that conflict but, instead, to bring to fruition a new vision of American society that had emerged from the Great Awakening. That society would be free of class conflict, sectarian strife, and the contentions that flowed from self-love. And, most important, it would provide for the lately divided Presbyterians an organic community, which in the late colonial period remained their social ideal.

Gilbert Tennent

Israel Evans

George Bryan

George Duffield

John Ewing

Samuel Miller

Charles Nisbet

CHAPTER IV

Colonial Educational Patterns

At Princeton the New Side Presbyterians hoped to produce leaders of colonial society who, in Davies's phrase, would be of "extensive Benefit to Mankind." That hope shaped the educational patterns established at Princeton in the late colonial period. Whether developing a psychology of education, deciding on the school's location or curriculum, or devising a system of student discipline, the Presbyterian educators were motivated by their conviction that only selfless and virtuous Christians could shape and direct the society that was emerging from the Great Awakening. During the Presbyterian schism that accompanied the revival, the New Sides had advanced a peculiarly evangelical idea of social leadership which they applied in particular to ministers. The educational patterns established at Princeton between 1746 and 1776 were intended to make that idea a reality and extend it to leadership in all areas of American life. That extension, the Presbyterians hoped, would hasten reformation of American society.

REDEFINING VIRTUE

The concept of "virtue" dominated the ideas and practice of the Presbyterian educators. References to the concept marked the Presbyterians' descriptions of their school, its curriculum, and, in particular, its

79

faculty. For instance, when William Livingston eulogized Aaron Burr in 1757, the leader of New York City's Presbyterians stressed that the late president never neglected at Princeton "any opportunity of imbuing the minds of his pupils with the seeds of virtue, at the same time that he enriched them, with the treasures of learning." The college's promotional literature assured prospective students and their parents that at the Presbyterian school the "utmost care is taken to discountenance vice, and to encourage the practice of virtue . . . ." [1] Young men who enrolled at Princeton soon learned to define as well as to practice virtue. As one of Samuel Finley's students informed the 1764 commencement audience, virtue was "a Disposition of Mind to whatever is morally good" and "consists in the Love of God and Man . . . ." [2]

The modern ear is not accustomed to serious public discussion of "virtue," but even to an untrained listener, these assertions seem perfunctory. Doubtless sometimes they were. But American evangelicals in the first half of the eighteenth century redefined virtue and revitalized that concept. At the beginning of the century the idea was a static one. The ancient concept of virtue first had been associated with the Ciceronian idea of *humanitas,* the willingness to subordinate one's own well-being to that of one's fellow man, and then with the Stoic emphasis on inner personal strength. In the early modern period Machiavelli had defined *virtù* as any action that was effective. Each of those emphases was foreign to the Enlightenment's more static understanding of the concept of virtue. The idea in 1700 connoted a willingness to acquiesce in prevailing norms of morality in any given society. In its social dimensions, that idea was the foundation of the eighteenth-century world of hierarchy and order. The editors of the French *Encyclopédie* assumed that the concept of virtue was the "foundation on which all human societies and all laws were built." It was defined by reasonable and usually optimistic philosophers and theologians as a general "benevolence to all things." Virtue for those thinkers consisted of doing one's duty and cheerfully functioning in one's allotted place in the social order. [3]

But that is not what colonial evangelicals meant by virtue. Jonathan Edwards was the first of them to suggest new connotations for the static concept. When Edwards analyzed *The Nature of True Virtue,* he ignored systems of morals and social arrangements. Instead, he concentrated on the nature of man and his relation to the cosmos and to God. Superficially, his definition of "true virtue" resembles that of some eighteenth-century moralists, especially the Scottish philosopher Francis Hutcheson.

Like that Scotsman, Edwards believed that "True virtue most essentially consists in benevolence in general." It was "that consent, propensity and union of heart to Being in general, that is immediately exercised in a general good will." But, unlike Hutcheson, Edwards did not believe man capable of a genial inclination to seek the good of his fellow men. In his essay on *Original Sin* Edwards described fallen man as selfish in his very nature. Then in *True Virtue* he carefully analyzed all the acts of natural man and found each of them, no matter how apparently selfless, based in a pervasive self-love. That love of self notwithstanding, Edwards defined true virtue as preferring above all else, not the good of one's fellow man, but the embodiment of all Being, God himself. The great gulf between fallen man and perfect God produced the creative tensions that permeate Edwards's thinking. That gulf, he believed, could be spanned only by God's unmerited and arbitrarily bestowed gift of divine grace to the elect. Only those elect were capable of aspiring to true virtue, which Edwards defined finally as an all-consuming desire for the holy.[4]

Had Edwards's definition of true virtue gone no further, it might have had little effect on colonial society. But he and his disciples added to Edwards's severe theological judgment a social dimension that gave the evangelical concept of virtue both immediacy and power. Edwards and the New Sides insisted that the truly virtuous man must not only lose himself in adoring God but also must selflessly exert himself for the good of society. It is difficult to escape the conclusion that during and after the Great Awakening selfless exertion became for the American evangelicals the essence of true virtue. That emphasis recalled the early Machiavellian emphasis on effective action and was made explicit in Edwards's popular edition of the diary of David Brainerd, a young evangel who had been expelled by the Old Side leaders of Yale and then became a missionary to the Indians. After Brainerd's untimely death Edwards published the young man's diary and in the introduction described the intense exertions of the young revivalist in the cause of Christ: "His obtaining rest of soul in Christ, after earnest striving to enter in at the strait gate, and being violent to take the kingdom of heaven, he did not look upon as putting an end to any further occasion for striving in religion; but these were continued still, and maintained constantly, through all changes, to the very end of his life. His work was not finished, nor his race ended, till his life was ended . . . ."[5]

This definition of true virtue was institutionalized in the New Side school at Princeton. It, for instance, permeated the 1760 commencement address of President Samuel Davies. To his charges Davies recommended as a model of true virtue the young King David. The shepherd boy had not been motivated by avarice, ambition, or revenge but had desired only to deliver his people from their oppressors. Without advantage of birth or education and lacking the wiles of the courtier, David rose by talent and exertion alone "to the Height of human Grandeur, and became an extensive Blessing to the Church and his Country." The knowledge he gained he dedicated to the service of his generation. So should Princeton's sons exert themselves for the good of their country and fellow men, President Davies declared. Whether in the "sacred Desk," the bar, the "chamber of Affliction," or even in private life, the young men should "Live not for your selves, but [for] the Publick." Therein, Davies believed, lay true virtue.[6]

The Presbyterians and other colonial educators agreed that, whatever else it might be, virtue had to be grounded in religion. Provost William Smith at the College of Philadelphia insisted that religion and virtue must be inculcated simultaneously, while Thomas Clap at Yale believed it was impossible to teach the arts and sciences, let alone virtue, without the aid of religion. And even William Livingston hoped that the virtuous citizens to be educated at his proposed nonsectarian school in New York would be exposed to a salutary version of innocuous, orthodox Protestantism.[7] Religion, it was believed, prepared the way for virtue by rendering a restless young man sober and reflective. Thus Livingston suggested that students at the proposed school in New York City be required to rise early in the morning for chapel because that rigorous exertion and consequent religious observance would "have a strong Tendency to preserve a due Decorum, Good Manners and Virtue amongst them, without which the College will sink into Profaness [sic] and Disrepute." [8]

The Presbyterian educators were convinced that virtue was grounded in religion, but they were not sure that virtue invariably was promoted by learning. For them the inculcation of virtue in an institution of higher learning was a problematical process; consequently, the New Sides carefully analyzed the relation of learning to virtue and prescribed the circumstances under which the young could be educated without danger to virtue or to piety. In 1760 Samuel Davies preached to the students and townspeople of Princeton a sermon on "The Rejection of Gospel-Light the Condemnation of men," in which he attacked the widely held assumption that education inevitably inculcated virtue. Davies welcomed the "light of human literature" that shone "with unusual splendors upon our age and nation . . . ." Happily situated students in British North America had only to bask in the rays of that light to polish their minds and "render them luminous." But, Davies warned, they must not thirst only for the "light of knowledge" and reject the more important "light of the gospel." Too often a student with a "turn for speculation" would follow with delight the beck of every branch of knowledge while shunning self-knowledge and confession of sin. That student desired a religion requiring "no vigorous exertion," and "attended with no dubious conflict"; he immersed himself in dissolute study, ignoring the convictions of his own heart.[9]

Davies, one of colonial America's leading orators, concluded his sermon on the dangers of rejecting the light of the gospel with effective imagery. He branded the "sins of men of learning and knowledge" the most "daring and gigantic" this side of hell. He reminded the young men of the fallen angels like Lucifer, "vast intellects" who had chosen to rebel against God and had fallen mightily. What good was knowledge to a man who lost his soul, the president demanded. Of what good to society was an institution of learning that produced "sinners of great parts [and] fine geniuses . . . ?" The New Side Presbyterians took very seriously the power of colleges to mold societies by producing the leaders of those organisms, and Samuel Davies believed that if Princeton produced only men of reason and intellect, it would have failed. Education untempered by religion was a social curse, not a blessing, and, far from inculcating virtue, unrestrained and untempered learning would raise to power haughty men whose inevitable downfall would also destroy the society they had been prepared to lead.[10]

If the inculcation of virtue was rendered problematical by an overemphasis on the intellect, so could virtue be subverted by the temptations of wealth. Presidents Dickinson, Burr, Davies, and Finley were all of middle-class origins, but they quickly observed that the Presbyterian school at Princeton attracted the sons of wealthy men from New York City, Philadelphia, and even the slave-holding south. Increasingly in the postrevival period the New Side educators feared that the morals of their students were threatened by the generosity of well-to-do parents. Those officials were especially concerned when members of a self-conscious and sometimes insecure colonial elite began to lavish upon their sons ostentatious signs of familial social status—fine clothing, large allowances, and servants. In 1757 the school's board moved to discourage parental indulgence by empowering any tutor or faculty member to forbid a student to contract any "needless" or "harmful" debt.[11]

The Presbyterian educators were especially concerned for the spiritual welfare of their wealthier students. Those young men seemed to Davies to exhibit a "Spirit of Pride and Contention" and appeared incapable of grasping that they too were sinners. There were among the rich boys no "public Outcries" of guilt but, instead, only a "decorous silent solemnity." Davies therefore made a special note of a wealthy young New Yorker who became so oppressed by his sins while ill that he communicated his apprehensions to his classmates and set a revival in motion! Soon Davies noted that the sons of the rich in particular began to "mourn for sin, and cry and long for Jesus." In that revival some students became so distressed that the president decided to use no further "Arguments of Terror in Public, lest some should sink under the Weight . . . ."[12] Davies did not mention that revival's effect on other students. Rich young men were believed to be particularly susceptible to dissipation and corruption, and their conversion appeared to the Presbyterian educators a particular triumph of virtue over luxury, the benefits of which would accrue to the entire student body and, eventually, to all of society.[13]

If parental wealth threatened virtue at the Presbyterian school, so too did its first location. Princeton was first sited in the villages of Newark and Elizabethtown, New Jersey, where the first two presidents, Jonathan Dickinson and Aaron Burr, ministered to the local Presbyterian congregations. While in Newark the school met in the county courthouse, much as medieval universities had convened amid the activity of urban centers. But, according to Samuel Blair, the temptations of even tiny Newark presented too many difficulties and dangers to the "morals and literary improvements of the youth" to be tolerated. Consequently, as soon as possible the school was moved to the even tinier village of Princeton, where presumably its students could escape the temptations of urban life and breathe the pure and salubrious air of the countryside.[14] Once in Princeton, President Burr immediately drew up plans for a dormitory, which would enable the faculty to gather all the students under one roof, out of temptation's way.[15] And even after the boys had been herded into Nassau Hall, one concerned mother would allow her son to enroll in the college only if he might live with President and Mrs. Burr.[16]

The aversion to urban centers as locations for educational institutions was one the New Sides shared with many colonial educators. For instance, when the Old Sides solicited support for their academy, they emphasized the virtues of rustic Newark, Delaware. The Reverend John Ewing noted that few people "are able to give their Children a regular Education in one of our Cities; and such as can bear the Expenses are not willing to attempt it, through an Apprehension that their Children might contract a Relish for that Manner of Living, which is inconsistent" with simplicity and self-denial.[17] But both King's College and the College of Philadelphia were located in leading urban centers. In New York the more urbane Presbyterians constructed an innovative defense of education in urban centers, where education was defined as participation in the daily activities of community life. Education, asserted the Presbyterian layman William Smith, was more than a simple matter of acquiring a knowledge of mathematics, languages, and philosophy. The future leaders of society must gain first-hand knowledge also of "Men and the World." In Europe that knowledge, that contact between the student and the world, had been a natural product of the urban locations of European universities and of their students' extensive travels. In America, Smith noted, young men do not travel widely; consequently, they should attend universities in the most cosmopolitan cities of the province. Smith also suggested that in urban institutions society could more easily superintend the education of its future leaders. In a city or town, members of society can observe at close range "the Fidelity of the Master" as well as the "industry of the Scholars" and easily register any dissatisfaction with either. Smith noted approvingly the educative functions of the courts that his fellow Presbyterians had just fled. He recommended personal visits to the courts rather than endless poring over dry legal texts, believing that such experiences would ably educate a future judge or legislator. That experience could not be had in a "sour Retreat from the World." [18]

The defenders of urban settings for colleges insisted that morals were as easily protected in towns as anywhere else. Smith even argued that young men would become stronger for having habitually exercised their wills in resisting temptation. In fact, students at the leading urban colleges were supervised as closely as at any rural institution. Benjamin Franklin suggested that students at the College of Philadelphia wear a uniform when mingling with townspeople so that they might be carefully watched by all concerned. And at both King's and the College of Philadelphia the morals of students were carefully guarded. In 1764 one Henry Lloyd III observed to one Joseph Lloyd II that a new addition had been made to the physical plant at King's. "We are now surrounded with a board fence eight foot high with Nails at the top which is just completed." [19]

In 1772 John Witherspoon took a position somewhere between fully endorsing and flatly rejecting cities as educational environments. In that year the new president of Princeton wrote a pamphlet aimed at persuading wealthy West Indies planters to send their sons to Princeton rather than dissolute Oxford or Cambridge. The Princeton president warned the planters that in the cities of England young men were constantly tempted by a succession of "intoxicating diversions, such as Balls, Concerts, Plays, Races" and other fatal attractions. And their sons would yield to temptation, Witherspoon predicted, because an acquaintance with each diversion was considered essential to good breeding in the corrupt urban centers of England. Rustic Princeton in provincial New Jersey, on the other hand, was a tiny village "so small that any irregularity is immediately and certainly discovered and therefore easily corrected." Having emphasized the ease with which the students' morals could be supervised in a small town, Witherspoon then acknowledged that there were certain advantages to being located near—but not in—an urban center. The college at Princeton, he informed the planters, was close enough to New York City "so as to be a center of intelligence, and have an easy conveyance of every thing necessary, and yet to be wholly free from the many temptations in every great city, both to the neglect of study and the practice of vice." The Princeton president even answered William Smith's objection that only in a city could students profit from the proximity of polished company. With great pride Witherspoon described the "vast concourse of the politest company" from nearby Philadelphia and New York City that attended the college's graduation services. While the Princetonians rusticated in virtuous solitude, the civilizing elements of the cities came to them, bringing to the students the undeniable advantages of an urban environment without exposing them to its contaminations. Witherspoon, at least, believed that virtue was best inculcated in an institution pristinely situated on the outer perimeter of an urban center.[20]

THE COLONIAL CURRICULUM

The Presbyterian educators believed that the problems in promoting vital piety and inculcating virtue simultaneously could be surmounted in a college rightly conceived and correctly administered. They believed that at Princeton they could balance piety and learning, that they could protect their charges from the dangers of their parents' indulgence and the village's temptations, that they could prepare their students for a life of extensive usefulness. That confidence, in part, measured the evangelical educators' confidence in the curriculum they created at Princeton. To be sure, much of that course of study was traditional, some borrowed from Yale, much more from the Scottish universities, and probably less than has been believed from the dissenting academies of England.[21] But the New Side Presbyterians at Princeton did innovate, and their tentative changes were pregnant with implications for the future.

At the basis of the Princeton curriculum was the New Side determination to produce selfless rulers for a reformed colonial society. That determination led the Presbyterians to reject the assumption that different parts of society should be educated in different ways, in different subjects, and possibly even in different institutions. That assumption was most clearly stated by Philadelphia's Provost William Smith in his celebrated proposal for a fictional "College of Mirania" in the 1750s. Smith divided his Miranians into an aristocracy whose sons would study philosophy, science, and the learned languages, and a "mechanical" class, the sons of which would be instructed in the "most plain and useful parts" of a college curriculum and concentrate on such subjects as animal husbandry. The curriculum of any college, Provost Smith believed, should be selected so as to cultivate the tastes of aristocratic young men while reconciling the sons of the lower classes to their naturally subordinate role while preparing them to function usefully in it.[22]

The Presbyterian founders of Princeton were no democrats. In 1755 Samuel Davies found it perfectly natural that God gave to some men "a turn for intellectual improvement," to others "a genius for trade," and to still others a "dexterity in mechanics." But Davies did not see in that distribution of gifts a divinely ordained system of social distinctions. Instead, the New Side Presbyterian saw the distribution as a providentially provided way for reforming all levels of colonial society. Only if intellectuals, traders, and mechanics alike were persuaded to renounce their selfishness would colonial society ever be revived and reformed, Davies believed. One suspects too that Davies's own middle-class background and his knowledge that education had aided his rise in the world inhibited him from viewing education as a means of controlling social mobility. Finally, Davies disagreed with Smith's clearly expressed hope to tranquilize society. Far from that, Davies and the New Sides hoped to arouse society from its lethargy and then lead it in reformation. To that end, higher education at Princeton had to be available to all levels of colonial society. Davies spent no time in devising a different curriculum for each different part of society. If society was to be united, that union had to begin at Princeton.[23]

The Presbyterian educators at Princeton, then, insisted that education be a unifying rather than a disruptive force in society. They also preferred that it be conveyed in ways that allowed for the maximum contact between professor and student. For that reason the New Sides withstood the trend at the midcentury toward the lecture method. The Scottish universities were the source of that trend, and Francis Alison, who had heard Francis Hutcheson's masterful lectures on moral philosophy at the University of Glasgow, used the lecture method with great effect at the Old Side Academy at New London. And, after John Witherspoon arrived at Princeton in 1768, students at the New Side school also were required to transcribe entire lectures into their notebooks.[24] But in the early years of the New Side school the Princeton faculty boasted of what they called its Socratic method of free dialogue and discussion between professor and student.[25] Promotional literature boasted that at Princeton no professor resorted to dry, dogmatic lectures that burdened the memory and imposed "heavy and disagreeable tasks" upon the students. Instead, through recitations, discussions, and demonstrations the "intention is engaged, the mind entertain'd, and the scholar animated in the pursuit of knowledge." Knowledge was thereby "convey'd into the minds of youth, in a method the most easy, natural, and familiar." [26] Samuel Blair stated in 1760 that the system of recitations at Princeton was far superior to the impersonal lecture system because it gave the students the opportunity "thoroughly to impress upon their memories" a particular concept or idea. And the system allowed the teachers frequent contact with their students, thus enabling the professors to supervise personally not only the young men's intellectual growth but also their development in virtue and piety.[27]

The terms in which they discussed the process of learning—"conveying" knowledge, "engaging the intention," "impressing" the memory—indicate the psychological foundation of the New Side curriculum. Like most educated men of the mid-eighteenth century, the evangelical educators subscribed to a form of "faculty" psychology. Medieval and early modern thinkers had conceived of the faculties as discrete spiritual entities that existed within the soul. During the Enlightenment, however, the faculties came to be viewed as "capacities" and as "potentialities." The Princeton curriculum was intended to develop those capacities and potentialities. The New Side educators assumed that the mind was divided into distinct faculties and that those faculties functioned interdependently to make up a student's mental "furniture." David Bostwick demonstrated the variety and number of the faculties when he listed the "uncommon [mental] Furniture" of Samuel Davies: "A large and capacious Understanding,—a solid unbiased and well regulated Judgment,—a quick Apprehension,—a Genius truly penetrating,—a fruitful Invention,—an elegant Taste,—a lively, florid and exuberant Fancy, were all happily united in *Him.*" [28]

Each of those faculties was to be developed. Often they were described in physical terms as muscles that were weak at birth but responsive to judicious exercise. The New Side Presbyterian educators believed that, like all good things in the eighteenth century, the faculties constituted a hierarchy. That hierarchy was ruled by the "reason" and the "understanding," the atrophied remnants of the mental powers that survived the Fall. The "reason" received all the information gathered by the "senses" of touch, feel, smell, taste, etc., from the physical world and then conveyed that information to the "understanding," the faculty that integrated those impressions and then related them to the ideal, supernatural reality behind the natural world. For the evangelical Christian in the first half of the eighteenth century, the "understanding" was closely identified with the "heart" and the affective dimensions of religion. The chief end of their pedagogy at Princeton was to sharpen the receiving powers of the "reason" while concentrating on the perceiving and integrating capacities of the "understanding" and the heart.

Their commitment to faculty psychology caused the Presbyterians to describe the process of education in almost physical terms. Faculties were to be exercised, sensations to be received, minds to be molded. In addition, that commitment intensified the New Side tendency to see the educational process as problematical. William Livingston asserted that the youthful mind was "susceptible of almost any Impression." And if that was true, the educator must be extremely careful to chose only those impressions that were exactly appropriate. But, by the same token, the evangelicals' pedagogy explains in part their confidence in their final success. If, as Livingston had said, the young mind was like "the ductile Wax," receiving "the Image of the Seal with the least Resistance," the educator had only to chose the right seal to be successful. [29]

Because they were believed particularly capable of exercising the mental faculties, the ancient and modern languages were the foundation of Princeton's curriculum.[30] William Livingston believed that language study should precede all other study because it developed the memory, a faculty that was essential to success in any area of inquiry. The memory was "a Faculty of the Mind which is generally exercised the first of any others in Youth." And, if elementary language study exercised the basic faculties, advanced work in the languages exercised the higher ones. In advanced language study, the students' "Capacities" were "gradually opened—their Curiosities raised—their Powers strengthened—their Views extended, and their Minds familiarized to Inquiry . . . ."[31]

Study of the classical languages seemed particularly important to the Presbyterian educators because they presented to youthful minds suitable models of virtue and selflessness. The ancient Hebrews, Greeks, and Romans were worthy of emulation because they had sustained the freest governments man had ever known. Of course, a knowledge of Greek and Hebrew enabled the student to read the scriptures in their original tongues and thereby opened a crucial source of moral instruction. And reading the lives and works of the virtuous ancients would cause students to emulate their selfless and noble actions. Furthermore, the exertion required to read the ancients in the originals, without benefit of translation, would indelibly imprint upon student minds the ideas contained in ancient works of poetry, history, and philosophy. At least one student at Princeton remembered that that process did in fact occur. Hugh Henry Brackenridge, a 1771 graduate and later a politician, judge, and writer, recalled that by slowly working his way through the originals of antique literature at colonial Princeton, the noble thoughts and examples in them "became more deeply impressed upon my mind."[32]

The Princeton faculty stressed the importance of concrete examples, especially biographies, because these gave substance to ideas. President Davies urged all of his charges to chose for themselves some illustrious man on whom to model their lives. He himself recommended King David and then attributed to the Jewish monarch those traits of character—virtue, selflessness, and patriotism—that he also ascribed to the ancient Greek and Roman republicans. In 1749, some years before he became Princeton's president, Samuel Finley addressed himself to the question of "general precepts" versus concrete examples when he analyzed the language appropriate to the sermons of an "Approved Minister of God." General precepts were useful, Finley allowed, because by them men were advised of their duties to God and to their fellow men. But specific examples, the biographies of virtuous citizens for instance, gave assurance that those duties were capable of being performed. "General Precepts form abstract ideas of Virtue, but in Examples, Virtues are made visible, in all their Circumstances." [33]

If language study at Princeton was intended to present concrete examples of virtue to the student, the study of oratory was intended to prepare the student to make an impression on the consciousness of others. The men who created Princeton were part of an evangelical revival that had revolutionized public address not only in America but in the Protestant countries of western Europe as well. Evangelical preachers experimented with all sorts of innovations—"pathetic" appeals to the emotion, extemporaneous harangues, colorful anecdotes in the vernacular of their hearers, emotive language—all intended to engage the affections and to set into motion a train of associations that would evoke purposive action. Much of the criticism of the revival was directed at those experiments. The evangelical educators at Princeton insisted that, in chastened form, those experiments become the foundation for oratorical instruction at Princeton. Before he became Princeton's president, Davies, already known as one of the colonies' most effective public speakers, visited the new Academy of Philadelphia and attended its student orations. Davies was disturbed to find that the young orators lacked the conviction of their assigned speeches and that, in particular, those who recited the speeches of Brutus and Marc Antony "were extremely languid and discovered Nothing of the Fire and Pathos of a Roman Soul." That lack of passion he believed to be the "great Defect of modern Oratory" but one "few seem sensible of, or labour to correct." [34]

At Princeton, Davies emphasized oratorical training in an evangelical frame of reference. He insisted that the orator be familiar with his subject and that he speak with conviction from an enlightened mind and an engaged heart. The boys read from Livy, Cicero, and Demosthenes and delivered orations from the ancients on Sundays to an audience that included the critical president and curious townspeople as well as their classmates. When Witherspoon arrived in 1768, he altered Davies's emphasis slightly and encouraged the students to deliver their own orations as well as those of the ancients. Oratory, Princeton's colonial publicists declared, was emphasized at the college because it clearly rendered a man "popular; and consequently useful." That emphasis, Samuel Blair assured prospective students, explained the frequency with which Princeton's sons immediately appeared "upon the stage of public action, employing their talents to the honour of the supreme Bestower, and in promoting the good of mankind." [35]

The study of the classical languages and the emphasis on oratory at Princeton were intended to inculcate virtue and to prepare a young man for social usefulness. But it remained for the study of religion and science to provide a larger framework into which all other parts of the curriculum had to fit. Far from being antithetical, Newtonian science and religion were joined into an intellectual system that set the tone for the entire curriculum. The college might use the Bible for its divinity courses, but Joseph Shippen, a student from Philadelphia, could also find himself in need of Isaac Watts's *Astronomy*. President Burr might train ministers, but he also arranged for demonstrations of the "electrical fluid" and in his spare time taught young men to calculate eclipses. The college might spend large sums of money to evangelize the Indians, but in 1751 Burr also spent the equivalent of thirty students' tuition on scientific equipment. Finally, the board persuaded one of America's leading scientists to construct for Princeton an orrery depicting the wonders of God's amazing creation. Installed in Nassau Hall in 1771, David Rittenhouse's great orrery depicted the movements of all the known bodies of the universe and was one of the wonders of the colonial world.[36]

The New Side attitude toward the relation of science to religion can be illustrated by the reaction of their most representative thinker, Samuel Davies, to an unusually long drought and a serious epidemic that plagued Virginia in 1756. When those disasters were followed by a rare earthquake, Davies felt obliged to explain the ways of God to a perplexed and distressed congregation. His was the explanation of a man who could no longer accept a totally supernatural explanation of causality but who also could not accept the explanations of those who denied the deity any part in the events of the natural world. For Samuel Davies the universe was a marvelous machine cleverly designed by a God who ordinarily worked His will not by miracles but through moral and physical agents. In extraordinary times, though, Davies's God still intervened in His creation, ordering His agents to "stand still and see the works of God . . . ." But Davies insisted that these divine interventions did not really disrupt the divine order of the universe. He regularized the irregular: "All the exigencies of such periods were known to the omniscient Creator when he first formed this vast machine, when he wound it up and put all its wheels in motion . . . ."

The creation was full of signals and hidden springs that the creator in His wisdom had foreordained to go off to deal with a foreseen extraordinary situation. Therefore, Davies was able to retain a Calvinistic belief in an absolutely sovereign God who foreknew all at the same time that he rejected an increasingly vulnerable belief in miracles.[37]

Other colonial thinkers, like Harvard's John Winthrop, had advanced an entirely natural explanation for the earthquake of 1756. These men Davies denounced as a "set of little, conceited smattering philosophers" who refused to see that the natural causes of which they spoke were "first *formed,* and are still *directed,* by the Divine hand." They were intellectually proud men who used their knowledge to set themselves apart from the rest of humanity. There could be no greater perversion of scientific knowledge, Davies believed, than to use it to further divide society. With Francis Bacon, Samuel Davies concluded that a little scientific knowledge encouraged atheism but that deep learning inculcated virtue and a veneration of the deity.[38]

But if Davies criticized Winthrop and those other "smattering Philosophers," he could not accept the unabashedly providential interpretation the clergy had put forth to explain the last major earthquake in the colonies in 1727. Those earlier men of God had tried to invoke a degraded tradition of using natural catastrophes to recall a covenanted people to God. Davies saw the 1756 earthquake in more sophisticated terms. In searching for an explanation for that later tremor, Davies represented the thinkers of an age that was beginning to seek in the embryonic natural and social sciences new ways of explaining the natural world. He was also a man of his times when he looked to history for enlightenment and interpreted what he found there scientifically. History, he insisted, reveals a "kind of *sympathy* between the *natural* and *moral* world" and demonstrates that some unusual occurrence in the natural world usually portends some revolution in the moral world. That observation was validated for Davies by the scientific principle that "When an hypothesis is supported by experiments and matters of fact, it ought to be received as true." The earthquake was not exactly punishment for sin; rather, it was an extraordinary signal sent by God in a planned and regular way to portend some important event in the world. For Davies it heralded the beginning of the millennium. The ultimate cause of the earthquake was still providential, but the method Davies used to arrive at that cause was a crudely scientific and historical one.[39]

Davies and the New Side Presbyterians were able to accept Newtonian science because it presented a universe created and controlled by God. That universe was but another form of divine revelation, the fixed laws of which could serve as models for constructing a social order as well regulated and harmonious as the cosmic order. Moreover, Newtonian science assumed man's ability to ferret out the rules of that divine order. Consequently, Davies was able to preach a sovereign God while marveling at the efficacy of man's reasoning powers. Davies's science was rational, not empirical. Students under his tutelage learned laws and rules and marveled at their regularity and predictability. They did not question the laws or seek new hypotheses. Newtonian science never got out of hand; it elevated man's position in the natural order; and it was thoroughly Christian. For these reasons the Presbyterians at Princeton welcomed it enthusiastically and forced all of their other subjects to conform to its "scientific" methodology. In practice that meant that each subject was dedicated to elucidating the natural, social, and spiritual laws that operated in a universe thoroughly subject and responsive to the will of God. When Samuel Springer, for instance, was called upon to defend before his classmates Newton's system of astronomy, he began bravely enough. But the marvelous system was too much for him. He was soon "overwhelmed with a sense of the Divine Majesty, and burst into tears . . . . [and] was unable to proceed." [40]

EDUCATION AND FREEDOM OF INQUIRY

The New Sides at Princeton believed that the curriculum they had devised would produce virtuous and selfless social leaders only if it was taught in an atmosphere of free inquiry. Therefore, they announced their intention at Princeton to "cherish a spirit of liberty, and free inquiry, and not only to permit, but even encourage . . . [their students'] right of private judgment, without presuming to dictate with an air of infallibility, or demanding an implicit assent to the decisions of the preceptor." [41] Varnum Collins, in his perceptive study of Princeton, rightly warns that a college's assertions do not always reflect reality. [42] At Princeton students encountered religious practice and theology that were recognizably Presbyterian. But to dismiss the evangelicals' pledge of free inquiry as promotional fluff or blatant hypocrisy is to ignore the revivalists' past and to miss an important insight into their educational theory and a clue to their confidence in its final success.

During the Great Awakening the men who created Princeton had insisted that ecclesiastical union could not be coerced by forced subscription to a doctrinal creed. Fragile bonds of social union could be maintained only by carefully tolerating those differences that occurred in even the most homogeneous societies. As educators, they asserted that virtue could be inculcated only in a climate of free inquiry. Like true social union, lasting reformation was the result of genuine convictions that could not be coerced. The New Sides found a dictatorial "air of infallibility" that demanded "implicit assent" to authority as obnoxious in the college classroom as it had been in the meetings of presbyteries and the synod. Presumably, then, they valued in practice as well as in theory the genial tolerance for which the evangelical educators were praised. Samuel Davies was eulogized as "strict, not bigoted, conscientious, not squeamishly scrupulous . . . , [a man who] gloried more in being a Christian, than in being a Presbyterian . . . ." And of Aaron Burr, William Livingston observed, "However steady to his own principles, he was perfectly free from every appearance of BIGOTRY." [43]

In a climate of benevolent tolerance and free inquiry the New Side educators were convinced that the delicate process of education and the inculcation of virtue could proceed with predictable results. Faculties would be judiciously exercised and minds rightly furnished. Having established those conditions at Princeton, the evangelicals were confident of their success. And their students seem to have justified that confidence. Students' evaluations of their professors are notoriously suspect, but one is struck when reading the memoirs of colonial Princetonians by the repeated references to the tolerance of the New Sides who superintended Princeton College and the several academies that fed it. [44] Young men obviously were stimulated by the Christian cosmos of Isaac Newton and by their teachers' assurances that the laws by which it was ordered also pointed the way to human happiness and social harmony. Thus stimulated, the students were exhilarated by their professors' encouragement to slough off the superstitions of the past. If anything, the young men at Princeton rather smugly decided that their minds had been liberated from all prejudice and could now discover truth in a logical, systematic, scientific manner. Thus, the young Joseph Shippen in 1751 informed his brother Neddy that he had just read Mr. Watts on logic, in which the Englishman throws out "all the Jargon & trappings of Art of the ancient Schools . . . ." Now, Joseph and his peers had made logic "a part of our Study, as well to direct us to judge aright ourselves as to detect Falsehood . . . in others." [45] Enamored of a scientific method that neatly explained the universe and promised increasing human felicity, the students at colonial Princeton had little reason to accuse their teachers of stifling free inquiry.[46]

In New York other Presbyterians went further than the New Sides at Princeton in defending freedom of inquiry. That defense was part of the unsuccessful Presbyterian opposition to Anglican control of King's College. Again, the layman William Livingston led the way. He asserted that a college, especially in a heterogeneous society, should never present any body of religious doctrine as absolute truth. At most schools, Livingston feared, students embraced their teachers' religious dogma as a matter of course and prepared to defend it against all challenges. Their minds were "circumscribed within the narrow Limits of Party-Prejudice . . . instead of being enlarged by Observation and [Experience]."[47] Livingston's observation was a sophistication of evangelical pedagogy, which was based on the teacher's power to influence his students. Because of that power, Livingston insisted, the teacher must be doubly careful not to force his charges into any sectarian mold. For that reason in part, when Livingston proposed a curriculum for King's, he banished theology from the course of study altogether. He suggested only innocuous morning and evening prayers in which all Protestants could freely join. The New Yorker was confident that "Truth is Omnipotent, and Reason must be finally victorious." But he was not willing that the college become a theological battleground. No professor, try as he might, could teach divinity without imposing his views on impressionable youth. And Livingston insisted that young men of college age should be allowed to make a "judicious Choice" in the controversial matter of theology. It followed then that no divinity at all should be taught.[48]

Livingston's radical proposal suggests the limitations of the Princeton New Sides' definition of free inquiry. Those evangelicals could never have agreed to banish theology from their school's curriculum. As the Presbyterians established Princeton, though, the rector of Yale instituted a controversial innovation that suggests the basic Presbyterian agreement on the issue of freedom of inquiry in a college community. In 1753 Rector Thomas Clap reacted to the alarming growth of Anglicanism in New Haven and the even more disturbing growth of rationalism at Yale. He withdrew the college's students from New Haven's First Church and ordered them—Anglicans as well as Congregationalists—to attend compulsory services on the campus. Clap's act produced a flurry of Anglican protests, and in response, the rector wrote a pamphlet that defended the *Religious Constitution of Colleges.* In it Clap had to defend coercing Anglican students to worship in a Congregational service in a school supported by the colony and by the voluntary donations from both Anglicans and Congregationalists. His basic position was that colleges were societies in and of themselves and could not allow unrestrained freedom of inquiry within their bounds. If students were allowed to disperse to churches of their own or their parents' choice, they would "break up all order in the Society, and defeat the Religious Design, and Instructions of It." He then advanced an argument that would become a staple of nineteenth-century sectarian defense. The founders of Yale in 1701 had prescribed beliefs to be taught in the school, exercising a "liberty of conscience" which he, Clap, was bound to protect. In addition, the founders had acquired a "property" in those beliefs. Consequently, to allow Yale's students to hear opposing beliefs violated both the founders' liberty of conscience and deprived them of their property. Collegiate education was a privilege to be had on those founders' terms. The students' liberty of conscience extended only to deciding if they would accept education on those terms.[49]

Despite the blatantly sectarian nature of his arguments, Clap asserted that Yale would serve the majority of Connecticut's society. Happily, the religious ideas of the founders of Yale coincided with those of Connecticut's Congregational majority. But, he asserted, he could not allow any of New Haven's churches to receive any of his students because there the boys might be subjected to "such Preaching, as would be contrary to the Minds, of the Generality . . . ." The rights of minorities who were taxed to support the school must be subordinated to the overriding rights of the Congregational majority. Clap apparently agreed with the Old Side Presbyterian equation of the majority and the whole. The benefit of each individual in a society could be consulted, Clap granted, but only insofar "as it is consistent, with the general Design, and the Good of the whole, or the Majority."[50] An Old Side Presbyterian would have agreed. But that formulation was alien to the New Side defense in the colonial period of minority rights, toleration, and free inquiry.

EDUCATION FOR A DEFERENTIAL SOCIETY

If the evangelical educators at Princeton believed coercion antithetical to effective social union, lasting individual reformation, and true education, they also found force destructive to effective discipline. Of course, the New Sides shared their age's commitment to deference. Samuel Blair asserted unabashedly that the college's system of discipline was intended to "habituate . . . [the students] to subjection, and yet maintain their respective ranks without insolence or servility . . . ." This end was achieved in part by requiring the students to stay one year in each of the four classes, "giving and receiving, in their turns, those tokens of respect and subjection, which belong to their standings, in order to preserve a due subordination."[51] Deference to constituted authority was as much a mark of the virtuous man as a concern for the welfare of society.

The Presbyterians, however, were not obsessed by deference and discipline. Students at Princeton, for instance, were never ranked according to social standing as they had been at Harvard. Each boy was required to make a copy of the school's rules upon entrance and to keep it with him at all times.[52] This rule was not intended primarily to make the student constantly aware of the school's regulations but, rather, to provide him with ready proof of matriculation. Moreover, the college's rules of moral conduct, though strict, were quite conventional. They were not proclaimed in shrill rhetoric that tied obedience to the student's salvation. Nor was a boy made to feel that the fate of Christianity hung upon his every action. The rules were simply stated and, with few exceptions, just as simply obeyed.

The school's officials were quite proud of Princeton's disciplinary system and insisted that it was completely scientific. Rather than relying on force, Blair insisted, Princeton's rules were meant "to work upon the nobler principle of humanity, and to move the more honourable springs of good order and submission to government." Seeking a medium between "too great a licentiousness on the one hand, or an excessive precision on the other," the board created a disciplinary system that attempted to fit punishment to crime, to treat each offense individually, and to provide mercy for the truly repentant. The students must agree to be governed by the principles of honor and shame or leave, insisted John Witherspoon in 1772. As a result, student Edward Crawford in 1772 could boast of the school's "laws and regularity," echoing Samuel Finley's earlier assertion that "Perhaps there can hardly be found so large a Number of Youth together, equally Sober, concordial, regular, & Studious."[53]

The Presbyterians at Princeton also evolved an ideal authority figure who measured justice with mercy. Livingston and David Bostwick described that ideal disciplinarian as they eulogized Presidents Burr and Davies. Burr had "the art of leading the will by invisible chains; and 'making reason, no less prevalent in authority' "; while Davies had "the peculiar Art, of mingling Authority and Lenity in such a due Proportion, as seldom or never failed of the desired Success." [54]

That is not to say that disruptions did not occur at colonial Princeton. But when they did, they were handled with restraint by the faculty and the board. For instance, in one of the few serious breaches of discipline in the colonial period, the freshmen and grammar students in 1758 petitioned the board to dismiss a tutor and the grammar school master because neither was "sufficiently qualified for the Business of Instruction." The board found no truth in the charge, but by the end of the year both men had been discharged for "the benefit of the Society." Moreover, when the student slated to make the salutatory address in 1774 led a student riot directed against Thomas Hutchinson, the Tory governor of Massachusetts, the board merely noted its high disapproval to Witherspoon and requested the president to provide a more discreet speaker to salute the class of '74. [55]

The faculty's paternalistic attitude toward the students also informs their attitudes toward education, virtue, and the family. Board and faculty accepted Benjamin Franklin's advice that officials should "look on the Students as in some Sort their Children" and should "treat them with Familiarity and Affection . . . ." Samuel Davies, for one, delighted to call the student body "that collected Family" over which he presided as a benevolent father. [56] Until the college moved to Princeton, many of the students boarded with Presidents Dickinson and Burr; in fact, this arrangement continued after the construction of Nassau Hall. After the dormitory's completion no student was allowed to board in the village without a physician's excuse. The founders of the college apparently agreed with William Smith of New York that virtue was best preserved when the boys lived together under the supervision of men they respected. [57]

The New Side ministers were acutely aware of young people because the Great Awakening had frequently been most successful among the young. Jonathan Dickinson in 1740 sensed that his lethargic congregation might be revived if he reached his young people. Consequently, he gathered a group of them and delivered a message prepared especially for them. As Jonathan Edwards had done in the mid-thirties in Northampton, he slowly caught the youthful spirit of his young hearers and moved them deeply. He was delighted to see many of the youth coming to him for spiritual advice, and within three months he counseled more young people than he had seen in the previous thirty years of his ministry. At Newark, Aaron Burr had a similar experience; after hearing the young Burr preach, numbers of young people came to him asking, "What shall we do to be saved?" [58] This awareness of youth was one crucial product of the Great Awakening. As the New Sides ministered to a congregation's spiritual needs, they were concerned especially with the needs of the young.[59] Consequently, they frequently entered into the home to discuss a child's welfare with his parents. This sometimes had the effect of introducing into the family a figure of authority that competed with the father.

Often the minister strengthened the hand of a mother who wanted to prepare a son for the ministry against a father who still needed him on the farm. For example, Samuel Davies's father tried to keep him on his Virginia farm until the youth's persistent attraction toward books forced the father to give in to his wife's entreaties that their son be educated.[60] The future founder of Washington College, William Graham, was also opposed by his father in his plans to enter the ministry until aided by his mother and his pastor, John Roan.[61] Caleb Wallace, future minister, jurist, and college founder in Virginia and Kentucky, was the eldest of four children, the son of a farmer in the valley of Virginia. He was influenced as a boy by two of his pastors, Robert Henry and Samuel Davies. Converted by Davies in a revival in 1756, Wallace was encouraged to continue his education by James and David Caldwell, two neighbors who had graduated from Princeton. When Davies became the president of Princeton in 1761, Wallace enlisted his aid and that of the Caldwells in persuading his father to allow him to further his education. The combination was eventually successful, but not until his son was twenty-five years old was the elder Wallace willing to forgo his services on the farm.[62] Some future ministers, such as John M'Knight, Robert Cooper, and Alexander McWhorter, were raised without fathers at all and were strongly influenced by their mothers in their career plans.[63]

It is perhaps not too much to say that the intrusion of the post-Awakening New Side ministry into families weakened the paternalistic nature of some colonial families. Certainly some disgruntled fathers believed that it did. To the extent that this is true, the development undermined an essential institution of a deferential society. This intrusion by the evangelical ministers into the home had another, more subtle, effect. By persuading poor young men to leave the farm and begin ministerial education, the New Side ministers made of their profession a significant instrument of social mobility. Just as some young men proved unwilling to defer to their fathers' dictum to remain on the farm, so too did many refuse to return to the farm upon graduation. By entering the ministry instead, these graduates contributed to a growing social mobility that was slowly undermining deference and hierarchy in colonial America.

The sons of the lower class mingled at Princeton with the sons of a colonial elite, and the two groups were separated by social class, age, and career plans. In the class of 1761, for instance, graduated one Isaac Handy, who was only eighteen years old. The son of a wealthy planter from Prince Anne County, Maryland, Isaac returned to that county upon graduating and practiced law for the rest of his life. Among Isaac's classmates was David Rice, the son of a poor Welsh farmer. Converted by Davies at age twenty, Rice raised tobacco and taught school to earn money for his education. At Princeton he received aid from one of the scholarships established by English dissenters. When he graduated in 1761, he was twenty-eight years old. Also in the class was David Caldwell, who served as a carpenter's apprentice until age twenty-four and graduated at thirty-six. And a Scotch-Irish immigrant, John Rosbrugh, left his trade after his wife's death and entered the college, sponsored by the fund for poor and pious youth. But he was no youth; he graduated in 1761 at the age of forty-four. These men were substantially older than young Handy, and the educational experience of Rice, Caldwell, and Rosbrugh differed from his in that they had been schooled only intermittently. That Handy should be educated at college was probably taken as a matter of course. For Rice, Caldwell, and Rosbrugh acquiring an education was a problematical process. Most important of all, while Handy entered the legal practice, each of the three older students entered the New Side ministry.[64]

The class of 1761 may be taken as representative of other classes. To the college came the sons of the Livingstons, Stocktons, Smiths, and Lees, who entered college at an early age and as a matter of course, and graduated to enter the legal or medical professions, inherit a family business, or retire to private life. But the sons of farmers and poorer merchants also found their way to colonial Princeton, often under the guidance of their ministers. Usually older than their classmates, they in effect created a separate student body in the college, and as divinity students under Witherspoon after 1768, they essentially became professional graduate students.[65] A few young men from the lower classes had always entered the ministry and, perhaps, gone to Harvard for an education. But in colonial Princeton their numbers rose dramatically as the vigorous New Side Presbyterians attempted to keep supplied the pulpits of their burgeoning denomination.

Colonial Princeton, then, was the institutional expression of ideas and forces that were suddenly released by the Great Awakening. The utopian nature of those ideas and forces has been greatly underestimated if not dismissed by historians. At best the New Sides are seen as naïve: surely the Presbyterians did not actually believe that they could halt the relentless progress of individualism and the resulting social conflict in America. Yet they did believe just that. Their belief led them to reunite with men they opposed on many basic issues. Moreover, the belief led them to elaborate a theory of social leadership to serve a Christian commonwealth that they expected to follow that reunion. And at Princeton they created an institution to make of that theory a vital reality. The Presbyterians of the late colonial period, then, only awaited a sign that the beginning of the millennium was at hand. That sign was not long in coming.

Part Two

Revolution
1775–1795

CHAPTER V

The Republic as Community

The American triumph in the war for independence appeared to be the sign the Presbyterians awaited. The colonists' amazing military success was attended by what the Presbyterians believed to be an even more astonishing transformation in colonial society. As they won their independence, the Americans also became republicans, and the creation of the republic appeared, almost miraculously, to end the disorder and conflict that had plagued colonial society. The enthusiasm with which Presbyterians embraced the ideology of republicanism and their extravagant visions of the republic's future are extraordinary. They believed that the Revolution had ushered in a new era of history in which the selfishness and contentions of the recent past would give way to a virtuous, ordered, and godly society. The Americans, in the act of opposing England, had themselves been transformed. Convinced of that transformation, the Presbyterians now turned their backs on the transatlantic Christian commonwealth and sought community in a distinctly American republic, a new society made possible by that amazing change.

THE EASY TRAVAIL OF ZION

During the Great Awakening the Presbyterians had been "surprised" by the "amazing works of God"; later they had been "astounded" by the triumph of Protestant arms over papist France. Neither reaction, though, approached their response to the extraordinary course of the American Revolution. Astonishment marked the sermons preached by Presbyterians in December of 1783 to celebrate the American victory. In Philadelphia's Pine Street Church, for instance, pastor George Duffield quoted the prophet Isaiah: "Who hath heard such a thing . . . ? Shall the earth be made to bring forth in one day? shall a nation be born at once?" In the case of America, apparently so. Unlike ancient Israel, the American Zion was not to be born after a "long continued sense of arduous dubious struggle." To the contrary, Duffield marveled, "almost as soon as our American Zion began to travail . . . she brought forth her children . . . ." In New York City a young Presbyterian chaplain was no less amazed. Israel Evans, who had graduated from Princeton only four years before hostilities began, predicted that historians, faced with the improbable American victory, would try to prove that "a revolution of such a magnitude, could not possibly be accomplished in so short a time by such an infant people . . . ." Their assertions, though, would be "destitute of truth." [1]

Presbyterians were amazed also at the ease with which American independence had been won. Though there had been trials and inconveniences, Duffield asserted, the travail of the American Zion had not been marked by the "pangs and pains which apprehensive fears expected." [2] The ease of the American victory appeared all the more remarkable when the Presbyterian clerics recalled the military might of England and contrasted it to the improvised colonial militia. Repeated references to David and Goliath dotted Presbyterian victory sermons. [3] Witherspoon, for instance, boasted that the celebrated discipline of the English professionals was "turned into confusion and dismay before the new and maiden courage of freemen in defense of their property and rights." Revealingly, Witherspoon attributed to the British soldiers the characteristics of selfishness and lack of patriotism that recently had been used to indict the colonists. The "redcoats" were "effeminate and delicate soldiers, who are nursed in the lap of self-indulgence," and consequently were no match for clear-eyed, selfless, brave young colonists sacrificing their all for the common good. And even worse than the English soldiers were the mercenary Hessians—hired thugs who sold their patriotism to the highest bidder. [4]

Having marveled at the "easy travail of Zion," the Presbyterian clergy endeavored to explain the American victory. In that effort the ministers resolved, at least temporarily, a deep ambivalence not only about the character of the American colonists but about the relation of human effort to divine providence in shaping history. During the Great Awakening and the war with France, the clergy had often marveled at instances of colonial selflessness. That exuberance, however, too often faded before a subsequent display of contention and greed which in turn provoked an unmistakable "frown of heaven." Between 1740 and 1763 the clergy had exhorted their members to pious exertions and then judged God's reactions to those efforts by the blessings or trials He visited upon the land. The problem for those clergymen had been to encourage exertion without necessarily binding God to reward it; that is, to evoke godly effort from men without producing a fatal pride in any divine favor that might follow. That ambivalence, born of revival and war, disappeared for the Presbyterian clergy during the American Revolution, the crisis that was both revival and war.[5]

The clergy, of course, dutifully attributed every aspect of the American victory to an all-powerful deity. Indeed, it seemed that God's providences had anticipated the imperial crisis. For instance, the war with France that once had been scorned as the nadir of colonial virtue appeared in the midst of the Revolution to have been a providentially appointed training ground for Washington and other colonial military leaders. Had England turned on the colonies before that proving-time, the Reverend Robert Smith believed that the colonies "must have fallen an easy prey" to the mother country.[6] And when it did come, the war for independence seemed replete with what John Witherspoon called the "singular interpositions of providence" in American affairs. God seemed to raise up the right man always at the right time and then to sow discord among the enemy, whose ineptness, at Saratoga for instance, suggested divine intervention to some. The disadvantages under which the colonists fought likewise were transformed by the clergy into advantages. The long seacoast, though it was admittedly difficult to defend, also brought all colonists into contact with the ennobling adversities of war; the depreciation of the colonial currency demonstrated the folly of greed, and those who were ruined by that lesson were usually sustained by Revolutionary virtue and were better for the instruction in any case. The clergy even had a providential explanation for the war's undeniable early disasters. The invasion of Canada, rout that it was, could be explained by Maine's John Murray because it had not been "strictly within the line of self-defence: and as that is the limit of lawful war, it was the kindness of

Heaven to hedge up our way so as to confine us to it . . . ."[7] Thus, colonial victories, such as Saratoga, were not attributed by the clergy to their countrymen's patience, perseverance, and courage. Instead, that particular victory was, in Israel Evans's words, "the work of the Lord, and marvellous in our eyes." But so epochal was the task at hand after 1776 that the Presbyterian clergy finally bound God to reward the exertions of His people, *not* because they were worthy, but because their cause was righteous and just. Affirmed the Pennsylvania Presbyterian, Hugh Williamson: "the Americans in a cause so righteous, cannot possibly be subdued by men so unjust, perfidious, and cruel as their present enemies." No people ever had been conquered in such a cause as now inspired the Americans. And in the victory sermons of 1783 and 1784 a few Presbyterians even suggested that heaven was dependent on the exertions of righteous men to obtain its ends. John Murray could find no reason for God to favor a "land swarming with the most audacious classes of gospel-sinners." But God had "declared himself to be still their God; theirs in a covenant-relation still." And God had been limited by that relationship: "The omnipotence of the agent never supersedes the use of means." True, God was not beholden "to any instrument." "Yet in all the business of Providence," Murray concluded, "means are employed as constantly as if they were necessary."[8]

TRANSFORMED AMERICANS

The clergy's willingness to bind the deity to reward the exertions of a virtuous people measures in part their conviction after 1776 that the Americans were becoming particularly virtuous, that the Revolution was transforming the colonists. The clergy's description of Americans, first during the war with France and then during the Revolution, is strikingly different. No longer profiteers who neglected the bonds of social union, the colonists appeared, under pressure, to become the selfless, virtuous citizens that for so long had been the clergy's social ideal.

Evidence of transformation was everywhere. John Joachim Zubly, a Swiss-born Presbyterian minister, believed that his adopted countrymen were turning from "trade, and the means of acquiring wealth, to agriculture and frugality . . . ." John Witherspoon hoped that, if Zubly was wrong, adversity would in time force "remiss and lax" Americans "back to the path of frugality and virtue." And Benjamin Rush in 1777 fretted lest the war end before adversity completed its work: "A peace at this time would be the greatest curse that could befall us . . . . Liberty without virtue would be no blessing to us." [9] Since the clergy had been most alarmed by the unrestrained pursuit of wealth in the late colonial period, they supported enthusiastically the associations formed early in the imperial crisis to boycott the luxuries of England. William Tennent III urged the ladies of Charleston, South Carolina, to "associate—resolve—burn your tea." [10] And clearly the significance of the tea boycott for Tennent was as much functional as substantive. It was not forswearing tea that was crucial, but *uniting* to renounce *all* baneful habits.

The transforming Revolution appeared to promote social union even while it halted the spread of luxury in the colonies. British cruelty and tyranny, it seemed, had succeeded in fostering colonial unity where all else had failed. Robert Davidson, Carlisle, Pennsylvania's Presbyterian minister, observed that during the Revolution, "Every friend of his country embraced another of the same spirit . . . strangers to national or party distinctions." And chaplain Israel Evans contrasted the divisions within the British army to the "happy union" of the patriot band, "where all strove to excel in bravery, and the service of our common cause and interest." George Duffield believed that the war miraculously had united America's "numerous husbandmen, her merchants and mechanics; and her sons of the learned professions, and students in every science," while John Murray was surprised that the colonists made "common cause" even when their own interests were not immediately threatened. And Witherspoon insisted—a little wistfully, no doubt—that the struggle had even erased most areas of contention among the colonies' religious groups and that only the cynical machinations of the British kept them alive at all.[11]

The transformed colonists appeared to survive even the most rigorous test of public virtue: the collapse of government. As royal government retreated and local authority filled the breach, Witherspoon for one found "public spirit" so pronounced as to elicit thanks for "its vigour and prevalence" rather than concern over occasional "dishonesty or disaffection." By "common consent," there was "a much greater degree of order and public peace, than men of reflexion and experience foretold or expected." Israel Evans could explain the stability of society only by the secret activities of public-minded citizens. Consequently, he believed, the final history of the "astonishing" Revolution would disclose "many things . . . which will raise the astonishment almost to the summit of unbelief." [12]

Of course, the change in the colonists during the Revolution was astonishing to the clergy not because it marked any permanent transformation in their countrymen but because the unity among patriots early in the war contrasted so vividly with the contentions of the recent past. Their confidence that a radical transformation had occurred measured the Presbyterian alarm at the abiding problem of selfishness in American society, rather than any actual, permanent change. They believed because they wanted to believe.

"THE MORNING OF THE WORLD"

The Presbyterian conviction that the Revolution had transformed once contentious colonists into selfless patriots also made possible the emergence of a much changed millennialism. Presbyterian eschatology during the Great Awakening had related the second coming of Christ to the universal spread of pietistic religion. When the pietist revival ran its course in 1745, the Presbyterians then invested the imperial wars with millennial implications, preaching the struggle with papist France as the battle with Antichrist. In that struggle the Catholic threat to civil liberty for the first time loomed as large to Presbyterians as did the perceived papist threat to religious freedom. During the Revolution, the Protestant mother country seemed an even more ominous threat to the civil and religious liberties of the colonies. The Presbyterians then embraced what recently has been called a "civil millennialism," in which America was seen not so much as the site of an imminent second coming of Christ but as the last refuge of liberty.[13]

The image of liberty flying to the New World from the oppressions of the Old was a venerable one. It had been used to describe the reasons for the first settlements of New England. The Revolution, though, gave that image new power and urgency. Tom Paine in the *Rights of Man* deplored the "tyranny and antiquity of habit" that precluded any political reformation in Asia, Europe, or Africa. "Freedom had been hunted round the globe," flying finally to America.[14] In 1752 the New York Presbyterian layman William Smith wrote a poem in which he traced freedom's flight from the ancient East, through Greece and Rome, and finally to England, where it remained until forced to flee the tyrannous Stuarts. Then, facing the great ocean, *"Empire and Liberty* their radiant Wings/ Expand to quit the sluggish *eastern* world;/ And cross the vast *Atlantic* meditate/ Their airy Passage to these western Climes,/ In quest of some Retreat to sojourn safe/ Till Time shall end . . . ." But in Smith's vision liberty is finally forced to flee the West, too. The American empire falls as even the virtuous westerners succumb to luxury, dissipation, and the ineluctable cycle of history. "Empire and liberty would sojourn in America only/ until again (when we/ Diseas'd and sunk, are ripe for Death) they're call'd/ By Fate to bless a Race of more Desert." Inevitably empire and liberty resume their westward course. America, for Smith, was simply one of many stages in the rhythm of history.[15]

In 1771 two young Princetonians, Philip M. Freneau and Hugh H. Brackenridge, collaborated on a commencement poem in which they described a different view of history and of America's millennial role. *A Poem on the Rising Glory of America* was suffused with a vision of America not as one episode in history alone but as its culmination. Like Smith, the young men described the cyclical course of past empires. When liberty took flight over the Atlantic in their poem, though, the rhythm of history had been broken. All that was past had been prelude to the "morning of the world" now dawning in America. Rather than another epoch in the cycle of history, America was the penultimate stage in an upward progression that would culminate in the millennium. In America the muse would finally sing "the final destiny of things." In those happy days "The bard enraptur'd scorns ignoble strains,/ Fair science smiling and full truth revealed,/ The world at peace, and all her tumults o'er,/ The blissful prelude to Emanuel's reign." [16]

The Presbyterian millennial enthusiasm was not limited to school-boys. More sedate and graver Presbyterians, such as Duffield and Zubly, agreed that America was the "last asylum of liberty," while Evans and Witherspoon vied with one another in praising America as the "last concluding scene" in perfecting human felicity.[17] Witherspoon was a staunch Calvinist who firmly believed in the depravity of human nature. But the Scotsman could nevertheless wax eloquent on the subject of America's future, even though that future depended, finally, on a trans-formation of human nature. In the Continental Congress he called the growth of America "next to miraculous" and described "A country growing every year in beauty and fertility, the people growing in num-bers and wealth, arts, and sciences, carefully cultivated, and constantly advancing . . . ." He would risk sounding "visionary and romantic" and declare that he expected in the colonies "a progress, as in every other human art, so in the order and perfection of human society, greater than we have yet seen." He even went so far as to make the very uncalvinistic statement that "There have been great improvements, not only in human knowledge, but in human nature." Those improvements, he asserted, would flourish best in a free and virtuous America, upon which the "state of the human race through a great part of the globe, for ages to come" depended.[18]

THE AMERICAN AS REPUBLICAN

If the Presbyterian conviction of a basic transformation in colonial society produced a fervent millennialism, it also enabled the Presbyterians to embrace republican ideas enthusiastically. The colonists in 1776 seem to have turned to republicanism almost by instinct, and that fact has intrigued historians. Some students of the Revolution have noted that until 1776 the word "republican" was a term of opprobrium for a set of ideas often rejected by thoughtful men convinced of the superiority of a constitutional monarchy.[19] Other historians, observing that republicanism is a representative form of government, have been surprised that it commanded the allegiance of Americans, who at the midcentury still held a rather pessimistic view of man. The idea of counterpoise— of checks and balances—was central to republican theory, and some historians have suggested that hard-headed colonists might have been attracted to that aspect of republicanism as a way of controlling naturally selfish men.[20] The suggestion is a useful one. But this theory fails to consider that republicanism was attractive to the colonists at least in part because it was a moral as well as a political system. The Presbyterians, at least, embraced republicanism not because it judiciously balanced power and liberty but because it promised to resolve their deepest fears about their society, because it promised to that society moral regeneration.

Historians have not appreciated the urgency of Tom Paine's cry that *"the time has found us."* His audience did. Few ideas were as compelling in *Common Sense* as the author's warning to the Americans to seize the day. "Youth," Paine warned, "is the seedtime of good habits, as well in nations as in individuals." Therefore, the colonists must be rid of corrupting England lest in fifty years they themselves become corrupt and incapable of virtuous exertion in liberty's behalf. Nations had but one chance to form the correct form of government. Paine urged the Americans not to miss theirs. Though new to America, Paine sensed the pervasive concern in the colonies with corruption.[21] He realized that the Americans, though young as a people, were obsessed with the dangers of disease and age. It was Paine's special contribution to the patriot cause to persuade the colonists that independence—if seized immediately—would rid them of the source of that corruption.[22]

In the "morning of the world" the Presbyterians were elated by Paine's challenge to "seize the day." A country "newly planted, and every day advancing to a maturer state affords the highest delight to a contemplative philosopher," Witherspoon declared in the early days of the war, "and is, at the same time, the strongest invitation to activity and usefulness." In a letter to John Adams in 1788 Benjamin Rush declared: "America has ever appeared to me to be the theater on which human nature will reach its greatest civil, literary, and religious honors. *Now* is the time to sow the seeds of each of them." And in Lancaster, Pennsylvania, the Presbyterian minister John King enjoined the members of the Franklin Society in 1789 to study civil government carefully because in America they had the unique opportunity to create new and perfect political systems.[23]

Not that the Presbyterians thought republicanism a perfect political system. Far from it. True, republicanism did have much to recommend it, and the Americans idealized it as a system of representative government with the potential for mediating between the excesses of aristocratic and democratic alternatives. Citizens, theoretically, elected the most virtuous of their peers to public office, where they prevented the excesses into which pure democracy inevitably ran while, at the same time, checking the naturally tyrannical tendencies of a monarchy. It was through that judicious balance between anarchy and tyranny that liberty survived.[24] But the Presbyterians—and all Americans—were attracted to republicanism despite its obvious liabilities. Republics were universally conceded to be the most vulnerable of all political systems. The ancient republics, Greece and Rome, had decayed and perished, and when the Americans sought republican models in the eighteenth century, they found only struggling miniscule states surrounded by rapacious monarchies. Therefore, Presbyterians frequently spoke, as Rush did in the 1780s, of the short lifespan of republics indicated by history and "the common opinions of mankind."[25]

Republics were believed to be of short duration because they were particularly intricate and delicate systems. The relations between the electorate, the representatives, and their ruler were of necessity more complicated than the tyranny of an unrestrained monarch or the anarchy of an uncontrolled democracy. Moreover, those intricate relations afforded numerous opportunities for corruption and the neglect of duty. A representative might be elected by appealing to the prejudices of the electorate; or the people might succumb to the blandishments of an artful demagogue. Beyond those problems, the delicate system of checks and balances that made republicanism attractive to the virtuous could still be subverted by the vicious.

Ultimately, though, republics were considered precarious because they depended for their success upon a virtuous citizenry. Only virtuous men were capable of choosing the best-qualified men for positions of leadership and of resisting the emotional appeals of scheming demagogues. Only virtuous men could rise above selfish interests and seek a larger common good. Charles Nisbet, the president of Dickinson College, noted in 1789 that virtue alone could balance the interests and ambitions of individuals. And in 1786 Rush observed that, even if virtuous men were elected to positions of leadership, public bodies in a republic could do no more good than the public allowed; if citizens were not virtuous, it did not matter how virtuous their leaders were. All agreed that only virtue and public knowledge could preserve republican government. Where the "common people are ignorant and vicious, a nation, and above all a republican nation, can never be long free and happy." Neither, added Nisbet, could it be just.[26]

Despite these vulnerabilities, the Presbyterians were convinced that republican governments should be established in each colony immediately; that the activity and exertion that accompanied the War for Independence provided the ideal opportunity for creating government; and that to hesitate would be to miss that crucial time described by Tom Paine. Witherspoon noted that "times of public commotion" rouse the mind and shake off "the incumbrances of sloth and self-indulgence"; Benjamin Rush spoke even more mechanistically of the "spring which the human mind acquired by the Revolution." It was as if the Revolution, like a searing flame, had softened the forms and habits of colonial society by agitating, or at least activating, the mental faculties of men. Like the Presbyterian New Sides during the Awakening, Rush sensed the malleability of an agitated society and, using the mechanical psychology acquired at Princeton, insisted that fundamental changes be made before society hardened into undesirable new forms or relapsed into unacceptable old ones. Possessed of the "yielding texture they acquired by the heat of the late Revolution," the people's minds could still receive new impressions, whereas in even three years that situation might be very different. The time had indeed found the Presbyterians, and Rush feared that the time allotted America for creating a virtuous government and society was much shorter than the fifty years allowed by Paine.[27]

Not all Presbyterians were convinced that Americans were virtuous enough to sustain a republican government. If Benjamin Rush was confident of the virtue of Americans, Charles Nisbet was not. When the Dickinson College Board began to seek a president for the new school in 1783, Rush suggested Nisbet, who he believed would administer Dickinson with the same vigor with which Witherspoon directed Princeton. "Come, sir," Rush implored, "and spread the influence of science and religion among us." He described to Nisbet a ductile society waiting to be molded: "Here everything is in a plastic state. Here the benefactor of mankind may realize all his schemes for promoting human happiness. Human nature here (unsubdued by the tyranny of European habits and customs) yields to reason, justice, and common sense." In this happy condition, Rush believed, America "seems destined by heaven to exhibit to the world the perfection which the mind of man is capable of receiving from the combined operation of liberty, learning, and the gospel upon it."[28]

Rush had every reason to believe that Nisbet would respond affirmatively to his invitation. The Scottish parson had supported the colonists during the war for independence, and he had been in the forefront of efforts to rid Scottish politics of patronage and corruption. To his friend the Earl of Buchan, Nisbet in 1782 had acknowledged that his opponents thought him visionary to expect from real men virtues that are found only in Plato's republic. "But surely," he insisted, "it is no utopian dream to expect a much higher degree of virtue and public spirit than is presently the *ton* among great men."[29] Both the Scottish minister and the American physician agreed, then, that men could be made more virtuous this side of utopia—or heaven.

Upon arriving on the Pennsylvania frontier in 1784 Nisbet discovered just how far from utopia he was. He was appalled at the selfishness rampant in America, and as for public virtue, he could find none. To the Scotsman it appeared that no revolution had taken place, and the transformation so clear to others escaped his careful examination. Change remained in the future and awaited the day when the Americans would have "more virtue, more industry," and more faith in each other than was presently the case.[30] Nisbet condemned in particular those characteristics of American society that had disturbed American Presbyterians at midcentury. The republic was composed of "discordant atoms, jumbled together by chance, and tossed by inconstancy in an immense vacuum." Also, the "industry, knowledge, and virtue" essential to republics had fallen victim in America to the "abuse of liberty and independence since the late revolution." Above all, society in America lacked "a principle of attraction and cohesion," because all men pursued self and ignored the imperatives of social union. Such men, Charles Nisbet was positive, were not the stuff of which republicans were made.[31]

Rush was undaunted, though. After he realized that Nisbet was not a second Witherspoon, Rush first attempted to ship him back to Scotland. Failing that, he met Nisbet's pessimism with unflagging optimism. For instance, in 1794, the year in which the Pennsylvania frontier produced the Whiskey Rebellion, Nisbet sarcastically informed one friend that he expected Carlisle's shoemaker (who was already the sheriff) to be elected to Congress by the "sovereign People" because of his expertise in conducting "Liberty Pole" meetings. At the same time, though, Rush assured an acquaintance that "The United States continue to demonstrate by their internal order and external prosperity the practicability, safety, and happiness of republican forms of government among a people too educated for monarchical principles and habits." [32] Finally, Rush buried the Scotsman in a torrent of invective and scorn. Nisbet, he charged, was himself a stranger to the virtue and public spirit he missed in America. His constant carping rendered him unable—even unworthy—to "inspire young men with the heroic principles of good republicans, or good Christians!" While Rush sought in Nisbet the "disinterested benevolence—the active public Spirit, and the fortitude in duty" that had characterized Finley (Rush's uncle), Burr, and Davies, Nisbet berated Rush for luring him to America with false estimates of American virtue. In the end, each man accused the other of lacking the expansive selflessness essential to republican success. Rush could easily have said of the Scotsman what Nisbet so pointedly observed of him: "There seems to be a want of Virtue and publick Spirit somewhere." [33]

THE REPUBLICAN AS CHRISTIAN

The pessimism of Charles Nisbet—and other Presbyterians—about the future of America must have been tempered in 1789. Almost simultaneously in that year George Washington was inaugurated as the first president of a newly unified republic, and the republic's Presbyterians created a General Assembly to unite the denomination. The conjunction of the two events seemed providential to the Presbyterians, who insisted upon the structural similarities between the ecclesiastical system of presbyterianism and the political system of republicanism. In each, ultimate power resided in the people, who elected representatives to ruling bodies subject to written constitutions and operated by majority rule. One was the surest defense against religious tyranny; the other, the strongest hedge against civil absolutism. Consequently, the Presbyterians embraced the one as enthusiastically as the other.[34]

Indeed, the Presbyterians' enthusiastic acceptance of republicanism measures the extent to which they identified that political system with Christianity, if not with Presbyterianism. That identification seemed embodied in the first president. For the Presbyterians, Washington was not just a selfless, virtuous republican. He was a *Christian* republican. In reality, the Virginia Anglican was a faithful vestryman but an irregular visitor at the Lord's table. For the Presbyterians, though, Washington's Christianity became the most important aspect of the president's public identity. When he resigned his commission, for instance, Washington was compared by John Murray first to Gideon and then to Cincinnatus. Murray noted that Washington left his office with "a public testimony in favor of religion" and a vow to devote his future days to encouraging "his people in the service of God."[35] In one of its first acts the General Assembly directed Witherspoon and his son-in-law, Samuel Stanhope Smith, to compose an address to Washington, expressing the Presbyterians' confidence in the republic's success under his leadership. In that address the Presbyterian leaders expressed succinctly the basis for their confidence: "Public virtue is the most certain means of public felicity; and religion is the surest basis of virtue." The statement was not original, nor was its sentiment unique to the Presbyterians. But it is important to realize the intensity with which it was held in order to understand the alacrity with which the American Presbyterians embraced republicanism. The new polity would succeed not because it was dependent upon republicans; in America, it would be sustained by *Christian* republicans.[36]

The equation of republicanism and Christianity was not an obvious one, either logically or historically. Other value systems could—and did —inculcate the selflessness and virtue necessary for republican success.

Moreover, the ancient republics of Greece and Rome had not been Christian, much less Presbyterian. The paganism of the first republicans sometimes embarrassed their eighteenth-century Christian admirers. However, just as Samuel Davies in the colonial period had endowed King David with Protestant virtues, so did republican Presbyterians stress those attributes which the virtuous pagans shared with orthodox Calvinists—a veneration of a supreme being, devotion to the common good, and above all, patriotism.[37]

At the basis of the Presbyterian equation of republicanism and Christianity was their insistence upon the unitary nature of truth. Benjamin Rush, for one, was convinced that "All truths are related, or rather there is but one truth." To Jeremy Belknap he asserted in 1791 that "Republicanism is a part of the truth of Christianity"; to John Adams, "The precepts of the Gospel and the maxims of republics in many instances agree with each other."[38] One would follow the other. Republican government might precede Christianity as the prelude to a "glorious manifestation of its power and influence upon the hearts of men"; republicanism playing John the Baptist to the Messiah of Christianity. Or the roles might be reversed; Christianity serving as the *"strong ground of republicanism."* In either case, it was "only necessary for republicanism to ally itself" with Christianity to "overturn all the corrupted political and religious institutions in the world."[39]

The relation of republicanism and Christianity to the "Influence of Religion in Civil Society" was thoroughly analyzed by a South Carolina Presbyterian, Thomas Reese, in 1788. The minister's essay was delivered among many heated discussions of civil society, and it reflected Reese's sensitivity to those debates and to the events that were shaping the republic. It was no simple encomium to the stabilizing influence of religion in society. Rather, the essay was a subtle analysis of the vulnerabilities of republican governments and of the relation of religion to those vulnerabilities. Reese found civil authority in a republic incapable of either encouraging or coercing virtuous conduct. Its operations were too crude, its sanctions too superficial. Civil authority could operate only through fear of punishment; it could not appeal to the hopes of men. Even on a negative level, civil authority could punish only those crimes openly committed. Those aspects of human relationships that were the true basis of social union—gratitude, hospitality, charity—were beyond its control. The sanctions of religion, though, were subtle and pervasive. They promoted virtue by promising heavenly bliss. They

thereby encouraged the exertion necessary to social union rather than a
sullen compliance to law that was destructive because coerced. Moreover, religion could legitimately concern itself with intangible human
relationships that civil authority rightly ignored. Divine punishment
pursued secret as well as open transgressions, impressing upon all "the
idea of a future state, an omniscient tribunal, and a punishment which
the guilty cannot possibly avoid." And, Reese concluded, the sanction
of divine law "falls in with, and strengthens" civil law. Religion, then,
added to the mechanical, superficial laws of men a force that at the same
time promoted virtuous activity while it promised eternal punishment to
the vicious.[40] Finally, for Benjamin Rush, for Thomas Reese, for all
Presbyterians, religion was essential to republicanism because it impressed upon men the fact that they were part of a larger community
to which they owed duties. Consequently, for Rush, "A Christian
cannot fail of being a republican, for every precept of the Gospel in-
culcates . . . humility, self-denial, and brotherly kindness . . . ." In
short, Christianity taught the one precept absolutely essential to the
success of republics: no man "liveth to himself." [41]

"NO MAN LIVETH TO HIMSELF"

Even after relating republicanism to Christianity, some Presbyterians
were still fearful for the future of the new nation. In part, those fears
measured the Presbyterians' response to a new and alarming force in
American life: the frontier. Henceforth, a much enlarged frontier would
influence all Presbyterian attitudes and decisions, always wrenching established patterns of thought and action into unexpected directions. It
was clear to the Presbyterians—as it was to most patriots after 1783—
that the success of the American republic would be decided upon the
banks of the Ohio and the Mississippi as well as the Hudson and the
Charles.

The Presbyterian response to the more limited colonial frontier had
been mixed. The New Sides tended to respond enthusiastically to its
challenges while the Old Sides worried about its threat to ordered society.
After 1783 the frontier became important because it seemed to menace
the success of the republican experiment itself. For just as the clergymen
convinced themselves that the colonists were uniting and abandoning
their former selfish and contentious ways, the opening frontier lured men
away from ordered society into the wilderness, where selfishness was

endemic and where man, by definition and necessity, did "live to himself."

The Presbyterians responded to the frontier with the same urgency with which they urged reformation upon their fellow Americans. In 1779, for instance, the Presbytery of Hanover reported to the Synod of Virginia a favorable disposition in Virginia toward religion in general and "towards the Presbyterian church in particular." But the presbytery urged immediate attention to the frontier lest the opportunity for progress be "utterly lost by the prevalency and preoccupying of many ignorant and irreligious sectaries." Immediate exertion was necessary to create on the frontier a sense of community that was already weak in settled society and that was doubly endangered in the wilderness. To that end religion was absolutely essential. In the midst of the frontier the new Transylvania Presbytery in Kentucky affirmed in 1792 that only religion could lead selfish men to "mutual love and good will" by gently compelling them "to consult the true interests of one another as individuals or societies, looking everyone not on his own things, but on the things of his neighbour." [42] Only Christianity could force men on the frontier to consult the good of a larger whole over their own selfish interests.

Just as they had divided over whether Americans were virtuous enough to support republican governments, so did Presbyterians disagree over the Americans' ability to sustain this indispensable sense of community on the frontier. Again, Benjamin Rush and Charles Nisbet took opposite, extreme positions, between which most Presbyterians probably found themselves. Nisbet did not realize the extent to which America was still a frontier society until he arrived in Carlisle in 1784. Upon making that discovery, he began a tirade against the American frontier that did not cease until his death in 1804. Indeed, the essence of his pessimism concerning America was his conviction that the frontier could not sustain communal life and that, for all practical purposes, the frontier was synonymous with American society.

In a series of letters to his friend Alexander Addison, a Presbyterian attorney in Pittsburgh, Nisbet in 1786 outlined his concern about the American republican as frontiersman. These "wandering Arabs" were driven by a "loco-motive tendency" that impels them to acquire ever more extensive and remote farms. On their estates they are thrown "so far from one another, as to bar social Intercourse" and are thereby deprived "of all the Advantages and Pleasures of Society." Thus, while they should "be mutual Helps" to each other, the frontiersmen instead become "distant Enemies to one another." [43]

Not the least of the advantages lost by isolated frontiersmen was mental stimulation, and Nisbet ingeniously linked that deprivation to the absence of virtue on the frontier. Separated from society, men were "deprived of that Stimulation which is necessary to excite their active Powers and convey Information to their Minds." Consequently, they quickly fell into "ignorance, Prejudice and Indolence." And, since the parts of the mind were intricately related, those weakened mental faculties inevitably diminished the moral faculties, which were dependent upon the mind for their strength. "The Restraint of Conscience must wear off," Nisbet warned, "and evil Appetites gather Strength in an imperfect and Scattered Society." Inevitably, mechanically, that process "unhinges Credit, overturns Decency, and destroys the Habits of Order and the Sense of Public Spirit." Those destroyed, Nisbet feared, the republic could not survive.[44]

Benjamin Rush too was convinced of the frontier's importance to the republic's success, and, to an extent, he shared Nisbet's concerns. He was particularly worried that Scotch-Irish Presbyterians composed the bulk of Pennsylvania's immigrants to the frontier, and lest the denomination be weakened on the seaboard, he sought to limit the Presbyterian flow to "the wilderness of the Ohio or Kentucke." Rush tried to convince his countrymen to stay in one place long enough to establish roots and a sense of community. He wished to see "the *paternal* house and farm more valued by our people." And the fastidious Rush was always horrified at what he believed was the state of disrepair of the Scotch-Irish farms; like many other Pennsylvanians he contrasted those farms to the estates of the tidy Germans and recommended the teutonic example to the sons of Ireland.[45]

But, unlike Nisbet, Rush did not view the frontier in apocalyptic terms. Rather, he saw the taming of the frontier as a process of three stages of pioneers, the first two quickly giving way to the third, when the frontier would become indistinguishable from the rest of society. Rush conceded that in the first phase the frontier was settled by vicious men who usually had been forced to flee from civilization. On the frontier they degenerated further and refused to give up any of their rights. But even those men Rush could praise for their friendliness and for their willingness to help each other in a crisis. In the second phase, the frontiersman characteristically owned a little property and began to take an interest in the larger community, even if he did spend too much time drinking and politicking. Rush felt that Pennsylvania was in this second phase in the 1780s, and he expected it soon to pass, bringing the third type of frontiersman west. He would be a man of property and character, usually the ambitious son of a respected eastern family. He would farm scientifically and "In proportion as he increases in wealth," he would value "the protection of the laws." He would therefore pay taxes and support the church and school "as the means of promoting order and happiness in society."[46]

Rush believed, then, that virtuous, industrious, and sober Americans would quickly settle the frontier and make of it an ordered and prosperous part of American society. The Christian virtue that would sustain the republic would do so, in part, by conquering the selfishness and contention of Americans on the frontier. The pessimism of Nisbet, accordingly, was totally uncongenial to Rush's enthusiasm about the future of the republic. Between those extremes were the majority of Presbyterian clergymen, many of whom shared some or most of Nisbet's doubts but who wanted to believe that Rush, in the final analysis, was the better prophet.

CHAPTER VI

Republican Tensions

The development of colonial Presbyterianism was characterized by a recurring tension. Presbyterian evangelicals encouraged in their followers a "spiritual individualism" they hoped would lead neither to Arminian nor antinomian extremes; they preached the primacy of individual conscience while endeavoring to restrain the socially destructive potentialities of that idea. Neither effort at restraint was entirely successful. The final effect of the Awakening was to maximize the individual in all sorts of ways and to legitimate, temporarily, competition between the supporters and opponents of the revival. Those tensions, never resolved in the colonial period, emerged with even greater force after 1776. The Revolution produced tensions within American Presbyterianism even more severe than those that accompanied the Great Awakening. Now the success of the republic depended upon exhorting virtuous activity from the colonists and thereby ridding American society once and for all of social conflict and competition. But, as did the revival, the Revolution divided American Presbyterians, and, in the process of dividing, they once again had to defend division and competition. More directly than in the colonial period, this division and its defense were related to the question of the cultural function of higher education.

INSTITUTIONS AND THE REVOLUTION

The founders of Princeton intended the New Side school to be a dynamic instrument of social reformation and integration. After 1776 the Presbyterians had every reason to believe that their school was having that effect on American society. In the year of independence graduates of Princeton began to lay the foundation for what by 1800 amounted to a Presbyterian educational empire. First in the Shenandoah valley and in the Southside of Virginia, then in central and western Pennsylvania, and finally in the bluegrass country of central Kentucky, Princeton's sons founded one college after another. Of course, graduates of Harvard and Yale were establishing colleges at the same time. But the Congregationalist founders of Williams, Middlebury, and the University of Vermont were not unified in the same ways as were the Presbyterian educators. Those men had, for the most part, been educated by the same Presbyterian scholars and had established lifelong connections with each other at Princeton. Moreover, by 1776 the Presbyterian educators were part of a purposive denominational hierarchy that unified and to an extent directed their educational ventures. And in at least two instances, the same Presbyterian educator was involved in creating more than one of the Presbyterian institutions established in the young republic.[1]

The first of those institutions was created by Virginia's Hanover Presbytery. That body had been one of the centers of New Side strength and had provided colonial Princeton with President Samuel Davies and with a large number of ministerial students as well. That connection with the Hanover Presbytery was the origin of Princeton's special relationship with the upper south in the nineteenth and early twentieth centuries. In 1749, only three years after Princeton received its first charter, the Reverend Robert Alexander established the Augusta Academy near Lexington in the Shenandoah valley for the purpose of training Presbyterian ministers to serve the first of the Scotch-Irish immigrants in the valley. For a generation the academy was supported spasmodically by the presbytery and served no function other than ministerial education. Then, late in the colonial period and apparently without the active encouragement of the presbytery, the Reverend Charles Jeffrey Smith, a Presbyterian minister from Long Island, attempted to establish what would have been an unofficial Presbyterian academy in New Kent County. However, Smith, who was an admirer of the educational efforts of the Reverend Eleazer Wheelock in New Hampshire, was accidentally killed before his own southern project could materialize.[2]

The educational efforts of the Hanover Presbytery were galvanized shortly thereafter by the arrival in the valley of the Reverend William Graham. A native of Pennsylvania and a 1773 Princeton graduate, Graham in 1774 was twenty-nine years old and had been appointed head of the Augusta Academy. In that capacity he urged upon the presbytery the necessity of invigorating and enlarging the school. The presbytery responded to his enthusiasm and declared in October of 1774 that it considered a school "for the liberal Education of Youth" to be "of great and immediate Importance."[3] To be sure, not everyone was enthusiastic about an enlarged educational role for the presbytery. The Reverend John Brown, himself an earlier teacher at Augusta, worried that "the Expectation is too high for the Plan that is laid." And, Brown believed, a "private school & the College of New Jersey will polish a young Man & fit him for usefullness better than any semenary [sic] that we can expect in Virginia."[4] Graham's enthusiasm prevailed, though, and near the end of 1774 the Hanover Presbytery officially assumed responsibility for the Augusta Academy and placed the young Princetonian in charge of the school. At the outbreak of hostilities with England the Presbyterians grandly changed the name of their academy to Liberty Hall.[5]

The second Presbyterian school in Virginia was also established by the Hanover Presbytery at the urging of one of Witherspoon's students. Samuel Stanhope Smith, the son of minister-educator Robert Smith, and Witherspoon's future son-in-law, graduated from Princeton in 1769 and arrived in Virginia as a missionary in 1773. The handsome and eloquent Smith greatly impressed not only the Presbyterian men of Hanover but important Anglicans on the Tidewater as well. It is not too much to say that the Anglicans and Presbyterians, who were on good terms in 1774, created a school for Smith in part to keep him in their midst. In 1774 the presbytery established under Smith's direction an academy in Prince Edward County that would serve the Anglican Southside, while Graham's academy served the Presbyterian valley to the west. The Southside academy opened its doors to more than one hundred students on January 1, 1776, and was self-consciously named Hampden-Sydney for two heroes of the English civil wars.[6]

Hampden-Sydney was established in the year of the Declaration of

Independence. The next Presbyterian college was founded in the year the war of independence ended, 1783. Again, a Princeton graduate was the principal force behind the school's creation. The details of the founding of Benjamin Rush's Dickinson College in Carlisle, Pennsylvania, are quite complicated and need not detain us here. In brief, they center on the efforts of Old Side Presbyterians—after the Reunion of 1758—to maintain an educational alternative to Princeton. The Old Sides failed in 1768 to take over the Princeton presidency. They determined, then, to support at least two secondary schools; one, the academy at Newark, Delaware, and another, further to the west. In 1770 Old Side Presbyterians led the move to create a grammar school in Carlisle in Cumberland County, Pennsylvania, and efforts to charter the school were under way when the Revolution broke out. In 1782 Rush joined with other Presbyterian laymen—John Armstrong, John Montgomery, James Wilson, and others—to revive plans for a college in the west. Those plans matured a year later in a charter for Dickinson College. The western school was intended in part to celebrate the triumph of republican principles and was named for John Dickinson, the "Pennsylvania Farmer" whose voice had been among the first raised in defense of those principles.[7]

While Benjamin Rush led the effort to establish Dickinson in Carlisle, other Princeton graduates contributed to the founding of Presbyterian colleges even further to the west. As the restraints that bound colonial Americans to the original English settlements disappeared after 1783, Presbyterian minister-educators followed and in some cases led the rush to the west. John McMillan, Joseph Smith, and Thaddeus Dod in the early 1780s established in Washington and Canonsburg, Pennsylvania, two academies named for the towns in which they were located and intended to serve the growing Presbyterian population in western Pennsylvania. At about the same time, migrating Virginians—Anglican and Presbyterian alike—established Lexington, Kentucky, in the center of the bluegrass country. And, again, Princetonians among them established an institution of higher learning. The Reverend David Rice, who had followed Davies to Princeton, and who had been instrumental in founding Hampden-Sydney before moving to Kentucky, took the lead in forming the Transylvania Presbytery in Kentucky and then in encouraging that body to establish a seminary in Lexington. In 1794 the presbytery responded, establishing the Transylvania Seminary. In that effort Rice was assisted by Judge Caleb Wallace, a Princeton graduate who had been instrumental in creating Hampden-Sydney and Liberty Hall as well.[8]

This flurry of college founding during and immediately following the Revolution demonstrates, among other things, a growing Presbyterian appreciation of the importance of institutions in a republican society. Colonial Americans had lived in a society in which social institutions—beyond the family and the church—little affected daily existence. The republican revolution, though, imparted urgency to the task of molding society in ways appropriate to a republic. That imperative, in turn, made Americans increasingly aware of the burden of social institutions. Of those, none seemed more important to the Presbyterians than the college. Of course all societies have invested the school with the task of molding citizens in prescribed ways. But having granted that generality, one must still explain the intensity with which nineteenth-century Americans came to believe that education could solve the most difficult problems and resolve the most persistent tensions in their society.

That conviction owes much to the republican revolution of the late eighteenth century. The revolution, it was believed, made necessary a reexamination of American institutions in order to expose those inappropriate to republican societies. Declared Rush in 1787: "It is high time . . . to study our own character—to examine the age of our country—and to adopt manners in everything that shall be accommodated to our state of society and to the forms of our government."[9] He reminded the Dickinson Board in 1786 that "It has pleased God to call us into existence at an important era." Then, in an essay on republican education, Rush asserted that the complexities of republican government gave to the "business of education" a "new complexion." Now Americans must reexamine their "former habits" relating to this and every other subject. For although America had changed her form of government, Rush warned the Englishman Richard Price in 1786, "it remains yet to effect a revolution in our principles, opinions, and manners so as to accommodate them to the forms of the government we have adopted."[10]

Rush firmly believed that such a revolution was possible because he also believed societies were infinitely malleable. He insisted that they were capable of being fashioned in an almost mechanical way. Indeed, it was possible, he believed, to "convert men into republican machines."[11] Most Americans shared Rush's confidence that republican institutions could reform American society; their embrace of republicanism was predicated on that belief. But some were less willing than Rush to see the process as a mechanical one. Samuel Stanhope Smith, for one, reminded Rush that institutions must be given time to remake a society. Smith acknowledged the transforming influence of educational institutions, but after reading Rush's essay on the education of women in 1787, Smith warned Rush against hoping for too much too soon. "It requires experience and Time to modify . . . [the ideas of a country], and to accommodate Them to new situations and states of society," he cautioned. "And it is not . . . effectively done till genius, prompted by virtuous zeal, and blessed with perseverance matures the system, and recommends it to Justice." [12]

Smith and Rush might disagree over the speed with which republican institutions would transform American society, but they agreed that those institutions must be created immediately in order to deliver the first, telling impression to a malleable society. That sense of urgency was shared by Presbyterian educators who faced the new frontier. Joseph Smith, one of the founders of the two academies in western Pennsylvania, warned that right direction must be given in particular to those communities that "are destined to germinate into mighty and widespread republics." [13] Smith's colleague, John McMillan, had been instructed by his mentor, Robert Smith, to raise on the frontier republican Christians who would give the right direction to social development in western Pennsylvania. [14] That McMillan felt he was heeding his teacher's advice is evident from his remarks at the opening of the Canonsburg Academy in 1791: "This is an important day in our history, affecting deeply the interests of the church, and of the country in the West; affecting our own interests for time and for eternity, and the interests . . . of thousands and thousands yet unborn." [15] McMillan expressed concisely the Presbyterian belief that on the frontier they were raising institutions that would transform a society made temporarily malleable by the Revolution and that would give permanent direction to the republic's development.

EDUCATION AND SOCIAL CONFLICT:
THE PENNSYLVANIA REVOLUTION

The Presbyterians soon found that it was easier to applaud than to create republican institutions. In Pennsylvania the Presbyterian effort to define and establish republican educational institutions was interwoven with the acrimonious debate over that state's revolutionary constitution.

Pennsylvanians split into opponents and supporters of that controversial document, and Presbyterians led both camps. As in the Great Schism, the Pennsylvania Presbyterians debated the legitimacy of social conflict and competition. That debate both reiterated and went beyond positions taken in the colonial schism. And this later debate was related directly to the creation and support of educational institutions. To single out the Pennsylvania constitution for discussion is not to deny the Presbyterian contribution to constitution-making in New Jersey, New York, and North Carolina, where their contribution was crucial. Nor is it to reduce the important Pennsylvania instance to a mere episode in the history of American Presbyterianism. The Presbyterian involvement in Pennsylvania is simply the most important of several instances and uniquely is related to the problem of creating and sustaining republican educational institutions.[16]

The patriot cause in Pennsylvania was supported by the Scotch-Irish Presbyterians that constituted a majority of Pennsylvania's frontiersmen in 1776, by the Presbyterian gentry of settled interior towns like Carlisle, and by the urbane Presbyterians who circulated freely in the cosmopolitan society of the Quaker capital. More so than in most colonies, the Revolution in Pennsylvania was made by Presbyterians, who were rewarded for their efforts by unprecedented power in the independent state. They were among those who cooperated with the radicals in the Continental Congress to undo the laggard Pennsylvania Assembly in the spring of 1776 and then, in the summer, to frame Pennsylvania's constitution, the second radical document to come from that sweltering season in Philadelphia. James Wilson, Daniel Roberdeau, George Bryan, Charles Thomson, Benjamin Rush, and John Ewing— all were leading Whigs; all, Presbyterian.[17]

The constitution framed by the Presbyterian leaders and their allies was the high point of radicalism in the American Revolution, and its provisions carried to its extreme the democratic thrust of the Revolution.[18] It provided for no executive, created a powerful unicameral legislature, extended the franchise, required the frequent rotation of officials, provided that acts passed in one legislative session be debated by the electorate before being promulgated by the next session, and created an innovative Council of Censors that provided a mechanism whereby the sovereign people could periodically inquire whether any branch of government was violating the constitution and could initiate changes to the frame of government when needed. The supporters of the controversial document were called Constitutionalists and were led by the Presbyterian merchant George Bryan and the Reverend John Ewing, professor of mathematics at the College of Philadelphia and Bryan's pastor at the First Presbyterian Church. Their chief support was in the Presbyterian frontier and, to a less extent, the Presbyterian-dominated militia companies. The Constitutionalists used the constitution of 1776 to gain control of the executive, legislative, and judicial branches of the state's government and then used controversial Test Acts to disfranchise any citizen who would not swear to uphold the constitution upon which they had based their drive to power. Well might Benjamin Franklin exclaim to a friend in 1784: "It is a fact that the Irish emigrants and their children are now in possession of the government of Pennsylvania, by their majority in the Assembly, as well as of the great part of the territory; and I remember well the first ship that brought any of them over." [19]

But not all the children of Ireland supported the constitution of 1776. Within days of its adoption there emerged a Presbyterian opposition to the document. First James Wilson, then Thomas McKean, and finally Benjamin Rush publicly denounced the document as tyrannous. Around them solidified an anticonstitution, or "Republican," party composed of much of the state's displaced leadership, most Anglicans and Quakers, some Presbyterian laymen, and much of the urban Presbyterian clergy. When the debate over the constitution began, it was immediately obvious that the Presbyterian Church in Pennsylvania was fundamentally divided.

The constitution's most controversial aspect was its provision for a unicameral legislature. It was in opposing and supporting that provision that the Presbyterians debated the legitimacy of social conflict and competition in a republic. The foes of the constitution denounced the unicameral assembly as a dangerous innovation. But in fact the single house simply continued the unicameral assembly stipulated in Pennsylvania's colonial frame of government. The provision thus exemplifies an idea, preservative in origin and intention, that was pulled into controversial new shapes by the Revolution. In debating those new shapes, each side posed as the defender of tradition. Each defense, though, impelled Pennsylvania's political and social theory into new directions.

The traditional defense of bicameralism was simple enough: the two houses represented different interests in society and protected liberty by providing a forum in which those interests checked and balanced each other. The Constitutionalists dismissed that function as irrelevant to American society. Only social inequalities had produced separate interest groups in the past, they argued, and since those inequalities did not exist in republican Pennsylvania, no bicameral legislature was necessary. In Pennsylvania men existed "naturally on a level" and should be represented by officials elected to a unicameral legislature that would be immune from the selfish jarrings of competing interests. In a land of equality and social unity that legislature would unite all "into one point of action" and would constitute an authority "commodiously fit for action without anarchy or confusion . . . ." Indeed, the Constitutionalists warned that a bicameral legislature would itself produce social distinctions and create *"separate, and jarring interests"* where they had not existed.[20]

Presbyterians outside Pennsylvania also rejected the idea that a legislature should reflect existing social divisions and dismissed as illusory the notion that competing interest groups in a bicameral legislature would serve as salutary checks on each other. In 1784 William Graham, the rector of Liberty Hall, was asked to propose a constitution for the state of Franklin, which was being carved out of land ceded to the Confederation Congress by North Carolina. The Presbyterian minister-educator modeled his draft on the Pennsylvania and North Carolina constitutions and reiterated the Pennsylvania Constitutionalists' critique of the conflict implied in a bicameral legislature. He noted that "Men agitated with a spirit of jealousy and contention are in no very promising situation to examine and judge of the tendency of measures to promote the public good . . . ." The only legitimate business of a republican legislature was to ascertain and promote the public good. That, Graham believed, could not be accomplished if distinctions were made between parts of government that continually competed with each other for power.[21]

The Republicans in Pennsylvania found it difficult to attack unicameralism without seeming to favor aristocracy and conflict in the midst of a democratic revolution based on republican unity. Benjamin Rush took up the challenge in 1777. He admitted that there were in Pennsylvania none of the "artificial distinctions" that historically had divided European societies. But neither could Rush find in Pennsylvania the "perfect equality, and an equal distribution of property, wisdom and virtue" that the constitution assumed existed in the state. Instead, Rush reasoned, "superior degrees of industry and capacity, and above all, commerce, have introduced inequality of property among us" and that inequality in turn had produced "natural distinctions of rank in Pennsylvania, as certain and general as the artificial distinctions of men in Europe."[22] It was those distinctions, perfectly permissible in a republic, that would be represented in a bicameral legislature.

The Constitutionalists pounced on such arguments. "Demophilus," probably the Presbyterian George Bryan, denounced the Republicans as "our gentry, to whose ears the words Liberty, Independence, Common-Wealth, [and] Free Constitution, have always been ungrateful sounds." Supporters of the constitution charged that the Republicans wanted to institutionalize class divisions in a bicameral legislature where the aristocrats of the upper house would overawe the plebeians in the lower.[23] The Republicans, in response, insisted that the upper house created an aristocracy of virtue and merit, not of wealth alone.[24] Moreover, Rush reminded his opponents that the men of the upper house would be elected by the same voters who selected the members of the lower chamber. Consequently, each house would be "the *annual* breath of the people," and Rush could not believe that "the same fountain of pure water, should send forth, at the same time wholesome and deadly streams." In short, the upper house of a bicameral legislature merely provided for a "double representation of the people."[25]

Then it was superfluous, countered the Constitutionalists, deftly marking the contradictions in the opposition to the constitution. The Republicans could not oppose a single house without appearing to favor aristocracy, and they could not advocate a traditional defense of checks and balances without seeming to endorse social conflicts. In fact, Rush did describe the bicameral legislature as a battlefield in which opposing social interests—but not social classes—clashed.[26] The Republicans were able to turn some of the Constitutionalists' arguments against them. Rush, for instance, charged that in fact unicameralism, not bicameralism, would lead to an aristocracy. The rich could control a unicameral legislature even more readily than they could overawe two houses and soon Pennsylvania, like Europe, would have only "two sort of animals, tyrants and slaves." The only protection, as far as Rush could see, was in an upper house that would serve as a check on the lower. The Republicans thus capitalized on the Americans' traditional fear of unrestrained power, carefully avoided discussing aristocracies, stressed the benefits of political competition, and put the Constitutionalists on the defensive.[27]

The adoption of the Pennsylvania Constitution inaugurated an educational as well as a political revolution. Almost immediately, the Constitutionalists abrogated the charter of the College of Philadelphia, replacing its basically Anglican board with an interdenominational body and its Anglican provost, William Smith, with the Presbyterian John Ewing.[28] They defended their controversial actions with arguments entirely consistent with their condemnation of social conflict and competition in a republic. The Presbyterians charged that under Smith the college had become a sectarian institution; under the Presbyterians it would be accessible to all denominations.[29] The Constitutionalists even argued in 1776 that *all* corporations—the College of Philadelphia, the Bank of North America—were repugnant in republics because they were endowed with extraordinary privileges and were therefore subversive of social equality. Corporations were opposed to "the spirit and policy of democracy," the Constitutionalists warned, and if left unchecked, would produce "an indirect, yet firm aristocracy over the state, before we be aware of the mischief." [30]

The attack on the College of Philadelphia was intended by the Constitutionalists to foster uniformity and unity. Instead it produced several new colleges to oppose the Pennsylvania revolution. Each was established by Republican Presbyterians and their allies. Provost William Smith went into voluntary exile in Maryland and there established St. John's and Washington colleges on the west and east shores of that state, respectively. He was assisted in that endeavor by the Reverend Patrick Allison of Baltimore and other Presbyterian opponents of Pennsylvania democracy. Likewise, Rush and other Presbyterian Republicans founded Dickinson in part to counter the Constitutionalist attack on the College of Philadelphia. Finally, presumably without any assistance from Presbyterian Republicans, the Anglicans of Philadelphia attempted to establish an academy to compete with the Presbyterians entrenched in the College of Philadelphia.

The Constitutionalists denounced all of those schools as aristocratic institutions designed to foster social conflicts. Maryland Presbyterians who supported the Pennsylvania constitution condemned Washington and St. John's as sectarian and aristocratic. Their founders "mean to establish ranks among us," one critic warned, and "begin their scheme by founding a College, wherein the lordly sons of our future nobility will be trained up, uncontaminated by a mixture with boys of plebeian mould ...." [31] And in Pennsylvania John Ewing denounced Dickinson's narrow "bottom" and insisted that all of Pennsylvania's Presbyterians unite behind him at the College of Philadelphia.[32] Also, the Presbyterian lay-man Joseph Reed insisted in 1783 that it was time "to drop religious dis-tinctions in Pennsylvania, and meet on the equal foot of generous catholicism." [33]

In contrast to these allegedly narrow, sectarian schools, the Constitu-tionalists advanced their own theory of republican education in Pennsyl-vania after 1776. They insisted that to be truly republican, education must be nonsectarian and, in one of their favorite phrases, "catholic." To that end, they believed that education must be controlled by the state and directed by Republicans who would create schools in which young men could be "early inspired with a love of their country, respect for its laws, and a taste for the principles and maxims of the state." That process, the Constitutionalists insisted, could not go forward in a narrow, sectarian institution.[34]

The supporters of the constitution were ready to act—to prevent social conflict and competition. They disfranchised all who would not swear to uphold the constitution, thus eliminating the possibility of effective political competition in the state. And they moved to eliminate any ac-tual or potential rivals of the College of Philadelphia. One Constitu-tionalist, appropriately calling himself "Uniformity" in print, argued against the chartering of an Episcopal academy in Philadelphia and suggested that those who "cannot be compelled to submit to the catholic spirit of our university" be required to secure a "license" from Provost Ewing and five of the college's trustees before being permitted to establish any competing institution of higher learning in Pennsylvania.[35]

The Republicans found it as difficult to answer the Constitutionalists' attack on sectarian education as to counter their rejection of the checks and balances of a bicameral assembly. Having insisted that the proposed upper house of that assembly was not an aristocratic counter to a demo-cratic lower house, the Republicans with equal vehemence asserted that their educational institutions were not divisive threats to the organic unity of a republican society. They countered that republican education, as they understood it, would reduce, not create, social conflict. Uneducated men, Charles Nisbet informed his students at Dickinson in 1786, see society as "so many loose, independent and unconnected individuals, having each a separate interest, and [being] naturally disposed to make war with one another." They therefore "nourish a selfish spirit" neglect social duty, and are totally indifferent to public needs. Only republican education, Nisbet concluded, could correct those "inaccurate" ideas.[36]

As their schools were not divisive, argued the Republicans, so were they not founded on sectarian foundations. Rush denied that Dickinson was the "offspring of personal resentments and party vices," and assured Carlisle's General John Armstrong that the school's board included both Republicans and Constitutionalists (there was in fact one supporter of the constitution on the board). To Nisbet, he boasted that all sects were represented on the board (at best a half-truth), thus proving that the Presbyterians were not "strangers to toleration."[37] Both Rush and the founders of the two Maryland schools made much of the guarantees of religious freedom in each school's charter and assured the public that in each instance the college's officers and faculties were chosen on the basis of their "literary and other necessary qualifications," not because of religious allegiances.[38]

The Republicans hoped that their schools would foster social unity in particular by educating together the sons of the Scotch-Irish Presbyterians and the German Calvinists who too frequently lived separately and in conflict in Pennsylvania. Rush anticipated that Dickinson would become a forum in which the industrious, thrifty Germans would "soften the tempers" of the Scotch-Irish, perhaps "inspire them with liberal sentiments in government and religion," even teach them moderation in their relations with other denominations and thereby "rescue them from the charges of bigotry and persecution that are so often brought against them." For their part, the Scotch-Irish might mitigate the German's notorious obsession with making money, might show them "men should live for other purposes than simply to cultivate the earth and to accumulate specie."[39]

But the Republicans could not discount a charge that essentially was true. Dickinson, in particular, *was* intended to be a Presbyterian stronghold. Rush was convinced that the Presbyterians had grown too powerful in Pennsylvania politics, that the Test Acts and the attack on the College of Philadelphia inevitably would backfire, and that the Presbyterians— Republicans *and* Constitutionalists—would soon fall and must prepare for that day. In 1783 he declared that "It is time for us to fortify before we are driven beyond the Mountains." The college at Carlisle would be the "principal Bulwark" of the Presbyterians, the "Asylum" of their hopes. Rush hoped that Dickinson would unite the embattled Presbyterians by creating and cementing loyalties, inculcating a uniform system of religion and knowledge, and by giving "system and consistency to our society however extended or scattered."[40]

While Rush continued to emphasize the importance of Dickinson to Pennsylvania's Presbyterians, he quickly abandoned his earlier emphasis on the college as an instrument of social integration. When the Germans proved reluctant to patronize the school in Carlisle and established their own college in Lancaster in 1786, Rush enthusiastically supported the project. He reasoned now that the Germans would become republicans only when their ignorance and prejudices were removed and that that process would proceed best where they could be instructed in their own language amid familiar cultural surroundings. The process complete, the German republicans could then unite with the English and with the Scotch-Irish "to form with them one homogeneous mass of people." Rush insisted that social unity was his ultimate goal. He had simply become convinced that his goal would be attained most readily by stressing the distinctions of the components of Pennsylvania's society and by allowing them to compete discreetly with each other.[41]

As they formed schools in opposition to the Pennsylvania Revolution, the Republican Presbyterians cautiously adumbrated a defense of sectarian education, much as they had been forced to defend a bicameral legislature as a forum for the competition of social interests. They insisted, though, that their ideas were not new. They noted that Quakers, Lutherans, and even Presbyterians had long maintained schools to serve their own denomination. It was true that colonial educational institutions characteristically had served a single religious denomination. But if denominational education was not new to America, a defense of sectarian education was, and the Republicans knew it. They insisted, therefore, that social unity was their ultimate goal. They believed now, though, that unity could best be attained when each sect educated its own young. "A Friend to Equal Liberty," obviously a Republican, warned in 1785 that "a body of Christians of different persuasions . . . could never unite in a form of worship, or a set of articles for their pupils"; therefore, religion could be safely transmitted only through denominational schools.[42] "An Episcopalian" believed that a boy must be educated in the tenets of a particular sect if he was to be inclined toward religion in general, and, that he must "chuse his principles" before he is twenty-one lest he turn out to be a "libertine or a Deist."[43] "A Friend to Equal Liberty" observed that sects, like families, *agree* best, when they are kept (to a certain degree) *separate* from each other." The Reverend John King insisted that, like a family, each sect should have the power to govern, preserve, and advance itself, of course, "without prejudice to others," and "in subservience to the common good." If each of those denominational families educated its own youth, Rush predicted in 1785, "the whole republic must soon be well educated."[44]

The Republican Presbyterians, in defending denominational education, did not so much abandon a traditional view of organic society as modify it to accommodate unexpected exigencies. Indeed, there is every reason to believe that the Republicans retained stronger allegiances to that view than did their radical opponents. But the experience of creating new institutions in a time of flux forced the Republicans, like the Old Sides in the Great Schism, to be flexible—even creative. Thus they turned the traditional argument against sectarian education on its head: sectarian schools, far from promoting discord, would foster unity by removing impressionable young men from those "opportunities of controversy" to be found in "catholic" institutions where a "variety of sects" provided the "certain fuel of bigotry." Protected from contention, the young man would not learn its ways, and instead would be indoctrinated with the tenets of his sect. Thus fortified, he could then lead his denomination in cooperation with others for the general welfare.[45] The young man in Ewing's "catholic" College of Philadelphia, on the other hand, would have to learn the ways of contention in self-defense. The school's catholicity, Rush warned, must soon yield "to the variety of its composition" and the school disintegrate into warring factions.[46]

But if the Republican Presbyterians and their Anglican allies abhorred rivalry among different sects within an individual school, they cautiously defended as a positive good competition among the schools of differing denominations. An Episcopal writer in the *Freeman's Journal* in 1785 even broached the novel idea of a collegiate marketplace within which parents could shop for an appropriate school for their son. And "A Friend to Equal Liberty" in the same year endorsed anything that would encourage "the competition of the different societies with each other." Likewise Rush welcomed any school that would compete with Dickinson, so long as its denominational affiliation was freely advertised. Rush was convinced that by "exciting emulation and increasing a taste for literature," those competing schools would even increase Dickinson's enrollment, "just as the cultivation of wheat on the Juniata has increased the price of it in Lancaster County."[47]

Thus, in Pennsylvania and in Maryland between 1776 and 1787 some Presbyterians endorsed controversial measures like the Pennsylvania Test Acts and the abrogation of the charter of the College of Philadelphia to rid the state of conflict and competition. Other Presbyterians at the same time reacted to those acts and began to defend social competition and conflict as positive goods. Each side was tentative, though. The Constitutionalists found it difficult to deny that, in the name of social unity, they were abrogating the political rights of all who did not accept the democratic thrust of the Pennsylvania revolution. On the other hand, the Republicans found it equally difficult to defend competition and conflict—whether in the legislature or the college—without appearing to renounce the ideals of the revolution. But in the turbulent first years of the republic, traditional ideas about social unions and the circumstances under which men might legitimately compete with each other within society were beginning to change. And they would continue to change at an accelerating pace.

EDUCATION AND SOCIAL CONFLICT:
THE VIRGINIA REVOLUTION

The pace was greatly accelerated by events in Virginia that paralleled the Pennsylvania revolution. In the Quaker state a controversial constitution forced Presbyterians to debate the proper relationship of education and social conflict in a republican society. A similar debate was prompted in Virginia by the efforts of Thomas Jefferson, James Madison, and the colony's Baptists to end the establishment of the Anglican Church; in effect, to extend into the area of religion the explosive ideas of equality and liberty that had just fueled the colonial political revolt. That extension seemed inevitable. Despite the weakening of establishments that attended the Awakening, in the majority of the colonies on the eve of independence a single denomination—the Congregational Church in New England and the Anglican Church in the south—was favored in some legal way by provincial governments. Dissenters in those colonies lectured patriot leaders, sometimes with ill-concealed relish, on the hypocrisy of protesting taxation without representation while requiring dissenters at home to support with their taxes ministers whose services they could not in faith attend. Any Whig defense of establishment in those circumstances would be lame. John Adams, assailed by Baptists at the Continental Congress in 1774, had to admit that there was a religious establishment in Massachusetts, but he then limply protested that it was "a very slender one, hardly to be called an establishment." [48]

Patriot leaders had an easier time of it where the established church was the Church of England: Jefferson and Madison could oppose both crown and miter in Virginia. They were supported by the colony's Baptists, who for a generation had lived under relatively severe restrictions in the Old Dominion.[49] The Baptists were united in their opposition to the Anglican establishment, and their pietistic fervor and petition campaigns were probably the decisive factors in a struggle led by deists like Jefferson. The contribution of Virginia's Presbyterians to that struggle is less clear. Presbyterians had fared rather well under the Anglican establishment in colonial Virginia,[50] and by 1770 some of them had forgotten that in 1740 Presbyterians had been harassed in the same ways the Anglicans now inconvenienced the Baptists. As late as 1774 the Hanover Presbytery assured the Virginia legislature that it was in no way hostile to the idea of an established church, that it desired only "an unlimited, impartial toleration."[51]

In 1776, though, the Presbyterians enthusiastically supported disestablishment. They had supported the colonial establishment only for "the sake of good order," they now declared. Moreover, they argued, establishment had minimized sectarian conflict and had ensured the public support of religion in Virginia.[52] After 1776, though, the Presbyterians discovered that social order and vital religion were, in fact, weakened by establishments. The men of Hanover argued that establishments were "highly injurious to the temporal interests of any community" because they retarded the growth of population and with it "the progress of arts, sciences, and manufactures."[53] And Caleb Wallace noted that the gospel flourished much more in those parts of America free of establishments than it did in Virginia. Wallace even looked forward to the competition among denominations that the colonial Presbyterians had feared. Rather than chaos, he predicted, only "freedom of inquiry and liberal sentiments" would result when each denomination was "left to stand or fall according to merit."[54]

Virginia's Presbyterians then welcomed without equivocation the final clause in the Virginia Bill of Rights stipulating that religion can be "directed only by reason and conviction, not by force or violence" and that men are therefore "equally entitled to the free exercise of religion, according to the dictates of conscience." The Buffalo congregation in Prince Edward County grandly hailed it as "the rising Sun of religious Liberty, to relieve us from a long night of ecclesiastical Bondage," and then urged the Virginia assembly to make of the colony—under that guarantee—"an Asylum for free enquiry, knowledge and the virtuous of every Denomination."[55]

The Presbyterians in 1776 also insisted that they were as opposed to a general assessment for the support of religion as they were to the Anglican establishment. The Hanover Presbytery was sure that Christ would provide for His own, that the church no more needed the forced contributions of the state's population than it required the protection of the state's sword. Moreover, the presbytery warned, a state that could levy an assessment for the support of all churches could in the future revert to a tax for a single denomination.[56] In the early days of the Revolution, then, Virginia's Presbyterians seemed to abandon their traditional equation of social order with a religious establishment and to embrace tentatively the revolutionary idea that denominational competition might be a positive social good.

They soon had second thoughts, though. Jefferson noted wryly in 1779 that the Presbyterian clergy, having achieved their "particular object" of weakening the Anglican establishment in Virginia now supported a general assessment for the support of religion.[57] He was right. The Virginia constitution of 1776 had not totally disestablished the Anglican Church, and Jefferson hoped to remedy that situation by a bill he introduced in 1779 calling for complete separation of church and state in Virginia. No Presbyterian petition appeared in support of that bill. Moreover, in the same year James Henry, a Presbyterian representative from the Eastern Shore, introduced a bill in the House of Burgesses calling for a general assessment.[58] By 1779 Presbyterians in other states—North Carolina and Pennsylvania, for instance—had been instrumental in framing state constitutions that limited political participation to those citizens who were Protestant and who affirmed the divine inspiration of the Bible in its entirety.[59] Now, in Virginia, a Presbyterian layman proposed that Christianity be made the official religion of the state and that all citizens be taxed alike for "the Support of Religious teachers and places of Worship." The revenue would be distributed by the state to the clergymen designated by church members to receive it. Introduced at a time of great distraction in the state, the bill died for lack of widespread support.[60]

After the cessation of hostilities, in 1784, the Virginia legislature simultaneously considered two bills that revealed the Presbyterian ambivalence about the complete separation of church and state in the new republic. One bill would incorporate the Protestant Episcopal Church. The other, drafted by Patrick Henry, provided for a general assessment for the public support of religion. The Presbyterians uniformly opposed the incorporation bill, arguing that for the legislature to grant special privileges to one sect of Christians would be "unworthy of the representatives of a people perfectly free." [61] That position was consistent with the Presbyterians' earlier attack on the establishment and with the assertion then made that the state should not single out one Christian denomination for special favors.

On the other hand, their reaction to the general assessment bill indicates that the Presbyterian clergy was not prepared to separate church and state completely. Madison noted a "shameful contrast" between the Presbyterian position of 1776 and 1784 and sarcastically observed to James Monroe that the Presbyterians "seem as ready to set up an establishment which is to take them in as they were to pull down one that shut them out." [62] One might have expected Madison to be more generous to the Presbyterians who had prepared him at Princeton for his role in the Revolution. And certainly he oversimplified their motives in supporting the assessment. They abandoned a hopeful position taken in the 1770s not because they expected the Presbyterian Church to be established anywhere but because in the troubled eighties they became convinced that social order could not be maintained without the public support of religion. And, if that support was not forthcoming voluntarily, it would have to be coerced.

The Presbyterian clergy had always subscribed to the general assessment bill's basic assumption that the "general diffusion of Christian knowledge" had a "natural tendency to correct the morals of men, restrain their vices, and preserve the peace of society." [63] Led by William Graham, still at Liberty Hall in 1784, the men of Hanover agreed that religion "as a Spiritual System" could not be "considered as an object of human legislation." But, taken in a "civil view," it preserved "the existence and welfare of every political combination of men in society" by sanctifying the oath, which was the "cement of the social union." Consequently, the presbytery urged, every man, "as a good Citizen," should be required "to declare himself attached to some religious Community, publicly known to profess the belief of one God—his righteous providence—our accountableness to him—and a future State of rewards and punishments." And, each citizen should be required to support a minister of that religious community. The Presbyterians, to be sure, always cautioned that any general assessment must be of the *"most liberal plan"* and should be used to force subscription only to those "articles of faith" that are "essential to the preservation of society." [64]

Beyond their conviction that the optimism of the seventies was inappropriate in the eighties, it is difficult to understand how the Presbyterian clergy in Virginia so thoroughly misread public sentiment on the issue of the general assessment. Some leading ministers, like John Blair Smith, the brother of Hampden-Sydney's president and a member of its faculty, were quite close to Henry and to other powerful Anglicans on the Southside of Virginia and may have supported the assessment because they simply were out of touch with the Presbyterian laity. More likely, the clergy believed that an assessment was going to be passed with or without their support and agreed to cooperate in order to have some impact upon the final form of the legislation. Most of Virginia's Presbyterian laymen, however, had not abandoned the stand on religious liberty taken by the denomination during the Revolution. The laity apparently did not equate public support of religion with social order and in 1784 they gathered at the Bethel Church to so inform the Hanover Presbytery. The laymen gladly acknowledged the "happy influences of Christianity upon the morals of men." But they noted that religion had been most effective "when left to its native excellence and evidence to recommend it, under the all-directing providence of God, and free from the intrusive hand of the civil magistrate." That had been the position of the men of Hanover in 1776 and 1777, and in May of 1784, under concerted lay pressure, they were forced to revert to it, voting unanimously to oppose any general assessment for the support of religion.[65]

The reversal was a grudging one. The clergy, if not the laity, in 1784 already had begun a reevaluation of the progress of the American Revolution that by 1800 would convince many of them that their earlier optimism about the republic had been ill-founded. Even under the Christian guidance of Washington many Presbyterians in the 1780s and early nineties despaired of a society so beset by luxury, corruption, and disregard of religion as was the American republic in the days following the Peace of Paris. Thus alarmed, the clergy began an unprecedented campaign to make America a visibly Christian nation. The campaign would not get into full swing until the early nineteenth century, but even in the late eighties and early nineties the evangelical clergy in general and the Presbyterians in particular began to propose ways to use the power of government—and public opinion—to oppose vice and support virtue. Chaplains were provided for the houses of the federal Congress and for the armed forces of the republic, such as they were. And in an effort to protect the purity of the scriptures upon which the republic was founded, the Baptists and the Congregationalists in 1790 petitioned Congress to establish a clerical committee to censure all versions of the Holy Bible that would circulate in the United States.[66]

In Virginia the Presbyterian clergy took official action to ensure that the portion of American society they influenced would be visibly Christian. In 1791 the Synod of Virginia instructed its members to "enjoin it upon all Magistrates in our communion to put the Laws [regarding the Sabbath] into execution within their respective spheres of observation." And the synod directed the clergy to publicly censure any Presbyterian magistrate who refused. The Hanover Presbytery went further and voted to refuse communion to all who profaned the Sabbath.[67] Deeply disturbed by the removal of all state support for religion in Virginia, the Presbyterian clergymen clearly attempted through their own powers of withholding communion and through the magisterial powers of Presbyterian office-holders to coerce the virtuous activity they feared the Americans were incapable of producing voluntarily.[68]

The tensions and ambivalences in the Presbyterian attitude toward the public support of religion found expression in 1784 when the Reverend William Graham was asked to draft a constitution for the proposed state of Franklin. As has been noted, Graham's draft was modeled upon the radical Pennsylvania constitution. While that document anticipated that Pennsylvania would be a Christian commonwealth, Graham proposed that the state of Franklin take steps to ensure that "citizens be visibly and really religious." He did not propose an establishment simply because he expected that all faiths would be "useful to the State." All would inculcate the "essential principles of temporal peace and happiness" and would cooperate with government "in strengthening the weakness of moral obligation." Then Graham proposed barring from office in Franklin all "whoremongers," swearers, drunkards, gamesters, and Sabbath-profaners.[69] Finally, the Franklin constitution stipulated that "Laws for the encouraging of virtue, and preventing and suppressing of vice and immorality, shall be made and constantly kept in force." [70]

For all his support of the Virginia assessment and the restrictive nature of some of his constitutional provisions, William Graham did not allow his alarm at the course of the eighties to turn him entirely from the ideals of the Revolution. This became dramatically clear in 1794 when the Pennsylvania backcountry rose in rebellion against Alexander Hamilton's whiskey tax. The Synod of Virginia happened to be sitting at Winchester near the site of the rebellion when it broke out. In attendance with

Graham at that session was the Reverend Moses Hoge, one of Graham's first graduates from Liberty Hall. Young Hoge was outraged by the whiskey rebels—most of whom were members of the Presbyterian churches in and around Washington and Canonsburg, just southwest of Pittsburgh—and he moved that the synod officially condemn the rebellion and remind their members of "their duty of obedience to the Laws of their Country." His teacher, though, was reluctant to condemn the right of citizens to dissent, even violently at times, from the actions of their government. After a brief but lively debate Graham persuaded the synod that Hoge was asking them to deplore the ideas that had sparked the American Revolution. When the vote came, the synod did recommend a fast day in which clergymen were instructed to admonish their members "to be subject to the powers that be." But the synod rejected Hoge's harsher words, not being ready to condemn officially the ideological foundation of the Revolution—yet.[71]

As in Pennsylvania, the course of the Revolution in Virginia had important implications for the Presbyterian schools in the colony. It is true that the Virginia Revolution did not involve Liberty Hall and Hampden-Sydney as directly as the College of Philadelphia was implicated in the Pennsylvania Revolution. But the attack on established religion in Virginia did raise important questions concerning the legitimacy of denominational education in a republican society. Not surprisingly, those questions were first raised by Jefferson, who hoped after 1776 to transform William and Mary from an Anglican seminary and training ground for the Tidewater elite into a broadly conceived university. To that end, he proposed abolishing theological instruction altogether, dividing the college into four schools, each with responsibility for part of the liberal arts, and replacing the Anglican board of trustees with a board of visitors that would include non-Anglicans.[72]

From Hampden-Sydney President Samuel Stanhope Smith, fresh from New Jersey, applauded all of Jefferson's proposals as liberal and enlightened. But he reminded Jefferson that the Anglican position in the state had only been weakened by the Revolution and that in 1779 they still had privileges at William and Mary, privileges that forced the Presbyterians to continue their opposition to the college.[73] It pained Smith to deliver an ultimatum to Jefferson. His "extreme love of peace" and the "benevolence" and "enlarged and liberal inquiry in matters of science" encouraged by the Presbyterian Church made Smith reluctant to embrace competition of any kind. The "partialities of sects ought to have no place in a system of liberal education," he advised Jefferson. "They are the disgrace of science and would to Heaven it were possible utterly to banish them from the society of men." He had hoped that the Revolution would eradicate denominational conflict in Virginia by ending the Anglican establishment, but he realized now that the "speculations of the closet are often very wide of the sentiments and manners of actual life." Even in a virtuous republic, it appeared, the "opposition of parties" will make all sects "solicitous for their own preservation and jealous of their antagonists." [74]

Smith's reaction to conflict and competition in a republic was ambivalent. He acknowledged that differences of forms and names would always preserve among Christians a narrow spirit that was "equally detrimental to religion and to learning." Smith rejected the new notion— later to be identified with Jefferson—that competition would force religious groups to better themselves in order to survive. Smith warned Jefferson that, to the contrary, competing groups would invariably defend "their characteristic peculiarities" and thereby "contract the free spirit and the sphere of science, and substitute bigotry and prejudice in the room of true philosophy." Thus rejecting any "ambition to become the leader of a sect," Smith suggested to Jefferson a union of Anglicans and Presbyterians in Virginia. The Presbyterians, he reminded Jefferson, were a numerous body and "not destitute of learning." Their concurrence, then, would be essential to any successful educational endeavor, and their opposition "may embarrass, if not disconcert any *general* scheme of education wherein they are neglected, and likely to be undermined." To allay Presbyterian opposition to Jefferson's educational plans Smith suggested a "coalition of the principal religious sects, and as many as were willing to unite upon the same catholic foundation." He disclaimed any wish for a legal establishment and called only for a union of Protestants that would end divisiveness and sectarian contention. But, when he descended from the theoretical to the practical, Smith embraced the very idea of salutary competition he had just denounced. Protesting that William and Mary would still draw her Visitors from the Anglican Tidewater, Smith insisted that the competition of a school in western Virginia—like Rush's Dickinson in Pennsylvania—would only benefit religion and science: "Would not two universities by their emulation have a favourable influence on learning?" [75]

HOMOGENEITY, SOCIAL CONFLICT, AND EDUCATION

The tentative defense of competition notwithstanding, the Presbyterians' social ideal in the early republic remained "one homogeneous mass of people" in which would be avoided the social conflict that threatened to destroy the republican experiment. It is crucial in understanding the Presbyterians' social and educational theories after 1776 to know that in some parts of the United States the Presbyterians lived in areas where that ideal could be approximated. In the Shenandoah valley, in Cumberland County in Pennsylvania, and in the far western frontier of that state, the Presbyterians were an overwhelming majority in a remarkably homogeneous population. In other areas—the Southside of Virginia, New Jersey, and central Kentucky—they were a minority in a more heterogeneous environment. The simple fact of numbers of Presbyterians in a given area influenced, first, the denominational nature of the Presbyterian school in that area, and, then, the Presbyterian attitude toward the legitimacy of denominational competition in a republican society.

In the Southside of Virginia the Presbyterian minority lived among a substantial Anglican population and was more often influenced by the Tidewater than by the Scotch-Irish valley of the Shenandoah. Consequently, the men of the Hanover Presbytery knew that Hampden-Sydney would survive only if it was supported by the leaders of the area's Anglican majority. In fact, the leading Presbyterians of the Southside maintained close relations with Anglicans such as Henry and Madison. As we have seen, John Blair Smith's ties with Patrick Henry probably influenced his decision to support Henry's general assessment bill. At any rate, when the Hanover Presbytery established Hampden-Sydney, it had the active cooperation of the Anglicans; indeed, the majority of the first board of trustees was Anglican, not Presbyterian. The Anglicans probably supported the Presbyterian school because it was an academy and therefore was no threat to William and Mary, which, in any case, was unpopular with many Anglicans at the time. Moreover, the urbane Samuel Stanhope Smith did not seem to the Anglican gentry at all like the uncouth Scotch-Irish Presbyterians who were flooding the valley. And none of the Presbyterians alarmed the Anglicans as the Baptists did.[76]

Having founded Hampden-Sydney on a "broad bottom," the Presbyterians stressed its availability to all denominations. They were therefore much disturbed when in 1790 several students charged their Presbyterian teachers with proselytizing. The trustees even met in special session to examine the charge. They interrogated a broad sample of the student body, as well as the aggrieved few, and elicited from the former the affirmation that they had seen or heard no proselytizing. To the contrary, the majority had encountered at the school only an "enlarged and liberal policy respecting religious parties." There is no reason to doubt the students' testimony about the situation in a Presbyterian school surrounded by an Anglican majority.[77]

The Presbyterians were also a minority in central Kentucky, where in the 1780s the sons of Virginia's Anglican gentry and unchurched frontiersmen created a Virginia at one remove. When they established the Transylvania Seminary, the minority Presbyterians stressed the school's catholicity. In 1787, for example, "Catholicus," possibly Transylvania Trustee Caleb Wallace, insisted in the *Kentucky Gazette* that the new school should not be dominated by one sect. He was quickly seconded by "A Transylvanian," who hoped that those inclined toward "superstition" and "party spirit" would not be able to use Transylvania to enlist youth "for the service of some sect or interest in church or state."[78]

Despite their minority status in Kentucky, there were Presbyterians in Lexington who defended sectarian education in the 1780s. One of them, proudly calling himself "A Sectarian," defended the "superstitious" and the "party-spirited" against the attacks of the "liberal and disinterested." The "Sectarian" insisted that the party-spirited and superstitious, as the "Transylvanian" called them, were interested only in protecting the morals of the young from the pernicious ideas of the "liberal" and the "disinterested." And if they had to embrace sectarian education to do so, they would. In the 1780s, though, most Presbyterians in Lexington would have subscribed to the broad views of the Anglican John Filson, Lexington's most respected citizen, who in 1788 hopefully declared that he anticipated at Transylvania a "spirit and practice of virtue" that would explode "party spirit."[79]

In areas of the republic where they constituted a majority of the population, the Presbyterians were not obliged to create "catholic" educational institutions in order to attract public support. In central and western Pennsylvania and in the Shenandoah valley of Virginia they could establish thoroughly Presbyterian schools that would at the same time serve the local public and the denomination. Lexington, Virginia, for instance, was virtually Presbyterian, and Liberty Hall Academy was dominated by the denomination. Its board of trustees was much more local and Presbyterian than the Hampden-Sydney Board; and when, as a condition of its charter in 1782, the state legislature transferred control of the school from the Hanover Presbytery to the board, Liberty Hall was still controlled in fact by the presbytery, which continued to support and examine the governance of the academy. The population of western Pennsylvania was almost as thoroughly Presbyterian as the Shenandoah valley; indeed, much of the valley's population came to Virginia from the west of Pennsylvania. Thus, as was the case at Liberty Hall, the boards of both the Washington and the Canonsburg academies were thoroughly Presbyterian.[80]

When the Synod of Virginia in the early 1790s decided to create two theological departments with explicit responsibility for ministerial education, it located them at the most thoroughly Presbyterian of its schools, Liberty Hall and the Canonsburg Academy. Under Graham, the former had become in effect a Presbyterian seminary.[81] In 1792 the school's function as a seminary was formalized when the synod created at Liberty Hall a theological department to offer courses "calculated to educate persons designed for the Gospel Ministry" by indoctrinating young men with a "course of religious instruction" to be "continually adhered to during their residence there according to the Principles of our Church." The Liberty Hall Board agreed to fill its vacancies from the Lexington Presbytery, which in turn agreed to support and periodically examine the school.[82] A similar agreement was arranged between the Canonsburg Academy and the Redstone Presbytery.[83]

As might be expected, the relationship between homogeneity and sectarian education was raised most pointedly at Dickinson. When the school was established, the overwhelming majority of Carlisle's families was Presbyterian; consequently, the college's trustees were heavily of that persuasion. But arrangements that went unchallenged in Virginia and in western Pennsylvania ignited an immediate furor when instituted at Dickinson. The crux of the matter was the contrast between the remarkable religious homogeneity of Carlisle and the unparalleled heterogeneity of the state as a whole. Even the friends of the college, that is, even Presbyterian Republicans, warned Rush that the plans for Dickinson excited alarm in the state about *all* Presbyterians, who were made to appear motivated by a "party partial Spirit" that needlessly aroused dormant "destructive animosities."[84] Rush replied by noting that the homogeneous population of Cumberland County made it inevitable that Dickinson would be patronized chiefly by Presbyterians. Rush also insisted that Presbyterian domination of the board was justified if it led one young man to a regard for true religion—even if at the risk of inculcating a bias for a particular sect. He remained uneasy, though, about Dickinson's obviously denominational nature. In his defense of the college, then, Rush discussed theory rather than practice: the school's charter was "catholic" even if Dickinson itself was not.[85] Presumably, if central Pennsylvania in general and Cumberland County in particular ever gave rise to a religiously heterogeneous population, the foundation for a subsequent change at Dickinson existed also. However, it is clear that in the early republic, even in those areas where they were a substantial majority, the Presbyterians were disturbed by the contradictions between the widely held belief that republican educational institutions should be expansive and integrative and the obvious fact that at least half of their new schools were thoroughly denominational institutions.

THE FINANCING AND CONTROL OF
REPUBLICAN INSTITUTIONS

Rush and other Presbyterians were disturbed—and challenged—by one of the crucial developments of the late eighteenth century, the emergence of the denomination as the characteristic form of religious life in America. A body of like-minded believers voluntarily joined to propagate their version of religious truth, the denomination has come to occupy a crucial mediating position in the United States between the exclusive "sect," which is usually alienated from a hostile society, and the inclusive "church," which endeavors to coexist with society. In America both sect and church have become denominations, voluntary organizations separate from the state but still committed to shape and direct society to the extent that society will allow.[86]

The heyday of American denominationalism began with two parallel developments in the early republic. On the one hand, the end of establishments in the states threw all religious groups back upon the voluntary support of their communicants. To attract members in a competitive, voluntaristic society, each denomination emphasized those doctrines that set it apart from other groups. At the same time, several religious bodies were forced after 1776 to sever discredited ties with mother "churches" in Europe and to establish creditable American identities. Thus impelled, in a decade of constitution-making, American Christians in the 1780s laid the foundations for the denominational communities of the nineteenth century. For the Anglicans that meant creating a full hierarchy in America, a process that began with the ordination of an American bishop in 1784. In the same year the fledgling Methodist Church began to overcome its double handicap of being associated in the public mind with both the Church of England and her discredited American daughter. A parallel drive toward autonomy in the Reformed Dutch Church in America culminated in 1794 with the creation of a full presbyterial system in the American church. And in the churches with no European connections, lines of authority were regularized, hierarchies strengthened, and colleges created to educate the denomination's young and train its clergy. Even the rigorously congregational Baptists between 1780 and 1800 organized their independent congregations into associations that invariably consolidated, stabilized, and gave direction to that rather amorphous denomination.[87]

These developments, visible everywhere, were epitomized within American Presbyterianism. The Presbyterians in 1783 clearly had the strongest denominational identity of any religious group in the new nation. Its hierarchy of session, presbytery, and synod was the only ecclesiastical hierarchy that existed in total in America before 1776, and that system unified the denomination as no other American group was unified. Moreover, the Presbyterians had been vastly stimulated by the revival of the midcentury and then greatly strengthened in numbers by the flood of Scotch-Irish immigrants in the 1770s. And the Presbyterians were virtually unified in their support of the Revolution and had little problem with the taint of treason.

Indeed, Presbyterian successes were becoming a problem by the 1780s. Almost five hundred congregations were spread from Maine to Georgia; attendance at the annual meeting of the synod was decreasing—in the 1788 meeting of the synod one-half of the sixteen presbyteries were unrepresented. With the coming of the peace, moves were made to create a General Assembly that would, in Witherspoon's words, be "the bond of union, peace, correspondence, and mutual confidence, among all our churches."[88] Efforts to create a more perfect union among the American Presbyterians paralleled similar attempts to strengthen the union of the American states. And both efforts reached fruition in 1789, when the General Assembly and the new federal government were inaugurated almost simultaneously. The General Assembly that saluted President Washington consisted of four synods, sixteen presbyteries, and almost five hundred congregations in every state of the new union.

In its first communication to the synods in 1789 the new General Assembly sounded two themes that would inform the denominational developments of the next half-century. All the innovations of the 1780s—the enlarged hierarchy, the detailed Form of Government with its close instructions as to the operations of the presbyteries, the General Assembly itself—all were necessary to preserve the Presbyterians' "character as a body; and our consequence in the republic, in comparison with other denominations of christians." They were to make the Presbyterians effective competitors in the denominational market place. And, to that end, the new measures would unify the denomination by supplying it with a "common intelligence" and concerted action, without which the Presbyterians' "respectability will be diminished," and their "efforts for the public good, and for the promotion of religion, will be weakened by becoming divided." [89]

The centralizing effect of the new hierarchy was immediately evident. The number of meetings increased dramatically: the New Brunswick Presbytery, for instance, was instructed to urge its sessions to meet twice a year and to make annual reports of its deliberations to the presbytery. And the synods and presbyteries began to insist that reports to the General Assembly be made in duplicate and be "particularly attentive to prescribed forms." Then, in an unprecedented display of concern for form and ritual, the General Assembly prescribed ways to handle contentions of various descriptions and steps to follow in bringing charges against a minister. And it published, for the first time, an elaborate description of prescribed ordination and installation services.[90]

Almost by definition, the innovations of the 1780s were intended to control and confine. In the years immediately following the peace, however, the move toward constriction and emphasis on the denomination had to compete with the expansive forces released by the republican revolution. The resulting tension is effectively illustrated by Presbyterian efforts between 1783 and 1795 to finance and control their institutions of higher learning.

Despite their emphasis on the "morning of the world" dawning over the new Israel in the west, the Presbyterians after 1783 turned for support for their colleges not to the American republicans but to the citizens of corrupt Europe. The ink was hardly dry on the Treaty of Paris before Witherspoon and William Bingham were dispatched on begging tours to Great Britain by Princeton and Dickinson respectively. The Presbyterians saw nothing foolish or naïve in petitioning their late enemy for aid. Were not Europe and England part of the same "republic of humanity and literature" of which the western refuge of liberty was the premier member? Benjamin Rush certainly believed so and actively promoted the idea that an international union of republicans would spring up in the wake of the American Revolution and that friends of republicanism everywhere would support generously republican higher education in America. In words reminiscent of the colonial Presbyterians' emphasis on a transatlantic Christian commonwealth, Rush prophesied that the Revolution would bind the "friends to truth and simplicity in worship and church government in every quarter of the world into a great Christian republic." [91]

Rush was wrong, of course, and friends at home and in Europe told him so. From England and Scotland came warnings that Great Britain was in no mood to finance the education of rebels, particularly successful rebels. And from Paris Benjamin Franklin cautioned Rush that to seek assistance abroad seemed to suggest that the new republic could not itself finance those institutions necessary to its survival. The efforts to raise money in England were, of course, disasters. Contemplating the £5.14 the able fund-raiser Witherspoon cleared, the Princeton Board concluded with grave understatement that the European venture "upon the whole, was very unsuccessful." [92] That failure does indicate a certain naïveté on the part of the Presbyterian educators. But it also reveals the extent to which the republican educators, like their colonial predecessors, believed they were part of an international community of evangelical Christians.

Shocked at the reaction of that community, the American Presbyterians turned—a little petulantly, it must be said—to their countrymen, for whom the colleges had been founded in the first place. The Princeton Board, for instance, announced plans for the first time to mount a subscription campaign making use of the denomination's hierarchical structure of presbytery and synod. [93] Between 1783 and 1795 all of the Presbyterian colleges followed Princeton's example and sent solicitors from New England to Georgia to raise funds and, incidentally, to assist in strengthening among Presbyterians a sense of denominational identity and purpose. [94] Those fund-raisers also began to standardize and systematize subscription drives. Ministers and trustees were sent in twos to beg for Dickinson and local ministers were authorized to collect what the fund-raisers were able to raise in the week spent in each location. And in Kentucky the Transylvania Presbytery in 1794 ordered each family to contribute a small amount to support the Transylvania Seminary and charged each session's moderator to record each contribution. [95]

This increase in denominational support immediately raised the issue of denominational control. The issue was first joined at Princeton. In

1791 the General Assembly requested to know from the Princeton Board the way in which the interest of the Tennent-Davies fund was being used. The Assembly then asserted the right both to name the recipient of the fund's interest and to direct the use of the fund. The board would concede the former but not the latter. Ashbel Green, minister, Princeton graduate, and trustee, denounced the board's claim and insisted that final control of the fund lay with the denomination's central body, the General Assembly, not with the Princeton Board. The explosive issue was not resolved in the eighteenth century. The Assembly's effort to dictate policy to the Princeton Board was perhaps the first constriction of the Presbyterians' generally expansive educational policy during the Revolutionary era. For the moment, though, those efforts were thwarted. Witherspoon and his son-in-law, Samuel Stanhope Smith, successfully opposed the Assembly's unprecedented effort to seize meaningful authority over the funding of Princeton.[96]

In essence, the Princeton Board and the General Assembly disagreed over the intentions of the British Christians who had responded to Tennent's and Davies's subscription trip in the early 1750s. The Assembly insisted that the money be used to educate ministers and the board asserted the right to dispose of the money as it chose. In point of fact, the philanthropists of the colonial period had not attempted to influence the shape of Princeton with their gifts. This trend continued during the Revolutionary period. For instance, when one William McConkey bequeathed £100 to Princeton in 1787, he stipulated only that it be used to educate poor and pious youth. Seven years later Azariah Horton gave the school some federal bonds for the same general purpose. Neither gift was designated for the education of Presbyterian ministers. In 1785, however, the board pledged that any money given for ministerial education would be "sacredly appropriated for that purpose alone." In 1792 Princeton received its first large bequest for the training of Presbyterian ministers. Princeton graduate and New York merchant James Leslie left his alma mater the princely sum of £4500, the interest from which was to be "appropriated to the Education of poor and pious youth of the presbyterian denomination, for the work of the gospel ministry."[97]

In the 1780s and 1790s the boards of the Presbyterian colleges intensified their efforts to locate benefactors. They recorded their names in special books, lauded their largesse at commencement exercises, and assigned student orators to declaim on the necessity for supporting literary institutions.[98] In the 1790s Samuel Stanhope Smith enlarged the scope of Princeton's fund drives until they involved a large part of the school's alumni. He circulated petitions among Princeton's graduates, urging them to raise money in their communities for specific needs of the college. It was an unprecedented technique, and it strengthened Princeton's denominational identity because fund drives were usually carried out by Presbyterian ministers within the local Presbyterian church. Moreover, Smith's efforts among the Princeton alumni helped build up loyalty to the school among a group of educated social leaders who were overwhelmingly Presbyterian.[99]

But if philanthropy began to contribute to the Presbyterian schools' denominational character during the Revolutionary period, it also sustained and even intensified their republican identity. Philanthropy in the young republic was expected to create republican institutions, and the leaders of the new nation were expected to contribute to the support of those institutions. The gifts of leading republicans were believed to obligate their recipients to create broad, nonsectarian institutions. Charles Nisbet, for one, sensed the power of republican philanthropy. He understood that to name the school at Carlisle for John Dickinson would help allay fears that it would be a denominational institution. He therefore was delighted when Dickinson allowed the school to be named for him and agreed to contribute land and 1,500 volumes from his celebrated library to the college. The "Pennsylvania Farmer" also gave Princeton £100 to purchase medals for orations on subjects that almost invariably dealt in some way with republicanism.[100]

George Washington's gifts to the Presbyterian schools best illustrate the symbolic and real impact that the republic's leaders had on republican education through their gifts. In 1783 Washington gave the Princeton Board fifty guineas in appreciation for their hospitality during the Continental Congress's brief stay in Princeton's Nassau Hall. The trustees would accept the money only if it were used to commission a portrait of Washington for the school. Washington agreed and sat for the portrait by Charles Willson Peale that still hangs in the faculty room of Nassau Hall. Thus, Washington's first contribution to Presbyterian higher education purchased a republican icon.[101]

Washington's second contribution to Presbyterian higher education came near the end of his life and precipitated a major crisis. In 1784 the Virginia legislature presented the general with one hundred shares of the James River Canal Stock. He accepted them on the condition that they would be applied to "objects of a public nature," and in 1796 announced that he would bestow them on a "public" institution of higher learning in western Virginia. Instantly, the Liberty Hall trustees instructed William Graham to apply for the stocks, worth almost $20,000. In applying for the funds Graham ignored the denominational nature of the Presbyterians' most closely controlled institution and instead represented Liberty Hall as a broadly based "public institution." No mention was made of the school's Presbyterian board of trustees or of its special relation with the theological department still maintained at Liberty Hall by the Synod of Virginia. Astonishingly, Washington was satisfied and bestowed the fund upon the school.[102]

The Washington bequest ignited an immediate confrontation between the proponents of sectarian and nonsectarian education in Virginia. The Virginia legislature in 1796 was controlled by Jeffersonians who opposed sectarian education in general and Presbyterian control of Liberty Hall in particular. Thus, as soon as Washington announced his decision, members of the legislature began to draw up plans for rechartering and remodeling the school. The plans closely resembled those suggested by Jefferson for William and Mary in 1779: the college was to be divided into four schools; the theological department was to be discontinued, and a Board of Visitors was to be given the power to remove faculty members. Moreover, the proposed board would include no Presbyterians and no clergymen. The Jeffersonian legislature clearly was unwilling to trust the Presbyterians to broaden their school's base and therefore determined to do it for them.[103]

But the Presbyterians fought back. Anticipating the Dartmouth College Case by twenty years, the Liberty Hall Board denounced the legislature's act as tyrannous and as a violation of the sanctity of contract, that is, the 1782 charter. And they applied political pressure. Again drawing upon their well-established relations with the Anglican Southside, the Hampden-Sydney Board joined with the Presbyterians of the valley to remonstrate with the legislature and to have the offending provisions repealed in 1797.[104] The Virginia Presbyterians in 1796 found themselves in the same position as their coreligionists at Dickinson when they attempted to appeal to as broad a constituency as possible while at the same time wanting to strengthen the denominational character of that school. In Virginia the Presbyterians certainly supported the expansive, integrative educational ideal that the Washington bequest came to symbolize. But they also wanted to strengthen the one part of society with which they were most closely identified. Therefore, in the end, like Rush, the Virginians decided that republican education could most safely be inculcated in denominational institutions, especially in those areas where one denomination was a preponderant majority. The Washington bequest, then, may be seen as the culmination of republican philanthropy. And the controversy it initiated raised issues that looked toward the democratic future more than they referred back to the republican past.

The Washington bequest and the Virginia legislature's efforts to reorganize Liberty Hall sharply focused the issue of public versus private control and support of higher education in a republic,[105] an issue that had surfaced at several points between 1776 and 1796. One of the central effects of the republican revolution had been to intensify Americans' appreciation for the importance of social institutions in republics dependent upon public and private virtue for their survival. Not surprisingly, that revolution increased the state's interest in controlling and directing all social institutions that influenced the development of the state by shaping its citizenry. The new state governments, then, tended to emphasize the civic, public nature of all institutions and to look with disfavor on those that obviously benefitted only a part of society. At the height of the Pennsylvania revolution the Presbyterian radicals abrogated the charter of the allegedly Anglican College of Philadelphia and replaced it with a broadly based institution, which they named the University of Pennsylvania. In the same year, 1779, Jefferson moved to reorganize the College of William and Mary in part because of its alleged sectarian connections with the Church of England. In 1784 the New York legislature reorganized Anglican-controlled King's College, renamed it Columbia, and put it under the control of a grand Board of Regents of the State University of New York. The board was to be made up of representatives of all the state's religious denominations and, rather mechanically, was to derive from those representatives a "common good" to be advanced by the several educational institutions that would make up the State University. Even in conservative Connecticut, dissenters were able in the early years of the republic to challenge seriously for the first time the Congregational monopoly of higher education in the state. Their representatives in the state legislature demanded either that Congregational control of Yale be diminished or that dissenters be allowed to establish their own college in Connecticut. And for a while in the 1790s it appeared that the dissenters might succeed in forcing change at Yale, thus obviating the need for their own college.[106]

Also in the 1780s and 1790s, the states of Vermont, Georgia, North Carolina, and South Carolina created the first educational institutions which the states exclusively financed and controlled. The charters of those first state universities emphasized their nonsectarian nature and their integrative social function. Especially in South Carolina, the state university was intended to ameliorate geographic animosities and social divisions that threatened the success of republican governments.[107] And what the new state universities were to do for the states, a proposed national university was to accomplish for the new federal union. The proposals for a "University of the United States" that appeared periodically in the early republic have too often been treated as quaint aberrations of Webster, Washington, and Rush, and deserve more serious study. The national university was intended to train leaders for the young republic and was to be rigorously nonsectarian, even to the point of prohibiting clerics from serving on its faculty. Free from sectarian strife, the young republicans would be taught at the national university the selflessness and dedication to the common good necessary for the success of the republic.[108]

Amid these developments Presbyterians grappled with the issue of whether or not to appeal for aid from the states for their colleges. Without exception, each of the Presbyterian schools did request state aid; invariably, those requests led the Presbyterians between 1776 and 1795 to emphasize the nonsectarian, expansive nature of their schools.[109] Not that the Presbyterians thought the schools' denominational nature precluded requests for state aid. The Dickinson Board, for instance, believed that the devastation suffered by the Carlisle area in the war and the service that the school would render to "a vast and growing western Territory" obligated the state to aid the school. And, the board argued in 1784 and 1785, was not the state bound to assist Dickinson after it subsidized the University of Pennsylvania?[110] The board did not argue that the state should aid one part of society simply because it assisted another, sensing perhaps that such reasoning might legitimize unbridled competition for the favors of the state and thereby destroy social order and union. Instead, the trustees suggested that the school deserved public aid because the Presbyterians represented a majority of the state's Christians; they were "a people probably the most numerous in the State." Thus the board did not hide Dickinson's denominational nature. They granted the obvious and embraced the idea that had undergirded the New England establishments for more than a century; that is, that the state should support financially the preponderant group of Christians in a society.[111] For the most part, the state legislatures seem to have agreed with the Presbyterian arguments; all of the Presbyterian schools received some form of aid from the states during the Revolutionary era, usually land, occasionally permission to have a lottery.[112]

That state aid forced the Presbyterian schools to emphasize their service to a wide constituency is most evident in the case of Princeton. The school had never received aid from the colonial government of New Jersey, and as late as 1784 Witherspoon argued that state aid might lead to state control that, in turn, might endanger the intentions of the "private gentlemen" who had established Princeton for the purpose of promoting religion as well as learning.[113] By the mid-1790s, though, the college's worsening financial condition forced the board and President Samuel Stanhope Smith to request $1,800 from the state.[114] The school had suffered in the cause of liberty, the board argued. Moreover, by conducting education with "skill, fidelity, attention to moral discipline, and yet liberty in religious opinions," Princeton had "attracted both reputation and wealth to the State," had produced citizens and leaders who attested to its "Utility," and in the future would attract students from north and south, become the Athens of the new republic, and educate jurists and statesmen who later, in councils of power, would give to New Jersey influence far disproportionate to its size.[115]

Despite their pledge that education at Princeton would be nonsectarian, the trustees charged with lobbying for state aid met the accusation that Princeton was "under the sole and exclusive control of one denomination of Christians," an allegation which the trustees were able to silence only by admitting that it had been true of the past. They argued, though, that denominational control of Princeton in the colonial period had been the result of Britain, who, "by her partial influence, supported the invidious distinctions among different denominations of Christians," a reply that was as disingenuous as it was ingenious. Happily, though, the late Revolution had removed the divisive English influence, and the trustees in 1796 assured the legislature that the Princeton Board "had determined hereafter to act upon all proper occasions, and particularly in the choice of Trustees, on a plan of most extended liberality." Mollified, the legislature granted the request.[116]

In their efforts to finance their institutions of higher learning, then, the Presbyterians revealed some of the same ambiguities and contradictions, some of the tensions, that had marked their reaction to the Pennsylvania revolution, to the drive for religious freedom in Virginia, indeed to the creation of a republican order dependent upon virtue for its life. They wanted desperately to believe that the Revolution provided a unique opportunity to halt the seemingly inevitable advance of selfishness and contention in American society; consequently, they embraced the revolutionary ideology of republicanism with its emphasis on social union and selflessness. But when the Revolution produced first the radical constitution of Pennsylvania, then Jefferson's religious revolution in Virginia, and finally the disorders of the 1780s and 1790s, many Presbyterians repented of their earlier ardor. Then, in order to oppose those unexpected results of the republican Revolution, those alarmed Presbyterians began in the 1780s and 1790s cautiously to defend social conflict as a positive good without appearing to renounce the Revolution altogether. Evident in their efforts to support and control their colleges, those same tensions would inform, in addition, the educational patterns of their institutions of higher learning in the early republic.

John McMillan's Original "Log College"

"Old West" of Dickinson College, 1811

Transylvania University, 1816–1829

CHAPTER VII

Republican Educational Patterns

The Presbyterians hoped that those institutions of higher education would be the instruments whereby America would be regenerated. Colonial Presbyterians, of course, also had envisioned their one college, Princeton, as a potent force for social reformation. But more so than their predecessors, republican Presbyterians wanted to know exactly *how* social institutions, and especially colleges, molded and transformed societies. They were more concerned because they believed their task was more urgent; its outcome, more portentous. Presbyterians in the last quarter of the eighteenth century, then, modified much of the educational theory that other Presbyterians had evolved in the late colonial period. Those changes invariably sought to extend the capacity of the Presbyterian colleges to produce the Christian republic made possible by the triumph of colonial arms. Specifically, republican Presbyterians embraced the Scottish philosophy of common sense and constructed on the foundation of that philosophy an expanded curriculum and a sophisticated "science of discipline." Having altered much of the educational experience available to students at their colleges, the Presbyterians then sought to make those colleges more accessible to larger numbers of young republicans.

THE PLAIN ROAD OF COMMON SENSE

At the basis of all those changes was the Scottish philosophy of common sense that John Witherspoon brought with him to Princeton in 1768. In a way, it is unfortunate that the origins of Scottish realism in British America can be traced so precisely to Witherspoon's arrival in the colonies. Students of early American thought have been satisfied to cite a few anecdotes about the Scotsman's campaign against idealism at Princeton and to attribute to Witherspoon's personality and energy the success in America of common-sense ideas. But the historian must do better than that if he would understand the process whereby the philosophy of the Scottish Enlightenment became within a generation of Witherspoon's arrival the reigning philosophy of the American republic.[1]

The ideas called Scottish "realism," or "common sense," are associated in general with the awakening of the Scottish intellect in the eighteenth century and, in particular, with the philosopher Thomas Reid (1710–1796). On one level, the philosophy of common sense was one of the less successful efforts by western thinkers to deal with the breakup of the grand unities of medieval Scholasticism. More specifically, it was intended to defend the empiricist tradition against the powerful assertion by David Hume that empiricism must of necessity lead to skepticism and even to atheism. In his own, earlier vindication of empiricism, John Locke had said of the process of cognition that men "knew" the material world only through sensory experience. Locke never demonstrated, though, whether or not the "ideas" derived from the senses corresponded to any material objects in the "real" world. Hume insisted that Locke's empiricism demonstrated that man, finally, could "know" nothing. If random sensory impressions were the only way in which man could have knowledge of his environment, then no external world could be said to exist in a permanent state. One could not even prove that he existed in the same body from moment to moment. And if the "real" world proved to be "unreal," how could men be persuaded to believe in an invisible, supernatural world? The implications of Hume's ideas for orthodox Christians were immediately obvious and disturbing. They were even more troubling when combined with the powerful assertion of Bishop Berkeley that "ideas" were themselves the objects of knowledge in the process of cognition and that the material world had no existence independent of those ideas.[2]

The Scottish realists were determined to refute both Hume's radical skepticism and Berkeley's negation of the material world. They insisted that sensible things—material objects themselves—were the object of knowledge in the process of cognition. That established, they could proceed to their central task: first, to assure western man that the material world *did* exist and that man, through reason and observation, could *know* it; and then to demonstrate that the world of matter moves according to laws of nature that are universal and immutable. Thomas Reid, in particular, developed a system of thought that attempted to combine realism and intuition, empiricism and idealism. He asserted that the mind perceived the material world through sensory impressions in reliable and verifiable ways and that the mind, in addition, apprehended other, intuitive, truths that were no less "real" than the objects in the material world. Those truths were the "first principles" of Thomas Reid's "philosophy of faith." They could not be explained or demonstrated. Nor were they innate with man. Instead, they were those propositions that, upon examination by the vast majority of men, appeared "self-evident," the "common sense" of mankind. Those self-evident first principles declared that men can be conscious and sure of their own personal existence, that the material world as perceived by the senses was real, that Nature was uniform and unchanging, and that every event in the material world had a "cause." On the basis of those principles, empirical philosophical investigation could safely proceed.[3]

When John Witherspoon arrived at Princeton in 1768, he discovered that the reigning philosophical system at the college looked distressingly like the idealism of Bishop Berkeley. Actually, Princeton's idealism was a home-grown Calvinist variety championed first by Edwards and then by his disciples, Samuel Hopkins, Joseph Bellamy, and the younger Jonathan Edwards. But Witherspoon was not one to make subtle distinctions. The whole lot of the idealists were "immaterialists," who made the fatal mistake of denying the existence of matter, and of relying solely upon the impressions made upon their minds in the process of cognition. Witherspoon insisted, often with ill-disguised impatience, that any idea the mind can produce "implies and supposes something external that communicates it" and cannot be separated from it. The idea of whiteness can be produced only by some white thing; the idea of "roundness," by the experience of seeing and feeling a ball or a globe. And because the idea of roundness resulted from actual sensory experience, it was a true idea verified by common-sense reliance on one's own senses. In addition, it was the result of an obvious cause-and-effect relationship. The effect—the "idea" of roundness in this case—was in some final sense "caused" by the process of touching and feeling. "The truth is," the Princeton president concluded, "the immaterial system is a wild and ridiculous attempt to unsettle the principles of common sense by metaphysical reasoning . . . ." At the basis of Witherspoon's quarrel with idealism was a disagreement over the passivity and activity of the mind in the process of cognition. To him, the idealists appeared to view the mind as an inert receptacle of the ideas that were themselves the active element in the process of knowing. Witherspoon simply insisted that the mind—not disembodied, evanescent ideas—was the locus of energy in that process.[4]

In Carlisle, twenty years after Witherspoon's arrival, Charles Nisbet attacked with more subtlety than his fellow Scotsman the notion that it is "by means of our ideas alone that we infer the existence of sensible objects around us, and discover their several properties and qualities." He refuted Locke's assertion that the qualities of matter do not exist in matter itself but in "the mind which perceives them," and laid down as a "childish quibble" the conclusions to be derived from idealism, for instance, that there is no heat in fire, no solidity in a wall. And, finally, Dr. Nisbet in a few concluding remarks in a 1788 lecture traced the entire history of the rise of Scottish realism as a refutation to Lockean ideas and subsequent idealism: "Mr. Locke and his followers, by affirming rashly that the mind perceives nothing except its own ideas, have laid a foundation for general scepticism, or doubting of the existence of external objects, which Mr. Hume has improved into a regular system without departing in the least from those principles which Mr. Locke had laid down in his celebrated Essay on the human Understanding. And it is truly a scandal to the philosophic reputation of the present age that the ingenious Dr. Reid was obliged to write [an] octavo volume, full of laborious reasoning, merely to prove the existence of external objects, which is rendered quite uncertain by Mr. Locke's hypothesis, and to bring us back to the level of children and savages, who have no doubts concerning the existence of objects that are perceivable by their senses."[5]

Eighteenth-century idealism, rightly understood, was a sophisticated defense of one of the most venerable ways of viewing the world. But Witherspoon and his disciples did not deal with the subtleties of the system. Instead they heaped ridicule and scorn on it. The story was told that Witherspoon observed, when a young men swallowed a hot drink too quickly, that the student's throat had been burned not by the hot toddy but by the "idea" of a hot toddy. And whether the story is apocryphal or not, a quarter of a century later his students, like William Graham, were still ridiculing before their own students those philosophers who argued that hot and cold existed only as ideas; those "wrong-headed metaphysicians" who denied that the world existed simply because they could not prove that it did. The "first principles" advanced by the Scottish realists could no more be proven than could a mathematical axiom, Witherspoon insisted. And Graham believed that, like the indisputable fact that two and two equal four, the postulates of common sense philosophy were too simple for definition and too basic to be proved. Instead they were "so plain that all men perceive the truth of them." [6]

Upon those principles, Graham believed, philosophers must erect systems of thought that rely solely on sensory perception, repeated experimentation, and the common experience of mankind. "All reason must be resolved into the testimony of our senses," he declared. Those senses must, in turn, be utilized in constant observation and experimentation. Nothing "but experiment will do." He would discover truth only "by accurately observing the operations" of his own mind. If those observations were the product of repeated experiment, they would not appear to be the "mere sensations of the brain, but what all men have believed to exist and do still continue to believe." Samuel Stanhope Smith agreed: "Experiment in morals as well as in physics is the only proper source of truth, and guide of reasoning." [7]

Their belief that the mind and its external surroundings interacted in the process of cognition served as the immediate basis of the Presbyterians' faith in the regenerative capacity of republican education. It seemed clear to them that, if exposed to proper stimuli, the mind would develop in a predictable fashion. "The cognition of man is formed for the world in which he acts," Graham believed, "and he is found susceptible of influence from the various objects with which he is conversant . . . ." [8] And, if that were true, the mind could be forced to develop habits of virtue and merit simply by surrounding it with meritorious stimuli. Smith reduced the process to a simple formula: "We usually think in a train and every idea almost is suggested by the one immediately before," he observed. Those ideas, or stimuli, are "linked together by the relations which objects bear to each other

. . . ." If virtuous examples were repeatedly presented to the active mind, in combination, they would produce virtuous action in a scientifically predictable way. If lost, those habits of virtue could even be regained. By "repeated" and "painful exertion" of the mind to recall the "lost images of virtue," by repeatedly contemplating those images, and then by "using them as motives of action," the images of virtue would "at length acquire the habitual superiority" over any vicious habits that might have momentarily superseded them.[9] That process, Smith believed, was aided by the inner connections that existed between truths. The mind must then be habituated to look for those "connexions and dependencies of things." All truths, he declared, are "consistent with one another," while error stands out, hideously, "from the general system, . . . refusing perfectly to coalesce with it . . . ." Thus, error was "more easily detected." [10]

While they embraced the Scottish school of common sense, the American Presbyterians also refined their view of faculty psychology. As we have seen, the Presbyterians had already abandoned the medieval concept of the faculties as discrete spiritual entities within the soul.[11] Instead they referred to the faculties as "capacities" and as "potentialities." Those faculties assisted man in determining action, in sorting out the data of sensory impressions. And in common sense philosophy as understood by the American Presbyterians, the faculties in general became very important and the moral faculty in particular became crucial. The existence of a moral faculty was one of the principal postulates of Reid's system and was at the basis of Presbyterian confidence in the regenerative capacities of republican education. For it was the existence of the moral faculty that made possible, finally, the inculcation of virtuous principles.

Benjamin Rush enthusiastically endorsed James Beattie's definition of the moral faculty as "a capacity in the human mind of distinguishing and choosing good and evil, or, in other words, virtue and vice." And, like the imagination, memory, and judgment, the moral faculty was extremely sensitive to stimuli of any kind. For Rush the list of stimuli was seemingly endless: climate, diet, idleness, pain, silence, music, odor, differing kinds of air, and so forth. All operated in a mechanical, predictable way upon the faculties, and especially upon the moral faculty. Borrowing a page from David Hartley, Rush emphasized the importance of "associations" upon morals and the moral faculty. Virtue should be promoted in the schools and in society by associating it with pleasure and reward. By the same token, vice should be discouraged by associating it with pain. By surrounding student and citizen with the appropriate stimuli it was possible, Rush believed, to turn them into "republican machines." [12]

INSTRUMENTS OF REPUBLICAN REGENERATION

Not all Presbyterians shared Rush's confidence in education's power to create "republican machines," but Presbyterian educators in the last quarter of the eighteenth century did make institutional changes that were self-consciously republican and that were intended to provide an academic environment where appropriate republican stimuli could be presented to the moral faculties of their students. One of the most important changes was the effort to construct a republican curriculum.

Some of the changes in the course of study after 1776 ratified developments that were well advanced in the late colonial period. One of those was an increasing emphasis on the study of history. Recent studies have shown that the colonists after the Great Awakening developed an intense interest in "social pathology." [13] They were fascinated by the reasons for the rise and fall of empires, why the millennium was destined to begin in America, why the British triumphed over France in the Seven Years' War, and so forth. With the rise of the American empire that interest had intensified and turned inward. The existence of an independent America had to be explained, and its problematical future had to be predicted. Any effort to do either had to be grounded firmly in an understanding of the history of past empires.

The Presbyterian educators believed that by studying history young Americans could understand the circumstances under which republics in the past had flourished and died. And the concrete example of the ancient republicans was deemed, by Charles Nisbet for example, to be superior to that of abstractions in "forming and assimilating the characters of men." [14] Nisbet believed that the languages and history of the ancient republicans should be the basis of all republican education. During the Revolutionary period, though, the usefulness of a classical education was intensely debated, and efforts were made to limit classical studies in the Presbyterian schools.[15] That debate reveals the dimensions of the Presbyterians' expectations of a republican education.

The Presbyterian defense of a classical education was grounded in both faculty psychology and republican ideology. Charles Nisbet believed that students should study the classical languages because they would "excite and exercise" their "taste and judgment." The ancient republicans were men "of a larger size, and sentiments and actions of much greater magnanimity, than can be found in the present dregs of time." And Nisbet insisted that their example would have an "assimilating effect on the manners of men" and teach them "by imitation and the principles of society" to "detest and abhor vice, disorder and indecency, and to exercise justice and benevolence to all." To begin to admire the great and virtuous ancients "is the first dawn of virtue," he concluded. And, if "properly improved," that admiration of virtue "will lead to the love and imitation of it." [16]

The defenders of classical education also urged that it begin as soon as possible, while young minds were still tractable and susceptible to virtuous stimuli and impressions. Just as they had argued that the colonists should create republican governments while they remained virtuous enough to sustain them, the Presbyterians now insisted that never again would a young man be as open to the impressions of wisdom and virtue as while in college. Both in creating the republic and in educating republican citizens, then, the Presbyterians were urged to the task while it was still capable of execution. [17]

It is clear that Nisbet, for one, defended classical learning because he believed the virtuous pagans worthy of emulation by young American republicans. The words he used to describe the ancients—virtuous, patriotic, selfless, disinterested, and noble—described also those characteristics Nisbet believed were sorely lacking in America. And he believed that only a classical education could enable young republicans to withstand the blandishments of the demagogues produced by the democratic thrust of the American Revolution. [18] But Charles Nisbet had to deal with the problem that confronted all Christians who urged the ancient republicans as models for the young: they were, after all, pagans. Nisbet granted that some of the scenes described in classical literature were not suitable for modern use. But he saw that as no insurmountable problem. The "discreet master" simply would pass over those passages, or, if adventurous, "convey the Antidote with the poison, and warn Youth against the temptations to which they are exposed." His lectures that survive in student notebooks indicate that Nisbet followed his own advice and thoroughly sanitized the ancients before passing them on to the lads at Carlisle. [19]

Like Nisbet's defense of classical education, the Presbyterian critique of the classics during the Revolutionary period was firmly based on the theories of cognition associated with Scottish realism. Like Nisbet, Benjamin Rush, for instance, spoke of the mind as actively responding to external stimuli. He simply did not believe that the classics were proper stimuli for young republicans. Rush believed, instead, that the early study of dead languages taught students only abstractions and neglected to teach them about "men" and "things." He pointed out that students "know" most "things" before they know the names of those things. And the teacher who filled the student's mind with words—abstractions—without attempting to convey to the youngster the meaning of those words lessened that boy's ability to acquire ideas about those real "things" at a later time. He became capable only of memorizing words and could make no connections between those words and the "things" for which they stood. The study of classical languages, then, gave the mind "an oblique direction." The process of cognition was a complicated affair, Rush declared. A student's mind had first to comprehend substances, then actions, then qualities, and finally all of the degrees of the "order of nature." At the end of that process the student should be able to "combine remote ideas upon plain subjects." Classical study simply was not adequate preparation for that complicated process. Rush recommended that a student first learn about the world that was immediately around him by studying "simple and truly delightful" natural history. By learning about the things in his immediate environment, the student would then begin to understand the relationship between "words" and "things" that was the absolute prerequisite for Rush's theory of republican education.[20]

Rush's rejection of the venerable notion that the ancient republicans were worthy models for the young was the most revolutionary aspect of his attack on the classics. The tales of the Caesars taught only vice, he asserted, and thereby diminished "respect for the unity and perfections of the true God." And by recounting tales of royal murder and military exploits, they led to a "universal preference of the military character to all others." To John Adams, Rush observed that "by enabling us to read agreeable histories of ancient crimes," a classical education "often leads us to imitate or to tolerate them." Henceforth, he grandly declared, he would view the study of the classics, along with the institution of slavery and the intemperate consumption of alcohol, as "unfriendly to the progress of morals, knowledge, and religion in the United States."[21]

Rush also refuted the defense of early training in the classical languages.

They neither exercised the mind nor taught clear, logical thinking, he asserted. And if a young man later decided to become a doctor, minister, or lawyer he could acquire in one year the requisite reading knowledge of Latin or Greek.[22] Rush seems to have been sensitive to the distinctive character of childhood and adolescense. He was sorry that language study often made miserable "that innocent period of life, which seems exclusively intended for happiness," and he often told the tale of the eleven-year-old who once confessed to him that he wished he had never been born into a world of trouble that required him to prepare two Latin lessons daily. Rush took the boy's lament seriously. If young men became disgusted with the schools of the republic because of their classical orientation, the republic, not the boys, was the ultimate loser.[23]

Benjamin Rush's critique of classical education was part of his continuing effort to declare the New World's cultural independence from the Old. He could not believe that Nature had exhausted herself when she created Greece and Rome, and he was certain that no one would surpass the ancients until he stopped studying them to the exclusion of all advances since the passing of the antique world.[24] And he rejected the contention that a knowledge of the classics was a prerequisite for understanding English. He noted that no one had taught the Greeks to understand their language by first teaching them a foreign tongue. The Greeks had excelled because they had something unusual in their blood or in the structure of their nerves, he believed. Rush insisted that Americans also were unique. America was like "a new planet" suddenly appearing in the solar system of established powers, facing new and boundless opportunities. For American youth to spend years studying dead languages was to turn their backs on a gold mine while chasing butterflies. Let the youth of Europe tramp about the ruins of Palmyra, memorize the intricacies of Greek grammar, and practice Latin conjugations. Young Americans should study only those subjects that "increase the convenience of life, lessen human misery, improve our country, promote population, exalt the human understanding, and establish domestic, social, and political happiness."[25]

Finally, Rush rejected classical education as elitist, and by definition, unrepublican. In a republic the entire citizenry must be educated, but the mysteries of Latin and Greek were revealed only to a few. Moreover, if the classical foundation of their privileges were rejected, perhaps educators would cease to lord it over the common people, who might then overcome their all too common prejudices against schools and schoolmen. College enrollments might increase and universal knowledge spread more rapidly throughout the land. The rejection of the classics, Rush concluded, might lead to nothing less than a "revolution in science, and in human affairs." [26]

The attack upon the classics in the Revolutionary period was not merely theoretical. At Pennsylvania's Washington Academy and at Hampden-Sydney, student societies debated the usefulness of a classical education and decided the issue in the negative.[27] And parents of students at Hampden-Sydney in the 1780s persuaded President Smith to exempt their sons "from learning the greek." The reprieve lasted for only two years, during which the boys studied more fashionable French. But when reinstated, obligatory Greek was a minor part of the school's curriculum. In their last session of the eighteenth century, Princeton's trustees inaugurated what amounted to America's first Bachelor of Science degree, which allowed students to complete all of the requirements for the B.A. except for Latin and Greek and to be rewarded with a new certificate, but not a diploma. The move was a dramatic break with the past and was the climax of the revolutionary attack on the classical foundation of American higher education.[28]

That attack did not extend to the most classical of disciplines, oratory, or to its companion, rhetoric. In fact, each was esteemed a proper instrument of republican education and was universally popular with educators and students. The evangelical fervor of the colonial educators had established oratory firmly in Princeton's curriculum, and the civil enthusiasms of the Revolution solidified and even extended that position. As with so much else in the period, oratory and rhetoric flourished at the Presbyterian schools because they were well adapted to prevailing psychological theory and especially relevant in republican societies.[29]

The proponents of oratorical training cast in secular terms the evangelical argument that public address was the only effective means of reaching large groups of people. The undeniable importance of oratory to the patriot cause—Rush believed it had been as important as the colonists' military endeavors—and the necessity of molding public opinion along republican lines made the Presbyterian educators particularly sensitive to the nuances and dynamics of oratorical training.[30] At Dickinson, Robert Davidson treated the art of oratory as a science and related it to current psychological theory. He emphasized the orator's power to stimulate his hearers and to elicit action from them. He divided the mind into three related parts and described the circumstances under which the orator could justifiably stimulate each of those parts. Invariably, a desired response was achieved by stimulating the prescribed "faculty." To instruct, the orator addressed the "reason"; to persuade, he approached the "moral sense"; and to please or excite, he aroused the "affections," or the passions. But, because the faculties were interdependent and related, they had to be approached cautiously and stimulated judiciously, and then only in proper sequence. The passions, for instance, were the seat of violent response and could be safely stimulated only after the reason had been first enlightened and, in any case, could be approached only after repeated efforts to arouse the moral sense had failed. Still, Davidson insisted, the passions were the "great springs of action" and must occasionally be used.[31]

Oratory, then, was a crucial instrument of republican regeneration because the orator could address himself directly to the mind and urge it to virtuous action. Thus, student debating societies regularly decided in the late eighteenth century that "eloquent speaking" was more to be desired than the "faculty of composing eloquently." And when the Liberty Hall Board dispatched Graham to New England in 1785 to purchase books for the school, they listed books on oratory as their first priority. Finally, in the 1780s the Hampden-Sydney Board petitioned the Virginia legislature for funds to build a hall in which student orators might appear. The board dared presume on the legislature's largesse because the lawmakers' "experience in the business of the state" undoubtedly had convinced them of the "importance of an early habit and address in oratory" in republican society. In other words, their experience with free republican institutions was believed to have demonstrated to the lawmakers the importance of oratory to the maintenance of this fragile form of government.[32] Apparently so. The hall was built.

THE SCIENCE OF DISCIPLINE

The same man who more than anyone else brought the common-sense philosophy to America also advocated a system of discipline thoroughly grounded in that philosophy. Just as common sense philosophy was the basis of Presbyterian faith in the regenerative capabilities of republicanism, so did Witherspoon's science of discipline serve as a principal means of accomplishing that process of regeneration. At Princeton and in the other schools founded by Princeton graduates, the Scottish parson's ideas provided the foundation for a system of discipline that better than anything else reflects the Presbyterian belief that Americans could indeed be transformed into virtuous "republican machines."

In a series of essays on discipline that was published posthumously, Witherspoon outlined a system of discipline worthy of an enlightened age. In former ages all education had been carried on by the "mere dint of authority," a "savage and barbarious method" that had been "terrible and disgusting" to all students. In contrast, Witherspoon's system was based on the pliability of young minds and the importance of example. Like a young tree, Witherspoon believed, the mind of youth could be bent in any direction and would receive "almost any form." And like Nisbet he was convinced that the mind was more influenced by concrete examples than by general precepts, which, no matter how "justly stated or fully proved," seldom leave a "strong or lasting impression." Examples, on the other hand, have "a constant and powerful influence, on our temper and carriage." And Witherspoon related the importance of examples to familiar cognitive theories. Children, he noticed, observe their parents' actions and begin to connect those actions with certain ideas. By connecting acts with ideas, they "acquire many sentiments of good and evil, right and wrong, in that early period of their life." They slowly build up "a great number of particulars," ideas which taken separately may not be important, but which, "by their union or frequent repetition, produce important and lasting effects." In fact, Witherspoon concluded, those ideas are the source of "national characters and national manners, and every characteristic distinction of age and place." [33]

With that kind of power in their hands, parents must deal with discipline in a scientific, reasonable manner, Witherspoon insisted. The president suggested that at an early age the child should learn that the parents' will must always prevail. That could be accomplished by arbitrarily withholding something from a child while graciously granting all other requests. He also cautioned parents never to present two different examples to the child, for that would only lead to the formation of conflicting ideas in his mind. And discipline should be rational. It should proceed from a "sense of duty" and be "directed by conscience." Under no circumstances should it be administered in a fit of rage, for the child would rightly see that as a sign of weakness. Finally, discipline, to be effective, had to be directed to the child's sense of honor, to his conscience. [34]

Benjamin Rush went even further than Witherspoon in insisting that republican discipline must be directed to the reason and moral sense of the young. He deplored the whipping schoolmaster as the last despot in a free society and asserted that, given the opportunity to promulgate only one law for the republic, he would make that tyranny impossible. Rush was no visionary. As a father, he was fully aware of the exasperating habits of adolescents. He simply believed that, like adults, schoolboys possessed the power to reason and a moral sense and that those faculties were affronted and harmed by harsh and irrational punishment. And that which weakened the moral sense of the young ultimately endangered the republic. Like Witherspoon, Rush believed that authority must be absolute. But for Rush—and the Princeton president—therein lay the key to the rationality and humanity of their ideas of discipline: both believed that strictness of discipline would always render severity unnecessary.[35]

When it was institutionalized at Princeton, John Witherspoon's "science of discipline" proved to be as precisely modulated and effective in practice as it was in theory. "Govern . . . govern always," was his motto. But he was careful to add, "beware of governing too much." Do not commit the authority of the school to laws not essential to its welfare, he warned his tutors, and be careful to distinguish between "youthful follies and foibles, and those acts which manifest a malignant spirit, or intentional insubordination."[36] Witherspoon's enlightened geniality appears to have prevailed at Princeton during the Revolutionary period and closely resembles the disciplinary ideas of that "gentle Puritan," Ezra Stiles, who superintended Yale during the same period.[37] The Princeton Board was proud that Princeton's discipline "was wholly of the moral kind, and addressed to the sense of duty and the principles of honour and shame . . . ." And the boys took the trustees at their word. One student successfully applied for readmission on the plausible grounds that his brief suspension had worked the reformation intended by the college's rules. And, usually, when students were suspended they were quickly readmitted. Discipline at Princeton, it appeared, was indeed to reform offenders, not to protect the school from those delinquents.[38] In one respect Witherspoon and his board were simply reacting to the obvious spirit of the times. Benjamin Rush was not the only American in the aftermath of the Revolution to decide that the "whipping schoolmaster" was a tyrant who had no place among free men or their children. College students—and their parents—were quite sensitive to their rights in the 1780s and it was a wise administrator who paid attention to those rights.[39]

The Presbyterian educators believed that a sensitive system of discipline could be maintained only in the proper environment; they disagreed, however, over what that environment might be. For instance, how were their charges to be housed? In the early years of almost all the colleges, the question of housing was a simple one. Students of necessity either lived and boarded with the president and faculty or in other approved lodgings.[40] When Princeton moved to the little village between New York and Philadelphia at the midcentury, though, it built Nassau Hall and attempted to force all students to live under its ample roof. Where they had once emphasized the advantages of familial living arrangements, the trustees now stressed the benefits of being able to supervise the students' morals more effectively when they were lodged in one place. Many students, however, preferred the earlier arrangement. The trustees and faculty were constantly having to force young men to return to Nassau Hall from the village, where they had illegally taken lodging in private homes and in taverns in search of female company and food more palatable than that available in the commons.[41]

Some Presbyterians, however, joined with the students in preferring the older familial arrangements to the dormitory. Benjamin Rush was the most vocal opponent of "herding" large numbers of young men into communal lodgings, and his critique of the dormitory was based on the tenets of common-sense psychology in general and, in particular, on the "associationalism" of David Hartley. Dormitories seemed to Rush to be the remains of "monkish ignorance" and were as useless in improving minds and morals as the monasteries had been in promoting true religion. Following Hartley, Rush warned that the "Vices of the same species attract each other with the most force"; consequently, the tendencies to mischief in all boys would only be magnified by their being brought into close proximity with other young men. Instead, Rush argued, the boys should live in private homes where they could be protected from corrupting influences "while we improve their manners by subjecting them to those restraints which the differences of age and sex naturally produce in private families." Rush spoke from bitter experience. He had allowed his son John to attend Princeton only when Professor John Minto agreed that the boy might live with his family. He was to enter Nassau Hall only to attend classes. John apparently succumbed to the temptation of the dorm, though, because he was caught playing cards there *on Sunday*. Rush immediately withdrew the boy from school and blamed John's downfall on "the temptations and opportunities of vice which are inseparably connected with a number of boys herding together under one roof without the restraints which arise from female and family society." George Clymer, a Philadelphian who signed the Declaration of Independence, even moved to Princeton for two years to superintend the education of his two sons and to enable them to live at home. And at Dickinson, Robert Davidson reported to the public that students lived in "good private homes" where they have the "polishing influence of the fair sex . . . ."[42]

Beyond the question of familial versus communal living arrangements was the issue of the proper locale for republican educational institutions. It made little difference if young republicans received appropriate stimuli in class if the college itself was set amid corruption and vice. In the opinion of most, then, young men could be converted into "republican machines" only when removed from the temptations that attended life in the city. Benjamin Rush believed that even tiny Princeton was a den of iniquity and had no hope at all for any young man educated in Philadelphia. Thus, even in tiny towns like Carlisle and Princeton the boards of the Presbyterian colleges exerted pressure on government to refuse licenses to tavern owners who sold drinks to their students. The Princeton Board sincerely believed that its actions would "not only promote the good government of the college, but also the peace and good order of the town." In Lexington, Virginia, the Liberty Hall trustees resisted all offers for financial assistance that were conditioned on the school's moving into the corrupting confines of the bustling frontier village. They chose, rather, to keep the school pristinely situated just out of the reach of iniquity at the village's edge.[43]

But with the exception of Hampden-Sydney, which was and remains situated among the fields of Prince Edward County, each of the Presbyterian schools *was* located in or just outside centers of population. As we have seen,[44] the defenders of King's College in the colonial period had outlined a defense of urban centers as appropriate locales for learning. Some Americans in the early republic improved on that defense. Each of the Presbyterian schools assured prospective students and their parents that the town in which it was located was as "free from luxury, and other evils, to as great a degree as perhaps any other town or village in the United States." But, particularly in the west, boosters of one town or another began to defend all cities in general—and theirs in particular—as ideal centers of learning that would stimulate the students even while protecting them from the problems peculiar to urban environments. In booming Lexington, Kentucky, for instance, the urbane John Filson offered to build a permanent home for Transylvania if the school would pledge to remain forever in Lexington and make it the "Athens of the West." And Filson contended that towns were better situated to protect morals than the country was. In the country, he noted, a schoolboy gets away with a great deal simply because "no eye beholds him." In a "respectable town," though, he would have to face the "contempt of ridicule" that any ill-bred behavior would immediately elicit. In a city, Filson insisted, a young man could become a gentleman as well as a scholar without endangering his morals. Like the attack on the cities, then, their defense was based on a desire to provide an educational setting that would present to the young mind those impressions and stimuli most likely to produce virtue and honor.[45]

EXTENDING THE LIMITS OF EDUCATION

To endorse republican education in the late eighteenth century was, by definition, to advocate the extension of education. The substance of education had to be made to conform to republican ideology, and that invariably meant extending the curriculum to subjects heretofore slighted or ignored in American colleges. And in a republic dependent upon an educated citizenry for its life, access to education had to be extended to as wide a range of Americans as possible.

Republicanism itself had to be taught. Their boast to the contrary notwithstanding, Americans were not "republicans by nature," and the Presbyterians knew it. Like all ideologies, republicanism would have to be systematically "inculcated" upon the young by republican educational institutions. To that end, patriots in the 1780s endowed prizes in the Presbyterian colleges for the best essays on subjects relating to republicanism.[46] And at the end of the period here under discussion the American Philosophical Society conducted a contest to discover the best plan for a system of education adapted in particular to republican societies. In the essay he submitted, Benjamin Rush suggested that in a society where anyone could become a legislator the art of republican politics had to be taught systematically in the schools. And he proposed that all colleges in the future be located in towns with courts to enable the students to see the republican system in operation. When Rush in 1784 urged Nisbet to come to America he proposed that the Scotsman prepare a "course of lectures on government, including not only the principles of constitutions but practical legislation," a course that would surely "be very acceptable in this country and very necessary in our republic."[47]

Boards of trustees in the early republic could become quite explicit in their demands for republican instruction. The Dickinson Board, for instance, became concerned when they discovered in the public examinations of 1797 that the graduating seniors had not been instructed in republican theory. The board reminded the graduates—and their teachers—that the subject merited their "most profound attention," and that "your country is interested in the formulation of these important principles by which your future conduct may be regulated." It was not enough for a student to assent lightly to republicanism. A good republican "must be a Republican from a just appreciation of its advantages over every other." Not content to scold, the board in the following year instructed the Professor of Belles Lettres to lecture extensively on republicanism.[48]

The effect on Dickinson was immediate. Professor Robert Davidson's lectures on grammar became vehicles for political indoctrination, suffused with allusions to the virtues of the antique republicans and to topics more directly related to modern republican theory. When he taught adverbs, he extolled the virtues of the ancients: "Cicero was eloquent, Pliny was *moderately eloquent,* Virgil wrote *admirably."* When conjunctions were the subject of the day, Davidson demonstrated the connection between ambition and slavery: "Rome was enslaved. Caesar was ambitious. Connect them by the conjunction *because* and then it will be Rome was enslaved *because* Caesar was ambitious." And, to illustrate the conjunction, "or," "manner must be reformed *or* liberty will be lost." To illustrate the "natural" order of syntax Davidson used a sentence that also warned of the dangers of a standing army, a fundamental of republican ideology: "In every kingdom where arbitrary power supported by a standing army prevails we hear daily complaints of cruel measurers [sic]."[49]

While the Presbyterians extended the curriculum to inculcate republicanism explicitly, they also broadened it to include subjects of a manifestly utilitarian nature and then related those subjects to republicanism. This was part of a much broader move at all American colleges to modify the classical curriculum in the early republic, to introduce the modern languages and the study of English literature, to emphasize mathematics and the natural sciences, and, in general, to provide a more utilitarian education.[50] At Princeton the classical curriculum was extended to include lectures on politics and the law and even to embrace navigation, surveying, and scientific agriculture. Tutor Ashbel Green trooped his young charges out of doors and taught them how to plot a field, while Witherspoon used the available manpower to farm scientifically his estate just outside Princeton. And at the Canonsburg Academy, Dickinson, and Liberty Hall youths were instructed in such practical subjects as mensuration, gauging, surveying, navigation, conic sections, and single- and double-entry bookkeeping.[51] Rush believed that those subjects were no less crucial to the survival of the republic than explicit courses in republican ideology. They were essential to the commercial and manufacturing enterprises that would give the young republic strength in a world of hostile monarchies, and they provided the basis for the military skills that might be necessary should those monarchies turn belligerent. For Rush no less than for Thomas Jefferson, agriculture was the "only true basis of national prosperity and of private happiness." In the final analysis, though, Benjamin Rush supported "practical" education because it satisfied his criteria for republican education: it made men publicly useful and privately happy.[52]

The most significant extension of the classical curriculum in the early republic was the amazing growth of the natural and mathematical sciences. Between 1787 and 1800 virtually all of the Presbyterian schools appointed a first professor of mathematics or natural philosophy, provided a series of scientific lectures for townspeople as well as students, and allotted a considerable portion of their limited funds to the purchase of scientific equipment, or "philosophical apparatus," as it was called—electrical machines, solar telescopes, thermometers, and sets of terrestrial globes.[53] Superficially, the sciences appear to have become popular in the late eighteenth century simply because they were an innovation in a stultifying curriculum. But there are more fundamental reasons. The new scientific knowledge was perceived as having a particular affinity with the new republic. Both science and the American republic seemed at the same time to offer new solutions to old problems, particularly to men who believed that the rules of the natural sciences could serve as prototypes for the laws of the embryonic social sciences.[54]

The Presbyterian educators grounded both these social sciences and the new natural sciences firmly in common-sense philosophy and the theory of cognition that grew out of that philosophy. That relationship was illustrated in a pamphlet published in 1796 by John Maclean, in which Princeton's first professor of chemistry attacked the theories and experimental techniques of that group of scientists who insisted that the phenomenon of combustion could be explained only by the existence of an element called "phlogiston." Phlogiston, they asserted, was an invisible substance present in all matter whose release accounted for the otherwise unexplainable loss of weight that occurred when a metal rusted or burned. Maclean denounced the phlogiston theory as "complicated, contradictory, and inadequate." Worse still, it was founded only on an "ideal principle" and was the mere creature of the imaginations of unscientific scientists. His own antiphlogiston position, on the other hand, was based on no "random conjectures," and was dependent upon "nothing whose existence cannot actually be demonstrated." His theory had been "submitted to the most rigorous examination," and had been verified at every step of experimentation by "the tests of weight and measures." [55] Like Witherspoon's attack on philosophical idealism, Maclean's challenge to the phlogistonists would admit of nothing incapable of demonstration and evaluation by the senses.

The natural scientist, in retrospect, appears to have been the ideal republican educator. When he performed experiments before amazed students and adults, the scientist addressed their senses directly, much as the orator did. But, unlike the orator, the scientist had the capacity to persuade finally, permanently. His was not a world of changing impressions and fleeting emotions, but of immutable, universal law. If the scientist combined two chemicals, he produced an invariable and predictable result. That result vindicated the law the scientist wished to demonstrate. And it graphically demonstrated the cause-and-effect relationship that was at the foundation of Scottish realism.

It was only a step from those scientific rules to the laws that governed social and moral behavior, and the Presbyterian educators invariably took that step. Walter Minto, Princeton's first professor of mathematics, recommended scientific study precisely for the sense of "order, regularity, and of dignity" which it conveyed to the student. Moreover, it "bridled" the imagination, which was prone to excess, while it moderated tempers and passions, and thereby enabled men to estimate "things according to their intrinsic value." Like Minto, Charles Nisbet believed that scientific study equipped a young man to find order in the chaos of the moral and the physical worlds by teaching him to think in analogies, to contemplate lofty matters of eternal consequence, and to appreciate the "connexions and dependencies" of more mundane considerations. All of which, Dickinson's president concluded, made students more appreciative of and susceptible to the laws that governed the moral relations of men and the universal order of the Deity: "In the certain and determined relations of numbers, lines and figures, you have been led to discern a specimen of that nice order and exact proportion in which God has created all things, and which we may trace in all the works of nature, in proportion as we are acquainted with them." [56]

"Moral philosophy" as well as "natural philosophy" now dominated the republican curriculum. Indeed, the former encompassed the latter. Witherspoon, who was largely responsible for the growth of both, believed natural philosophy was the necessary preparation for and companion to moral philosophy. Moral philosophy was usually taught to seniors and was intended to recapitulate the entire educational experience, bringing into focus the reasons for which it had been undertaken and the responsibilities it supposedly had prepared the student to assume. Its scope was virtually unlimited and its character was determined finally by the personality of the president teaching it.[57]

In his course in moral philosophy, which would influence Presbyterian ministers for at least a half-century, John Witherspoon endeavored to shape from the embryonic social sciences—anthropology, economics, psychology, sociology—an integrated system of public and private ethics. His principal concern was to demonstrate that religion and morality, rightly perceived, had nothing to fear and everything to gain from the scientific methods of induction, experimentation, and demonstration. In discussing ancient history, political economy, or the nature of true virtue, Witherspoon welcomed the opportunity to ferret from the most unlikely sources some demonstrable support or vindication of revealed religion and, by extension, republican government. He knew of nothing that supported religion more firmly "than to see, from the different and opposite systems of philosophers, that there is nothing certain in their schemes, but what is coincident with the word of God." He sought to demonstrate *real* truth by critically examining different *versions* of truth, and he never doubted that such a demonstration was possible. The process would pose no danger to scripture, which, being true, could not be contrary to discoveries of reason. Witherspoon hoped someday to be able to establish the exactitude and certainty in moral investigations that characterized scientific research. He looked forward to the time "when men, treating moral philosophy as Newton and his successors" had treated natural philosophy would make that former science as exact and beneficial as the latter.[58]

Most Presbyterians applauded the increased emphasis on republicanism, utilitarian subjects, and the sciences, but the extension of the scope of education during the Revolutionary period produced some results that troubled many of the denomination's educators. They were concerned in particular about the Revolution's effect on educational standards. Nisbet was appalled to find that in Dickinson there was no provision for classifying students according to age and educational progress. The grammar school and the college met in one room, he lamented, and confusion was total. "To erect a College in the Corner of a grammar school," he observed to Rush, "is a scheme that never was thought of in any other Age or Place in the World." Moreover, he found that boys entered school at any time they chose and also left at their convenience.[59] At Liberty Hall there was no required curriculum, and students were allowed to study in areas of their own choice. In Kentucky the Transylvania Board stipulated that boys who could write a "legible hand" and read the *Spectator* or a novel with "tolerable propriety" should be admitted in good standing by the English teacher, their "ages or sizes" being immaterial. At Hampden-Sydney the board directed that boys who did not wish to go through the regular course of study might join any class and study "those parts of science which they wish to obtain the knowledge of." And at Princeton in 1780 the board found it necessary to proclaim that a traditional two year residence requirement was henceforth to be enforced. It was not.[60]

This lack of classification and standards during the Revolutionary period was largely the result of unprecedented and effective student and parental pressure. At Hampden-Sydney students agitated successfully for the dismissal of an unpopular tutor and at Dickinson young frontiersmen exploited the already bad relations between the board and Nisbet, and persuaded the board to lower Nisbet's rigorous standards. The young men complained that the president required them to take down every word of his lectures. The trustees informed Nisbet that Dickinson was acquiring an unwanted reputation for academic rigor and was consequently losing students to other schools. They therefore requested the harassed president to lighten the students' work load, without sacrificing essentials or quality, of course.[61]

Student pressure on the boards during the early republic was effective because it was often attended by parental pressure. Parents in particular were interested in shortening the time required to receive a college degree. A frustrated Witherspoon in 1786 blasted "the mistakes of parents and their desire to precipitate the education of their children," and resolved to admit to Princeton only those who could enter one of the lower classes in good standing and to graduate only those who completed the entire required course of study. Smith was even more resentful of republican parents, who, he believed, only wanted Princeton to equip their sons for making money as quickly and as inexpensively as possible. He would not, he declared, turn Princeton into a grammar school in order better to accommodate their "great babies." [62]

Student and parental pressures reached a climax at Dickinson in the late 1790s. To his dismay Nisbet found that the board in 1797 was seriously considering a one-year degree. To his friend Alexander Addison, Nisbet lamented that such a move would at least enable Dickinson to compete with the "University of Parkinson's Ferry," Nisbet's fictional expression of contempt for the state of higher education in America. In 1798 the board overruled Nisbet's almost apoplectic objections that a one-year course would produce "only raw and ignorant Graduates, to the Hurt of Society," and provided for just such a course. In 1799, 1800, and 1801 young men graduated from Dickinson College after one year. An extreme instance, the disastrous experiment was the climax of the attack on academic standards that attended the extension of the classical curriculum during the late eighteenth century.[63]

The attack on standards in the Presbyterian schools was paralleled by related efforts to revise educational qualifications for the ministry. At issue were the growing number of vacant pulpits on the frontier and the requirement that all Presbyterian clerics have at least the equivalent of a college education. Many Presbyterians believed those pulpits would not be filled until that requirement was modified. Even Samuel Stanhope Smith warned that the educational background required of a minister "ought to be regulated by the demands of the church, the state of society," and other changing circumstances. In some ways, then, he supported the 1785 proposal that the synod relax the "literary qualifications required of entrants into the ministry." [64] Others vehemently opposed any lowering of standards. And in 1792 the Assembly not only refused to reduce the educational requirements but instead proposed that the period of required theological study be extended to at least three years. In a show of force and unanimity every one of the presbyteries opposed the proposal.[65] Then some of the presbyteries began on their own actually to shorten candidacies. The men of Hanover, for instance, sought ways legally to license mature men with little education, who might still be "extensively useful" as lay exhorters on the Methodist model. But when the presbytery actually licensed one such man in 1789, they affirmed their general approbation of the rule to which they were making an exception.[66] Other presbyteries followed suit and also abbreviated the length of candidacy, which was uniformly shorter in the Revolutionary period than it had ever been in the colonial period.[67] Finally, the Assembly relented and agreed in 1800 to license men of "piety and good sense" who, though they had little education, might still catechize blacks, Indians, and *unchurched* frontiersmen, but could do nothing else.[68]

The final way in which the Presbyterians made significant extensions of education in the Revolutionary period was to make education itself more accessible to an ever larger number of Americans. As we have noted, during the colonial period increasing numbers of small-farmers' sons found their way to Princeton, often with the help of their Presbyterian pastors and over the objections of their fathers. This pattern continued in the Revolutionary period, as did the pattern whereby Princeton, especially, educated the sons of the American elite. To these two patterns now was added a third, different one.

In the Revolutionary period Princeton continued to prepare the sons of the elite of the middle states and the upper south for the learned professions and social leadership. For example, Morgan Lewis of the class of 1773 was the eighteen-year-old son of Francis Lewis, a signer of the Declaration of Independence. Lewis became a lawyer and served as the attorney general and the governor of New York. Likewise, the seventeen-year-old scion of the great Livingston family, Edward, graduated in 1781 and entered upon a legal career, becoming a congressman, a district attorney, a United States senator, mayor of New York City, secretary of state, and minister to France. The class of 1792 included the eighteen- and twenty-year-old sons of the Willing family of Philadelphia and the Lee dynasty of Virginia. George Willing entered his father's successful countinghouse, while Henry Lee became a gentleman lawyer. Benjamin Rush's son Richard, who graduated in 1797 at seventeen and entered the bar, attended classes with a son of the governor of Delaware, who would graduate at nineteen, and the son of a wealthy Georgia Huguenot family who returned to the south with a Princeton degree at the age of fifteen.[69] As had been the case in the colonial period, these wealthy young men entered Princeton earlier than their peers, graduated at an earlier age, and characteristically followed their fathers into legal and mercantile careers.

The Revolutionary period also saw the emergence of a new group of students at Princeton. During that period the sons, grandsons, and nephews of Presbyterian ministers enrolled at Princeton in increasing numbers. These young men did not come from the upper classes, but their educated kinsmen often endeavored to begin their education at an early age. Consequently, many of them were able to graduate as early as did their wealthier colleagues. Those students were often the beginning of virtual dynasties of Presbyterian ministers, and their heirs would attend and support Princeton throughout the nineteenth century. Many of the relatives of Presbyterian ministers followed their fathers and uncles into the clerical profession; others—Aaron Burr, Jr.—obviously did not. Like the sons of the aristocracy, those sons of the clergy did not utilize Princeton as an instrument of social mobility. That step had usually been taken by their fathers in the previous generation.[70]

On the other hand, Princeton continued to serve as an instrument of social mobility for a significant number of students. As had been true in the colonial period, this was particularly true for the sons of farmers who came to Princeton to prepare for the Presbyterian ministry. These young men frequently were considerably older than either the sons of the elite or of the Presbyterian ministers. One Joseph Clark, for instance, was trained to become a carpenter in his home in Elizabethtown, New Jersey. But Clark was encouraged by his minister, James Caldwell, and by his mother to prepare for the ministry, and he entered Princeton at age twenty. He served in the Revolutionary army, returned to college, and graduated in 1781—at the age of thirty. He was then licensed by the Presbytery of New Brunswick and served the Presbyterian Church in Allentown, Pennsylvania, for twelve years. The Presbyterian educators sometimes filled the role of father for orphaned young men. One such orphan was John Watson, who was born in western Pennsylvania in 1771. While working in a tavern in the Presbyterian stronghold of Washington, Pennsylvania, young Watson was noticed by Judge James Allison, who brought him some Latin books to study. The judge then introduced Watson to John McMillan at the Canonsburg Academy. McMillan took a great liking to Watson, who studied with him from 1794 to 1795 and proved a most apt student. McMillan then sent the young man to his alma mater at Princeton, where he graduated first in his class at the age of twenty-eight. He returned to western Pennsylvania, then, was ordained to the ministry, and eventually became the first president of Jefferson College, the successor to McMillan's Canonsburg Academy.[71]

Watson's experience demonstrates the crucial role that Presbyterian ministers and the frontier schools, especially, played as instruments of social mobility in the Revolutionary period. At the Canonsburg Academy, McMillan, Thaddeus Dod, and Joseph Smith encouraged many young men like John Watson to abandon their farms or their trades to embark on a new clerical career at twenty-five or even thirty. One such young man was Thomas Marquis, the fourth son of an Irish farmer, who died when Thomas was a boy. Living with his uncle, a Presbyterian elder, Thomas was apprenticed to a weaver at the age of thirteen. After receiving a crude elementary education, Marquis moved to western Pennsylvania in 1775. There his exceptionally pious demeanor attracted the attention of several members of the new Presbytery of Redstone, who urged him to prepare himself for the ministry. Finally he gave in and at thirty-six began to study with Joseph Smith and John McMillan, leaving his wife to care for the farm while he carried on his studies. He was quickly ordained and served the Presbyterian Church at Cross Creek for thirty-two years. Thomas Marquis, however, was but one of several young men whose social status—indeed whose entire life—was changed dramatically by the coming of the Princeton educators to western Pennsylvania.[72]

In central Pennsylvania Dickinson College affected the lives of young men in a similar manner. Nisbet's school enrolled an exceedingly large number of older students; of the 148 students who graduated before 1800 only twenty-two were under twenty, and eight were over twenty-five. William Stewart, for example, was a ministerial student who graduated in 1795 at the age of forty-six.[73] More typical of the older students at Dickinson was Robert Cunningham, a North Carolinian whose desire to obtain an education met the strong resistance of his farmer father. However, with the aid of his Presbyterian minister, Robert Finley, Cunningham left the farm at twenty-two and began his education in the homes of several nearby Presbyterian clergymen. He entered Dickinson in 1787 and graduated two years later at the age of twenty-nine. Ordained into the Presbyterian ministry, he then served churches in Alabama and Tennessee.[74]

The Presbyterian schools in Virginia and Tennessee likewise served as the means of social mobility for young men who entered the ministry. Hampden-Sydney, of course, served the wealthy local planters of the Southside, characteristically preparing the teenage sons of the Cabells, Carringtons, and Harrisons to enter the law school of William and Mary. But the little school also enabled young adults like Drury Lacy, James Blythe, and Moses Waddell to leave the small farms of their fathers and to prepare for a professional career in the Presbyterian ministry and in education.[75] Possibly because there was no real planter class in the valley of Virginia in the late eighteenth century, Liberty Hall served almost exclusively the small farmers of the valley and served as a vehicle whereby many of their sons entered the professional classes through the Presbyterian ministry.[76] And that Transylvania Seminary served the same function in central Kentucky is demonstrated by the career of Archibald Cameron. Born in Scotland, Cameron was brought to western Pennsylvania by his parents at an early age. He moved then to Bardstown, Kentucky, in 1781 and received his elementary education from an elder brother. Cameron was converted at nineteen by the Presbyterian cleric, Terah Templin, who then encouraged him to enter the ministry. At Templin's urging, he left his father's modest farm and entered Transylvania, graduating at about the age of twenty-four and entering the ministry.[77]

In 1797, at the end of the period here under discussion, President Smith preached a sermon "On Industry" to the assembled students at Princeton, addressing himself directly to the question of social mobility in America. The opportunities for rising, he assured his charges, were limited only by their own capacity for exertion. The president cautioned against an unseemly ambition to break out of one's place in society, but he also reminded the students that a true republican would assiduously apply himself to making the best of all available opportunities for advancement. He would not believe that one of his students would "prove so unworthy and degenerate as to be contented to drag through the inferior grades of society useless and undistinguished and to yield the palm of excellence and merit wholly to others." [78] The careers of at least the ministerial students at the Presbyterian colleges in the first years of the republic indicate that many young men took such rhetoric at face value and used those colleges as vehicles for rising in an increasingly open society.

Samuel Eusebius McCorkle had used colonial Princeton to enter the clerical profession, and in 1795 was superintending the thriving Zion-Parnassus Academy in North Carolina. That school was replicating for young men on the Carolina frontier the process that had led Reverend Mr. McCorkle to the ministry. In 1795 McCorkle preached a sermon on the "comparative Happiness and Duty of the United States of America" in which he expressed succinctly the high expectations that had come to dominate republican Presbyterianism. "As to the future our hopes can scarcely soar too high. Led on by the lights of revelation and reason what revolutions in favour of liberty may we not expect?" Revelation, reason, and revolution. For a generation after 1776 the republican Presbyterians were able to embrace each of those three R's without fear. Revelation by definition could not contradict the discoveries of reason, and vice versa. And any revolution in favor of liberty was not to be feared but warmly supported as a child of the American struggle for independence. But McCorkle spoke at the end of an era. Already some Presbyterians were deciding that indeed their hopes had soared too high, that the lights of revelation and reason could not burn simultaneously, and that the late revolution in favor of liberty had begun to devour its children.[79]

Part Three

Retrogression
1795–1820

CHAPTER VIII

The Denomination as Community

This study thus far has traced two important shifts in the American Presbyterians' sense of community. In the late colonial period the Presbyterians in general and the New Sides in particular sought community in an invigorated union of American revivalists that was part of a reformed transatlantic Christian commonwealth charged with preparing the way for the millennium. During the Revolution that international context was secularized. The glorious day dawning in the west was given important secular as well as sacred dimensions. And for twenty years after 1776 the Presbyterians were concerned primarily with establishing a Christian republic and creating within it a denominational community that could influence the development of the new nation by uniting and energizing the nation's Presbyterians. Between 1795 and 1820 a significant shift of emphasis in that development occurred. In 1789 the American Presbyterians simultaneously entered two new communities—the federal union created by the Constitution and the new denominational union organized under the General Assembly. In Jeffersonian America those Presbyterians created a denomination that functioned as one of several religious communities within the larger republican community. Gradually, between 1795 and 1820, they transferred to that denominational community the hopes they had invested in the colonial Christian commonwealth and expended on it the energies they had recently given to the creation and defense of the American republic.

"WATCHMAN, WHAT OF THE NIGHT?"

In 1804 the venerable David Rice addressed the Synod of Kentucky for what he believed would be the last time. "Father" Rice, a graduate of colonial Princeton, a founder of Hampden-Sydney, Liberty Hall, and Transylvania Seminary, and the acknowledged leader of Kentucky Presbyterianism, indulged himself in a bit of the retrospective judging that had accompanied the passing of the eighteenth century. He took for his text the arresting words of Isaiah 21: 11-12: "Watchman, what of the night? The Watchman said, the morning cometh, and also the night." For Rice the morning in the scripture verse was the birth of the American republic and the subsequent outbreak of a great revival in the west at the turn of the century, a revival that was still raging in Kentucky as he spoke. But the old pastor was troubled. In the hopeful dawn of a glorious day, already he sensed the approach of night. "A day of national prosperity is often succeeded by great national judgments and sore afflictions," he warned, "and so a time of revival in religion is frequently followed by great error and delusion." [1]

David Rice was not the only American in the first years of the nineteenth century to see encroaching darkness where they had recently hailed the "morning of the world." He, along with many other Presbyterians, reevaluated his revolutionary optimism and found it dangerously naïve. Some reassessment of the republic's origins, of course, was to be expected as circumstances changed and, particularly, as the nation's political institutions developed. The republican ideology that undergirded the move toward independence could not be expected to sustain, unaltered, a complex democratic empire of continental dimensions. Then, too, the ideals that had fueled the Revolution had to be reassessed in the light of many later developments that greatly disturbed many Americans who had supported the Revolution wholeheartedly. The radical turn taken by the French Revolution after 1794; the alarming emergence of savage political contention in the wake of the adoption of the Jay Treaty in 1795; and the rising of the whiskey rebels in western Pennsylvania—all of those political developments disturbed Presbyterians who had expected the Revolution to establish a republic in which selfish interests would be subjugated to the common good. The Presbyterians after 1795 were even more alarmed, perhaps, by the effect the Revolution had on religion. Religious fervor and attendance at services plummeted to unprecedented lows, and deism ceased to be an easily ridiculed affectation of the rich and appeared to compete openly for converts among all parts of American society, often with distressing success.[2]

For some Presbyterians alarm turned to despair as the eighteenth century waned. As they approached the passing of the century, they did not hopefully stress the dawn of a new era but instead concentrated on the gloomy portents at the expiring of the old. Charles Nisbet, for instance, had probably seemed to many to be morbidly preoccupied with death and insensitive to the promise of the age when he observed in 1793 that "We live in an expiring Century and a decaying World, and our Piety seems to be worn out by Length of Years." In the last year of the eighteenth century, though, he probably sounded less out of step when he predicted that America's iniquities, if unrepented, "must soon bring forth our Destruction." In the same year the Virginia minister Drury Lacy gloomily observed that "Dark prospects hang over the church. Infidelity is ready to overwhelm the Land—the Bible to be entirely rejected, and the Christian name to be forgotten." The Synod of Virginia, of which Lacy was a member, even believed that God was calling his most faithful servants home to spare them from the necessity of witnessing the imminent triumph of iniquity. Noting the unusually large number of ministers who died in 1799, the synod in that year appointed a day of fasting to forestall the "progress of iniquity in our land." But only two months after the synod met, God withdrew his most faithful servant, George Washington, the very personification of the Christian republican. Significantly, when the Presbyterians eulogized the American Moses, they did not bewail his death as untimely. Rather, their sermons reflected the Presbyterians' own grave doubts about the promised land, the American Canaan.[3]

Thus alarmed, the Presbyterians around the turn of the century reexamined many of the tenets of their republican faith. The most vulnerable of those revolutionary ideas in 1800 was the notion that the Americans were by nature virtuous and, consequently, "republicans by nature." At Princeton in 1795 Samuel Stanhope Smith tried to understand what had happened in the twenty years since the Presbyterians had first made that hopeful assertion. During the war for independence, he began, the "pressure of imminent danger" repressed all other passions among Americans "but love of the public." In 1776 "the public will anticipated the resolutions of the legislature—every citizen contended who should serve his country best, and who should make to it the most illustrious sacrifices." The patriots had "fondly hoped" that this was the virtue "not of the occasion, but of the people—that it was peculiar to their country—and that when she should be emancipated it would be eternal." But the Founding Fathers had not understood that the Revolution was calling forth "revolutionary virtue," that "it is the character of great and generous passions to draw every other principle to their service, and to elevate human nature to their own dignity." In the flush of Revolutionary fervor, they had forgotten "those unjust, and selfish principles which take possession of the human heart in the ordinary state of society . . . ." Thus, when the unifying force of common hopes and shared dangers disappeared, so did the Americans' extraordinary virtue. As they then began to jar and clash, David Rice observed, "the Americans did not appear to be wiser than other people." [4]

Some Americans in the last years of the eighteenth century even challenged the fundamental tenet of republican ideology—that fragile, representative republican governments depended upon the public and private virtue of their citizens for their survival. In 1779 Alexander McDougall, a Presbyterian leader of the patriot cause in New York, noted in a letter to the Presbyterian Joseph Reed in Pennsylvania that an alarming disjuncture was opening between the "Spartan" spirit of the republican constitutions being framed by the several states and the "Roman" manners that seemed to pervade all ranks of American society. [5] A way must be found to force public morals to conform to the rigorous spirit of those constitutions, McDougall warned, or they must fall. McDougall did not consider the possibility that a "Spartan" constitution could survive among "Roman" manners because he assumed, as did almost all patriots, that governments must inevitably reflect the character of the people they govern.

In the 1780s, though, some Whigs, while accepting that general proposition, insisted that republican governments could succeed even among selfish men *if* laws were written and power divided in such ways as to force public officials and citizens alike to equate their selfish ends with the public good. Noah Webster was arguing by 1785 that it was useless to hope that all men would willingly subordinate their private gain to the common good without hope of reward. But, he continued, since even self-interested men must seek the approval of the electorate before assuming public office in America, they would be forced to make the people's interest theirs.[6] And when Princeton-educated James Madison led the move to frame a federal constitution in 1787, he constructed the charter on the assumption that men, even in republican America, would always be motivated by selfishness and pride, not by virtue. Through its systems of checks and balances the federal constitution was to ensure that no one part of government gathered all power to itself. Madison in *Federalist #10* turned Montesquieu's conventional wisdom on its head and asserted, for the first time, that republics would *best* survive in a large, heterogeneous nation, whose very size and diverse population would guarantee that no one interest group or geographical section could become a permanent, tyrannical majority. To be sure, many Americans only very reluctantly accepted this defense of self-interest as the basis of a republican polity; many, with John Adams, were not prepared to abandon the belief that public and private virtue was the essence of republicanism.[7] However, by the 1790s some Presbyterians, like Pennsylvania's James Wilson, were arguing that the systems of checks and balances of the American federal and state constitutions for the first time made it "advantageous even for bad men to act for the public." That being the case, it remained only to find constitutional and legal formulas to encourage the equation of selfish ends with the public interest. In that situation the question of virtue in America became a moot issue and, in fact, ceased to inform American political discourse in the early nineteenth century.[8]

The Presbyterians' renunciation of their optimistic view of their fellow Americans appears to have been only partially the result of that "other" revolution in France. In fact, the Presbyterian clergy by and large supported the French Revolution before 1795, the years in which it was most violent.[9] Moreover, their support was sophisticated and discriminating. They were perfectly capable in those early years of deploring the violence of the French rebellion while at the same time relating it to ancient oppressions that at least explained, if they did not justify, that violence.[10] More important, the Presbyterians usually asserted that if the American Revolution had not actually kindled the fire of rebellion in France, it had certainly fanned the flame once it was ignited.[11] The clergy believed that, in supporting the French rebels, the Americans for the first time had reversed the westward course of liberty. Invigorated by her stay in America, liberty after 1783 had turned eastward for the first time and set about the task of freeing those nations which lately had banished her. And, the clergy hoped, from the French flame would blaze a "general flame" that would not be extinguished until liberty illuminated the "darkest and remotest corner of the earth." [12]

The Presbyterians before 1795 also analyzed the French Revolution in the same terms in which they had understood their own rebellion against England. For instance, the French rebels like the American amateurs triumphed over impossible odds with astonishing ease.[13] And on that triumph depended those same portentous causes lately vindicated in America—liberty, republicanism, and religion. Of course, the American clergy had to explain the disturbing French attack on religion. If the French fought in the "cause of humanity, the cause of religion, the cause of God," as had been alleged, how explain the infidelity obviously rampant in France?[14] The Presbyterians had several responses. Perhaps the tales of French infidelity were merely lies propagated by alarmed monarchical neighbors. More likely, the alleged death of true religion in France was merely the long-overdue demise of papist priestcraft. Even granting the worst, the clergy reverted to an explanation last used by the colonial Old Sides: God could use even the most wicked men—or infidel nation—to work His will in the world.[15] At any rate, before 1795 the Presbyterians reacted sensitively to the French Revolution and condemned the causes of the rebellion as well as the violence that attended it. As the Reverend James Malcomson put it, "The troubles of revolutions ought to be a lesson to mankind to prevent the necessity of them." [16]

The Presbyterian attitude toward the French Revolution changed after 1795, apparently not so much because of anything that happened in Europe as in response to alarming developments in America. After the Whiskey Rebellion and the rise of political contention and aggressive deism, the revolution in France appeared less the laudable sequel of the American rebellion and more an example of once pure republicanism now subverted by "national deism." Once the hopeful emulator of American virtue, the nation that would "plant the tree of liberty before the capitol of Rome," France now stood as a reminder of the fate of all nations that reject revelation for the ephemeral charms of reason.[17]

In the years after 1795 it became obvious that many Presbyterian ministers were much more disturbed by spiritual declension and social chaos at home than by the course of a revolution gone wrong abroad. In the decade after the Whiskey Rebellion many Presbyterians began to fear that rebellion was to be the permanent condition of the republic.

Most were not as vocally violent as Charles Nisbet, who constantly referred in the nineties to the "Sovereign People" as those "four-footed Beasts" that "will be the End of the World." A society composed of such beasts was not "properly a Nation," he asserted, but a random "Assemblage of loose and unconnected Individuals, collected from sundry Nations, having no common Faith or Bond of Union."[18] The Presbyterians' pessimistic estimate of their post-Revolutionary society was epitomized in 1796 by Samuel Stanhope Smith. Two years earlier Witherspoon had died, a venerated republican relic tending his garden at Tusculum outside Princeton while his son-in-law superintended the college. In 1796 Ashbel Green, one of Witherspoon's students and tutors, suggested that his mentor's works be collected and published in a memorial volume. Smith had grave reservations. He worried that the works of the virtuous old revolutionary would find no market in the society that had succeeded the Revolution he had helped make. In that world, Smith declared, religion and morals have been effectively supplanted "by politics, infidelity, and frivolous entertainment."[19] Green disagreed, though, and Smith reluctantly approved the publication. The Witherspoon memorial volumes appeared in 1802. And to Smith's considerable surprise, by the time they appeared there was a great demand for Witherspoon's works. For they appeared in 1802 in a world not marked by "politics, infidelity, and frivolous entertainment," but by an astonishing revival of religion, the Second Great Awakening.

The nineteenth-century revival, even more than its colonial predecessor, appeared as a "surprising work of God" in the eyes of Christian America.[20] It seemed, amazingly, to reverse the religious decline of the 1790s by generating on an unprecedented scale evangelical energy both on the rural frontier of the Ohio River valley and on the urban frontier of the industrializing eastern cities. In the west the revival was characterized by extraordinary camp meetings that produced religious fervor and ecstasy without example in American history. That energy, in turn, was harnessed by the vigorous denominational and then inter-denominational agencies that were the most significant product of the revival's eastern phase. The wedding of these interrelated revivals produced an evangelical Protestant empire that as early as 1820 had vanquished the fashionable deism of the late eighteenth century and had shaped for the new nation an evangelical orthodoxy which, quite simply, served as the unofficially established religion of the American republic.[21]

But the Awakening began inconspicuously enough. In the late 1780s, in the midst of the post-Revolutionary religious depression, a small band of Presbyterian students at Hampden-Sydney became concerned for the condition of their souls and began to meet with their teachers for prayer and Bible study. A local revival soon broke out in Prince Edward County, which was instantly communicated across the Blue Ridge to Liberty Hall. That revival soon burned itself out, but not before it had touched the lives of several young Presbyterian ministers who shortly thereafter left Virginia to toil on the Kentucky frontier. Meanwhile, in Connecticut in 1795 the young Timothy Dwight succeeded Ezra Stiles as the president of Yale College. In the last years of the eighteenth century, in Connecticut and on the frontier, Dwight and the young Presbyterian evangelists ignited two different revivals of religion. At Yale, Dwight determined to check what he perceived as French infidelity among the undergraduates and began to issue to them godly devotional literature to serve as the antidote to atheism and free thought. At the same time he encouraged interested young men to organize themselves into holy bands to support virtue and repress vice in Connecticut. The result, by 1800, was a carefully controlled revival of religion at Yale that was concerned primarily to influence public and private moral behavior in the land of steady habits.[22] On the western frontier young Presbyterian evangelicals cooperated with Baptist and Methodist preachers in perfecting techniques of mass evangelism that would thereafter dominate American revivalism.[23]

The Presbyterian hierarchy reacted first to the more spectacular western revival. Aware of the Presbyterian involvement in the frontier awakening, the General Assembly in 1801 remarked on the "very extraordinary manner" in which the Lord was manifesting himself in Kentucky and Tennessee. The Assembly did not criticize the extraordinary dimensions of the revival but instead rejoiced that "infidelity does not assume that bold and threatening aspect which it did for some years past." The Presbytery of New Brunswick remarked on the "unexampled rapidity" with which the "American Zion" was expanding in the revival's wake, while from the center of the religious agitation the Synod of Kentucky reported that the Lord had "made the wilderness a fruitful field," and that "the prospects of vital religion in America, are more favorable and encouraging, than at any period within the last forty years." Then, in 1804, the Assembly announced that the great revival had begun to move northward. In the synods of New York, New Jersey, and Albany, "Trophies are continually raised to the grace of the

Redeemer." The western revival seemed to carry all before it and to herald an unanticipated but welcomed reversal of the spiritual declension threatening all of America; consequently it was embraced both officially and unofficially by American Presbyterianism in its first days as the hopeful dawn of a new century.[24]

There was a note of apprehension, though, even in the Presbyterians' first reaction to the frontier revival. As the news spread eastward that the west was being secured for Christ, disturbed Presbyterians heard stories that caused them to worry about the means by which that laudable end was being won. Tales circulated of Baptist, Methodist, and even Presbyterian ministers encouraging a cacophony of jumping, barking, fainting, and jerking in meetings that sometimes turned into sexual as well as emotional orgies. John Montgomery, safe in 1801 in the settled comfort of the older frontier of Carlisle, Pennsylvania, passed on to Benjamin Rush the extraordinary stories he had heard about the religious excesses on the new frontier of Bourbon County, Kentucky. Montgomery of course welcomed the revival, especially since it occurred on the vulnerable fringe of settlement. Still, he did not know what to make of it. In 1801 Montgomery was willing to wait on the Lord, who had "his own ways of Conducting those things" that sometimes appeared mysterious to mortals, who must "waite and hope for the Best." Rush agreed. He too had heard astonishing stories, but from North Carolina. Rush hoped that the "novelty of the Scenes which are described," would not discredit them. God, for His own reasons, had chosen to move "in a manner unprecedented in former ages." Had not the patriots just argued that a nation could be born in a day? Surely, Rush believed, a sinner might be as instantly transformed, even if that transformation was accompanied by extraordinary physical manifestations.[25]

The "wait-and-see" attitude of Montgomery and Rush did not long characterize official Presbyterian reaction to the great western revival. By 1802 Samuel Miller, a powerful Presbyterian minister in New York City, while he still thanked the Lord "for so rich a shower of his grace," now found the "very singular" occurrences on the frontier to be suspicious to "those who have been accustomed only to the still, small voice of the gospel." Still, small voices were heard with difficulty in a Kentucky camp meeting, and in 1803 the Synod of Kentucky ominously noted that "some who once were under great awakenings, and appeared to bid fair for the kingdom of heaven, have since turned aside to the paths of the destroyer." In the next year the General Assembly felt compelled to condemn, for the first time, "antic gestures, ridiculous contortions . . . , and apparent levity" that accompanied the revival, while at the same time the Lexington Presbytery ordered its members to prevent in their churches "all extraordinary bodily exercises which appear voluntary and ostentatious." By 1805 the General Assembly clearly had decided officially that the revival's excesses threatened to outweigh any benefits it might bring. "God is a God of order, and not of confusion," the body asserted in that year, finding a firm tone it would not lose again while discussing the revival. The Assembly warned that "bodily affections have been of such a nature, and proceeded to such lengths, as greatly tended to impede the progress and to tarnish the glory of what, in its first stages, was so highly promising." [26] Henceforth the hierarchy would reserve its approbation for the orderly revivals of religion of the kind reported by the Synod of North Carolina in 1821. They were "carried on, without noise or tumult, during public worship." "Everything like enthusiasm was discouraged" in the Carolina revivals of the 1820s, where the movement of the Spirit was acceptable because it was "deep, and often extensive; but yet a still solemnity seemed to prevail." [27]

The "bodily exercises" of the frontier revival were troublesome enough for the hierarchy. The jerks, barks, and contortions were so much more alarming than the few moans that had disturbed Jonathan Edwards and other colonial Presbyterians, and they seemed completely to remove the afflicted person from any external or even internal control. But for all of that, the Presbyterians were probably more alarmed by the theology being preached on the frontier than by the "antics" that sometimes accompanied the revival. The hierarchy was distressed to hear that Baptists, Methodists, and even some Presbyterians were preaching the "universalist" doctrine that Christ died for all men, who then might either accept or reject the gift of grace. Those ideas had not always alarmed the hierarchy. As late as 1799 the Synod of the Carolinas had overruled the Abingdon Presbytery's censure of one John Bowman for preaching "universalism" and "self-sufficiency." The synod commended the lower body's vigilance in defending the truths of the gospel but reminded the zealots that it was "extremely difficult if not altogether impracticable" to preach the "freeness and fulness of the Gospel" to large crowds of sinners without saying some things that might be construed "to be directly contrary to our confession and catechism." The synod therefore urged the presbytery to regard both "truth and charity; and in so doing we shall all fulfill the law of our common Lord." [28]

That tolerance did not survive the passing of the eighteenth century. In the wake of the revival the hierarchy regularly condemned all "universalist" ideas and rejected the revivalists' contention that an "inner light" enabled the Christian to interpret the Bible as validly as did the institutional churches through their creeds. The doctrine of the inner light surely would disintegrate the bonds of society, the hierarchy warned. From Kentucky, David Rice insisted that no man could make the "exercises" of his own mind a "new or an additional revelation from heaven." Then, in 1807, the General Assembly attributed to the preaching of free will the "increasing dereliction of truth" on the frontier, which "pervades all classes of society." The doctrine inevitably led to the prevalence of unbelief, to a "state of mind which is enmity against God," which "reproaches his truth," and which condemns "the amiable glories of redeeming love." [29] In short, it threatened all order in ecclesiastical and civil society.

THE "NATURAL AND SALUTARY COLLISIONS OF PARTIES"

The Second Great Awakening produced the second great schism in American Presbyterianism. On the Kentucky frontier the Presbyterians discovered that, as in the colonial revival, disputes over theology became disagreements over the nature of social unions—over the location of authority in those unions, over the rights of majorities and minorities, over the circumstances in which social unions might be legitimately dissolved. The frontier schism, in addition, dramatically demonstrated that the revolutionary era separating the two Awakenings had profoundly affected the Presbyterian attitude toward social conflict in general and toward denominational competition in particular. Alike in many respects, the colonial schism and the later division on the frontier were quite different in their resolution.

Whereas the colonial division eventually had been healed, the frontier schism produced three permanent divisions within the American Presbyterian Church. Some Presbyterians joined the "christian fellowship" of Barton W. Stone and Richard McNemar. Others followed the men of the Cumberland Presbytery into a separate Cumberland Presbyterian Church. And still others succumbed to the radical pietism of the Shaker movement. All of these groups were part of a larger development on the southern and western frontier that, in general, emphasized an Arminian theology over the "fatalism" of Calvinism and that sought to substitute "christian unity" for the sharp sectarian divisions that often marked frontier Protestantism. Within Methodism this development, first in Virginia and in North Carolina and then in Kentucky, produced the Republican Methodist Church of Reverend James O'Kelly. And among Baptists it sharpened already clear divisions between the more conservative Regular Baptists of the coastal regions and the revivalistically inclined Separate Baptists of the backcountry.[30]

In the Presbyterian instance, the frontier schism consisted of two parallel divisions that occurred within the new Synod of Kentucky between 1802 and 1809. The first centered around Cane Ridge and was dominated by Barton W. Stone and Richard McNemar. Stone, a son of the Virginia frontier, had been educated at David Caldwell's Presbyterian Academy in North Carolina, where he was converted by the Presbyterian revivalist James McGready. Stone then itinerated in North Carolina and Tennessee before accepting appointment from the Transylvania Presbytery to the Cane Ridge Church in Kentucky. By the time he settled in Kentucky, Barton Stone had met and been influenced by a wide range of Presbyterian, Methodist, and Baptist clerics with whom he shared a growing dissatisfaction with the theological and ecclesiological bases of frontier Protestantism.[31]

One of those he met was Richard McNemar, a young Scotch-Irish Presbyterian with no known ties to the Presbyterian academies of his native western Pennsylvania.[32] Both Stone and McNemar found themselves preaching at the controversial camp meeting at Cane Ridge in August of 1801. By November of that year, McNemar was summoned by the Washington Presbytery to answer charges that, in that meeting, he had preached Arminian principles and denigrated the importance of church discipline. McNemar refused to appear and even renounced the presbytery's jurisdiction over him. In the following year the presbytery again examined McNemar's teachings, found them "dangerous to the souls of men, and hostile to the interests of all true religion," and submitted its case against the revivalist to the newly created Synod of Kentucky.[33] In its first significant decision the synod moved quickly to protect orthodoxy on the vulnerable frontier by expelling the party that had gathered around McNemar and Stone. The evangelicals, or "New Lights" as they were called, first organized themselves into the Presbytery of Springfield and in 1804 issued *An Apology for Renouncing the Jurisdiction of the Synod of Kentucky*. Within a few months, though, McNemar and Stone had decided that the existence of the presbytery savored itself of a "party spirit" that threatened the Christian unity that was their ultimate goal. Accordingly, the presbytery issued a "Last Will and Testament" that spelled out the evangelicals' objections to sectarian distinctions among the people of God, and then dissolved itself. Having renounced the unifying bonds of the presbytery, the evangelicals then drifted apart.[34] Some followed McNemar into the Shaker fold; others joined with Stone in creating the "christian fellowship" that coalesced with the followers of Alexander Campbell in the 1820s to create the Disciples of Christ.[35]

This "New Light" schism was followed almost immediately by the division that created the Cumberland Presbyterian Church. That schism centered in the Cumberland region of Kentucky and was dominated at first by the Reverend James McGready, a young evangel who had studied with John McMillan in his native western Pennsylvania and who had converted Barton Stone at David Caldwell's North Carolina academy. The Cumberland evangelicals were disturbed by their inability to provide an adequate number of ministers to convert the frontier, and they ran afoul of the Presbyterian hierarchy in the first years of the revival when they attempted to license uneducated but pious "exhorters" to spread the gospel. The Synod of Kentucky, which had just defended orthodoxy by expelling the New Lights, now moved quickly to discipline the men from Cumberland. In doing so, the synod initiated a schism over the related issues of congregational and presbyterial autonomy, the nature of the conversion experience, and the educational requirements of the ministry. In 1806 the synod expelled the recalcitrant Cumberland men, who by 1813 organized an independent Cumberland Synod and, by the 1820s, an independent Cumberland Presbyterian Church.[36]

In both the New Light and the Cumberland schisms the synod and the dissidents proceeded in ways that pointedly demonstrate the differences between the colonial schism and the later controversies on the western frontier. For instance, when complaints were lodged with the Washington Presbytery about McNemar's theology, the aggrieved Presbyterians who made the complaints expected that the charges would work their way through the ecclesiastical hierarchy that had already been established on the frontier. They expected McNemar to be tried by the Presbytery of Washington and then by the synod and even by the General Assembly if necessary. They were very much surprised, then, when McNemar refused even to appear before the constituent bodies of the hierarchy and, instead, organized his own presbytery. At a parallel stage in the first Great Awakening, the New Sides too had formed a synod and had claimed to be as thoroughly Presbyterian as the Old Side synod. Then, within five years, the leaders of both sides had begun to seek ways to end the schism for the sake of Christian unity. On the frontier, though, the synod— almost gratefully—allowed the erring brothers to go in peace. And the erring brothers went, not to establish a parallel synod but to establish two entirely new, competitive denominations. Clearly, while the colonial Presbyterians only tentatively defended the legitimacy of conflict and then hastily retreated from that defense, on the frontier both sides from the beginning found ways to stress the benefits of competition and conflict. The Synod of Kentucky defended its actions on the basis of the necessity for that uniformity and orthodoxy within the Presbyterian denomination that would enable it to compete with other denominations in the market place of faiths.

Basic to the issue of uniformity and orthodoxy was the dual nature of the Presbyterian creed, the Westminster Confession of Faith. The creed was at the same time a statement of personal conviction and the bond that united the Presbyterian Church. The revivalists seem to have emphasized the first function; the hierarchy, the second. When called before presbytery or synod the New Lights and the Cumberland dissidents disdained any hierarchical effort to bind their conscience. The New Lights, for instance, in 1803 protested to the synod that they were not allowed the privilege of interpreting scripture but were bound "to such explanations of the word of God as preclude all further enquiry after truth." [37] The synod replied that it only intended "to establish the minds of sincere enquirers on the firm basis of truth." And truth for the synod was contained in the Westminster Confession and must be acknowledged by all who ministered in the name of the church.[38] The synod insisted that it had no desire to prevent its members from interpreting the Bible. It simply reserved the right to examine those interpretations. If, on examination, its members were found to be "honest enquirers after truth," the synod would gladly acquit them with honor and repair any reputations that might have been damaged by the synodical trial. If, on the other hand, that examination revealed heretical views among its members, the synod would have no alternative but to follow the biblical injunction to cast the heretics out.[39]

The synod recognized the severity of that injunction but thought it imperative to establish and protect the denomination's unity. And that bond of union was the denomination's confession of faith, its creed. Embattled, the Synod of Kentucky declared that it was not ashamed of adhering to a creed; rather, its members proudly confessed their creed openly, as "children of light." Once agreed upon, that creed could not be altered. Changes would enable infidels to charge that there was no revealed truth because the people of God kept changing their view of it. Also, alterations might confuse weak believers and even accustom them to frequent changes, thereby leading to "lasting uneasiness, constant altercations, and, finally to the adoption of errors." [40] When dealing with the Cumberland dissidents in 1812, even the General Assembly refused to alter any part of the Confession because the creed was the bond that united the entire church; consequently, no individual *or* judicatory— not even the Assembly—could lawfully alter it in any way. And, the Assembly asked, if changes were made for one part of a union, would not other parts of that union demand further alterations, and where would strength and purpose be then? [41]

Unquestioned acceptance of a denomination's unifying creed seemed particularly crucial to the hierarchy in a society in which denominations were forced to compete with each other for members. In the denominational marketplace it seemed only fair to provide prospective members with a clear statement of the denomination's tenets. Those hopeful communicants would be asked to enter into "tender and endearing bonds" with the Presbyterians, and the Synod of Kentucky did not believe that its future members should be left "at a loss to know whether we believe or disbelieve what they esteem the essential doctrines of christianity . . . ." [42] And, the General Assembly insisted in 1812, since the Presbyterian union was an entirely voluntary one, since no one was forced to adopt its creed, no minority could ever ask the majority to alter the Confession for their scruples: "there is no oppression exercised over any by our adherence to our own principles." Indeed, the contrary was true. The "intolerance of a few over the many" must produce "ruinous effects." [43]

On the western frontier in the early nineteenth century, the Presbyterian hierarchy accepted some implications of their arguments which their colonial forebears had, ultimately, rejected. When insisting upon a confession of faith to unify and distinguish American Presbyterians, the synod and General Assembly did not feel obliged to embrace the catholicity that had remained at least the theoretical ideal of both Old and New Sides in the colonial period. Thus the Presbytery of West Tennessee in 1812 could denounce that "universal Catholicism which embraces all professions, without respect to order or truth," and which is no better than the infidelity that "arraigns the word of God." [44] Nor was the General Assembly willing—as the colonial Presbyterians had been—to "relinquish principles for the sake of peace." To do so was "too dear a sacrifice." For in the final analysis, the Assembly assured the world, the Cumberland men left the Presbyterian union because *they* felt they had to: they "went out from us, because they were not of us." And, if they should ever wish to reconsider and rejoin the true Presbyterian Church, "They know the terms." [45]

Unlike the colonial Presbyterians, the frontier hierarchy obviously could conceive of, and was ready to tolerate, the permanent existence of erring Presbyterians outside its jurisdiction and concern. In both the New Light and the Cumberland schisms the hierarchy was quite willing to tolerate and even to compete with the dissidents if only they would admit they were no longer true Presbyterians, leave the denomination, and clearly announce their beliefs to the world. In the Cumberland dispute the Presbytery of West Tennessee seemed at times to be taunting the dissidents, badgering them into giving up the name "Presbyterian." "If the doctrines and discipline of our church were really so obnoxious to you as to produce a separation, why would you still desire to retain the name of Presbyterians—and hold communion with our body?" It was clear to the hierarchy that the Cumberland men called themselves Presbyterians merely to "gain currency" in their proselytizing even though "in their doctrines & modes of worship, they are nearly with the Methodists." [46] In 1820 the Virginia Synod stated explicitly what the Kentucky Synod had hinted at. When the Abingdon Presbytery complained to the synod that some members of the presbytery were preaching heterodox views, the synod replied that, while members of the Presbyterian union, ministers must uniformly and enthusiastically preach its published doctrines. When they could no longer do so in good conscience, they should be encouraged to leave that fellowship and declare their own creed. Once the dissidents entered the denominational market place as the members of another denomination or the creators of a new one, the Presbyterians would tolerate them—and compete with them—as they did with all other denominations. The synod, of course, renounced controversy for its own sake. But, it asked, "was it not an apostle who said contend earnestly for the faith once delivered to the saints?" [47]

All of the discussion about creeds and confessions might suggest that the frontier schisms were the product of theological disagreements. Certainly the revivalists never tired of denouncing Calvinistic "fatalism." Moreover, the hierarchy was obliged to be always on the defensive, at times insisting that the doctrine of election did not mean simple "blind fate," and at other times retreating into the warning that the doctrine is "a high Mystery which should be handled with special prudence and care."[48] The most careful student of the frontier divisions believes that the New Lights and the Cumberland men were anathema to the hierarchy because they preached free will while subscribing to a creed that was based on the doctrine of election.[49] It is possible, though, that the dissidents were expelled not for teaching heresy but for refusing to be *tried* for teaching heresy. The difference is a crucial one.

The Presbyterian opponents of the revival insisted that by refusing to appear before the various judicatories of the hierarchy, the revivalists had forfeited their membership in the denomination that had delegated its authority to those judicatories. The hierarchy simply did not know what to do with men who regularly asserted that they "had no tho't of appealing to any earthly tribunal."[50] The Presbyterian hierarchy, even on the frontier, was a carefully graduated union of "earthly tribunals" that were to be appealed to in prescribed ways. The Synod of Kentucky was constantly reprimanding the dissidents for failing to carry out proceedings in "the institutional way," for appealing irregularly to the General Assembly while ignoring the synod, or for approaching the synod without first answering the charges of local presbyteries.[51]

At a time when authority of all sort seemed on the defensive in all places, the maintenance of authority on the vulnerable American frontier was the crucial issue for the Presbyterian hierarchy. Consequently the frontier hierarchy in the early nineteenth century defended ecclesiastical authority in terms that even the colonial Old Sides had avoided. For example, the Synod of Kentucky in 1802 insisted that it must be obeyed simply because it acted as the surrogate of God. Sending the revivalists scurrying to the history of the Reformation for rebuttal, the synod declared that "whatever the ambassadors of Christ or rulers of his church, do in his name, agreeably to his word, is to all intents and purposes as valid as if he had done it in his own person." The assertion was carefully hedged—all things must be done in ways that conform to scripture. But that qualification clearly was lost on the revivalists, who instead caught the unmistakable central message of the hierarchy's claim: to denounce the authority of the Synod of Kentucky was, ultimately, to despise the authority of Christ.[52]

Astonished at the hierarchy's extravagant defense of authority, the frontier revivalists attacked it with an amalgam of the ideas of the colonial New Sides and the natural-rights ideas that had animated the Revolution. Harking back to both the colonial schism and the war for independence, the Springfield Presbytery in 1804 insisted that all authority be divided and limited. No authority—not that of the synod, not that of any government—was absolute. If it was, then the Revolution had been fought and won for naught. If there was a "sovereignty in government, unlawful to pry into," the presbytery warned, then men must be content to "reason not but resign." This they were unwilling to do. Moreover, it was the "unalienable right of every moral agent to withdraw from any society, when he thinks the rights of conscience are invaded." And, if the Synod of Kentucky "deprives its subjects of this privilege," it "must be tyrannical." [53]

When the colonial New Sides renounced the authority of the Synod of Philadelphia, they too had invoked the right of conscience and had branded as tyrannous any abridgment of that right. At all times, though, the New Sides had considered the Presbyterian Church in America an organic union and had worried over the painful necessity of rending the fabric of that unit. At no time did they describe the denomination as a voluntary association that they could enter and leave at will. The Kentucky revivalists, though, used just those terms. The authority of any society over an individual, they asserted, was "in consequence of a voluntary compact tacitly or explicitly made." That compact bound the individual to the society and put him under its laws. But it remained a voluntary agreement and, for that reason, might be dissolved "at any time, by the voluntary act of the individual" or of the society itself.[54]

Richard McNemar insisted that the synod's authority over the dissidents had ended when the synod attempted to examine the doctrines of the revivalists and then to expel them on the basis of that examination. He asserted the right of all Christians to interpret the Bible "according to their own proper sense" because the will of God and scriptural truth was "made manifest to each individual who honestly sought after it, by an inward light, which shone into the heart." The promptings of the inner light were much more trustworthy than creeds that were, after all, only the opinions of men temporarily in positions of hierarchical authority. The revivalists, therefore, refused to appear before synod or presbytery "so long as human opinions were esteemed the standard of orthodoxy." [55]

From that defense of the unfettered conscience the revivalists moved easily to denounce the creeds the hierarchy deemed crucial to denominational survival in America. McNemar announced for his followers that they would be bound only by the Bible and asserted that all "systems" were "detrimental to the life and power of religion." [56] He, Stone, and other revivalists assured the synod in 1804 that they did not "desire to separate from your communion, or exclude you from ours." They wished only to "bear, & forbear, in matters of human order, or opinion and unite our joint supplications with yours for the increasing effusions of that divine Spirit which is the bond of peace . . . ." [57] Then, to the General Assembly, the Kentucky dissidents in 1805 declared that "We feel ourselves citizens of the world: God our common father: all men our brethren by nature, and all christians our brethren in Christ." This principle of *"universal love to christians,"* they continued, "gains ground in our hearts, in proportion as we get clear of particular attachments to party." [58] And the revivalists were convinced that they alone in America abhorred party strife. They were appalled as the American Christians split into "a thousand little kingdoms"; were alarmed as a "great Christian empire" proved to be full of worms, "biting and devouring one another, each pursuing a distinct cause to which he presumes all others must finally give way," each sect hoping to "reduce the whole commonwealth" to its laws and government, each ready to make the "grand mistake" of converting the Bible into a "civil law-book." [59]

The frontier revivalists, then, appeared to abhor party strife and denominational competition. They insisted that they left the synod under coercion, not from choice, and loudly disclaimed any intention of establishing a party. [60] And they formed the nucleus of a significant movement in American history that was characterized by an overriding emphasis on Christian unity. But, in several significant ways, those frontier "christians" weakened the idea of Christian unity as surely as did the synod's defense of competition and its insistence on denominational orthodoxy and uniformity. From outside the denomination the revivalists insisted that "merely forming a separate association, is not schism" so long as that association was not intended "to dissolve the union and communion of the church." They referred, of course, to the *universal* church, not to the particular denomination of American Presbyterians. But it seemed to the revivalists that the synod equated the two, a separation from the one becoming automatically a secession from the other. To the dissidents, the synod appeared to believe that "they are the only church on earth." In point of fact, the Kentucky Synod probably expelled the revivalists precisely because it realized that the Presbyterian Church was *not* the only church on earth. Having accepted that disturbing but undeniable fact, the synod purged its membership of all elements that would prevent it from competing effectively with other religious groups on the frontier. And the dissidents' protests at their expulsion diverted attention from their own schismatic acts and their practical endorsement of denominational competition. They insisted, in their defense, that they had simply renounced the tyrannical jurisdiction of the Synod of Kentucky. They had *not* seceded from the larger, immaterial body that was the one true church.[61]

The revivalists probably further weakened the idea of Christian unity by denigrating the significance of creedal statements as bonds of spiritual union. McNemar, for instance, confidently assured his readers that "all who received the true light of the spirit in the inner man, and faithfully followed it, would naturally see eye to eye," that they would then "understand the things of the spirit alike, without any written tenet or learned expositor." The inner light thus understood was no threat to order because all honest inquirers would receive the same impressions from that inner illumination. No belief could have been further removed from the synod's insistence on creedal subscriptions, but both beliefs had the same practical effect in the end. They both justified schism and the formation of associations of Christians that would think and function as one.[62]

Finally, the revivalists attacked the use of creeds—and justified their own schism—by insisting that true social union could be affected only by spiritual forces. In doing so, they added a new dimension to the ancient analogy between society and the human body. They insisted that the human body was united by organic rather than mechanical bonds; it required nothing to cause the parts to act in concert beyond "that spirit which animates the whole." Mankind, likewise, is not "bound together like the parts of a machine, nor put in motion by external force"; rather, men "must be influenced by motive, and that motive must be in the heart." By analogy, the Presbytery of Springfield reasoned, the church was bound not by creedal subscriptions but by the spirit of Jesus Christ. That being the case, the presbytery concluded, the church's union would survive external differences among its parts.[63]

Thus the Second Great Awakening produced the second great division in the history of the American Presbyterian Church, a schism that was different in significant ways from the Great Schism that followed the colonial revival. That first schism was much more acrimonious than the frontier division. It had enlisted the passions of the entire leadership of the denomination and inaugurated a long-lived pamphlet war. The frontier schism did neither of these things, despite the fact that the Second Great Awakening was as traumatic and widespread as was the colonial revival. The new hierarchical machinery was in part responsible for the difference. While the embryonic hierarchy in the colonial period had probably prolonged the Great Schism by becoming first a weapon and then a prize for which both sides contended, the more intricate and widespread machinery at the turn of the century served to contain the repercussions of the frontier schism, even though it could not prosecute the schismatics.

But the colonial schism ended with reunion and the frontier division did not. Even though it was highly acrimonious, the Great Schism was healing within a decade, and the Presbyterians entered the Revolutionary period a united denomination. The less acrimonious frontier division, though, proved permanent, resulting in the creation of two new denominations. No more dramatic evidence could be found that in the last half of the eighteenth century the Presbyterians gradually had accepted social conflict in general and denominational competition in particular. Whereas the Old and New Sides could not accept the anomaly of two distinct and competing Presbyterian synods in America, the Synod of Kentucky allowed the revivalists to go in peace simply because the church—and society—were no longer viewed as organic units animated by a common good to which all selfish interests must be subordinated. Rather, society was seen as a collection of interest groups in which the Presbyterian Church had to compete for members and power. In order to compete effectively, the denomination had to be united and firmly orthodox. Those elements that threatened the union were summarily expelled, and they did not return. Rather, they established other unified, orthodox denominational communities to compete in the denominational market place of the young republic. Clearly, Presbyterians at the end of the Revolutionary period had begun to accept that competition as legitimate. With New York City's Samuel Miller they could speak approvingly of "the natural and salutary collisions of parties," forgetting a very recent past in which all parties of any kind had been anathematized. With Samuel Stanhope Smith at Princeton they could at the turn of the century assert as a settled conviction what the colonial Presbyterians had only gingerly suggested for a moment: "a fair and generous competition among the different denominations of christians, while it does not extinguish their mutual charity, promotes an emulation that will have a beneficial influence on the public morals." Some Reformed Christians, like John Mitchell Mason of the Associate Reformed Church, were even willing now to accept the once-despised idea that truth inevitably would emerge from the competition of the nation's denominations: "Religious controversy, properly conducted, has often proved highly beneficial to the interests of truth." [64]

THE REPUBLICAN AS *VISIBLE* CHRISTIAN

Even in the early nineteenth century, though, the Presbyterians were uneasy competitors—they did not abandon lightly an organicism that had been normative in western thought for at least a millennium. We have already noted the reluctance with which the colonial Presbyterians accepted, even briefly, the existence of competing Presbyterian synods. And we have seen the hesitancy with which some Presbyterians of the Revolutionary era embraced a complete separation of church and state with its corollary of competitive denominations. Now, in Jeffersonian America, the Presbyterians had to come to terms with religious voluntarism at a time when voices from the highest and lowest levels of American society condemned as aristocratic meddling and "priestcraft" any effort by the churches to influence the development of the republic. The Presbyterian efforts to adjust to that voluntarism took the form of two simultaneous campaigns, each of which was necessary before they would accept as a final, positive good the denominational competition endemic to voluntarism. First, the Presbyterians sought a way to ensure—without arousing animosity—that the republic and its citizens were visibly Christian. Then, the Presbyterians were determined to create a denominational community through which to influence their society and in which to find the identity and community that the republic had failed to provide.

That former campaign is part of one of the most interesting and controversial chapters in American religious history. Their contemporaries and their historians have disagreed over the means and the ends of the Congregational and Presbyterian clergy as they sought to ensure the Christian nature of the American republic in the first decades of the nineteenth century. They were often denounced as "jesuitical" by those contemporaries who deftly marked the clergy's uneasiness with the ecclesiastical arrangements necessitated by the end of established religion in America. And many historians of the "benevolent empire" erected by the clergy between 1800 and 1830 have often described a "malevolent empire" erected by a displaced clerical elite trying to regain, through a massive reform movement, control of a society that would no longer tolerate the formal arrangements whereby churchmen heretofore had influenced society in America. Of late, though, historians of the righteous reformers have been kinder. They have noted that, by and large, the clergy in Jeffersonian America did, of necessity, accept the liberalizing effects of the "revolutionary settlement" in religion, and those historians have been intrigued by the various ways in which clergymen made peace with their new world. Most significantly, they have focused on the "Christian republicanism" of the clergy and have found it both a complex and a creative effort to address the many problems created by the revolutionary settlement in religion.[65]

Although the Presbyterian Church had been established in several European countries, it had been officially favored by no government in the New World and could therefore accept the end of establishment more easily than, say, the New England Congregationalists who in 1800 enjoyed a much diminished but nonetheless real preferment in both Connecticut and Massachusetts. By 1795 the Presbyterians with virtual unanimity applauded the benefits of the separation of church and state as vigorously as they once had extolled the virtues of an "unlimited toleration." Samuel Stanhope Smith in that year endorsed the idea of which the laymen of the Hanover Presbytery had been forced to remind their pastors during the general assessment controversy in Virginia: religion flourished best where it was free of the state and was supported by the voluntary contributions of the faithful. In America, Smith bragged, religion "is left to propagate itself by its native evidence and beauty" and was better off for it. He was glad to see religion stripped "of those meretricious charms that, under the splendor of an establishment, intoxicate the senses . . . ." Smith's Presbytery of New Brunswick went even further. It was certain that the free churches of republican America closely approximated the condition of the first-century church, for none of them demanded or received "any civil protection, but depends . . . on the voluntary bounty of its disciples." And the Synod of Virginia in 1814 rejoiced that "Happily for us, while the State is bound to protect all Christians in the exercises of religious worship, she is not particularly connected with any church." [66]

But for all their acceptance of disestablishment, the Presbyterians did not believe that the church and government could be completely divorced if the republic was to survive. They could not subscribe to the radical separatism of the Baptists John Leland and Isaac Backus, who insisted that the coercive, contaminating state must not be allowed to interfere with the people of God; nor could they accept the ideas of Jefferson and Madison, who, in essence, wished to protect the state and its citizens from the grasping ambitions of the "priests" and their tyrannous churches.[67] Instead, the Presbyterians sought ways in which free men, organized into voluntary denominations, could influence the basic nature of their society without appearing to threaten the liberties of their fellow Americans.

It was an impossible task. Even the most simple efforts proved controversial. The Presbyterians believed, for instance, that at the very least the ceremonial occasions of the new government should be visibly Christian; consequently, the hierarchy insisted that chaplains be appointed to invoke God's blessings on both houses of Congress. At the same time, they suggested that Protestant chaplains be appointed to serve each of the republic's armed services. The chaplains, of course, would teach only the "essentials" of Christianity, which remained purposely vague. Madison, though, opposed the appointment of chaplains, and he did so in ways that indicate he had learned a great deal from his New Side education at colonial Princeton and that he had retained more of it than had many Presbyterians. Writing after the chaplains had been appointed, James Madison suggested, in good New Side fashion, that the experiment "be tried by its fruits." Are not "the daily devotions conducted by these legal Ecclesiastics," he asked, "already degenerating into a scanty attendance, and a tiresome formality?" He also condemned the appointments as a "palpable violation of the constitutional rights" of, say, Catholics, who certainly would never hear a familiar prayer in either camp or Congress. If the republic's legislators were not by nature pious, Madison asserted, the perfunctory prayers of a hired cleric were not going to make them so. And, as for the armed services, Madison reminded his readers that righteous fervor could not be induced by hirelings but, instead, is "more likely to flow from the labours of a spontaneous zeal."[68]

The Presbyterians also had difficulties when they encouraged the Virginians who monopolized the presidency to proclaim ceremonial days of fast and thanksgiving, a practice of New England origin. The Anglican Washington cooperated—to a point. He pleased the Presbyterians by writing his own fast-day proclamations, but he then withstood all entreaties to make a public, personal commitment to Christianity. New

Englander John Adams arranged with the Congressional chaplains or with leading clerics to compose his fast-day proclamations—in 1799, for instance, the Presbyterian Ashbel Green was drafted for that congenial task.[69] The administrations of Thomas Jefferson, though, were a great trial for those Presbyterians who sought a president to lead the nation in abasement before God. After several failures by others, the intrepid Samuel Miller in 1808 implored the Virginian to declare a national day of fasting and mourning. As he watched his foreign policy disintegrate in the final year of his presidency, Jefferson may indeed have felt the need for divine assistance, but the deist president was not likely to seek it in Samuel Miller's stern God. Rather, Jefferson graciously replied that he could not comply for several important constitutional reasons. Those reasons indicate that Jefferson understood perfectly the informal relationship between government and religion desired by his old Presbyterian foes. He could not recommend a fast day, he said, without assuming an "unconstitutional authority over religious exercises." Miller had suggested that Jefferson merely recommend a day of humiliation, of course without any sort of sanctions. Jefferson still declined, asserting, correctly no doubt, that the citizen who refused to follow the recommendation would still encounter "some sort of proscription" in public opinion. And to *enjoin* fasting and praying was an "act of discipline" totally abhorrent to the president.[70]

It was abhorrent to his successor, too, but Madison did revert to the tradition of Adams and Washington, possibly in order to enlist the Deity, and presumably his Federalist followers in New England, in the War of 1812. Later, though, Madison was critical of fast days, and his criticism is important because it was made by other critics, some of whom were Presbyterian. Fast days, Madison suggested, "seem to imply and certainly nourish the erroneous idea of a *national* religion." Madison did not object to the "imposing idea" of a "union of all to form one nation under one Govt in acts of devotion to the God of all . . . ." But, particularly in a heterogeneous society, reason and Christian principles seemed to dictate that such a union "ought to be effected thro' the intervention" of religious rather than political leaders.[71] And some Presbyterians wondered if even religious leaders should organize fast days. After all, argued New York's Synod of Geneva in 1814, fast days and days of humiliation were supposed to be the Christian's response to the *"extraordinary* dispensations of divine Providence." Should they not then be spontaneous? Formal calls for fasts and humiliations, then, were inappropriate because they were mechanical.[72]

Despite critics within and without the denomination, the Presbyterians in the early nineteenth century led a successful crusade to ensure that the ceremonial aspects of the republic's government were visibly Christian. That effort was controversial enough, but infinitely more controversial was the Protestant effort to use that government to make American society as visibly Christian as those ceremonies. To that end the American Presbyterians assisted in creating a far-flung "benevolent empire" of non-denominational, voluntary associations of Protestants dedicated to encouraging virtue, suppressing vice, and generally working a thorough reformation in every facet of American life. Societies to promote temperance, Sunday Schools, domestic and foreign missions, pious literature, and a godly Sabbath were often modeled on English organizations that sprang up as part of a conservative reaction to the French Revolution. Like their English counterparts, American clergymen, usually Presbyterian or Congregationalist, sought ways to counter what they perceived as a fundamental challenge to constituted authority in the Atlantic community, in church as well as in state. But the voluntary societies created in the first years of the nineteenth century by Lyman Beecher, Jedidiah Morse, John Mitchell Mason, Ashbel Green, and many other leading Protestants do not resemble the often reactionary agencies of England so much as they seem to continue a native reform movement that had been interrupted by the American Revolution. In the late colonial period American Protestants had begun to cooperate with each other and with Christians in Great Britain to create a transatlantic Christian commonwealth that would, among other things, prepare the way for the millennium. The creation of that commonwealth had been interrupted by the war between the participants, but with the cessation of hostilities cooperation resumed. For the American Christians, the task now was to find ways in which, working with their own colonial models and with the example of contemporary Englishmen before them, they could create powerful agencies through which men committed to the ideals of the American Revolution could reform the society it created without appearing to renounce the Revolution's basic ideals.[73]

The nondenominational voluntary association seemed the ideal means to that end. In an age of sharpened denominational rivalries the nonsectarian agency could unite, at least temporarily, the leaders of those denominations into a powerful reforming phalanx. Moreover, the agencies' voluntary basis disarmed critics who were prone to sniff out a clerical conspiracy in any organized Protestant effort at social reform. Recent studies have suggested that the voluntary associations, at least in the first decades of the century, supplied a convenient remedy to several theoretical and practical problems that arose when republican ideology was institutionalized. For instance, the nondenominational agencies, operating outside politics, were able to exert power in a society that looked with suspicion on all political power, whether embodied in the executive or legislative branch of government. It has even been suggested that through the agencies of the benevolent empire, Protestants were able to shape and direct American society in ways that were forbidden for ideological reasons to the federal and state governments. It is true that clergymen themselves were prohibited by some state constitutions from engaging in political activities. But, again through the nondenominational agencies, they were able to exert considerable political influence at both state and federal level. Much of that influence flowed from the fact that the voluntary associations provided an outlet for the energies of an engaged laity—successful businessmen, politicians, and lawyers who brought to the benevolent empire, in addition to their zeal, a considerable experience in organizing and executing various entrepreneurial activities. Finally, at a time when republican theorists were becoming alarmed at the forces of disintegration gnawing at American society, the voluntary associations had the incalculable advantage of being able first to organize citizens at the local level and then to unite those local units into a purposive, cohesive national structure.[74]

The records of the Presbyterian hierarchy between 1795 and 1820 are dominated by concern for the agencies of the benevolent empire. Presbyteries, synods, and the General Assembly in hundreds, perhaps thousands, of instances moved in some way to cooperate with other Protestants in promoting what the Assembly in 1815 called the "social principle." That principle, a basic urge among people to associate, was "mighty in its operations" and, according to the Assembly, "constitutes a powerful law of our nature." Out of the social principle, "a multitude of associations of a pious and benevolent nature have spread themselves through the churches." The Assembly was pleased in particular with the societies that were formed to spread Bibles through the republic. Those pious bands embodied "all the zeal of all Christian denominations" and "knitted" them to other Christians who, "however they may differ on many points of greater, or of minor importance, agree in affirming the word of God to be the only infallible rule of faith and practice; neutralize the asperity of the bigot and the sectarian, and reconcile the contending members of the same great brotherhood." [75]

The Presbyterians had to be very careful about the way in which they cooperated with efforts to reform American society. An old saying popular at the Stuart Restoration had it that "Nothing is more dangerous than a Presbyterian just off his knees," and the Presbyterians in republican America were well aware of abiding suspicions about their intentions. Consequently, they urged all Presbyterian ministers who held civil offices to give them up. [76] Presbyterians also were encouraged to avoid the clash of partisan conflict, "to have no participation whatever in the angry strife, falsehood, slander & party violence which too often attend the election of civil officers." [77] The Presbyterians also shied away from any suggestion of a "Christian party in politics," such as the chilling "Christian Constitutional Society," a voluntary association proposed by Alexander Hamilton in 1802 to support the Christian religion and the federal constitution by ensuring the election of Christian Federalists instead of atheistic Jeffersonian Republicans to public office. [78] And even when Presbyterian Ezra Stiles Ely suggested in the 1820s the creation of an explicitly Christian party to run a ticket of Christian politicians, most Presbyterians held back. [79] To be sure, Presbyterians were encouraged to ask of a candidate, "Is he a Christian," and to "neglect" those "known to be unfriendly to Christianity." [80] The Presbyterians' intention was to support the most godly candidates of the regular political parties and then to create "voluntary associations of the most respectable citizens of our country" to "aid the civil magistrates" in suppressing vice and immorality. [81]

That intention is most clearly demonstrated in the Presbyterian campaign for a pure Sabbath in the first thirty years of the nineteenth century. The sabbatarian campaign immediately focused upon the delivery of the mails on Sunday, a problem involving, of course, the federal government. The Synod of Kentucky in 1811 declared that the objections against the delivery of Sunday mails were "too many to admit enumeration, and too obvious to be discovered." But the Presbyterians did enumerate at every opportunity the objections to "desecrating" the Sabbath. [82] The General Assembly in 1815 declared that a pure Sabbath was the "grand pillar of the Christian fabric"; and presbyteries and synods darkly warned that profanation of the Lord's day was "one of the great national sins of America" and "one of the darkest signs of the times." The Presbytery of West Tennessee did not exaggerate the Presbyterian position when it declared in 1816 that without the Sabbath "there will be no religion. Without religion, no morality[;] and without correct and sound morality, the bonds of society must be dissolved . . . ."[83]

The campaign for a pure Sabbath was particularly well suited to the nonsectarian nature of the benevolent empire. The necessity to remember the Sabbath, to keep it holy, was one of the "essentials" on which most Protestants could agree. The explicit command involved no worrisome questions of election or free will; it would not set Christian against Christian. The Protestants were confident that only those who profited from its desecration would oppose their efforts to consecrate the Sabbath.[84]

The sabbatarian campaign revealed that both the denominations and the agencies of the benevolent empire could effectively organize local support for a measure and then successfully press that measure upon the federal government. All levels of the Presbyterian hierarchy cooperated in censuring those Presbyterians who traveled unnecessarily on Sunday and were particularly harsh on any Presbyterian unlucky enough to own a stage, packet, or ferry that operated on the Christian Sabbath. Presbyterians were encouraged to patronize only those companies that ceased operations on Sunday and to organize companies to compete with those that persisted in sin.[85] A full twenty years before Lyman Beecher organized the General Union for Promoting the Observance of the Christian Sabbath in 1828, Presbyterian synods and presbyteries were circulating thousands of petitions against Sunday mail deliveries, were securing the cooperation of other denominations, and then were presenting those petitions to the federal Congress.[86] They organized mass meetings and utilized with great effect a wide array of new denominational periodicals in that campaign. At least one representative, Frelinghuysen of New Jersey, was elected to Congress on a sabbatarian platform; others who ran on that same platform, though, were soundly rejected by a populace that grew suspicious very quickly of the apparently well-financed clerics who learned so quickly from the politicians how to use new techniques of organization and promotion and who taught the politicos a little about the use of the periodical press.[87]

Much of the opposition to the Protestant sabbatarian campaign came from within the Presbyterian communion. John Holt Rice, perhaps

the leading southern Presbyterian of the early nineteenth century, dis-
approved of the campaign because it seemed to enforce morality by the
use of political conflict and force.[88] More fundamentally, the Synod of
Ohio in the 1820s registered its general disapproval of reformation by
legislation. Such legislative efforts appeared to the synod to involve the
clergy in unchristian political turmoil, to ignore the biblical injunction
to reform by godly example, and appeared to be based on an unrealistic
estimate of human nature. Dissidents in the conservative Synod of
Philadelphia in 1815 protested that synod's participation in the sabbatarian campaign as an "improper interference" in civil affairs. The
campaign directly contradicted Christ's assertion that His Kingdom was
not of this world and would not be won by "carnal" weapons. With
Thomas Jefferson, the Philadelphia minority deplored sabbatarian
legislation "Because it maintains the principle on which the Inquisition
with all its antichristian train is founded." [89] Other citizens were more
direct in their opposition to the zealous sabbatarians. When one unlucky
man was arrested in Washington County, Pennsylvania, for traveling on
Sunday, he sued the local Presbyterian moral society for false arrest—
and won.[90]

FROM REPUBLIC TO DENOMINATION

Despite the vocal protests of wealthy deists, who charged the clergy
with jesuitical ambitions and methods, and despite the less vocal complaints of the poor, who resented the moralistic conformity that seemed
to be the final goal of the benevolent empire, evangelical Protestantism
by 1820 was the unofficially established religion of the American republic. The triumph of the Protestant churchmen over "aristocratic infidelity" and popular apathy was complete. That triumph was one of
two necessary preconditions to the clergy's unconditional acceptance of
the voluntarism and competition now endemic to American religious
life. The other precondition was equally important. For the Presbyterians, at any rate, it was necessary also to create a denominational
community within which they could find identity and security and
through which the Presbyterians could compete effectively in the voluntary society of the early nineteenth century. That denominational community, it was hoped, would be the organic community that the
heterogeneous republic could never become. Thus, as the Presbyterians
reached outward to shape the broad contours of American society, they

also turned inward. And the energy they had expended in creating and defining the American republic they now lavished on that new form of religious life in America, the denomination.

It was particularly important that a denominational community be created on the vulnerable frontier. To that end, Presbyterians sought out only Presbyterians in the west and ignored the throngs of unchurched people among whom the Presbyterian minority was interspersed. The General Assembly in 1807 noted with approval that settlers from central Pennsylvania had banded together to form a tightly knit Presbyterian congregation on the southwestern frontier and gladly agreed to supply the new church with a settled minister. On the other hand, a missionary to the Carolina frontier reported to the Synod of the Carolinas in the same year that he had organized no congregations on his last trip, "for, to be plain, the people were in general so ignorant of the very first principles of the gospel" and especially of "the forms, doctrines, and discipline of our church, that they did not appear fit for organizing." And in 1811 missionaries from the Abingdon Presbytery reported that they had had little effect among the "impenitent sinners" of Georgia but that they fondly hoped "that the children of God have been edified" by their ministrations.[91] Concern for those "children of God" was the principal reason for the denomination's early support of the western revival. Presbyterians like David Rice saw the great revival as a way of reclaiming backsliding Presbyterians, not as a means of saving sinners. The Synod of the Carolinas in 1802 rejoiced that God had lately shed His blessings upon "many societies of his professing people." Clearly the revival was welcomed at first because it seemed to bring those professing people together. When it threatened instead to drive them apart, the revival was condemned.[92]

The Presbyterians depended upon the denomination's hierarchical machinery to create and maintain a Presbyterian community on the frontier. It was essential, then, that the hierarchy be able to reach all Presbyterians in the west. Of course, individual Presbyterians could be disciplined by the denomination's intricate judicial system only if they submitted themselves to the authority of an established congregation and to its session. That, many apparently failed to do. Consequently, the hierarchy frequently deplored the growing number of "scattering individuals calling themselves presbyterians, but not connected with any of our churches," and urged a concerted effort to remedy that dangerous situation.[93]

The hierarchy was concerned that Presbyterians on the frontier be accessible to sessional discipline because in the west the local Presbyterian session often was more than an ecclesiastical court. It frequently was the only tribunal concerned with moral behavior in a frontier town, and, since it often included the town's leading citizens, it was a potent instrument for maintaining social as well as ecclesiastical order. Some Presbyterians on the frontier—and in the settled east, too—complained that the sessions were not vested with authority adequate to that crucial task. The Presbytery of Philadelphia, for instance, wondered how a session could discipline members who refused to take the Lord's Supper when the only penalty available to the tribunal was to bar delinquents from communion. And other presbyteries and synods in the early nineteenth century even sought ways for the Presbyterian session to exercise discipline over people who had no connection with the denomination at all. The Synod of Virginia, in particular, was forever being pestered by its presbyteries and sessions for a ruling on the legality of extending discipline outside the church. The synod, in turn, passed the buck on to the Assembly, which stalled for ten years before warning the hierarchy against the public outcry that would inevitably follow such an aggressive act on the Presbyterians' part.[94]

The Presbyterian community, united by discipline, was to be strengthened on the frontier in particular by a marked emphasis on ceremonial and sacramental occasions. In response to directions from a synod or the Assembly, congregations would meet on stated occasions for what was revealingly called "social prayer," periods of communal supplication for particular blessings. The Synod of Virginia, for one, found those communal gatherings very gratifying and in 1799 congratulated itself that, while vital piety might languish elsewhere, it flourished "where particular attention had been paid to the exercise of social prayer, especially in the stated seasons recommended by the Synod."[95] On the frontier, too, the hierarchy soon realized the power of sacramental occasions to foster discipline and a sense of community among Presbyterians. In the early nineteenth century they ever more adamantly demanded that delinquent Presbyterian parents be forced to accept sessional discipline before having their children baptized.[96] The clergy discovered also that the sacraments gained unifying force when they were part of impressive ceremonial occasions. The Virginia Synod directed that ministers baptize converts only irregularly, and then only on solemn, stated occasions that would impress all the people with the importance of "Covenanting with God therein" and impress parents in particular "with a sense of their duty."[97] Even more impressive was the Presbyterian practice—emphasized on the frontier—of issuing communion tokens, small metal medallions issued before communion, that set the communicant off from the sinful multitude and signified in concrete form his worthiness to sit with the minister and the faithful at the Lord's table. On the frontier, at least, the celebration of the two sacraments became a significant ceremonial occasion with powers of unification that were not overlooked by the Presbyterian clergy.

The frontier camp meeting was a ceremonial, sacramental occasion elevated to high drama. The high point of any camp meeting was a mass communion and a mass baptism. Christians who seldom saw more than a few people a year watched—and joined in—as thousands of Christians partook of their Savior's body and blood and then rejoiced to see the baptismal waters of a wilderness stream wash away the sins of thousands. Indeed, it was as miraculous communities that the camp meetings were most attractive to the isolated—and often fearful—frontiersman. Descriptions of the camp meetings always emphasized their numbers, and incredulous observers marveled at the way in which the frontiersmen immediately transformed the huge clearings into ordered communities.

Richard McNemar noted that there had been four thousand at a meeting in Bourbon County, Kentucky, and possibly as many as twenty thousand at one Cane Ridge gathering. But, he marveled: "How striking to see hundreds who never saw each other in the face before, moving uniformly into action, without any preconcerted plan, and each without intruding upon another, taking that part assigned him by a conscious feeling, and in this manner, dividing into bands over a large extent of ground, interspersed with tents and wagons . . . ." He considered it "one of the greatest wonders that ever the world beheld," that "persons, so different in their education, manners and natural dispositions, without any visible commander, could enter upon such a scene, and continue in it for days and nights in perfect harmony . . . ." Here was the communal cooperation that many Presbyterians in the early nineteenth century longed for. And, it should be noted, they abandoned the revivalist community for a denominational community that was more amenable to their control.[98]

Increasingly in the early nineteenth century that community was to be distinguished by its doctrines from other Protestant groups. During the 1780s and even occasionally in the nineties Presbyterians on the frontier had joined with other Protestants for services and, infrequently, communion. But in the early nineteenth century a different spirit prevailed. As early as 1791 the Virginia Synod ruled that its churches must not hold even occasional communion with Christians who did not subscribe to the Presbyterian view of the essentials of Christianity. In practice, that eliminated just about everyone. The Abingdon Presbytery warned its ministers against all who preached universal atonement; the Synod of Pittsburgh's churches were to avoid all who denied the depravity of human nature; and the hierarchy in the Carolinas was constantly warning Presbyterians against the newcomer Methodists, who apparently delighted in badgering Presbyterian ministers about their doctrines and their insistence on an adequate salary.[99] The new spirit of exclusion that was in full force after 1815 was epitomized in a carefully worded pronouncement of the General Assembly in 1818. In the previous year the Assembly had cautioned the American Presbyterians to be careful that "no bigotry, or prejudice, no party rancour or offensive crimination, pollute your testimony" to the *"faith once delivered to the saints . . . ."* In 1818 the emphasis had changed. The Assembly, rather grandly, asserted that if there is "a religion revealed by God," then it was important to "have correct views on its principles." The Assembly would have no more to do with tentative searches for the "truth" among the various faiths of the land: "To be ever learning and never coming to the knowledge of the truth, is characteristic of none but those who assume for the human understanding, the prerogative of sitting in judgment upon the inspired truth of God . . . ." Truth existed. It was based on scripture. And the Presbyterians believed that their ecclesiology and doctrines most nearly approximated that truth among the imperfect American faiths.[100]

Important as they were, the efforts of the Presbyterians to ensure doctrinal uniformity were not as crucial to their achieving a strong denominational identity as was a simultaneous flurry of organizational activity. Between 1789 and 1820 the new General Assembly created new presbyteries and synods that in turn brought the authority of the Assembly closer to the sessions and thus increased its ability to unify the denomination. In the colonial period an annual synodical meeting, an occasional publication, and informal, irregular relations among ministers and elders had united Presbyterians, who looked to their presbytery as the most significant element of the hierarchy. In the competitive nineteenth century, though, all levels of the hierarchy were brought into precisely graded relations with each other. In several significant ways the General Assembly thereby gained the ascendancy and used its power to unite the denomination.[101]

The Assembly, first of all, retained the right to intervene in any disturbance anywhere in its jurisdiction, as in 1805, when it sent a committee to investigate the situation in Kentucky and to prevent wavering Presbyterians from joining the revivalists. The satisfied committee believed that its visit had the "happy tendency to reclaim some, and establish others, who were wavering and seemed to 'halt between two opinions.' "[102] And they were probably right. Normally, though, the Assembly maintained the stratification essential to any hierarchy. For instance, in 1805 it refused to recognize the Presbytery of Charleston because it would not place itself under the intermediate authority of the Synod of the Carolinas; in that anomalous situation, the Assembly ruled, "it would not be so easy to subject them to discipline, should they be found in censurable errors, either in principle or practise."[103] The Assembly further strengthened the hierarchy by using it both to gather and to distribute information of interest to Presbyterians. It sent thousands of copies of the extracts of its annual meetings through the hierarchy, spreading the news of its deliberations and directives through channels that connected east with west and north with south.[104] Reversing the procedure, the hierarchy collected the facts and figures required by a growing bureaucracy—numbers of converts, number and size of churches, contributions, etc. Often the two processes were really part of one unifying operation. For instance, the Assembly annually directed each level of the hierarchy to submit a "narrative of the state of religion" within its bounds. The narratives were sent up the hierarchy and incorporated into an annual report by the Assembly on the state of religion throughout the denomination. That narrative, describing the year's advances and setbacks, was then sent down the hierarchy from whence it came for the information and edification of all.[105]

The hierarchy also strengthened the Presbyterian community in the early republic by publishing denominational magazines. At just about the time the nascent political parties were discovering the periodical press as an instrument of mobilization, the Synod of Pittsburgh and then the Synod of Virginia decided to publish synodical magazines. And in 1804 the General Assembly considered publishing a journal "sacred to religion and morals."[106] Like the political newspapers, the Presbyterian periodicals were described in the most altruistic and noncontroversial language; the religious papers were benevolent attempts to further the cause in general, just as the political newspapers were patriotic efforts to defend republican ideas. But the Presbyterian papers obviously were intended to unite the denomination and to serve as a weapon of denominational competition. Samuel Miller hoped that the Assembly's magazine would compete successfully with a new Episcopalian periodical, and the Virginia Synod's *Evangelical and Literary Magazine* was from its inception dedicated to "the diffusion of Christian knowledge, according to the doctrines and discipline of the Presbyterian church . . . ." Finally, the hierarchy endeavored to create a denominational community by encouraging the various parts of the community—session, presbytery, and synod—to compile and publish their individual histories, to legitimate the young denomination by re-creating its past.[107]

In the early nineteenth century the Presbyterian hierarchy established benevolent societies that were of a specifically Presbyterian nature and that sometimes cooperated, sometimes coexisted, with the interdenominational agencies of the benevolent empire. Those Presbyterian societies characteristically were established at the presbyterial level and were intended to promote missions activity at home and abroad, to distribute free copies of Presbyterian literature, hymnals, and Bibles, to aid the poor, to minister to slaves and to Indians, to establish church libraries, and to promote morality and piety in general.[108] They were usually local in nature and control and were often the Presbyterian element in a particular endeavor of the benevolent empire. After 1815, however, a new, denominational emphasis began to emerge in the Presbyterians' benevolent agencies. Certain Presbyterian leaders, especially some more conservative minister-educators in Philadelphia and Princeton, began to insist that the Presbyterians create denominational equivalents of all the agencies of the benevolent empire. The debate occasioned by that insistence would dominate the history of the Presbyterian Church between 1820 and 1837. It had its beginning, though, in the efforts of the Philadelphia-Princeton "axis," as it came to be called, to assert denominational control over all Presbyterian educational affairs. In 1819 the Assembly reminded all Presbyterians that it "forms the bond of union of the Presbyterian Church in the United States, and affords the acknowledged means of combining the intelligence and concentrating the efforts of the denomination . . . ." To that end, the Assembly had determined that it was "necessary to originate new and more efficient measures" to "systematize and unite" the educational efforts of the denomination. The Assembly then established its first major denominational agency, the Presbyterian Board of Education, and directed that the hierarchy create educational societies at the presbyterial and synodical level to support the central denominational board.[109]

Between 1795 and 1820 the American Presbyterians created an ecclesiastical system that contradicts every assertion that American institutions were weakened when hurled into the frontier. That system, in effect, made possible all the Presbyterian efforts to create and sustain a denominational community in the early republic. At its most mundane level, the ecclesiastical system made it possible for each element of the hierarchy to examine for heterodox procedures the records of the elements below it.[110] At the same time, all elements of the hierarchy carefully maintained the boundaries between the denomination's geographical units in order to prevent unseemly jurisdictional disputes that would disturb the unity and peace of the church.[111]

Of much more importance, though, was the hierarchy's increasingly close supervision of the clergy's movements through the denomination's ecclesiastical system. One measure of that supervision is the disappearance of itineration as an issue in the nineteenth century. By 1820 the Presbyterians had erected an elaborate system for supervising the placement of ministers, which they were enforcing with vigor. Each minister was required to join the presbytery within whose bounds he served. The Hanover Presbytery in 1803, therefore, refused to dismiss one Conrad Speece from its care until he produced a letter affirming that he had been called to serve a church under the jurisdiction of the Baltimore Presbytery. And a dismissed minister was instructed to join immediately the presbytery to which he was dismissed. To delay, delinquents were warned, perpetuated an unacceptable "disconnected state."[112] Presbyteries also were required to state in writing the reasons for each dismissal, and no presbytery could accept a minister without that testimonial to his good standing in his former presbytery.[113]

After 1790 the presbyteries required of a minister seeking admission not only a letter of dismissal but also letters of recommendation from well-known members of the presbytery from which he came. In the colonial period most of the presbyteries had established committees to inspect the credentials and the letters of recommendation of all ministers desiring membership, and in the post-Revolutionary period those committees' functions became increasingly important. In a representative action, the committee of the Redstone Presbytery in Pennsylvania in 1791 refused to accept the credentials one Thomas Cooley presented from the Presbytery of Charleston, South Carolina, simply because no one on the committee had ever heard of the Presbytery of Charleston. When Cooley refused to write for letters from Presbyterians in South Carolina who were known to the men of Redstone, the presbytery turned the case over to the Synod of Virginia. The synod in turn presented them to the General Assembly, which pronounced the credentials "spurious" (incorrectly, as it turned out). Thus did the entire hierarchical system protect the Pennsylvania presbytery from fraud.[114]

The Assembly even ventured into tentative cooperation with the Congregational General Association of Connecticut to establish a joint committee to protect both denominations from impostors. In 1794 the committee recommended that private letters between members be used as testimonials rather than the easily forged form letters then in use. The Presbyterian members noted that they had used such private letters to detect unfit foreign ministers and now recommended that they be used to regulate "the admission of those who may come from distant parts of our nation." Even if no Presbyterian in the town which a minister left knew anyone at his destination, the committee reasoned, "sufficient intercourse prevails between intermediate places, to admit of his being regularly handed, and sufficiently recommended, till he reach the object of his destination." A number of well-known men, "most conveniently situated for the purpose," would authenticate the certificate of any minister passing through their towns. The name of at least one of those men had to appear on his certificate before a minister could be accepted by a new presbytery. Thus the Presbyterians made it virtually impossible for a minister to move from Portsmouth to Charleston or from Baltimore to Louisville and escape the institutionalized surveillance of the denomination's hierarchy.[115]

If the hierarchy believed that a well-regulated clergy was essential to the creation of a cohesive denominational community, it believed also that ministers must be adequately supported if that community was to be sustained. The records of the post-Revolutionary hierarchy bristle with arch references to "the difficulties under which gospel ministers labour, for want of liberal maintenance from the congregations they serve."[116] Determined to remedy the situation, the Presbyterians took actions that invariably made them appear mercenary. Vacant congregations were instructed to pay supply ministers in cash and to be ready to pay extra if they expected the supply either to baptize or to celebrate communion. Such action compared poorly with the Baptists and Methodists who frequently served on the frontier without pay. And it lent credence to the charge that the Presbyterians were mercenary—as one ancient adage had it, "The Presbyterians kept the sabbath, and everything else." Public reaction to the clergy's demands for compensation was reflected in a poem written by one Tom Johnson, the local wag of Danville, Kentucky, after David Rice refused to celebrate communion until his arrears were paid:

> Ye fools! I told you once or twice,
> You'd hear no more from canting R——e;
> He cannot settle his affairs,
> Nor pay attention unto pray'rs,
> Unless you pay up your arrears.
> O how he would in pulpit storm,
> and fit all hell with dire alarm!
> Vengeance pronounce against each vice,
> And, more than all, curs'd avarice;
> Preach'd money was the root of ill,
> Consign'd each rich man unto hell;
> But since he finds you will not pay,
> Both rich and poor may go that way.
> 'Tis no more than I expected—
> The meeting-house is now neglected:
> All trades are subject to this chance,
> No longer pipe—no longer dance.[117]

The Presbyterian ministers were, of course, no more or less avaricious than any other group of men. But the hierarchy believed firmly that a minister must labor full time to be effective, and even on the frontier it insisted that ministers hold no secular employment.[118] Without a full-time ministry, Alexander Addison warned in 1803, "we shall then see congregations multiply and pastors decrease, or congregations starving their pastors." And the New Brunswick Presbytery worried that unless "their situation be rendered tolerably easy," the best men would not be attracted to the ministry, with lamentable results for the church and the republic.[119]

The final way in which the post-Revolutionary Presbyterians created a denominational community was by crushing a contention advanced first during the Great Schism and again briefly during the frontier schism. Like the colonial New Sides the Presbyterian frontier revivalists unsettled their fellow Presbyterians by defending an "internal call" to the ministry. Like their colonial predecessors the dissidents attacked the settled clergy as cold, lifeless men who, by their own admission, often were strangers to the gospel they preached. McNemar charged that they were "proud, aspiring, contentious men, striving who should be the greatest, over-looking common people as an inferior rank of beings— deeply immersed in the cares of the world—eager after salaries . . . ." [120] Such men were not fit to minister to the Lord's church; certainly they should not decide if *other* men should be admitted to the ministry. The true minister was called directly by God, the revivalists asserted. And when the representatives of the church examined that man, they could rightly only "inquire into that validity and authority which he professes to have received from God." They could not judge the original, internal call and surely could not annul it. [121]

The hierarchy denounced the "internal" call in ways that recalled the colonial Old Sides. Since God alone could judge the validity of the internal call, the "judicatories of the church can judge only of the life and conversations of men; their knowledge and their talents to teach." In other words, orthodoxy was the only acceptable criterion of judgment. The Synod of Kentucky condemned the idea that ministers are ordained of God and not of men. God did not choose ministers immediately "but mediately, that is, by the instrumentality of a certain description of men, to whom the business is assigned." [122] In the heat of revival, the Assembly warned, men "who are destitute of any liberal culture of mind" conclude that they have "peculiar and extraordinary gifts . . . which ought not to be suffered to lie useless and unemployed." The hierarchy admitted that those enthusiastic Christians might have a place in the church; they simply insisted that it was not in the sacred desk. Let them then serve, the Assembly urged, where "they appear destined by providence to move." Every Christian was required to "exercise his pious and benevolent dispositions, and exert his talents, whatever they may be," the Assembly concluded. But men must be very careful not to throw open the gates of the church to "weakness and ignorance," not to see it "overflowed with errors, and with the wildest disorders." [123]

The Presbyterians of the post-Revolutionary period were above all else determined that their church would not be "overflowed" by error and wild disorder. Their determination led them to take constrictive actions that were at great variance with their expansive actions in the period between the Great Awakening and 1795. The change was fundamental and it was permanent. And it can be explained, finally, only as part of the Presbyterian disillusionment that succeeded the extravagant expectations of the Revolutionary period. The ideology of republicanism proved unable to end contention and strife in America. Consequently, the Presbyterians reluctantly accepted them as an unavoidable fact of life within the republic. But they then turned to the denomination, and within that smaller unit vigorously established a community that would at the same time be free of contention and conflict in itself and enable the denomination to compete in a society that was soon to be defined in terms of competition.

CHAPTER IX

The Denominational College

In 1822 the aged Thomas Jefferson wrote to his old friend the deist Thomas Cooper, president of South Carolina College. A few years earlier Jefferson had hoped that Cooper would become a professor at his beloved University of Virginia, but the Virginia Presbyterians had successfully campaigned against the appointment. Cooper, then, was predisposed to appreciate Jefferson's denunciations of the Presbyterian "priests." They charged the country's atmosphere "with a threatening cloud of fanaticism," the old republican charged. They were "systematical in grasping at an ascendancy over all other sects," and Jefferson was convinced that the Presbyterians' "ambition and tyranny would tolerate no rival if they had power." From bitter personal experience Jefferson had concluded that the Presbyterians would always be "hostile" to every educational institution that they did not control, that they would forever be "jealous at seeing others begin to attend at all" to the task of raising institutions of higher learning. As always, he caught the essence of a Presbyterian threat while he exaggerated it by seeing it as aimed personally at himself. Certainly one of the most obvious and significant results of the Presbyterians' turn from the republic to the denomination after 1800 was their effort to control higher education and to make of their colleges weapons of denominational competition. That effort, though, was not produced by Presbyterian antipathy to

235

Thomas Jefferson. It measured, instead, Presbyterian realization of their minority status in a voluntaristic society.[1]

THE TRIUMPH OF DENOMINATIONALISM

While they constituted the majority in a few scattered sections of the republic, the Presbyterians had always been a minority of America's total population. In the colonial and Revolutionary periods that minority status had led the Presbyterians to emphasize toleration and inter-denominational cooperation. After 1800, though, Presbyterian hostility to the excesses of the Second Great Awakening precluded any significant growth in the denomination while the Methodists and Baptists reaped the numerical rewards of their enthusiastic support of the revival. To their great alarm, the Presbyterians in the first years of the nineteenth century discovered that they were even a smaller percentage of America's population than they had been in the eighteenth century. That realization, especially on the frontier, contributed to an unprecedented Presbyterian defense of denominational education. That triumph of denominationalism is most clearly seen in the early history of two of the schools established by the Presbyterians in the 1790s.

Significantly, the first thoroughly denominational Presbyterian school was the Transylvania Seminary, located far into the Kentucky frontier where the Presbyterians were a tiny minority.[2] From its inception in the early 1780s until 1794 the Presbyterians cooperated with the transplanted Virginia Anglicans and skeptics in supporting the seminary in Lexington. The board was composed of Anglicans and Presbyterians, although the latter effectively controlled the school through the new Transylvania Presbytery. In 1794 the non-Presbyterians on the board outmaneuvered the Presbyterians and elected as the president of the school one Henry Toulmin, an English-born disciple of Joseph Priestley and Thomas Jefferson, and a Unitarian. The Presbyterians were appalled at the prospect of a Unitarian governing the one college in a new land. So they determined to establish another. They shattered the coalition that had governed Transylvania for a decade and established the Kentucky Academy, which they hoped would unite their own ranks and oppose the infidelity momentarily triumphant at Transylvania.

The Kentucky Academy was proudly Presbyterian. The Transylvania Presbytery appointed from its own ranks the board of trustees and the president, who had to be a zealous promoter of the "interest of real and practical religion." The presbytery also reserved the right to appoint all faculty and to inspect both their lectures and the readings they assigned. And, while the charter solemnly pledged that "No endeavours shall be used . . . to influence the minds of any student to change his religious tenets, or embrace those of a different denomination," the presbytery added the significant qualification that they would tolerate at the academy only those beliefs consistent with the "gospel system, and the practice of vital piety." The Presbyterians, with an "indignant frown," informed the new governors of Transylvania that "if you appoint men who despise our religion and religious institutions, rather than endanger the morals of our children, we will abandon you." And they did. They took the unprecedented step of urging Presbyterians to send their children to the Kentucky Academy and nowhere else.[3]

The ease with which the Presbyterians fractured the unity of the seminary anticipated the ease with which the denomination itself would divide in the frontier schism. In each instance, a shattered larger unit was replaced with a smaller one from which all dissidents were expelled in the name of orthodoxy, unity, and strength. Unlike the denominational schism, though, the educational division was temporarily healed. After four years of competition, the seminary and the academy were reunited in 1799 as Transylvania University. To some extent a practical necessity, the reunion was primarily the result of the efforts of Judge Caleb Wallace, a graduate of Witherspoon's Princeton, who had assisted in establishing Liberty Hall and Hampden-Sydney as well as the original Transylvania Seminary. Wallace was still imbued with an earlier Presbyterian emphasis on Christian unity as the only means to reform American society and was able finally to overcome the opposition of David Rice and other Presbyterians to the reunion.[4]

By 1804 the Presbyterians regained control of Transylvania. They quickly alienated the majority of the state's people with their view of the proper relationship between religion and state in a republican government. The depth of that alienation became apparent in 1815. At the conclusion of the War of 1812 James Blythe, the Presbyterian minister who was the acting president of Transylvania, observed the national fast day proclaimed by Madison with a remarkable sermon entitled, "Our Sins Acknowledged." Blythe informed the citizens of Kentucky that the war with England had been deserved punishment for the lamentable decline of visible Christianity during the administrations of Jefferson and Madison. Forgetting that public morality and

Christianity were inseparable, the Jeffersonian Congresses had promulgated laws without reference to *"God the Saviour."* And, despite America's being "confessedly a christian nation," the state legislatures met and adjourned year after year "without once acknowledging God in all their ways, that he might direct their steps." It is probable that some Kentuckians, perhaps many of them, shared Blythe's alarm at the state of American society in 1815. But he clearly alienated most of those potential allies with a forceful description of church-state relations that was highly offensive to Kentucky's non-Presbyterian majority. He spoke forcefully of "the intimate, and indeed, indissoluble union there is between a manly and ardent piety, and an equitable administration of our government." And he hoped that no one would challenge the desirability of that relationship between religion and politics simply because in the past it had occasionally proven "highly injurious to the liberties of the people, and the free exercise of conscience." Nor did he advocate an establishment of religion. The "celestial goddess" of religion had no need of feeble, temporal establishments; she could captivate "by her own power." But, Blythe concluded darkly, while religion could flourish without government's support, the reverse was not true. Government could not survive without the support of religion.[5]

The reaction to Blythe's sermon revealed just how controversial even a trite discussion of church-state relations could be in Kentucky when delivered by a spokesman for the tiny minority whose clergy controlled the state's only college and who had rather consistently opposed the war effort. Critics charged immediately—and effectively—that Blythe had advocated a Presbyterian establishment in Kentucky. One anonymous critic denounced as "downright sectarian bigotry" and an unconstitutional arrogation of power Blythe's demand that legislatures acknowledge their dependence on the God of a "confessedly christian nation." Blythe was reminded that there were "other religions beside the Christian" in the republic and that not even all Christians in America would agree with his decidedly trinitarian theology. The critics dismissed Blythe's disavowal of an establishment as "vile, hypocritical canting" and directed the public's attention to his revealing assertion that "the *government* is bound to be religious—to sanctify the Sabbath, and keep it holy—*by law of course."* [6]

To the potent charge that the Presbyterians sought an establishment in Kentucky, the critics added the equally effective accusation that the Presbyterians had turned Transylvania into an aristocratic institution.

The Presbyterians numbered fewer than one in every hundred of Kentucky's citizens in 1815. Such a minority should control no public institution, certainly not the state's only college, the Presbyterians' opponents charged.[7] Apparently many Kentuckians agreed. In 1817 the Presbyterians were driven from power in Transylvania when the non-Presbyterian part of the board proved strong enough to elect as president another eastern Unitarian, Boston's distinguished Horace Holley.

From outside the university the Presbyterians in the late 'teens and early twenties vigorously defended their own administration of the school and viciously attacked the ensuing regime of Dr. Holley. The Presbyterian offensive reached its peak in 1823 in a series of essays published in *The Literary Pamphleteer* by John McFarland, a leading Presbyterian minister. McFarland began by admitting the obvious: a major change was occurring in the Presbyterian attitude toward denominational education. He noted with some pride that colonial Princeton—and eighteenth-century Transylvania, for that matter—had been broadly based and had never been used to proselytize for the supporting Presbyterian Church. Now, unfortunately, the triumph of infidelity at Transylvania dictated an immediate change in that perfectly laudable policy.[8]

When McFarland attempted to explain and then to justify that change, he became entangled in a morass of contradictions. He insisted, for instance, that the Presbyterians had no desire to drive the "liberals" from Transylvania in order to transform the school into a denominational institution where Presbyterian doctrine would be taught as the only revealed truth. He found it difficult, though, to defend the minority Presbyterians' control of Transylvania. And the Presbyterians themselves had advertised their minority status when they sought to illustrate the desperate condition of Christianity in Kentucky. Then it suited their purpose to divide the population of Kentucky into Christians and "infidels," to bemoan the fact that the "infidel part" had a "considerable majority" of the population, and sadly conclude that Kentucky was not "a Christian but a heathen land."[9] At other times, though, as when they endeavored to discredit Holley, it was convenient for the Presbyterians to appear to be the majority in Kentucky, or at least to appear to be *part* of a religious majority. McFarland began that seemingly impossible feat by asserting that Holley was a Socinian, one who denied the divinity of Christ. Holley had taught Socinianism as the only revealed truth at Transylvania, had forced the legislature to appoint only infidels to the board, had, in fact, established infidelity at Transylvania, McFarland charged.[10] That infidelity was the religion of only a few in Kentucky, though. The Presbyterians were careful at that point to refer to Holley not as a liberal or a skeptic, of which there were many in early nineteenth-century Kentucky. Instead, he was an avowed Socinian, of which there were admittedly few anywhere. It was this tiny minority that controlled Transylvania, McFarland charged.[11]

To the Socinian minority McFarland opposed what he considered the religious majority in Kentucky. Not even a determined partisan like McFarland could assert in the face of obvious facts that the Presbyterians alone constituted a majority of the state's Christians. But McFarland believed that with the Baptists, Methodists, and Episcopalians, the Presbyterians did constitute a majority that agreed upon certain basic principles of religion and morality. That majority had the right, indeed the duty, to manage Transylvania. McFarland hastened to disavow control of the school by any one denomination; such an establishment would outrage "the principles of the social compact." Representatives of the leading Protestant denominations should control the board, though, and determine the doctrines to be taught in the school, thereby assuring that religion, properly understood, would not be separated from the other parts of the course of education. "Infidels, Atheistical, and Socinian parents" obviously could never be satisfied with such a school, for they "can never unite and harmonize in education with those who are really christian . . . ." They should support their own private schools, then. McFarland concluded with the gratuitous assertion that, should the infidels ever really constitute a majority of the population of the state, control of Transylvania should revert to them immediately.[12]

McFarland, then, seemed to advocate a common front of orthodoxy against infidelity. Well he might in a state in which Baptists and Methodists outnumbered Presbyterians seven to one and in which all church members accounted for no more than fifty thousand in an adult population of more than three hundred thousand.[13] But the other Protestants in Kentucky did not respond to his call for interdenominational cooperation, probably because they realized the extent to which the Presbyterians had become determined advocates of denominational education. They had only to pay attention to McFarland's arguments. If a group of Christians had received the truth, how could they fail to support it and oppose all contesting beliefs, he wondered. It simply followed that if one had received the truth, one could recognize its opposite. "I am at a loss to determine," McFarland confessed, how "one can believe a proposition, and at the same time not disbelieve its opposite . . . ." [14]

The Presbyterian belief that each sect should defend its version of revealed truth led McFarland to make a condemnation of Holley that is at first perplexing. On the one hand, McFarland criticized the president for sedulously inculcating Socinianism at Transylvania. But on the other hand, McFarland had to grant what was perfectly obvious: many people in and around Lexington had no idea what Holley's religious views were because he resolutely refused to discuss them in public. Holley, it seems, carefully practiced what the Presbyterians preached. He taught no sectarian doctrines at Transylvania and refused to engage in the sectarian wars that raged in the Kentucky press. And for that, McFarland condemned him. That Holley's creed was a matter of "doubt or dispute" at this late date was the deplorable result of his "extreme caution not to appear in a tangible form from the Press . . . ." McFarland urged the president into the fray. Holley ought to speak honestly and specifically to enable prospective students to "know satisfactorily what he is." In the collegiate marketplace McFarland expected each college, through its president, to identify itself clearly and to compete for students on that basis. The Presbyterians might praise "liberal" and nonsectarian schools, but their opposition to the man who made of Transylvania such a school eloquently demonstrates their practical acceptance of denominational education. The Presbyterians, McFarland boasted, at least "own their sect and defend it openly." [15]

While waging their eventually successful campaign to drive Holley from Transylvania, the Presbyterians attempted to establish at nearby Danville a college to be controlled completely by the Synod of Kentucky. Such a school would provide "the youth of the West the opportunity of obtaining a liberal education under circumstances to guard their morals and best interests from those snares which are at present planted in the principal seat of science among us." Responding to the Transylvania Presbytery's urging that the synod establish a "literary and biblical institution" under its patronage, the Presbyterians petitioned the liberal-dominated legislature to charter Centre College. However, when the lawmakers stipulated that "No religious doctrines peculiar to any one sect of Christians, shall be inculcated by any professor in said college," the Presbyterians rejected the charter since it "did not embrace the principles contemplated by the Synod of Kentucky in their plan for establishing a college." [16]

The school at Danville was chartered despite the Presbyterians' reaction, and from 1819 to 1823 it operated independently of the denomination. At the height of its campaign against Holley, though, the synod made another effort to transform Centre into a "Seminary of Learning . . . entirely under its direction and control," where young people could be taught a "course of Biblical and Religious Instruction according to the Confession of Faith in this Church." This time they were successful. In 1824 a more cooperative legislature vested control of the school in the Synod of Kentucky, made the wording of its constitution more palatable to the Presbyterians, and Centre College quickly became as thoroughly Presbyterian as Kentucky Academy had been. Three years later Holley finally tired of fighting the Presbyterians and returned to the east, leaving both of Kentucky's colleges in the control of the state's smallest religious denomination.[17]

In the year that the Kentucky Presbyterians gained control of Centre College, a young Princeton graduate named Philip Lindsley became the president of Cumberland College in Nashville, Tennessee, a tiny Presbyterian school that became, after several transformations, the George Peabody College for Teachers. A learned and tolerant graduate of Samuel Stanhope Smith's Princeton, Lindsley elaborated in the 1820s a sophisticated defense of denominational education as at least a necessary evil if not yet a positive good.

Lindsley deplored "sectarian" education as a "grievous and growing evil" in the republic. If schools were sectarian, he wondered, why should there not be sectarian penitentiaries, road and canal companies, and even sectarian banks? (Actually, through the 1820s there was an "Episcopalian Bank" in Hartford, Connecticut.) Lindsley further ridiculed the idea of "sectarian" education by speculating on the nature of sectarian Greek, mathematics, logic and philosophy. But he clearly distinguished between "sectarian" and "denominational" institutions. He realized that denominational competition was an unavoidable condition of American religious life and, as such, had to be dealt with. *True* Christianity, he declared "breathes a pure angelic charity, and is as much a stranger to the strife, and intrigue, and rancour, and intolerance, and pharisaism of party, as science and philosophy can be." But men refused to be "honest Christians" and instead took the field as "zealous Presbyterians, Episcopalians, Methodists, Baptists, Quakers or Romanists."[18] Those zealous Christians ought to be allowed to establish denominational schools, Lindsley contended, so long as the denominational nature of their institutions was openly and clearly advertised. He especially abhorred as "specious and very hypocritical" the obviously denominational college that, upon receiving its charter, becomes "all of a sudden, wonderously liberal and catholic," and its supporters totally free of the "odious taint of sectarianism." "Their college *is* sectarian, and they know it," Lindsley charged. "It is established by a party—governed by a party —taught by a party—and designed to promote the ends of a party." It should be so labeled.[19]

Lindsley charged that state legislators were responsible for allowing the denominations to foist their sectarian schools upon an unsuspecting public as liberal, broadly based "public" institutions. The people's representatives allowed the denomination to insert in its charter a pledge of toleration and liberality that would never be honored in practice. The "sectarian manufactory [then] goes into operation under the smiles, patronage and recommendation of the people's representatives." The sectarians then insist that their "liberal" charter is "the talisman that is to guard the people against every insidious attempt at proselytism . . . ." The bait is seized, and the unsuspecting student finds himself at a school in a "small village or retired part of the country" under the exclusive control of a sect where he is required to attend prescribed religious services. And in the meantime the sectarians who publicly "profess the greatest liberality" privately "boast among themselves of the converts which they have made from their dissenting pupils."[20]

Lindsley, then, did not object to the creation of schools intended to unify and sustain America's Protestant denominations. He simply insisted that, in a land of competing denominations, the nature of the religious instruction at each school be explicitly labeled and conspicuously advertised. Lindsley also believed that as a necessary complement to those "private" denominational institutions, each state should support one "public" college that would be "independent of all religious sectarian bias, or tendency, or influence." Lindsley did not speculate as to how such an institution would be able to survive in sectarian America, but he did insist that it be above all else *safe,* a place where "all may intrust their sons . . . without fear of danger to their religious faith." Thus, a religious family had two choices, as Lindsley saw them. They might send their son to a denominational school to be instructed in the ways of the righteous. Or, he might instead go to the state's public, nondenominational college, where his earlier denominational religious training would not be challenged or in any way harmed. In both cases, Lindsley's primary concern was the preservation of the religious doctrines that were at the core of the developing denominational communities in republican America.[21]

Twenty years before Lindsley wrote, North Carolina Presbyterians were intimately involved in creating precisely the sort of state university Lindsley later envisioned. The nature of that involvement, though, indicates that most Presbyterians in the early republic probably disagreed with Lindsley's hopes for a system of scrupulously nondenominational state universities. In 1789 the North Carolina legislature created the first state university actually to go into operation. The charter of the University of North Carolina explicitly acknowledged the state's particular responsibility for supporting liberal education in a republic, and in 1794 the state acted on that responsibility by vesting in the university's board all lands escheated to the state. Problems soon emerged, though, from the influence of the Presbyterian clergy in the school. Impetus for the school had come from the Presbyterians, who by 1800 virtually controlled the university. Members of other denominations and liberal deists, who were almost as numerous and powerful in North Carolina as they were in Jefferson's Virginia, urged the legislature to annul the 1794 land grant, arguing that the Presbyterians had taken a charter granted for the public good and used it to advance the interests of a tiny minority. The legislature was persuaded and repealed the land grant. Immediately the university's trustees brought suit against the state, a suit which in 1805 they won. The North Carolina Supreme Court agreed with the plaintiffs that all corporations were by definition established for the public good—a corporation established for private gain was a contradiction in terms. But the court rejected the allegation that the Presbyterians had perverted the intention of the charter: the school had been created to serve the public good and it was doing so. At the same time, though, the court ruled that the school was the private property of the board and that the charter was an inviolate contract between that board and the legislature. The court reminded the plaintiffs that the school had been created in 1789 by the state constitution, the permanent expression of the people's will. It could not, then, be destroyed by the legislators who only temporarily represented the people.[22]

The court thus put the University of North Carolina beyond the control of the legislature that supported it and anticipated by fifteen years the landmark decision in the Dartmouth College case of 1819. Indeed, when Webster successfully argued that the "tiny school" in New Hampshire was the private property of its board of trustees and that its charter was an inviolate contract, he used the North Carolina case as a judicial precedent. That decision, Webster argued, had made all charter grants "sacred" and had clothed all chartered institutions "with all the security and inviolability of private property." Then, when Chief Justice Marshall ruled in Webster's favor, he gave the highest judicial sanction to developments that by 1819 had made of the Presbyterian schools denominational institutions whose primary functions were to foster denominational unity and to serve as weapons of sectarian conflict.[23]

It is clear that the Presbyterians were not unique in defending openly denominational colleges by 1820. For example, Connecticut's Episcopalians used arguments similar to Lindsley's when they challenged Yale's educational monopoly in that state in 1822. That monopoly had been under attack since the 1790s, and it became increasingly vulnerable as support for the Congregational establishment in the state crumbled after 1800. In 1822 the Episcopalians (who supported the "Episcopalian Bank" in Hartford) petitioned the legislature for a charter for Washington College, a school in Hartford that was openly advertised as being under the complete control of the Episcopal Church.[24] The sons of Eli rushed to the defense of Yale's monopoly, an increasingly difficult and thankless task. Chauncey Goodrich could not deny the Congregational domination at Yale and therefore argued that, in the normal course of events, colleges *ought* to be managed by men of like beliefs. But that did not mean that the school should serve only one denomination. As far as Goodrich was concerned, the Episcopalians' open avowal of their denominational intentions was not normal. It was alarming. They brandished the "name of a single denomination in their public and recorded acts," and by that indicated "the character and design of their institution." Certainly, Goodrich argued, the legislature should not charter a school whose sole purpose was to *"give influence and patronage to a particular sect of Christian."* Goodrich's description of the ideal collegiate environment approximated his perception of the situation at Yale. The college ought to be a "common ground, on which the youth of all denominations meet" during the week while pursuing literary studies. On Sunday, though, each should retire to his own place of worship to be edified in the tenets of his particular denomination. For that laudable intercourse among the denominations, Goodrich charged, the Episcopalians would substitute a school to be patronized by only one group of Christians. And surely, he concluded, if one denomination were allowed to establish such a school, all would insist on one.[25]

The Episcopalians replied that they merely desired what the Congregationalists already had—a school completely under their control. Yale might denounce that wish as "sectarian," but it had in fact long been "sanctioned by the *practice* of every other denomination." The Episcopalians were ready to admit what the supporters of Yale's educational monopoly would not: the preponderance of one denomination on a college campus fundamentally affected the educational experience a student would have there. They freely advertised the denominational character of Washington College and encouraged all of Connecticut's Episcopalians to patronize it. And they welcomed all non-Episcopalians who would accept the education available at Washington College on the terms set by the supporting denomination.[26] Philip Lindsley would have understood and approved.

PROFESSIONALIZATION AND DENOMINATIONALISM

One of the crucial dynamics in the development of Presbyterianism in the early republic was the interaction between Presbyterian efforts to create a denominational community and to professionalize the ministry that would serve that community. Education was central to both those efforts. In the early nineteenth century the Presbyterians developed a defense of denominational education. In addition, they sought to intensify the denominational character of each of their colleges and to establish institutions with explicit responsibility for theological education. The result of those developments was to hasten Presbyterian embrace of the voluntaristic denominationalism characteristic of the early nineteenth century.

The first step the Presbyterians took to professionalize the clergy was to institutionalize ministerial education. In the eighteenth century a ministerial candidate might have studied "divinity" with his college president—Witherspoon, Nisbet, Smith, etc. But usually upon graduation he would have returned to his home to study with a local pastor while preparing for ordination, a process that was almost always under the control of a young man's home presbytery. At the turn of the nineteenth century, however, the Presbyterians experimented with several ways to provide systematic theological instruction in their colleges. In 1803 the

Princeton board of trustees named the Reverend Henry Kollack, of the class of '94, to be his alma mater's first professor of theology.[27] In expectation of Kollack's arrival President Smith pledged that the school would in the future better fulfill its primary function of training Presbyterian ministers. And, in anticipation of the arrival of large numbers of those students, the board made special arrangements for their room and board—fees were halved or dispensed with, a special house was furnished, and firewood was provided at no expense to the students.[28]

But few students materialized. In 1806 Kollack was forced to resign his professorship, and some prominent Presbyterians began to wonder why Smith's Princeton had failed to attract pious ministerial students. In the following year the students mounted a rebellion against the school's administration, which was forced finally to expel more than one half the student body. For reasons which will be discussed in the following chapter, many Presbyterians withdrew their support from Smith as Princeton's president. The Presbyterians, led by Samuel Miller and Ashbel Green, had decided that the college was not a suitable environment for theological education and as early as 1805 had expressed an interest in creating a theological seminary completely independent of the college. "I fear," Miller had told Green in that year, that "the theological students would not be better for habitual intercourse with the students in the arts." To protect those students Miller recommended a seminary completely separate from the college—"its government unfettered and its orthodoxy and purity perpetual."[29] In Philadelphia Benjamin Rush endorsed the idea, hoping that a separate seminary would protect pious ministerial candidates from both the contamination and the ridicule of corrupt secular students.[30] After those students rose in rebellion in 1807, Miller wondered if Princeton should be "purged and elevated, or totally destroyed." For the moment, the disaffected Presbyterians did neither. Rather, between 1808 and 1812 they boycotted the college. "Princeton has lately lost its popularity among us," Rush admitted in 1808, and in 1810 Ashbel Green sent his son not to riot-torn Princeton but to Dickinson, now safely under the stern direction of the Reverend Jeremiah Atwater, former president of Middlebury College.[31]

By 1812 virtually all Presbyterian clerics conceded the desirability of institutionalizing theological instruction in a separate seminary created especially for that purpose. The only issue, then, was whether there should be one seminary or several. Some who opposed a single seminary worried that it would be inaccessible to many prospective students in a far-flung denomination. Others feared the power of a single institution to mold the denomination in its own image. Those astute critics isolated exactly the reason for which Miller and others insisted on a single seminary. Those Presbyterians understood that only in a single, central institution could the clergy be molded into a cohesive unit. For the sake of "order and uniformity," clerical education could no longer be left to the "individual enterprize and caprice" of an apprentice system that too often produced heterodox views. Nor could theological education proceed in their colleges, where the Presbyterians had to cooperate with other denominations and could not, for that reason, inculcate the doctrines necessary to mold a ministerial community. "Harmony and unity of sentiment," among the clergy, Miller insisted, could be attained only "by educating a large body of them under the same teachers, and in the same course of study." The only truly effective means to that end was a single, central seminary that would produce among its students "an enlightened attachment, not only to the same doctrines, but to the same plan of government." [32]

The Presbyterian supporters of a single seminary believed that its students would develop there a consciousness of belonging to a Presbyterian clerical community, an awareness that could not be encouraged while ministerial candidates studied with individual pastors. The Synod of New York and New Jersey argued that pursuing their studies together would stimulate and arouse the mental exertions of candidates. From "daily conversation on the subjects studied, mutual assistance, and societies for aiding them in their preparations for discharging the duties of the pastoral office," those students surely would "derive advantages which cannot possibly be commanded by the private student." [33] Not the least of these would be lifelong Presbyterian connections. Samuel Miller hoped that those connections would be the foundation for a professional clerical community, which he believed essential to the survival of the denomination in a competitive, voluntaristic society. In the late eighteenth century clerics in several denominations began to correspond with each other on a regular basis, in conscious imitation of mercantile and legal associations. Samuel Stanhope Smith, for one, believed that ministers could foster both a professional and a denominational identity by meeting upon stated occasions for fellowship and mutual encouragement. [34] And Samuel Miller hoped that the "early and lasting friendships" established at a single Presbyterian seminary would produce "confidence and mutual assistance" among old friends and hence advance the cause of religion.

Doubtless a scattered denomination would be more firmly united if its leaders could reminisce in convivial reunions amid the serious work of synodical and General Assembly meetings.[35]

While most Presbyterian clergymen probably shared many of Miller's enthusiasms for a unified clergy and may even have shared his reservations about earlier methods of educating ministerial candidates, the majority of them probably favored the creation of several seminaries under the control of the individual presbyteries and synods rather than a single institution under the direction of the Assembly. The western and southern states, for instance, were virtually unanimous in their opposition to a single seminary, and even Miller had to admit in 1810 that a "large majority" of the clergy opposed a central institution.[36] The supporters of a single seminary, then, arranged that the matter of the seminary was never put to an actual vote, and in 1812 the General Assembly created the Princeton Theological Seminary and started construction at a safe distance from the rejected college.

The creation of the Presbyterian seminary was a singular triumph of institutional centralization at a time when, according to many historians, American institutions were being weakened and decentralized. The seminary at Princeton was to be totally controlled by the General Assembly. That central body appointed the seminary's board of trustees, which in turn appointed the faculty and then inspected every aspect of faculty and student performance, both curricular and extracurricular.[37] That rigor was essential not only to unify the Presbyterian clerical community but, in addition, to make the Presbyterian seminary competitive. In the years at the turn of the nineteenth century, the Dutch Reformed, the Associate Reformed, the Congregational, and Episcopal churches established theological seminaries that were intended to do for those denominations what the Presbyterian seminary was expected to do for the Presbyterians. As early as 1805 Samuel Miller was warning his fellow Presbyterians of the "aggressive intentions" of other denominations, and he later believed that the threat of other seminaries finally persuaded the Presbyterians to create the institution at Princeton. Those other denominations were taking steps to elevate the level of ministerial education and to strengthen denominational union, he warned. If the Presbyterians did not do likewise, their church would "inevitably decline" and fall into "discouraging weakness, inferiority, and comparative uselessness." [38]

In response to the "aggressive intentions" of other denominations, the Presbyterians intensified the denominational identities of their colleges and established a denominational seminary. At Dickinson the new Yankee president, Jeremiah Atwater, welcomed young men fleeing corrupt Princeton and promoted the college in Carlisle as a pure, alternate site for the seminary proposed for Princeton. He knew that Ashbel Green was leading the movement to establish a seminary in Princeton, but he was most gratified when Green in 1810 chose to send his son to Carlisle rather than to Nassau Hall. He then pledged his college to "aid the cause of religion, and [to] be of assistance, in particular, to the Presbyterian church—in connection with a theological institution." And, despite the opposition of an increasingly anticlerical board of trustees, Atwater noted regularly that "it is by the special countenance of the clergy, that such institutions have flourished and must continue to flourish." The principal responsibility of the college, then, was to replenish that clergy.[39]

The denominational nature of the other Presbyterian schools was likewise intensified. At Virginia's Washington Academy the denominational character that had so galled the Jeffersonian legislatures in the eighteenth century was, if anything, strengthened in the first decades of the nineteenth. The Lexington Presbytery continued to inspect the school's students and faculty on behalf of the Synod of Virginia; that synod's theological department remained a vigorous part of the college; and its students were required to attend the only church in Lexington—Presbyterian, of course.[40] The situation was much the same at the Canonsburg Academy in western Pennsylvania. The academy was chartered—ironically—as Jefferson College in 1802, but retained the theological department created by the Virginia Synod in the 1790s. Its clerically dominated Presbyterian board even worked with the Synod of Pittsburgh in the teens and early twenties to enlarge that department. Largely for that reason, Jefferson College by 1825 was the center of a strong, unified clerical community, largely alumni. And when reproached about the college's obvious denominational nature, the board merely noted "the apparent necessity for adopting the principle of ecclesiastical supervision in the founding of new institutions, in those parts of our country where all other denominations are pursuing the same course . . . ."[41]

The most dramatic change occurred at Hampden-Sydney, where the Presbyterian-dominated board in the early nineteenth century transformed into a denominational seminary the broadly based eighteenth-century college of Madison, Henry, and Smith. Under a new president, Reverend Moses Hoge, the board and the Hanover Presbytery created a theology department in the college in 1807; by 1819 more than one-half of the college's students were enrolled in that department.[42] By 1821 the theology department had transformed the nature of the college, and in 1823 that transformation was formalized when the Hanover Presbytery created the Union Theological Seminary at Hampden-Sydney. The seminary was not intended to compete with the central institution at Princeton, and it succeeded where other efforts to create local seminaries failed because it was supported by the men of Hanover. Since the days of Samuel Davies the Hanover Presbytery had stressed presbyterial organization, and in the post-Revolutionary period it had been in the forefront of the move to create presbyterial societies to enforce uniformity and orthodoxy and to lend strength and respectability to the denomination. The creation of Union was only the most visible and significant expression of that movement in Virginia. At another level of the hierarchy, the Princeton seminary had been established for identical reasons. By 1825 both seminaries stood as concrete manifestations of the Presbyterians' search for community at all levels of the ecclesiastical hierarchy.[43]

As they established new institutions and transformed others, the Presbyterians in the early nineteenth century also made more rigorous the process whereby young men entered an increasingly self-conscious professional ministry. A significant part of that process, the "ministerial trials," took place outside both the college and seminary. By making those trials more difficult, the Presbyterians hoped to raise the level of ministerial education and, by extension, the caliber of the members of the Presbyterian ministerial community. They insisted, though, that they did not favor a learned ministry over a fervently pious one. By 1800 the debate over a learned clergy was a very old one and, in the Presbyterian Church, had long since been won by the advocates of learning. Consequently, the pronouncements on the subject in the early nineteenth century sound ritualistic. Samuel Miller, Thaddeus Dod, and Samuel Stanhope Smith insisted that they advocated a learned *and* a pious ministry; that a clergyman must be educated if he hoped to appeal to sophisticated audiences; and that the message of God was associated inevitably with the men who bore it.[44] In the Presbyterian tradition in 1800 there was simply no basis for an effective rebuttal to those assertions.

Other Protestant traditions, of course, emphasized the necessity of a pious ministry as effectively as the Presbyterians stressed the need for a learned one. And on the American frontier the Presbyterians faced the competition of Baptist and Methodist preachers with little or no education whose ministrations swelled the ranks of those two popular denominations. The Presbyterians reacted to that challenge by intensifying their efforts to produce a learned ministry. At the height of the Kentucky revival, while the Baptists and Methodists enlisted the aid of lay exhorters in harvesting the rewards of the awakening, the Transylvania Presbytery between 1803 and 1806 admitted virtually no candidate to the ministry. The ministerial "trials" became just that. One young man was dropped from candidacy because he lacked "that aptness to teach which the nature of that office requires" and because he had no prospect of "ever obtaining the degree of literary knowledge and distinctness of expression which would make him an edifying minister of the word . . . ."[45] And when a candidate finally was ordained, it was only after a rigorous process: exercises had to be repeated; examinations on Latin and Greek sometimes had to be repeated several times; *ad hoc* committees were appointed to tutor the candidate in more difficult areas; and years—sometimes more than a decade—were spent in fulfilling the presbytery's requirements.[46]

There was nothing like the Presbyterian "trials" in other denominations on the frontier, and the Transylvania Presbytery paid for its rigor. Between 1806 and 1816 it licensed and ordained very few men. And when it decided in 1816 to support a ministerial candidate at Princeton, it refused to accept any additional candidates for a decade.[47]

The seminaries in New Jersey and in Virginia immediately affected the subject matter of the Presbyterian "trials." The Virginia Synod, for instance, directed that an education at Union should prepare a ministerial candidate to defend the essentials of Christianity against "every assailant." The defensive synod deplored combat for its own sake, and it did not want young men to spend years at Union "turning over large volumes of religious controversy." But it did insist that Union prepare potential candidates to defend Presbyterian dogma against skeptic and enthusiast alike. To that end, the synod directed that Union provide a two-year course in biblical criticism, systematic theology, languages, and ecclesiastical history.[48] And when that course was instituted, it tended immediately to make ministerial examinations at the presbyterial level more systematic, more rigorous, more closely regulated—in short, more professional. Candidates were examined for the first time on ecclesiastical history and government, "didactic theology," and the "evidences of Christianity." Latin exegeses, which had all but disappeared on the frontier in the 1780s and '90s, were again required of candidates after the presbyteries began to support students at Union and Princeton, where they would be instructed in all of those subjects. And soon the force of hierarchical support made the movement toward more professionalized candidacies a denominationwide phenomenon.[49]

The Presbyterians, of course, were not blind to the dearth of ministerial candidates and did attempt to recruit *suitable* young men for the ministry. Eastern presbyteries warned their fellow Presbyterians that urban as well as frontier pulpits were vacant and that solutions must be found to that "serious and alarming" problem. Most suggested remedies were traditional—the New York Presbytery, for instance, in 1805 urged parents and ministers to seek out promising candidates for the clergy.[50] Others, though, experimented with new bureaucratic techniques, as when the presbytery in 1806, noting that the cry, "Give us ministers," came from "large and important congregations, in our most populous cities and towns" as well as the frontier, created a "Standing Committee for the Education of pious youth for the Gospel ministry." Chaired by Green, the committee was to locate and arrange support for young men deemed suitable for the ministry. By 1825 similar organizations were established in virtually every presbytery. Characteristically, a presbytery constituted itself into an education society and carried out searches for "poor and pious youth" throughout its bounds.[51] In 1818 those local societies were unified under the Education Society of the Presbyterian Church, a bureaucratic, hierarchical culmination of local beginnings. In the words of the General Assembly in 1819, the "present state" of the nation demanded "new and more efficient measures" for educating ministers. The Education Society was the Assembly's effort to meet that demand, to "systemize and unite" all efforts at theological education throughout the Presbyterian Church.[52]

Not all Presbyterians approved of the drive to professionalize the ministry. And in 1822 the board of the Education Society found it necessary to refute the charge that the new board and seminaries were merely "fitting men" for the "trade" of preaching. The board asserted that it would not be "intimidated" by such "scurrilous" accusations. But the board's detractors had caught the change in emphasis that the new arrangements reflected. While it was not true that the Presbyterian ministry had become a "trade," it certainly had become a profession, and the change was fundamental.[53] In the colonial period, the New Sides had attempted to professionalize the ministry. But they had simultaneously expanded access to the ministry. Then during the Revolutionary period, efforts to professionalize the ministry had at times a confining and at other times an expansive effect on the denomination. But in the post-Revolutionary period Presbyterian efforts to professionalize the ministry were almost invariably constrictive and stultifying in their impact. Educated in colleges that were increasingly denominational and molded into a Presbyterian phalanx in theological seminaries, the members of the Presbyterian clerical community were intended to make their denomination a unified community free of dissent and conflict. For the time being, they were remarkably successful.

DENOMINATIONAL FINANCES

The intensified denominational character of the Presbyterian schools in part reflected a marked change in the sources of their support. In a change that began around the turn of the century and that was well advanced by 1820, denominational support for the first time became the colleges' principal source of income outside of student tuition. That change, in turn, was a product of the proliferation of denominationwide agencies and societies during the early nineteenth century. Just as they formed themselves into societies to support missions and other causes, the Presbyterians at the sessional, presbyterial, and synodical levels organized societies for supporting the education of "poor and pious youths" for the Presbyterian ministry. Those agencies, with no eighteenth-century equivalent, had an immediate impact on the Presbyterian colleges.

The experience of Hampden-Sydney, Union, and the Synod of Virginia is instructive. The synod in 1801 recommended in rather general terms that sessions and presbyteries under its control raise money for ministerial education.[54] In the period after 1812, then, its methods of raising funds became more explicit and systematic: committees were appointed and subscription papers drawn up to be circulated among presbyteries and sessions. Those efforts were further systematized and focused by the effort to establish Union. In 1813 the synod established a special fund for the seminary; in the following year it required each minister to make a special effort to raise money for Union; and in the next year the synod required of each minister an annual report of his efforts in the seminary's behalf. In 1816 the seminary's board itself proposed to the synod that every session be organized into a society for the support of Union, and by 1818 a committee of the synod was checking on sessional compliance with a directive to that effect. One of those committees reported back that the seminary was being cheerfully supported by "those benevolent associations which have been the invention of the present age, and have given it so precious a character."[55] With little variation, other presbyteries and synods followed the example of the Virginia synod and organized agencies to raise money for the support of the poor and pious youth who wished to study theology and enter the presbyterian ministry: the Synod of Pittsburgh in 1808 and all its presbyteries by 1815; the Lexington Presbytery by 1819; and the Redstone and Transylvania Presbyteries in the following year.[56]

The Presbyterian schools proved quite willing to emphasize their denominational character in order to receive this increased Presbyterian support. This was especially true when any of the colleges was faced with a financial crisis, as was the case after the main buildings of both Princeton and Dickinson burned in 1802 and 1803 respectively. As was noted earlier, Princeton's board in 1796 had emphasized the school's "catholic" nature when applying for state aid. But when they appealed to the General Assembly for aid in 1803, they represented it as a thoroughly denominational school. Princeton, the board now asserted, had been "the child of piety and individual munificence," not the offspring of the fickle state. And the board trusted that the school would be restored by the same forces "by which it was established." If not, the school was doomed: "it has no other resources." The board proudly resorted "to the aid of that munificent piety by which the Institution was originally [created]" and applied to the Assembly "as the fountain which puts its stream into motion over so large a body of this Continent . . . ." The board did not appeal in vain. The Assembly set in motion a denominationwide campaign that vindicated the board's faith in the Assembly's power, and that almost immediately rebuilt Nassau Hall.[57]

While the hierarchy erected an institutional framework through which the schools were supported, the colleges themselves elaborated a philanthropic structure through which individual Presbyterians could make bequests that were explicitly intended to increase the denominational character of the colleges. Virtually all monetary bequests to Princeton between 1800 and 1820 were for the express purpose of training young men for the Presbyterian ministry. By 1810 the board had ruled that the charity funds of the eighteenth century, never intended solely for the support of theological education, would henceforth be applied exclusively to that purpose.[58] And by 1818 the board ruled that earlier bequests intended for ministerial education, such as the large Hodge and Leslie funds, could be used to support ministerial students at Princeton itself *or* at a school *better* suited to train Presbyterian clergymen, that is, at Princeton Theological Seminary.[59] At Hampden-Sydney, too, individual philanthropy intensified the school's denominational character and was largely responsible for the creation of the theological department that quickly dominated the school.[60]

The college and seminary boards in the second decade of the nineteenth century for the first time began to campaign actively for specific purposes. Trustees would appeal to the vanity of prospective donors for the purpose of endowing a specific professorship or scholarship. After one John Whitehead endowed a $2,500 scholarship at the Princeton seminary in 1818 the General Assembly announced that the donor of any large scholarship or professorship would have it named for him. Six years later the Kentucky Synod put a price tag on a similar arrangement: a donor could have a scholarship named after him for $2,500 and a professorship for $20,000. The Hampden-Sydney Board even promised that a donor could name the professor to fill the chair he endowed—subject, of course, to the board's approval.[61]

Appeals to Presbyterian philanthropists' vanity were sometimes fruitless, but the far-flung subscription drives launched by the Presbyterian schools in the early nineteenth century were enormously successful. They were invariably more profitable than similar eighteenth-century efforts. The obvious difference in the post-Revolutionary period was the maturation of the Presbyterian denominational structure. When representatives of the Princeton, Hampden-Sydney, or Dickinson boards ventured forth in the early republic they methodically worked their way through the intricate relationships of session, presbytery, and synod, going from town to town recommended on their way from one local elder or minister to the next. In other words, the same machinery that united and protected the denomination against undesirable ministers also facilitated the raising of funds for the support of its schools. The system worked remarkably well. Even though he called himself the "worst beggar in the world," Samuel Stanhope Smith raised $8,000 in the vicinity of Princeton alone before touring the south, where he raised an astonishing $100,000.[62] In the eighteenth century the wide-ranging trips of Witherspoon and others had broadened Princeton's appeal and widened its clientele. Now, equally extensive fund-raising drives instead intensified its denominational character both by strengthening the hierarchy's machinery and by appealing almost exclusively to Presbyterians.

Denominational support, especially for the seminary at Princeton, was often conditioned on the maintenance of orthodoxy at the Presbyterian institutions. The Synod of New York and New Jersey, for instance, in

1819 agreed to endow a professorship at the seminary provided that its faculty be required always to subscribe to a Confession of Faith, as stipulated in the seminary's constitution. Should that stipulation be changed, the synod instructed the Assembly to retrieve the money and to use it to support a minister who would pledge to instruct young men privately in doctrines consistent with the Westminster Confession. And to ensure that the crucial section remained intact, the synod recommended that the *written* consent of two-thirds of all presbyteries be required before any changes could be made in that part of the constitution that pertained to the Confession.[63]

The increase of organized and individual denominational support for the Presbyterian schools in the early nineteenth century was accompanied by a marked unwillingness of state legislatures to support those colleges financially. There was, to be sure, no simultaneous lessening of the Presbyterian conviction that the states *should* support their schools. On the contrary, Atwater voiced a widely held belief when in his inaugural address at Dickinson he spoke of the "intimate connexion of religion with civil government." And he believed that the state's willingness to support the Presbyterian colleges would indicate that there was still in America "a sort of national acknowledgment of a belief in the importance of Christianity." [64] It is true that some of the Presbyterian schools continued to stress their services to the public as sufficient justification of their requests for state aid. Both of the academies in western Pennsylvania in the last years of the eighteenth century petitioned for state aid, assuring the legislature that it would be a "public injury" to allow the academies to perish "after having been productive of so much good," and after their usefulness had been "so well established." [65] And all of the Presbyterian schools continued to appeal for state aid regularly, sometimes stressing their public usefulness, sometimes not.[66]

But the Presbyterians discovered that the state legislatures were beginning to differentiate between "public" and "private" institutions, that the people's representatives were increasingly uncomfortable with the ambiguities of past arrangements of support and control, that they were ever more reluctant to support institutions that they did not also clearly control. To their considerable distress, the Presbyterians found that the more they treated their colleges as denominational institutions, the more the state legislatures were prone to treat them in exactly the same way. It is true that legislatures did occasionally aid the Presbyterian schools, especially in a state like North Carolina, where Presbyterians controlled both the state legislature and what was supposed to be the state university. But in states where the Presbyterians were not in political control, they found the state legislatures increasingly unwilling to grant public funds to institutions that were obviously private.[67]

The legislators' willingness to distinguish between public and private institutions was most obvious in their reluctance to grant charters to various Presbyterian organizations in the early nineteenth century. As has been noted, charters of incorporation in perpetuity were granted regularly in the eighteenth century to organizations that were conceived as serving the public good and not private interests. In 1811 the Synod of Pittsburgh was shocked when the Pennsylvania legislature proposed to charter the synod's missionary society for only twenty-one years, not in perpetuity. Moreover, the legislature insisted the synod use the society's funds for no purpose other than missionary work. Outraged, the Presbyterians refused the charter.[68] In a similar situation, the Jeffersonian Virginia legislature in 1816 refused to charter Union Seminary. When the Presbyterians had applied for charters for their colleges, they stressed the usefulness of such schools in training secular as well as clerical leaders. They could not argue that a seminary would do anything but train ministers, though. And the Jeffersonians were not willing to charter an institution for that purpose.[69]

Clearly something had changed. In the eighteenth century, the idea of a corporation that served private interests was a contradiction in terms. Corporations by definition served the public good. That idea, in turn, was part of a view of society that made no allowances for conflict between differing interest groups. As we have seen, in the post-Revolutionary period that view of society began to be replaced by one in which social conflict was accepted at least as legitimate, if not a positive good. The Presbyterians in the early nineteenth century created a denominational community within which they would compete in a voluntaristic society. They now demanded that the definition of a corporation be changed to reflect a society in which competition was normative. They did not argue that their institutions served the public good. Instead, they insisted that in a democratic society the service of private interest was a legitimate function of social institutions.

CHAPTER X

The Great Retrogression

At one o'clock on the night of March 6, 1802, the interior of Princeton's Nassau Hall was gutted by fire. There was much debate at Princeton about the fire's origin, but when he heard the news at Dickinson, Charles Nisbet did not hesitate to afix the blame for the conflagration. The old Scotsman noted sarcastically that "The Students of Princeton College have shown a noble Spirit by burning the Place of their Confinement . . . ." Perhaps, he mused, the "Burning of Colleges is a part of the new Order of things . . . ."[1] In this instance, Nisbet's sarcasm may be forgiven him. The "new Order of things" to which he referred truly was alarming, even to those Americans who were less easily alarmed than the Dickinson president. The burning of Nassau Hall occurred at the crest of a wave of unprecedented student rebellions that swept over American college campuses between 1798 and 1815. Virtually every institution of higher learning in the land was affected. In 1798 President Maxcy at Rhode Island College was forced to sign an extraordinary "Treaty of Amity & Intercourse" with a party of rebellious students who were boycotting the college commons; in the following year the president and two of the trustees of the University of North Carolina were beaten by aggrieved students who clearly were not interested in signing treaties with the administration. After 1800 the pace of violence quickened. The students at Transylvania in 1801 prosecuted a mock trial of a professor charged with suppressing free thought and succeeded in having the man dismissed from his position. In 1805 and 1807 the majority of students at North Carolina and at Princeton left their respective schools rather than accept unpopular administrative actions. Those Presbyterian schools as well as Harvard and Williams were closed down for weeks at a time between 1805 and 1808 by full-scale student rebellions. Finally, the commencement at Columbia in 1811 degenerated into a riot that involved students, alumni, spectators—and the courts.[2]

Alarming though they were to contemporary observers and fascinating though they are to historians, these student rebellions are not the most significant development of Charles Nisbet's "new Order of things." Instead the rebellions were the reaction of students to their teachers' repudiation of the Enlightenment, to what one scholar has called the "great retrogression" of the early nineteenth century and what another has termed the "Protestant Counter-Reformation."[3] On American college campuses, that fundamental shift saw the faculty repudiate the eighteenth century's "science of discipline" and in its place institute a hard line of authority sharply at odds with the balanced practices of colonial and Revolutionary educators. That repression, in turn, fomented student rebellions that appeared to educators to justify more repression. The early nineteenth century, then, saw the swift unfolding of a self-perpetuating cycle of repression and rebellion from which none of the Presbyterian colleges emerged unscathed. That cycle, in turn, intensified the Presbyterians' efforts to transform their colleges into narrow bastions of denominational orthodoxy.

THE SCIENCE OF DISCIPLINE ABANDONED

The Princeton Trustees announced to the world that the fire of 1802 was a "great frown of divine providence," yet, somewhat inconsistently, charged that Nassau Hall had been "intentionally set on fire."[4] After the blaze, even President Smith abandoned his usual optimism to confide to Jedidiah Morse that many believed the fire was a result "of those irreligious and demoralizing principles which are tearing the bonds of society asunder . . . ." He found a disturbing similarity between the Princeton fire and a recent fracas at the College of William and Mary in which students had broken into the chapel, desecrated the Holy Scriptures, and then by threat of further violence had "obliged the faculty to renounce the right of interrogating a student on any part of his conduct, or his studies . . . ." Both deplorable episodes appeared to be "the signs of the days which are coming upon us."[5]

Assembled students, faculty, and fellow trustees two months after the fire heard Trustee Ashbel Green describe the flames much more dramatically. The Philadelphia conservative was superintending the college while President Smith undertook a "begging tour" of the south to raise funds to rebuild Nassau Hall, and Green took his responsibility seriously. He heard in the burning of Nassau Hall the "warning voice" of God urging him to purge Princeton "of the dross which it now contains, and to provide for its future purity."[6] The "friends of piety and rational education," he asserted, are "looking around them with more than ordinary anxiety, and asking where they may send their children with safety and advantage . . . ." They seek a refuge where they might send their children with a "reasonable expectation that their religious principles will be guarded, their morals carefully inspected, the habits of order, industry and due submission to superiors formed . . . while science shall enlighten their minds and exertion invigorate their faculties . . . ." Green, speaking for the board, promised to make Princeton such a school—an "asylum for the soundest principles of religion"—and he kept that pledge.[7]

The "science of discipline" had asserted that young men could be made virtuous by proper stimuli; it argued that each act of discipline must be self-evidently just. Real order and true reformation would follow justice rationally and fairly applied. But in their post-Revolutionary disillusionment Presbyterian educators concluded that their expectations had been naïve. Watching the virtuous republic become, as they saw it, a hotbed of licentiousness, they determined to make of their denomination the ordered moral community that the turbulent republic plainly was not. That process would begin in their colleges, those small, self-contained communities that were to be the prototypes for a united denomination. Witherspoon's science of discipline was, therefore, sacrificed.

The Presbyterian educators began by insisting that even the most insignificant regulation be obeyed. In 1803, for instance, the Princeton faculty suspended a boy merely for defacing the new walls of Nassau Hall.[8] In 1802 Green had warned that the faculty and board stood "ready to dismiss the whole college rather than suffer the least infringement or contempt of its authority." And he meant it. The

Princeton trustees not only insisted on absolute obedience to their laws, but invested their corporate authority in all officers of the school, thus violating Witherspoon's dictum that authority was effective only when vested in mature men respected by those they ruled. Green's 1802 speech reflected the "collective sentiments of the guardians of the college" and his pronouncements were therefore "clothed with their authority." Like the officials of Transylvania, North Carolina, Williams, Union, and South Carolina College, the Princeton Board adopted more stringent student regulations in 1802, and in those revisions they explicitly delegated to each faculty member—even the lowest tutor—"sufficient authority to make himself and the laws respected," and directed those surrogates never to "suffer" any crime to pass their notice "without its due reprehension or punishment." [9] At the University of North Carolina the Presbyterian president, Joseph Caldwell, even vested the authority of the board in a few student "monitors," who were appointed, in effect, to spy on their fellow students. When Caldwell in 1805 made it a misdemeanor to insult the monitors and vested them with the authority of a faculty member, a majority of the student body "seceded" from the university rather than live under those conditions.[10]

The Presbyterian educators also enhanced institutional authority by surrounding it with ceremony. After 1802 Princetonians no longer carried a copy of the school's rules merely as a means of identification. Instead, "to impose stronger ties on the minds of all the students to good order," each boy was required annually to solemnly pledge obedience to the college's revised rules. After the 1807 riot the board demanded that the pledge of obedience be made in writing in a book prepared especially for that purpose. Then, when Ashbel Green became president of Princeton in 1812, he had the boys sign the pledge in an elaborate and solemn ceremony which he himself conducted with "studied gravity and emphasis." Under Green, signing the oath to obey the college's laws became a "sacred obligation" and was enforced as such.[11]

The Presbyterian educators in the early nineteenth century also rediscovered the rod. Eighteenth-century educators had virtually abandoned corporal punishment, sometimes under pressure from parents but usually on Benjamin Rush's theory that discipline administered by force deformed rather than reformed delinquents. After 1800 one after another of the Presbyterian colleges renounced its Revolutionary leniency. Hampden-Sydney and Transylvania freed teachers to whip boys under fourteen, while at Virginia's Washington Academy the faculty were allowed to paddle large, but not small, twelve-year-olds.[12] To be sure, parents complained of Presbyterian cruelty and often refused to send their sons back to colleges in which they had been firmly disciplined.[13] But the Presbyterian educators were undaunted. Green bluntly reminded the Princetonians that as long as they resided in Nassau Hall, their parents "give you up to us." He assured the young men that their teachers would not be tyrants. Like every good parent, Princeton's administrators would allow "every indulgence consistent with your good and the good of the seminary." But, *unlike* most parents, the Princeton faculty would not "suffer you to ruin yourself by vice, nor to waste your time in idleness, nor to contract habits of extravagance, disorder, disobedience or resistance to lawful authority." Green insisted that only vicious students would object to the school's revised laws, and he trusted that virtuous students would recognize any resentment of those laws as an indication of corruption. At any rate, he concluded, the virtuous in any society must suffer some inconvenience and restraint that would be unnecessary if all members of the society were virtuous. Each student, then, must submit to the revised laws for the "general good, and as the condition on which alone he can himself receive the benefits of society." [14]

The Presbyterians anticipated parental and student resistance to stricter discipline and prepared to meet it. Green in 1802 assured the Princetonians that if the board were forced to dismiss them all, that act itself would so impress the friends of virtue and piety that within a few months the school would be filled with the most virtuous young men in the nation.[15] The president of the North Carolina Board worried that the board might have to abolish the office of monitor but consoled himself with the knowledge that the spies could at any time be reintroduced.[16] President Caldwell, though, asserted his absolute determination to resist the criticisms of vicious students and the threats of their weak-willed parents: "If so many of the youth of our country can so easily sacrifice the opportunity of science and aim with so little reluctance a fatal blow at the very existence of the University, it is for those who know by greater experience the value of such an institution to baffle the waves of adversity and steer the bark safely from the storm which assails it." [17]

The leaders of the student rebellions at the turn of the nineteenth century were usually the sons of the American elite, Federalist in political persuasion, and, especially at Princeton, southern. These "young bloods" rebelled for a multitude of reasons. Poor food in commons still produced traditional "bread and butter" riots that recalled colonial days. Rejection of the often miserable food available in the antebellum college also suggests that the contrast between the conditions of life at home and at school became increasingly important as the colleges enrolled wealthy young men. It is clear, too, that there is an important connection between the beginning of student violence and the emergence at the turn of the century of the literary societies in the colleges. Those organizations dominated virtually every facet of a student's life. The literary societies' extracurriculum in many cases became a more vital forum for effective education than the course of studies formally offered by the colleges. It may be that the student rebellions were in some sense a contest between the societies and the faculty for control of student life, a contest which the faculty finally won only by coopting the societies.[18]

It is clear, though, that the students believed they were defending what the faculty were rejecting. As always, it is impossible to separate rhetoric from reality. But the rhetoric of the rebellions was that of the eighteenth century, of "scientific discipline," and of the American Revolution. The rebels insisted that they abhorred violence for its own sake. Even as the disorders began at Princeton in 1807, the students "respectfully" protested the suspension of four of their colleagues in a thoroughly subservient petition. They suggested "humbly" that their teachers had heard only prejudiced witnesses before suspending the four. They assured the faculty that "With you we detest Jacobinism. With you we love due subordination." But the young men were convinced that "respectable remonstrance" did not constitute Jacobinism.[19]

For a generation the Presbyterian educators had inculcated veneration for the republican ideals of the American Revolution. Now their students revolted under the banner of those same principles. In their remonstrance to the board the Princeton rebels of 1807 reminded the trustees that if "order and harmony" were to be preserved in any society, "it is essential that there should be correspondent duties and rights." If the students acknowledged their duty to be subordinate to authority, the faculty must agree to be fair and not arbitrary. The school, they insisted, was a civil society, the several parts of which must not infringe on the recognized rights of other parts. Two years earlier a student at the University of North Carolina had argued that the student remonstrances accompanying the Great Secession of 1805 had been the triumph of republican principles in the southern school.[20] In 1807 Abel P. Usher, one of the leaders of the Princeton rebellion and a Virginian, referred explicitly to the republican Revolution when he testified before the board of trustees. Any people dissatisfied with their government, he declared, "have a right to resist or even overthrow it."[21] His colleague in rebellion, the Kentuckian Joseph C. Breckenridge, was even more explicit in relating the present rebellion to the American struggle for independence: "If men have no right to associate themselves for the purpose of consulting about things which most materially concern their dearest interests, they have no rights at all . . . . It is astonishing to me that any set of men should be so weak as to make such an observation in a country the fundamental principle of whose government is liberty of action."[22]

Like many other Americans, the Presbyterian educators were quite uncomfortable with the ideas of 1776 in the early nineteenth century. Organized resistance—combinations—against "tyranny" had been exactly appropriate when directed at the sorry remnants of royal government in America. Now, directed at the duly constituted authority of republican governments, they were simply licentious and intolerable.[23] The Princeton Board dismissed any idea that the comparison with the American Revolution was in any way appropriate in the current crisis. In response to the students' 1807 remonstrance the board noted their contention that the college was a civil society "which the people, if they are dissatisfied with the government, have a right to rise and resist, or even overthrow it." That might have been the case had the students founded the school and appointed its officers, the board conceded. But the school was the board's property and the students were there at the trustees' pleasure. Their only *right* in the case was to accept education on the owners' terms—or leave.[24]

The colleges seem to have learned from the rebellions only that discipline was not adequately severe. North Carolina's lay founder, William R. Davie, blasted the students' references to the "sacred regard to their rights" and to the "high and imposing duty of remonstrance." Once, those slogans had fueled the American Revolution. Now, the students' ideas were dismissed as the "general Slang of the times culled from the columns of Newspapers" and deplored by Davie as "attended with the most mischievous consequences."[25] The students insisted, though, that they were moved to remonstrate not by the "general Slang" of newspapers and surely not by French radicals or even Jeffersonian democracy. Instead, the students appear to have resisted an innovative, controversial practice they believed to be inconsistent with republicanism in general and with rational discipline in particular.

The Presbyterian educators in the early nineteenth century became increasingly obsessed by the need to gather information about the boys under their care. After 1800 they demanded that students testify before faculties and boards concerning their own actions and those of their peers. First at Hampden-Sydney and then at Princeton, boys were required to give evidence in any case being considered by the faculty or board.[26] At the same time the two Presbyterian schools in Virginia worked closely with William and Mary to devise a "more effectual mode of obtaining evidence for the purpose of preserving order in literary institutions . . . ."[27] In 1807 the vigilant schoolmen petitioned the Virginia legislature for a law requiring a student—or any citizen—to testify under oath in any case deemed important to the well-being of any of the state's colleges.[28] The North Carolina "monitors" were the most striking result of the Presbyterian obsession with surveillance. But the Transylvania Board accomplished the same purpose when it ruled in 1803 that "it shall be the duty particularly of the senior students to cooperate with the officers in the preservation of order and decorum in the University."[29]

The Presbyterian educators denied that they were creating a network of spies. The Princeton trustees in 1810 assured young Daniel Fitzhugh that they required no boy to become a spy, but they maintained their right to examine anyone in their charge. Fitzhugh therefore must tell them who had started a certain disturbance in the refectory or be expelled. When he refused, the board made good its threat.[30] The educators believed they had no choice. If the boys would not give information about crimes voluntarily, they must be forced to cooperate. Force was required, then, for the students proved remarkably reluctant. The minutes of all the Presbyterian schools contain episodes similar to the one at Hampden-Sydney in 1806, when the trustees were questioning a student charged with shooting a pistol near the college building. Rather than testify, the boy showed "the utmost contempt of the Board, by leaving their presence, and telling them they might do what they could."[31] The Princeton Board in fact believed that the students' refusal to testify against each other was the real cause of the 1807 rebellion because that refusal had made necessary the close official surveillance that had triggered the revolt. Finally, Benjamin Rush, approaching the last year of his life in 1812, lent his enormous prestige to the effort to "prevent or abolish the obligation the students enter into not to inform of each other," a determination Rush found wholly pernicious in its tendencies and based on a "deep-seated immoral principle." [32]

Far from being rooted in immorality, the students insisted that their refusal to testify against each other was lawful resistance to an odious policy that threatened their rights against self-incrimination and that was thus inconsistent with republicanism. At North Carolina student Henry Chambers justified the Great Secession by declaring the monitors' appointment "odious" and reprehensible to every "friend of science." At Princeton students charged that their teachers now advocated actions they had only recently condemned. Men who had congratulated boys for not informing on their friends now expelled them for that refusal. How then could the students take seriously the faculty's assurance that they wanted only to treat the students as their sons? If they truly wished to serve as fathers, the students advised, the faculty might begin by doing more to "avert the rigor of the Inquisition." [33]

The students had some allies in charging the Presbyterians with turning inquisitors. William Davie of North Carolina strenuously opposed the appointment of the student monitors at the university because they were "not a species of Magistrates, but *real spies.*" Like the Princeton remonstrants Davie urged the North Carolina trustees to demonstrate that the school's discipline was really of a "domestic" nature. Just as no father would attempt to regulate every movement of each member of his family, so Davie believed that the trustees must not try to control all the actions of their students by detailed, usually anticipatory legislation. Such precision only transformed the students themselves into "lawyers and legislators," constantly "deliberating, remonstrating, and revolting." The best-governed colleges, instead, were those with "the most respectable Faculties, and the fewest *written* laws." [34] But the Presbyterian educators continued to legislate for everything and to retreat from the eighteenth century's fragile science of discipline. By 1812 the "great retrogression" was well under way. At Princeton in 1810 the board created a Committee of Visitors to ensure that President Smith enforced the rigorous discipline it demanded. In 1812 the genial Smith was driven from office, and the Enlightenment came to an end at Princeton. Smith was replaced as president by Ashbel Green, a man who had connived at his downfall for a decade, and a man on whom the trustees could rely to do their bidding—and more.

CERTIFICATES AND FENCES

On September 24, 1806, the Princeton trustees hired four men to stand guard as they met in Nassau Hall; on the next day the same men kept watchful eyes on commencement proceedings. Henceforth, the board decided, guards would maintain surveillance on important occasions at Princeton to prevent "all riotous and disorderly practices" on the campus.[35] That decision epitomizes the Presbyterians' efforts in the early nineteenth century to erect legal and sometimes physical fences around their schools to keep out the pernicious forces which they blamed for their students' riotous behavior.

The Presbyterians first closed their schools to undesirable students. The Virginia colleges in the first years of the century empowered their faculties to refuse admission to any applicant deemed potentially injurious to the good order of either school. At Washington Academy in Lexington the faculty could reject any applicant for any reason. At Hampden-Sydney the faculty after 1813 had the authority to deny admission to anyone who refused to give "satisfaction" that he would obey the laws of the college.[36] Before *any* student was admitted to any Presbyterian school, he was required to produce a certificate attesting to his moral character. With the acceleration of student violence after 1798, those certificates became increasingly important to the guardians of the Presbyterian colleges. After the 1802 fire the Princeton Board required that anyone wishing to transfer to Princeton from another college must first produce a statement from the head of his former college attesting that the student left without censure. Any student caught with a forged certificate would be expelled immediately. To ensure that *their* certificates would not be counterfeited, the boards of Princeton and of Hampden-Sydney prepared a special stamp with which to mark all certificates of honorable dismissal.[37]

Between 1802 and 1808—at the height of the wave of student rebellions —the presidents of virtually all the American colleges organized an informal but effective system of correspondence that served as an unofficial blacklist of all students expelled from any of those schools. They followed the lead of liberal William and Mary, whose board announced to the public in April of 1802 that henceforth they would send the name of every young man expelled from the Virginia school to "all other public seminaries in the United States." [38] After the rebellions of 1807 at Harvard and Princeton the boards of each school sent the names of all expelled students to all college presidents with the request that none of the disciplined students be admitted to any other American college. Only the student-hungry University of Pennsylvania declined the request. In the same year the North Carolina Board requested a list of expelled students from every campus and required that every transfer declare in writing that he had not been expelled from any other college. [39]

Having expelled troublesome students, the Presbyterian educators found to their annoyance that they were sometimes a greater problem outside than inside the college. An expelled boy might loiter about just outside the campus, flaunting his freedom, and enticing virtuous young men into license. The exasperated Princeton trustees first threatened to publish the names and offenses of hangers-on, and after the 1807 riot the board did take firmer action. During Green's tough-minded regime the board even availed itself of the local civil authorities to hurry expelled students out of the village limits. [40]

The various Presbyterian boards endeavored not only to protect their colleges from vicious students but also attempted to isolate them from their immediate environment and from taverns, in particular. The Presbyterians in western Pennsylvania were especially anxious to keep college students out of the taverns of Canonsburg and Washington. Innkeepers were threatened with the full force of the law if they served students, and state legislatures were encouraged to forbid the licensing of a tavern near an institution of higher learning. [41] At Princeton, too, the board lobbied for laws against selling liquor to minors and led the move to incorporate the village, hoping in that way to provide a more orderly and respectable environment for the college. In 1819 the board even instructed the college's steward to hire—at the students' expense—several carriages to pick the students up at the college gates on the last day of classes and take them to their respective homes immediately, without stopping at the local taverns. [42]

The Presbyterian educators came to believe, however, that the greatest threat to their schools came not from taverns or even from immoral students. A more insidious threat was posed by the students' parents—their indulgent, extravagant, weak-willed parents, who provided the money that led their sons into temptation. That danger could not be met by erecting legal—or physical—fences, requiring various kinds of certificates, or by enacting repressive legislation. Instead, parents had to be persuaded somehow of the evil consequences of their ill-considered liberality.

The Princeton Board decided only two weeks after the 1802 fire to set a limit to the amount of money a Princetonian might receive from home, to send a letter to all parents informing them of that limit, and to require each student to swear to spend no more. "Few things corrupt the heart of a young man more than the power of gratifying his vanity or his passions whenever he pleases," the board warned students and their parents. The liberality of some parents also lowered student morale, the trustees feared. While some boys had much and others little, the latter could not help but "become discontented and impatient." Then, lest wily students continue to exaggerate to their parents the funds necessary to attend Princeton in comfort, the board circulated to parents a list of expenses normally incurred in supporting a boy "genteely and prudently" at the college.[43]

These and other efforts were in vain. The trustees attributed the 1807 rebellion to "the almost unlimited allowance of money, or of credit" extended to the students by indulgent parents. And the board once again set a limit on student allowances. But now the young mens' parents were requested to send those allowances to a college bursar, who would in turn dole out funds as required. And parents were asked to pledge—in person or in writing—to abide by the financial limits set by the board. But to no avail. As late as 1819 the Princeton Board was admitting that nothing attempted in the previous twenty years had caused indulgent parents to limit their sons' allowances.[44]

The Presbyterian educators persisted in their almost fanatical opposition to parental indulgence in part because they subscribed to the traditional idea that money in all cases was a corrupting influence. But, specifically, they believed that money was a disruptive force in their institutions. It set the rich against the merely comfortable and the poor. Worse, it gave students the wherewithal to leave the college campus and to encounter unacceptable models of moral behavior. Worse yet, it strengthened the bond between student and parent and to that extent weakened the institution's control over the boys. The educators believed firmly that lax familial discipline and parental indulgence were at the root of all the disciplinary problems in the colleges. And they saw parents persist in encouraging extravagance even after they had delivered their sons into the educators' hands. Familial indulgence was the most pernicious of all evils because the educators could do nothing about it. And they knew it.

THE ATTACK ON "UNRESTRAINED PHILOSOPHY"

The Presbyterian educators could not control parental extravagance, but they could and did closely regulate the curriculum of their colleges in the early nineteenth century. Green's statement in 1802 that "this hour a new era commences" at Princeton applied as much to the school's curriculum as to its government and discipline. As the Presbyterian educators abandoned the eighteenth-century science of discipline and raised all sorts of fences around their colleges, they also launched a vigorous attack on what they called "unrestrained philosophy," the pejorative term that conveyed the Presbyterians' conviction that somehow learning had got out of control during the Revolutionary era.

When Joseph Caldwell spoke to his graduates at the University of North Carolina in 1802, he failed even to mention the relation of education to republicanism; indeed, he did not mention the republic at all. Rather, he stressed in somber terms the necessity for duty, control, and due submission on the students' part. The Presbyterian educators of course continued to chant the now traditional litany that related education to the republic's success. For example, in his 1809 inaugural address at Dickinson Jeremiah Atwater echoed the wisdom of the past century, now a cliché: "knowledge has ever been acknowledged to be the very life, and ignorance the bane" of republican governments. In those governments "where all power emanates from the people, and where men in public office are always responsible to the people for the faithful discharge of their trust, it is important, now indispensable, that the people be enlightened." The words were those of the eighteenth century, but in the first years of the nineteenth, they no longer conveyed the sense of expectation and urgency they once had.[45]

Their reluctance to link republican success to learning measures the Presbyterian retreat from the eighteenth-century belief in the transforming powers of education. They rejected that conviction in part because William Godwin and others began to transform it into a "perfectionist" confidence in the possibility of infinite improvement in the lot of man through education. The Presbyterians were particularly alarmed by this perfectionism when it appeared that Samuel Stanhope Smith was advocating it at Princeton. Smith did, in fact, assert to his students his conviction that man was "susceptible of improvement" and then used the theme of human improvement as an organizing principle around which he discussed the rise of human communication. Needless to say, Samuel Stanhope Smith, although a product of the Enlightenment, was no disciple of the anarchist Godwin. He did, however, retain the eighteenth-century conviction that education, rightly conceived and executed, could alter the "state of society" fundamentally. That conviction, in the final analysis, was what had made him a *republican* educator and was what marked him as an anachronism in the post-Revolutionary period.[46]

Most Presbyterian educators in the early nineteenth century no longer shared Smith's confidence in the improvability of man and the transforming power of education. Both ideas now seemed to deny the innate depravity of man and to encourage human pride and atheism. In his *Brief Retrospect of the Eighteenth Century* the scholarly Samuel Miller in 1803 blasted any kind of "perfectionism" as "unsupported by any facts," as contrary "to the experience of mankind," and as opposed to human nature and divine revelation. Specifically, he denounced the idea that education has a "kind of intellectual and moral omnipotence." And he denied that "to its different forms are to be ascribed the chief, if not all the differences observable in the genius, talents, and dispositions of men." [47]

Presbyterians of the Revolutionary period had been confident that republican educational institutions would produce virtuous citizens capable of sustaining republican government. For Benjamin Rush the process had appeared to be mechanical. To provide the proper stimuli necessary to that process, Rush had suggested that colleges be established in court towns. There young men could observe the daily functions of local political and judicial leaders and be impressed with the necessity of virtue in the leaders of republican polities. By 1800, though, many Presbyterian educators saw the relationship among virtue, education, and republicanism as much more problematical. It was no longer clear that the courts of the republic were the proper stimuli for young republicans, nor did the Presbyterian educators view the courts primarily as instruments of education. The charter of the University of North Carolina directed that the school be located no closer than five miles to the state capital or any court of law or equity. In 1809 the Hampden-Sydney Board ruled that the students' attendance at court days and militia musters was a waste of time and "generates vice and a corruption of Morals and ought not to be tolerated." But, when that board prohibited any student from visiting the court house unless legally compelled to, they found that the ruling created some apprehension among the public. For the next three years the board alternated between their desire to protect the morals of their students and the demands of parents that their sons be allowed to attend court days. While the trustees obviously felt that the hurly-burly of court day threatened the morals of their charges, many citizens believed just as firmly that the observation of the working institutions of republican government was indispensable to a republican education.[48] Clearly, the Presbyterian educators of the early nineteenth century were as concerned about the contaminating as well as the instructive force of the courts of the republic.

A crucial change had occurred. In 1807 Benjamin Rush, once education's surest American friend, delivered himself of an estimation of learning that is astonishing for its negative judgment. "Learning," Rush suggested, should be considered a luxury in the present state of American society. He insisted that "practical knowledge" should always "be as common and as cheap as air" in a republic. But "learning" was a different matter altogether. It should be placed "only within the reach of persons in easy circumstances," Rush suggested. For should it "become universal," it would "be as destructive to civilization as universal barbarism." [49]

American Presbyterians, in short, had come to fear learning. Rush—like many other American educators—became convinced that in the years following the American Revolution "learning" or "philosophy" had become "unrestrained." In the eighteenth century Americans had described "power" as masculine and aggressive, always threatening feminine, retiring "liberty." In much the same way, the Presbyterians now saw voracious "unrestrained philosophy" threatening defenseless "religion." Presbyterians of course had always insisted that faith and intellect be carefully balanced. In the early nineteenth century they became convinced that the latter had grasped the ascendancy and threatened to vanquish religion. The "unrestrained philosopher" became a stock character in Presbyterian sermons and lectures, always a man overleaping bounds and reaching for forbidden goals. John Henry Hobart, a tutor at Princeton in 1796 and later one of the fathers of the American Episcopal Church, described "mere Philosophy" to his friend

Joseph Caldwell in precisely those terms. "There is no knowing . . . where mere Philosophy will lead men. Unfortunate indeed is her influence when she exalts the pride of human reason and extinguishes those lights which only can guide her to truth." And in Kentucky the *Literary Pamphleteer,* written by the Reverend John McFarland, even more vividly described the vaunting career of the young man who sought only to improve his intellect. The *Pamphleteer* pictured "the ardent and aspiring youth rising in a splendid balloon, piercing the clouds, where cold storms toss and drive him in wild career, until precipitated with awful horror, into the arms of death." [50]

At one level, the Presbyterians' unease about "unrestrained philosophy" was indiscriminate. Thus, Jeremiah Atwater in 1809 could assert that "There is no study . . . from which, through perversion, evils may not flow." On another more important level, though, the fear of "learning" was specific. The Presbyterians sensed, correctly, that the traditional complementary, mutually supportive relationship between religion and science was changing in fundamental ways. That shift occurred, Samuel Stanhope Smith believed, when the scientist in all his pride began to "pry into the essential constitution of things," directly contradicting the dictate of God that those secrets were "beyond the reach of human faculties." Samuel Miller singled out the chemist for special censure. Once lauded as the ideal republican educator who invariably demonstrated essential cause-and-effect relationships, the chemist now was criticized for attempting to account "for all the phenomenon of motion, life, and mind." Additionally, on those facts "which clearly prove wise design, and the superintending care of an *INFINITE INTELLIGENCE,*" the chemist attempted to erect "a fabric of *atheistical* philosophy." And mathematicians were no better. The mathematical scientists demanded proof "where demonstration is not to be expected," Atwater charged. Many of life's truths are incapable of demonstration, and men must often act without "waiting for the certainty of mathematical demonstration." Even Smith believed that modern "philosophers of the mind" too often left the "plain but tedious road of experience and fact" and, under the guise of science, recklessly plunged into the "region of conjecture, where philosophy has often wandered, and perhaps, must always wander in inextricable error." [51]

Smith's criticisms of "unrestrained philosophy" are significant, because it was at his Princeton that the Presbyterians believed science was becoming most aggressive and destructive. It will be recalled that in their last session of the eighteenth century the Princeton Board had approved a non-language diploma for those young men who wished to study only the sciences at Princeton. But in a notably symbolic act, at its first meeting of the nineteenth century the board decided to suspend consideration of the granting of diplomas to "irregular" students. Then, in the wake of the 1807 riot, the board's dislike of the scientific diploma matured into a settled determination to be rid of it. The first professor to be dismissed when the faculty was reduced in 1808 was Alexander Hunter, the professor of mathematics and astronomy.[52] In that same year Archibald Alexander stood before the General Assembly and charged that "The great extension of the physical sciences, and the taste and fashion of the age, have given such a shape and direction to the academical course that I confess it appears to me to be little adapted to introduce youth to the study of the Sacred Scriptures." Thus the scientific bent of the college's curriculum was produced as yet another compelling reason for the creation of a separate, safer seminary. In 1809 the board officially discontinued the scientific diploma, and in 1812 both Smith and the chemistry professor, John Maclean, were forced to resign their positions.[53]

In light of the opposition to him, Samuel Stanhope Smith's views on science are important. Those views were, essentially, those of his father-in-law and were based firmly in a particular understanding of the philosophy of common sense. He believed that all scientific investigation must follow "the method of analysis and "reason from particular facts" that are collected "by extensive and careful observation." That investigation would produce a "uniformity of a multitude of facts" in the objects being studied. That uniformity, in turn, indicates "some principle or power in that subject, which, tho' unknown in its essence, we conclude, from our experience of the constancy of nature, will, in similar circumstances, always operate in the same way." That uniformity and predictability constituted one of the laws of nature. Those laws alone enabled the scientist "to infer the future from what we know of the past." [54]

In that process of inference, Smith refused to be trammeled. "I do not intend to wrap myself in the shroud of orthodoxy with lifeless acquiescence in established systems," he had asserted in 1788.[55] Nor would he make the Bible a scientific textbook. Instead he used an impressive grasp of the embryonic natural sciences to grapple with unresolved questions. His use of those sciences was rigorous and discriminating, and his investigations were intended to discover laws and truths supported by scientific observations, not, primarily, to vindicate revealed truth at the expense of observed facts.

Examples of Smith's use of the social and the natural sciences abound in his Princeton lectures. Of those, his discussion of the building of the Tower of Babel in particular illustrates the president's willingness to challenge orthodoxy. Smith believed that most efforts to understand the confusion of tongues at the great tower did not take into account the "laws and economy of the natural, or moral world." Those explanations had recourse only to the Bible and inevitably concluded that the confusion of tongues had a supernatural explanation, that is, the miraculous intervention of God. In opposing that explanation Smith utilized the latest information concerning ancient languages and architecture and thereby established that the tower was to have been a place of idol worship. He then referred to the "state of society" in the ancient fertile crescent. He noted that the tower's builders intended to establish an empire over the entire world and that, following "the prevalent ideas of those early eastern nations," they had determined to build a central place of worship with which to unify conquered races. Smith's explanation of the confusion of tongues at the tower reflected his command of eighteenth-century theories of social development and decay. The tower was built before the rise of absolute power; consequently, a "great division of sentiment, and violent contests" born of political and religious dissension sprang up among the conquered but uncontrollable people who were building the temple. Groups were then alienated from each other not by a miraculous confusion of tongues, but by unavoidable differences in "sentiments, projects, and designs." These caused "violent and conflicting parties that ended, at last, in total separation from one another." Then, after rejecting a supernatural explanation for an event with obvious social causes, Smith also noted that there were errors in the translations of the biblical account of the tower—the Hebrew word translated usually as "tongue" more frequently had meant "sentiment" or "opinion." Clearly, a man who admitted to one translation error would point out others.[56]

President Smith's views on science are important also because he was advocating them at a significant moment of transition in the development of common-sense philosophy in the United States. He condemned both the idealism of the eighteenth century and what he chose to call the "materialism" of the nineteenth. Idealism was "too subtle, and too far removed from the apprehensions of common sense, to be true." Accordingly, he dismissed the entire eighteenth-century controversy over cognition. No matter if an object was communicated to the brain by an image or by an "idea," it was beyond doubt for Smith that "the object itself, not its idea," was "discerned by the senses." To believe otherwise was to "annihilate the spiritual no less than the material world" and to usher in "universal skepticism." But Smith was equally severe with the "materialists." If the soul was reduced to "the condition of perishable matter," he reasoned, "the most reasonable foundation of gratitude to our creator for existence is removed; the most powerful encouragements to virtue, and restraints from vice are effectively destroyed," and mankind loses "the natural hopes, and apprehensions of a future being." [57]

Ashbel Green, Archibald Alexander, and Samuel Miller also adhered to the Scottish school. But that system of thought clearly had come to mean something different to those conservative Presbyterians than it meant to Samuel Stanhope Smith and had meant to Witherspoon and other eighteenth-century Presbyterians. The potential for an illiberal and stultifying defense of the status quo, for equating what is with what ought to be, had always been present in the Scottish school. It was, after all, built upon a firm foundation of principles that were undebatable and incapable of demonstration. And those principles, in turn, were based on something called the "common sense" of man, a phrase that could be used to justify virtually any system of values. During the last quarter of the eighteenth century, the illiberal tendencies of the Scottish school had been held in check. However they quickly became an important support of the early nineteenth century counter-reformation.

The common sense school could serve those who wished to develop the natural sciences through empirical investigation. And it could also serve those who wished only to appeal to its unassailable foundations. Presbyterian educators in the early nineteenth century clearly fell into the latter category. For them, the evidence of the senses was admissible only if it vindicated revealed truth and contributed to social order. When it did not, sensory evidence was dismissed as "speculative," "superficial," and "unsystematic." And the "common sense of mankind" gave way to the opinions of men charged with systematizing revealed truth as perceived by the Presbyterians.[58]

It is easy to make too much of the differences between Smith and his critics. Certainly in some ways the president was as conservative as Green and Miller; for him no less than for Green, the "essence" of knowledge was as closed to the scientist as it was to any other mortal. And of course Smith's opponents did not absolutely reject learning. They could hardly have done so and remained in a venerable Presbyterian tradition. Yet there is a basic difference. It was perhaps best caught by Archibald Alexander when he tried to defend "the study of mental and moral science" from the charge that no benefit was derived from such study. Alexander found much merit in the assertion that "plain common sense and the Bible, are our surest guides" and that "the speculations of philosophers have tended to perplex rather than elucidate the great practical principles which should be the guides of our lives." Alexander insisted on the "necessity of paying diligent attention to these subjects," but his reasons for so urging were defensive if not combative. The faithful must attend to philosophical speculation "in order that the errors of speculative men may be refuted, and that truth may be established on its true foundation." But Alexander would admit of no sensory evidence that contradicted his conception of the self-evident foundations of common-sense truths. "Objections to self-evident principles, however plausible, should not be regarded; for in the nature of things, no reasoning can overthrow plain intuitive truths, as no reasoning can be founded on principles more certain." [59]

The differences between the conceptions of "common sense" held by Smith and his opponents were most obvious in their attitudes toward science. The eighteenth century had systematized the discoveries of Newton and had venerated that great man. Smith's science, too, was systematic, and it was also flexible and open. For men like Ashbel Green, though, an ossified version of Newtonian science held the answer to all past, present, and future problems. Samuel Miller venerated a science "founded on principles so precise, connected and firm" that it explained with "luminous clearness" all previous and subsequent astronomical discoveries.[60] Newtonian science was also attractive because it was controlled, the celestial spheres of Newtonian astronomy always describing their divinely appointed rounds. And, of course, Newton had been a *Christian* scientist. With the "humble disposition" that befitted the scientist, Newton had had recourse at all times to the word of God, that "unerring standard of truth." [61] Samuel Miller insisted that science be used to vindicate and strengthen that "unerring standard." He noted approvingly that "Enlightened mineralogists, practical miners, and patient experimenters" were gathering information that would establish the historicity of the flood and the biblical estimate of the earth's age. From that research, Miller concluded, "has arisen a new presumptive argument in support of the authenticity of that Volume, which contains the most ancient, and the most precise of all records." [62] Other Presbyterians agreed. Virginia's John Holt Rice also defended subordinating scientific inquiry to scriptural truths. And he insisted that the submission would not repress the "boldness of the human mind" or in any way dampen the scientist's "ardour of discovery." Rather, it would promote truth by preventing "that rashness of decision, that overweening confidence in our own powers which invariably drives man into error." [63]

Thus the Presbyterian educators insisted that science be harnessed to the service of Christianity and that its place in the college curriculum be greatly reduced. Green expressed this determination in 1802. He urged the Princeton students always to remember the "somewhat peculiar" original designs of Princeton's pious founders: "the promotion of science in union with evangelical fervor." Science without religion, Green warned, was most dangerous. Likewise, religion without science is "apt to run into enthusiasm, fanaticism, superstition, bigotry and persecution . . . ." Together, he concluded, they form a "respectable and happy individual, who is also the blessing and ornament of society." [64]

But in the Presbyterian schools in the early nineteenth century the subordination of science to religion neither promoted science nor intensified evangelical fervor. On the contrary, it led to stultifying orthodoxy and to a drastic reduction of what freedom of thought had existed in the schools in the eighteenth century. James Moore, Transylvania's president, reflected this change in 1800 when he urged his students to have confidence in the judgments of their professors and thereby save themselves "from the hesitation and anxiety of perplexing doubts" caused by making up their own minds about speculative questions. The president, of course, hastened to assure his audience that he did not require "your assent to any doctrine without the conviction of your own minds." At Princeton Ashbel Green would not make even that meaningless concession. "We are not . . . going to turn inquisitors, and to search your minds, or require you to avow your secret sentiments," he told the Princetonians in 1802. But, he added a qualification that epitomized the spirit of post-Revolutionary Presbyterianism: "if any student voluntarily avows opinions hostile to revelation he must leave this institution." In practice, these informal pressures led the students to become their own censors. In 1805 the American Whig Society at Princeton voluntarily prohibited any future student "composition, orations or debates, inconsistent with the tenets of Christianity or operating against the belief in its truths and influence." [65]

THE TRIUMPH OF THE CLASSICS

In addition to the attack on "unrestrained philosophy," the early nine-teenth century saw the classics triumph in the Presbyterian colleges over the criticism of the Revolutionary period. In fact, the two developments were closely related. Princeton's scientific diploma had been accompanied by efforts to relax the requirement that all students study Greek as well as Latin to qualify for the B.A. But after the scientific diploma was abolished in 1809, the board returned the classical languages to the center of the curriculum. And the first act of Joseph Caldwell as the president of the University of North Carolina was to do away with the six-year-old rule that had abolished required classical languages for the B.A. Under Caldwell the students at North Carolina were required to conquer Greek as well as Latin.[66]

To be sure, there were still critics of classical learning in the early nineteenth century. Their critique grew out of the attack on the classics that had accompanied the republican Revolution and, in some ways, anticipated the much more effective attack that businessmen and scientists would mount in the 1820s and 1830s. For instance, shortly after the merging of Transylvania Seminary and the Kentucky Academy in 1799, the proponents and opponents of classical education carried on a lively debate in the *Kentucky Gazette*. Because the debate occurred during the battle for control of the reunited school, it is probable that the opponents' representative, "Philanthropist," was a liberal opposed to Presbyterian con-trol of Transylvania, and that the proponents' "Philologus" was a Presby-terian, possibly the Reverend James Blythe.

For the liberals, "Philanthropist" in 1802 charged that in America sub-servience to the past—even to the classical past—was inconsistent with the revolutionary present and false to the republican future. This is an age in which men have discovered errors in government, overthrown ancient laws, and disputed "almost at the point of the sword for the minutest political right," he observed. In contrast to that innovation, "in our sys-tems of education, we are content to sit down in the same errors which our ancestors taught two centuries ago." [67]

"Philanthropist" made much of the charge that language study taught a knowledge of "words" rather than "things." With Benjamin Rush, he believed that learning only words "tends to keep the mind vacant." And "Philanthropist" noted that the meanings of words change as rapidly as new words are invented. At any rate, it mattered little if a writer knew what a word meant to some dead civilization so long as he was aware of its meaning for his own culture.[68] He also rejected the idea that a classical education was a prerequisite for learning English. By analogy, he observed, a student of English should conquer French, Anglo-Saxon, and Dutch, all languages from which English was more directly descended than Latin and Greek. To learn English, "we must study that language, and that only."[69] In all his charges "Philanthropist" dismissed the contention that language study was valuable because it exercised the mental faculties at an early age. He rejected early language study as preparation for more rigorous investigations by insisting that surely boys were capable of reason before age fifteen. Moreover, he pointed out a real contradiction. If language training was difficult enough to exercise and indeed form the faculties, how could it also be simple enough to precede all other study? And, at any rate, did not mathematics—admittedly difficult and still accessible to youth—also fulfill the functions desired by the defenders of the classics? Rather than forcing disgruntled young boys to conquer the classics, "Philanthropist," like Rush, suggested that adolescence be recognized as a distinct and significant part of life and that it be spent in studying geography, biography, and natural history, all of which would introduce a young man not to dead words and men but to the world immediately around him.[70]

"Philanthropist's" articles elicited a flurry of response in the Kentucky press. The most interesting and complete reaction was from one "Philologus," possibly James Blythe. Significantly, he spent little time defending the power of the classics to exercise and form the faculties. Rather, he concentrated on their capacity to produce a certain kind of man. "The principal object of Education is to make youth wise and virtuous citizens and thereby qualify them for being useful members of society," he began, traditionally enough. But moving to a rather new emphasis, "Philologus" asserted that the classics were "exceedingly well-calculated" to achieve that object because they furnish "excellent precepts of morality, sage observations, wise maxims, and prudent directions, for the regulation of our passions, and for the conduct of our lives." The ancient historians examined the past and held up that which was virtuous for emulation and that which was not, for scorn. The classical orators used oratory only in the cause of humanity and patriotism, and rather than stirring the ill-bred mob to vicious acts of destruction, they aroused the faculties of lethargic citizens to acts of benevolence. The poets in like manner presented virtue in the most becoming garments and portrayed vice in a manner that invited the reader's disgust. A classical education, then, was above all else intended to produce right conduct inspired by the example of the virtuous ancients.[71]

The Revolutionary defenders of the classics had said no less. But in the aftermath of Mr. Jefferson's "Revolution of 1800," "Philologus" invested the classics with an almost mystical power to produce citizens immune to the blandishments of democratic demagogues. A classical education "humanizes the wildness of nature, and tranquilizes the passions of youth," and teaches them, as adults, to hate excess in others. Studying the Greeks and Romans somehow made the young honest and simple, not easily dazzled by outward appearances or overly fond of the graces. Moreover, a boy who could read the classical authors had always available to him an innocent and instructive form of entertainment. Rather than seek out low company, the classically educated youth could always entertain himself in the privacy of his own study. Finally, when that young man reached maturity, he would be able to judge men and things by the "intrinsic merit of their actions," not by superficial appearances. He would be able to overcome the prejudices of mobs and would not be fooled by show, always "preferring real merit in rags, to ignorant audacity in brocade." [72]

Like Nisbet in the Revolutionary era, "Philologus" insisted that the classics be thoroughly sanitized. He even went beyond Nisbet in describing the Greeks and Romans as Christians before their times. Poets like Ovid might have written about the popular religions of the pagans, but the great philosophers had clung stubbornly to a purer belief in a religion of one supreme deity. Moreover, those classical philosophers taught the immortality of the soul and a system of rewards and punishments in an afterlife. In short, the pagans had practiced a religion that closely approximated the "outlines of natural and revealed religion" and had elaborated a system of morals very like that of the Gospels.[73]

Thus were the sanitized Greeks and Romans thrown into the breach to save the republic from the unleashed mob that had put Mr. Jefferson into the White House. The man who had been educated in the classics was described by the Presbyterians as virtuous, temperate, just, discriminating, somewhat aloof, and in complete control of his passions. He was the man who traditionally had ruled American society but whose continued right to rule was being challenged in a society increasingly reluctant to honor his classical virtues. As much as anything else, the realization of that rejection fueled the Presbyterians' determination to tighten the discipline in their schools, to isolate those schools from the contamination of the outside world, to restrain the alarming emphasis in their curriculum on the natural and mathematical sciences, and finally to restore to the center of that curriculum the study of the classics.[74]

STAGNATION AND DECLINE

When the Princeton Board dismissed 125 of the school's more than two hundred students after the 1807 rebellion, one of the trustees remarked, "We will probably have fewer students . . . but a few under discipline is better than a mob without any." [75] The trustee was partially correct. Princeton did indeed have fewer students after 1807 as parents refused to subject their sons to the harsh regime inaugurated by Green after 1812. But those students who did enroll proved resistant to that regime. The new president negated earlier curriculum revisions, tightened up discipline, and, perhaps most important, encouraged pious young men to organize into religious bands to encourage each other in the faith and to prepare Princeton for a revival of evangelical religion. And in 1815 those efforts were rewarded with the first of several extraordinary revivals that marked Green's tenure. But the impact of those revivals was temporary. What was permanent was student rebellion and intellectual stultification. Between 1812 and 1815 the leading Presbyterian college fell into a period of decline from which it did not recover before the Civil War.[76] The same was true of every other Presbyterian school. Hampden-Sydney and Washington College between 1800 and 1825 became stagnating centers of Presbyterian orthodoxy increasingly dominated by Union Seminary. In western Pennsylvania the Washington Academy and Jefferson College were absorbed in competing with each other to produce Presbyterian ministers. And in Kentucky Transylvania did not recover in the antebellum period from the Presbyterian assault on Holley's administration, while the Presbyterians' college at Danville, Centre, had to fight for survival in a growing field of fiercely denominational colleges.

That process of decline was most evident at Dickinson. By the time of his death in 1805, Charles Nisbet had alienated much of Dickinson's natural clientele in central and western Pennsylvania with his outspoken Federalism and harsh criticism of most things American. His successor, Jeremiah Atwater, was no improvement. The former president of Middlebury College promulgated the first code of student regulations at the college, built the first dormitory at Dickinson, and unsuccessfully tried to transform the frontier school into a replica of Middlebury by emphasizing ministerial education and encouraging the forming of religious organizations. To no avail. In 1811 an increasingly anticlerical board of trustees, dominated by independent laymen from Carlisle, presented Atwater with an astonishing *fait accompli*. They engaged as the college's professor of chemistry the celebrated—even notorious—Thomas Cooper, a friend of Joseph Priestley, a deist, and, it was whispered, an infidel. Thomas Jefferson might call Cooper "the greatest man in America in the powers of the mind and in acquired information, and that without a single exception," but to Atwater his appointment was simply "a fatal blow." [77] The hiring of the great scientist excited the students and townspeople alike. They attended his scientific "demonstrations," and the students in particular responded to his lectures because their "relevant" nature contrasted markedly with the classical curriculum favored by Atwater. Between 1811 and 1815 the campus was in chaos. The board was divided between the supporters of Cooper and of Atwater. Discipline degenerated to the point that students openly offered and accepted challenges to duels. In 1815 one student was killed in a duel and the entire faculty resigned, Atwater and Cooper having hopelessly divided the professors as to the ends and means of higher education in the early nineteenth century. Shortly thereafter the college at Carlisle closed its doors, the first republican educational institution to do so. The school would be reopened briefly under Presbyterian auspices in the 1820s, only to cease operations again. And when the doors reopened permanently in 1833, Dickinson was in no way connected with the Presbyterian Church. It was, instead, part of the Methodist wave of the future. [78]

The Presbyterian schools, then, by 1800 were bastions of orthodoxy, dedicated to advancing Presbyterianism in the fierce denominational competition that characterized American religious life. They were, therefore, quite different from the broadly based, energetic college established in colonial Princeton by the expansive New Side Presbyterians. Nor did the denominational schools resemble very closely the republican institutions of the Revolutionary period. The New Sides had conceived of Princeton as the center of a Christian commonwealth and intended it to assist in the reformation of American society, while the Revolutionary Presbyterians had been convinced that the schools they established would sustain a moral reformation to accompany the political revolution the Americans had successfully prosecuted. But the reformation never came, and the Revolution threatened to devour its children. In the wake of that turbulent experience, the Presbyterians renounced their Revolutionary ardor and fundamentally transformed their institutions of higher learning.

But these later Presbyterians were more revolutionary than they knew. By 1820 they had, albeit reluctantly, embraced a view of society radically different from the view that had sustained American society from its inception. The eighteenth-century Presbyterians had slowly modified their vision of an America free of selfishness and contention. First the Christian commonwealth and then the republic failed to become the organic community that was the Presbyterians' social ideal. Gradually the Presbyterians evolved a view of society that allowed them to accept as inevitable the social conflict and competition that appeared to be endemic in America. But at the same time, they made of their denomination the organic community they had failed to find in commonwealth or republic. That community would compete with other denominational communities, with no obvious concern for the "common good" of society. After a half-century of struggling with the reality of conflict and competition in American life, the Presbyterians in the early nineteenth century finally abandoned their organic view of society, fortified their denominational community and its colleges, and entered the fray. Few changes in American history have been more revolutionary.

Epilogue: Toward 1837

Just beyond the chronological limits of the present study looms the Presbyterian schism of 1837.[1] By all measures the most acrimonious of the denomination's divisions, the 1837 schism in fact created two Presbyterian denominations that for a generation competed with each other as vigorously as they contended with Baptists, Methodists, and Congregationalists. Not until 1869, not until the tragedy of the Civil War had eclipsed their disagreements, were the Old and New Sides of the 1837 schism reunited. And eight years before that reunion, the contentious example of the earlier division contributed to yet another schism, this one the apparently permanent division of the American Presbyterian Church into northern and southern denominations. For forty years after 1830, then, the history of American Presbyterianism was one of unremitting warfare, the major battles of which occurred between 1830 and 1838. The president of the United States during those years was himself an Old Side Presbyterian, and Andrew Jackson reportedly once observed that the celebrated political donnybrooks of his contentious administrations were neither as acrimonious nor as troublesome as the "dissensions in the Presbyterian Church."[2]

Indeed, the Presbyterian schism of 1837 provides a useful vehicle for understanding much of Jacksonian America. Like many of that period's significant political confrontations, the ecclesiastical schism was, to some

287

extent, a conflict over slavery. Old Sides, by no means all of whom were southerners, believed that the New Side ranks were infested with Abolitionists who would force the church to take a stand on a civil issue beyond its purview, a fear that surely was exaggerated in the extreme. Many historians of the schism have emphasized yet another Old Side charge, that the New Sides were heretics who preached an Arminian theology with increasing boldness in the Age of Jackson. The charge was an ancient one and was probably no more accurate in 1830 than it had been in 1800. It was an accusation, though, that became notorious through the sensational heresy trial of the Reverend Albert Barnes in 1831.[3]

The immediate cause of the schism is beyond debate. In 1801 the Presbyterian General Assembly joined the Congregational General Association of Connecticut in a Plan of Union under which the two denominations agreed to evangelize the old northwest in concert. By 1830 it was clear to all concerned that the Presbyterians had gained the most from the union: far more churches were organized on presbyterian than on congregational lines, and three new synods in the northwest attested to the vigor of the Presbyterian half of "Presbygationalism." That undeniable fact notwithstanding, Old Sides insisted that the churches established under the Plan of Union were only nominally Presbyterian, that they were in fact Congregational, and increasingly a threat to the denominational integrity of Presbyterianism. The Old Sides believed that the cooperative spirit that produced the Plan of Union also opened the coffers and territory of the Presbyterian Church to the depredations of the voluntary associations that proliferated after 1810.[4] By 1830 the largest of those associations—the American Home Missionary Society and the American Education Society—were nationwide in scope, controlled not by clergymen but by laymen, and were directed not from Philadelphia but from New York City and Boston.

Stymied by New Side majorities in the General Assemblies that convened between 1830 and 1834, the Old Sides finally took the extraordinary measure of convening in 1835 before the Assembly's annual meeting. The meeting was held in Pittsburgh—in the heart of New Side territory—and was in effect a council of war. The Old Sides were determined to gain control of the 1835 Assembly, to abrogate the Plan of Union, to withdraw Presbyterian support from the voluntary societies, and to ensure that the Assembly in the future controlled its own missionary and educational activities.[5] Since the New Sides opposed each of those aims, they would have to be expelled. Fired with the enthusiasm of the

Pittsburgh Convention, the Old Sides for two years mounted an un-precedented organizational campaign aimed at solidifying their ranks and at capturing the General Assembly at the earliest date. Their day came not in 1835 but two years later. Finally in command of a scant majority, the Old Sides at the 1837 meeting of the General Assembly declared the Plan of Union unconstitutional and made their decree retroactive; conse-quently, they expelled as not truly Presbyterian the three northwestern synods organized after 1801 under the Plan.[6] Those synods were the center of New Side strength, which now ceased almost to exist in the Assembly. After expelling their opponents, the Old Sides in quick succes-sion withdrew Presbyterian support from the interdenominational mis-sion and education societies, forbade their operation in Presbyterian churches, and organized denominational societies to direct those activities instead. In the tumultuous Assembly of 1838 the New Sides attempted to challenge the amazing proceedings of the 1837 Assembly, only to hear the Old Side moderator declare, "We know you not." For the next thirty-one years, that retort would characterize the attitude of Old and New Sides toward their former brothers.[7]

The Presbyterian schism of 1837 and the competing denominations that emerged from it appear to call into question, if they do not outright invalidate, the central conclusion of the present study. If by 1820 the Presbyterians had established a denominational community that would allow them to compete with other denominations, how explain the fact that only seventeen years later that community divided, its two parts competing with each other as well as with Baptists and Congregational-ists? Actually, the contradiction is more apparent than real.

Virtually all Presbyterians of the early nineteenth century accepted two related propositions. First, in a voluntaristic society the denomination would be the primary focus of religious life. A New Side would yield to no one in his esteem for Presbyterian polity, and Old and New Side alike insisted on the benefits of denominational competition. But as a precon-dition to that competition, all Presbyterians demanded that the republic be visibly Christian. To that end, they endorsed in the early years of the nineteenth century the first efforts to organize the faithful of all denomina-tions into voluntary associations to support domestic and foreign missions, to establish theological seminaries, and to eradicate every vice of which evil men were capable. It was argued that individual denominations were not equal to the task, that united action was itself laudable, and that the voluntary societies were noble experiments peculiarly suited to the free conditions of the new republic.[8] But above all else, the voluntary societies were intended to establish an environment in which Christians might in clear conscience erect denominational communities to propagate their particular version of the Christian faith.

The first hint that the means might destroy the end came in 1818. In that year Elias Boudinot, a New Jersey Presbyterian, led several men with strong ties to New England Congregationalism in establishing the Education Society of the Presbyterian Church in the United States of America. Around him the New Jersey layman gathered ministers and other laymen who opposed denominational control of missions, who had strong allegiances to the voluntary empire, and who then became the nucleus of the New Side party. Not a month later the "Princeton-Philadelphia axis" began to coalesce around clergymen like Archibald Alexander, Princeton President Ashbel Green, and Princeton Seminary Professor Samuel Miller. That group of clerics then created the Educational Society of the Presbyterian Church, which was to be under the sole control of the General Assembly.[9] All efforts by third parties to unite the groups failed. By the late twenties the New Sides' board actively cooperated with the American Education Society, while after 1831 the opposing board of the General Assembly became the center of Old Side strength.

Gradually the lines were drawn. The Pittsburgh Convention blasted the American Home Mission Board. That board's goal of evangelizing the west had once been applauded by all Presbyterians as a necessary step to the creation of a Christian republic. Now the Convention warned darkly that "the Assembly's own Board of Missions, created by herself, governed by herself, and amenable to herself, finds a great and powerful rival in her own house, with whom she comes in perpetual conflict." [10] Samuel Miller for a while tried to point out carefully those functions which voluntary societies might legitimately perform, but by 1837 the time for precision and moderation was past.[11] As in the late 1730s, reason gave way to rhetoric, and the church was split by men convinced of the righteousness of their cause.

The Old and New Sides in 1837 apparently were convinced that they had to choose. The choice seemed to be between the denomination, the new institutional form of American Christianity, and the voluntary societies, those even newer institutions that were intended to produce an environment in which the denominations could flourish. The Old Sides, for their part, could see in the voluntary societies only "great and powerful" rivals in their own house, while the New Sides condemned the Old

Side denominational emphasis as *"exclusive* and *sectarian,"* and thus unfit for "freemen" who have "breathed an air too liberal and elastic, to feel ourselves at home, and in our own element, when hemmed in by such confined and narrow walls." [12]

But the New Sides had assisted in raising those walls. And the Old Sides had nourished the first voluntary societies. In truth, no choice had to be made in 1837 between the voluntary society as a purposive instrument and the denomination as an ecclesiastical—or community—form. By 1830 the great engine of the "benevolent empire" and its voluntary societies had done its work. In 1829 William Ellery Channing marveled, "without much exaggeration," that "everything is done now by Societies. Men have learned what wonders can be accomplished in certain cases by union, and seem to think that union is competent to everything. You can scarcely name an object for which some institution has not been formed." [13] Channing's fellow New Englander, Orestes Brownson, was more impatient with the ubiquitous societies: "matters have come to such a pass that a peaceable man can hardly venture to eat or drink, to go to bed or get up, to correct his children or kiss his wife, without obtaining the permission and direction of some . . . society." [14] Through those societies, and through the great revival that spread them, evangelical Protestants by 1830 had vanquished deism, fashioned an evangelical orthodoxy for the republic, and stood ready to exclude from the religious life of the nation the Mormons, the Catholics, the eccentric Transcendentalists—all who might dissent from that evangelical orthodoxy. And both Old and New Side Presbyterians were among the most orthodox of the orthodox. In a very real sense, the schism of 1837 was a luxury, a luxury purchased by thirty years of unrelenting evangelical effort. Now, in separate and competing camps, each side could look to its purity, tidy up its ecclesiology, and go about the business of erecting a denominational community, a community based on doctrinal uniformity, of course, but also on shared educational and increasingly significant kinship patterns.

Finally, it must be said that the experience of the Great Schism of the colonial period and the schism that accompanied the frontier revival made easier the division of 1837. Nothing is clearer in the records of the 1837 schism than that both sides had learned well the lessons of those earlier divisions and, more important, were giving close attention to the emerging art of partisan politics. Thus Ashbel Green could urge his compatriots in the Old Side to organize and propagandize: ". . . when parties exist, and are earnestly opposed to each other, the one that uses no means to obtain or preserve an ascendancy, will almost inevitably be crushed, by the one that actively employs such means."[15] Other Presbyterians might deplore Green's advice, but they all took it to heart. The Presbyterians now lived in the world of Martin Van Buren, who first advanced a defense of political competition as a positive good.[16] As did the wily president in politics, American Protestants in the 1840s and 1850s developed a full-blown defense of denominational competition. In religion as well as in politics Americans in the antebellum period emphasized not the shared interests, the common good, of society but, instead, the ambitions of political and religious groups and now defended as a positive good any competition among those groups.

It remained for the trauma of the Civil War to reveal the logical conclusions of that fundamental change. In his last formal address to the United States Senate John C. Calhoun in 1850 discussed the schisms in the Baptist, Methodist, and Presbyterian churches as the prelude to the inevitable disruption of the American union. "It is a great mistake to suppose that disunion can be effected by a single blow," he warned. "The cords which bound these States together in one common Union, are far too numerous and powerful for that." Disunion, Calhoun believed, "must be the work of time. It is only through a long process, and successively that the cords can be snapped, until the whole fabric falls asunder." The Senator from South Carolina then traced with keen insight the process whereby the three great evangelical denominations had created ecclesiastical communities that in the early antebellum period "embraced the whole Union." Principal laymen and clerics of each denomination had met annually "to transact business relating to their common concerns." There they devised plans for "disseminating the Bible—establishing missions, distributing tracts—and of establishing presses for the publication of tracts, newspapers, and periodicals, with a view of diffusing religious information—and for the support of their respective doctrines and creeds." Taken as a whole, those efforts "contributed greatly to strengthen the bonds of the Union. The ties which held each denomination together formed a strong cord to hold the Union together . . . ." Those ecclesiastical bonds, however, had not been able "to resist the explosive effect of slavery agitation." First in the Presbyterian Church, then in the Baptist and Methodist communities, those cords had broken with "explosive force" and instead of exhibiting "that feeling of attachment and devotion to the interests of the whole church which was formerly felt," each of the great evangelical churches in 1850 was "arrayed into two hostile bodies, engaged in litigation about what was formerly their common property." [17]

Calhoun, of course, was right. But the American evangelical denominations in the thirty years before the Civil War did more than simply debate the pros and cons of slavery. Those debates, and the fundamental differences that they revealed within each ecclesiastical community, forced American Protestants to grapple with fundamental questions about the nature of social unions: what constitutes a bond of union? what are the origins of that bond? under what circumstances may it be broken? what are the rights of majorities and minorities within a social union? For the American Presbyterians at least, those were familiar questions. In that sense, their entire history in the New World had been a rehearsal for disunion.

Notes

Chapter I

1. See especially James T. Lemon, *The Best Poor Man's Country: A Geographical Study of Early Southeastern Pennsylvania* (Baltimore, 1972), pp. 1–41; and Conrad M. Arensberg, "American Communities," *American Anthropologist*, 57 (December, 1955): 1143–1162, for the best discussions of the implications of land-settlement patterns for cultural configurations.

2. John C. Rainbolt, "The Absence of Towns in Seventeenth-Century Virginia," *The Journal of Southern History*, 35 (August, 1969): 343–360. The Clayton quotation is on p. 343.

3. Francis Makemie, *A Plain and Friendly Perswasive to the Inhabitants of Virginia and Maryland, For Promoting Towns and Cohabitation* (London, 1705), in Boyd S. Schlenther, *The Life and Writings of Francis Makemie* (Philadelphia, 1971), p. 141.

4. There is no adequate published study of presbyterianism as a decision-making and administrative system, but see, Boyd S. Schlenther, "The Presbytery as Organ of Church Life and Government in American Presbyterianism, 1706–1788," unpublished Ph.D. dissertation, University of Edinburgh, 1965. Sessional, presbyterial, and synodical records provide ample material for a much more ambitious study than Schlenther's, and the Presbyterian Historical Society in Philadelphia has succeeded in assembling virtually all extant eighteenth-century records in some form.

5. This is not to deny the very real differences in the historical development

295

of a group of Protestants who were, still, multinational, but merely to urge the crucial role of the Confession as both a response to and source of unity. For a needed reminder of the diversity of the European Presbyterian experience see, C. G. Bolam, *et al.* (eds.), *The English Presbyterians: From Elizabethan Puritanism to Modern Unitarianism* (Boston, 1968).

6. The most thoughtful analysis of the covenant theology remains Perry Miller, "The Marrow of Puritan Divinity," in *Errand into the Wilderness* (New York, Harper Torchbook edition, 1964), pp. 48–98.

7. For one such biography see Edmund S. Morgan, *The Puritan Dilemma: The Story of John Winthrop* (Boston, 1958). Michael Walzer has observed astutely that future studies of the English Puritans ought to be based on collections of these biographies, and, although he does not follow his own advice in the work, any serious student of Puritanism must now take into account the psychological and sociological theories advanced by Walzer in *The Revolution of the Saints: A Study in the Origins of Radical Politics* (Cambridge, Mass., 1965).

8. Leonard J. Trinterud, *The Forming of an American Tradition: A Re-examination of Colonial Presbyterianism* (Philadelphia, 1949), pp. 13–37, remains the most detailed and thoughtful discussion of the founding of American Presbyterianism. Keith J. Hardman, "Jonathan Dickinson and the Course of American Presbyterianism, 1717–1747," unpublished Ph.D. dissertation, University of Pennsylvania, 1971, discusses the origins of Presbyterianism in Long Island and in New Jersey. For the beginnings in Pennsylvania and Maryland see Guy S. Klett, *Presbyterians in Colonial Pennsylvania* (Philadelphia, 1937), pp. 36–38; and Robert Pickens Davis, "Makemie Churches in the First Presbytery," *Journal of the Presbyterian Historical Society,* 29 (June, 1951): 115–125. For New England see, Walter M. Boston, Jr., "A Study of Presbyterianism in Colonial New England," unpublished Ph.D. dissertation, Michigan State University, 1971.

9. John Calam, *Parsons and Pedagogues: The S.P.G. Adventure in American Education* (New York, 1971); William G. McLoughlin, *New England Dissent, 1630–1833: The Baptists and the Separation of Church and State* (Cambridge, Mass., 1971), 1: 305; Leonard J. Kramer, "The Political Ethics of the American Presbyterian Clergy in the Eighteenth Century," (unpublished Ph.D. dissertation, Yale University, 1942), p. 13n, for the statistics.

10. September 23, 1728, *Records of the Presbyterian Church in the United States of America* . . . (Philadelphia, 1904), p. 92; William J. Hinke (ed.), "Church Records of Neshaminy and Bensalem, Bucks County, 1710–1738," *Journal of the Presbyterian Historical Society,* 1 (May, 1900): 129.

11. Jonathan Dickinson, *A Sermon Preached at the opening of the Synod of Philadelphia . . . 1722 . . .* (Boston, 1723), pp. 5–6.

12. Klett, *Colonial Pennsylvania,* pp. 116–126, 169–171. Quotation on p. 170.

13. For a representative denial, this one by the Philadelphia Presbytery to preserve a congregation from "rupture," see, May 20, 1708, *Presbyterian Records,* pp. 11–12.

14. Dickinson, *Sermon . . . 1722,* p. 14.

15. The best discussions of the controversy are now to be found in two dissertations: Hardman, "Dickinson," pp. 42–65; and especially the analysis in Elizabeth A. Ingersoll's superb "Francis Alison: American Philosophe, 1705–1799," (unpublished Ph.D. dissertation, University of Delaware, 1974), pp. 3–38. Ingersoll's is among the most sophisticated of the work yet done in colonial Presbyterianism.

16. Efforts to trace the Subscription Controversy and subsequent Presbyterian divisions to differences between liberal New Englanders and rigid Ulstermen tend to become simplistic and ignore especially the extent to which the Scotch-Irish were divided by generations.

17. John Thomson, *An Overture Presented to the Reverend Synod of dissenting Ministers, Sitting in Philadelphia, in the Month of September, 1728* (Philadelphia, 1729), pp. 8, 26, 27.

18. Jonathan Dickinson, *Remarks Upon a Discourse Intituled An Overture* . . . (New York, 1729), pp. 6, 8–9, 20, 22.

19. Thomson, *An Overture,* pp. 8–15, 20–24.

20. *Ibid.,* p. 12; Dickinson, *Remarks,* pp. 24, 3. For another press war that involved Presbyterians and Benjamin Franklin in the 1730s, see the discussion of the Samuel Hemphill affair in Melvin H. Buxbaum, *Benjamin Franklin and the Zealous Presbyterians* (University Park, Pa., 1975), pp. 80–83.

21. September 19, 1729, *Presbyterian Records,* p. 94.

22. April 4, 1735, Minutes of the Donegal Presbytery (microfilm in the Union Theological Seminary, Richmond, Va.), 1: 58; June 11, September 18, 1735, *ibid.,* 1: 64, 82–83. Hereafter cited as Don. Pby. Min.

23. May 15, 1733, *ibid.,* 1: 7.

24. May 4 (?), 1738, June 19, September 4, 1739, May 31, 1740, *ibid.,* 1: 162, 179, 182, 192.

25. October 25, 1738, Minutes of the Presbytery of Philadelphia (microfilm in the Presbyterian Historical Society, Philadelphia, Pa.), 2: 63.

26. September 1, 1737, October 18–19, 1738, April 4–5, 1739, Don. Pby. Min., 1: 149, 169, 171, 174–175.

27. George Gillespie, *A Sermon Against Divisions in Christ's Churches* . . . (Philadelphia, 1740), pp. 1, 16; Jonathan Dickinson, *Danger of Schisms and Contentions* . . . (New York, 1739), p. 4.

28. Thomson, *Overture,* pp. 12, 26–27.

29. Dickinson, *Remarks,* pp. 6, 24.

30. Dickinson, *Danger of Schisms,* p. 12.

31. Samuel Finley, *Christ Triumphing, and Satan Raging* . . . (Philadelphia, 1741), pp. 10, 30.

32. Gilbert Tennent, *The Danger of an Unconverted Ministry* . . . , in Alan Heimert and Perry Miller (eds.), *The Great Awakening* (Indianapolis, 1967), p. 77; Gilbert Tennent, *Remarks Upon a Protestation Presented to the Synod of Philadelphia* . . . (Philadelphia, 1741), pp. 13, 40.

33. Tennent, *Unconverted Ministry,* p. 93.

34. Synod of Philadelphia, *An Examination and Refutation of Mr. Gilbert Tennent's Remarks* . . . (Philadelphia, 1742), pp. 5, 35.

35. [Robert Cross], *A Protestation Presented to the Synod of Philadelphia* . . . (Philadelphia, 1741), p. 13.

36. Syn. of Phil., *Examination and Refutation,* pp. 44, 65.

37. *Ibid.,* p. 43.

38. For the campaign against the licensing of John Rowland by the New Brunswick Presbytery see Trinterud, *American Tradition,* pp. 80–85.

39. John Thomson, *The Government of the Church of Christ, And the Authority of Church Judicatories established on a Scripture Foundation* . . . (Philadelphia, 1741), pp. xii, 5, 55, 56.

40. *Ibid.,* pp. 7, 63.

41. Finley, *Christ Triumphing,* p. 30.

42. Thomson, *Overture,* pp. 8, 25–29, 32.

43. Syn. of Phil., *Examination,* p. 11.

44. Thomson, *Overture,* p. 22.

45. May 24, 1744, *Presbyterian Records,* p. 174.

46. Samuel Blair, *A Vindication of the Brethren who were unjustly and illegally cast out of the Synod of Philadelphia* . . . . (Philadelphia, 1744), pp. 8, 21.

47. Dickinson, *Sermon* . . . *1722,* pp. 2, 3, 11; Tennent, *Remarks Upon a Protestation,* pp. 31, 67; Dickinson, *Remarks Upon an Overture,* p. 16; Blair, *Vindication,* p. 46.

48. Dickinson, *Sermon* . . . *1722,* pp. 15, 12.

49. Tennent, *Remarks Upon a Protestation,* p. 63.

50. Blair, *Vindication,* pp. 17, 20; Dickinson, *Remarks Upon a Discourse,* p. 28.

51. Tennent, *Remarks Upon a Protestation,* pp. 58, 59.

52. Dickinson, *Remarks Upon a Discourse,* pp. 9–13, 20, 24; Blair, *Vindication,* p. 30; Tennent, *Remarks Upon a Protestation,* p. 30.

53. Thomson, *Government of the Church of Christ,* pp. 6, 60, 63, 69.

54. *Ibid.,* pp. 6, 64, 89, 91, 107.

55. October 7, 1732, Don. Pby. Min., 1: 2.

56. May 27, 1741, *Presbyterian Records,* p. 155; June 1, 1741, *ibid.,* p. 160n; Syn. of Phil., *Examination and Refutation,* pp. 135–136, 143.

57. June 1, 1741, *Presbyterian Records*, pp. 158–159; [Cross], *Protestation*, p. 9; Syn. of Phil., *Examination and Refutation*, p. 137.

58. Tennent, *Remarks Upon a Protestation*, pp. 14–15, 40; Syn. of Phil., *Examination and Refutation*, p. 137.

59. Syn. of Phil., *Examination and Refutation*, p. 137; Thomson, *Government of the Church of Christ*, pp. 62, 64, 67, 80.

60. Syn. of Phil., *Examination and Refutation*, pp. 56, 61, 62, 64; Thomson, *Government of the Church of Christ*, p. 55.

61. May 28, 1742, *Presbyterian Records*, p. 162.

62. May 30, 1743, *ibid.*, p. 168.

63. May 24, 1744, *ibid.*, p. 174.

64. *Ibid.*

65. Blair, *Vindication*, pp. 24, 26, 36.

66. Tennent, *Remarks Upon a Protestation*, p. 34; *A Declaration of the Presbyteries of New-Brunswick and New-Castle* . . . (Philadelphia, 1743), pp. 2, 7.

67. The graphic phrase is from an Old Side complaint against the New Sides' alleged plans to invade their territory by holding the 1755 meeting of the Synod of New York in Philadelphia. See May 31, 1755, *Presbyterian Records*, p. 219.

68. The best discussion of the impact of the Moravians' arrival on the Presbyterians is in Ingersoll, "Francis Alison," pp. 415–426.

69. September 28, 1750, *Presbyterian Records*, p. 244.

70. September 19, 1745, *ibid.*, p. 233.

71. September 27, 1751, *ibid.*, p. 246; October 5, 1753, *ibid.*, p. 254.

72. September 6, 1751, *ibid.*, p. 204.

73. May 22, 1758, *ibid.*, p. 286; Francis Alison, *Peace and Union recommended* . . . (Philadelphia, 1758), pp. 12, 13–20. Ingersoll's "Francis Alison" is an exhaustive study of Alison that is never exhausting.

74. October 5, 1753, *Presbyterian Records*, p. 253.

75. May 27, 1756, *ibid.*, p. 222.

76. *Ibid.*, p. 223.

77. May 22, 1758, *ibid.*, p. 286.

78. Ingersoll, "Francis Alison," pp. 429–431.

79. Francis Alison to Ezra Stiles, December 12, 1767, Alison-Stiles Correspondence (copy in the Presbyterian Historical Society of MSS in the Archives of Yale University, New Haven, Conn.).

80. Gilbert Tennent, *Irenicum Ecclesiasticum* . . . (Philadelphia, 1749), p. 10; Alison, *Peace and Union*, pp. 12, 41–42.

81. Tennent, *Irenicum*, p. 8; Alison, *Peace and Union*, p. 12. See also Tennent, *The Blessedness of Peace-Makers* . . . (Philadelphia, 1765), p. 17.

82. Alison, *Peace and Union,* pp. 21, 34, 39; Tennent, *Blessedness of Peace-Makers,* p. 9.

83. May 31, 1755, *Presbyterian Records,* p. 218.

84. At this point the Presbyterians confirm James Henretta's useful criticism of Michael Zuckerman's *Peaceable Kingdoms: New England Towns in the Eighteenth Century* (New York, 1970). Henretta notes that the communal values that Zuckerman argues persist unchanged though challenged right up to the American Revolution were "enunciated most clearly and most frequently" when under attack, that is, during the decade immediately following the revival. Henretta sees the colonists, caught up in social and economic change, invoking "the old precepts of uniformity, harmony, and community" until a new value system can be found. In the cases of the Presbyterians in the middle and southern colonies, at least as far as religion was concerned, those older precepts remained remarkably powerful. Their invocation at the reunion may indeed have been in some sense a futile call to "a vanished past." But those precepts in their residual power had in fact fueled the Presbyterian reunion. If they no longer reflected reality precisely, they were certainly more than what is described by Henretta—convenient way stations on the road to a more modern concept of community. See James H. Henretta, "The Morphology of New England in the Colonial Period," *The Journal of Interdisciplinary History,* 2 (Autumn, 1971): 395.

Chapter II

1. David Bostwick, *Self disclaimed and Christ exalted: A Sermon, preached at Philadelphia, before the Reverend Synod of New-York, May 25, 1758* (Philadelphia, 1758), pp. viii, 13–15. My understanding of the concept of individualism has been greatly influenced by C. B. Macpherson, *The Political Theory of Possessive Individualism* (Oxford, 1962).

2. For a somewhat dated discussion of New England's Great Awakening as a social conflict, see John C. Miller, "Religion, Finance, and Democracy in Massachusetts," *New England Quarterly,* 6 (1933): 29–58. For a weak refutation of Miller's argument, see Edwin S. Gaustad, "Society and the Great Awakening in New England," *William and Mary Quarterly,* Third Series, 11 (October, 1954): 566–577. The best treatment of the Great Awakening as an effort at social reformation is Alan Heimert's overenthusiastic discussion of the Calvinist clergy in *Religion and the American Mind from the Great Awakening to the Revolution* (Cambridge, Mass., 1966), especially Chapter III. The most successful efforts to recapture the crisis of confidence of colonial society at the midcentury have been in the articles of Jack P. Greene: "Search for Identity: An Interpretation of the Meaning of Selected Patterns of Social Response in Eighteenth-Century America," *Journal of Social History,*

3 (1970): 189–220; and "An Uneasy Connection: An Analysis of the Pre-conditions of the American Revolution," in Stephen G. Kurtz and James H. Hutson (eds.), *Essays on the American Revolution* (Chapel Hill, 1973), pp. 33–80. Particularly helpful for the neglected period between the revival and Revolution is Kerry Arnold Trask, "In the Pursuit of Shadows: A Study of Collective Hope and Despair in Provincial Massachusetts in the Era of the Seven Years War, 1748–1764," unpublished Ph.D. dissertation, University of Minnesota, 1971. Finally, in one of his last works Richard Hofstadter used the sharp eye of the nonspecialist to catch much of the unsettledness, tension, and trauma that has escaped other students of the late colonial period. See *America at 1750: A Social Portrait* (New York, 1971).

3. September 2, 1735, Minutes of the Presbytery of Donegal (microfilm in Union Theological Seminary, Richmond, Va.), 1: 72; October 10, 1739, November 5–6, 1740, April 7–8, 1741, *ibid.*, 1: 187, 200, 202, 212, 213; December 4, 1739, Minutes of the Presbytery of Philadelphia (microfilm in the Presbyterian Historical Society, Philadelphia, Pa.), 2: 79–80; April 23, 1740, June 20, 1740, *ibid.*, 2: 86–87, 91.

4. December 4, 1739, Phil. Pby. Min., 2: 79–80; August 28, 1734, Don. Pby. Min., 1: 37.

5. March 14, 1738, Phil. Pby. Min., 2: 52.

6. October 27, 1736, Don. Pby. Min., 1: 137–148; November 11, 1740, *ibid.*, 1: 208, 210.

7. Gilbert Tennent, *The Danger of an Unconverted Ministry . . .* , in Alan Heimert and Perry Miller (eds.), *The Great Awakening* (Indianapolis, 1967), pp. 79, 82, 98.

8. Samuel Finley, *Christ Triumphing, and Satan Raging . . .* (Philadelphia, 1741), p. 24.

9. Tennent, *Unconverted Ministry,* p. 83.

10. April 14, 13, 1736, November 5, 1740, Don. Pby. Min., 1: 111–112, 199.

11. George William Franz, "Paxton: A Study of Community Structure and Mobility in the Colonial Backcountry of Pennsylvania," (unpublished Ph.D. dissertation, Rutgers: The State University, 1974), pp. 273–7. Franz's study is one of the first of the current wave of demographic studies of early American communities to venture outside of New England, and the contrasts that he discovers are most instructive. Especially intriguing is his idea of the "ad hoc community" on the frontier.

12. April 11, 1738, Don. Pby. Min., 1: 159–162.

13. In one of his most incisive essays, Perry Miller suggested that the Great Awakening was that crucial point in early American history where the man who would rule in the New World began to have to earn that right by demonstrating his capacity for managing public affairs in ways that would promote the public welfare. Miller sees the idea as an Edwardsian one, but it

more appropriately can be seen as part of a broader evangelical redefinition of social leadership in America, one which emphasized identity between ruler and ruled and the importance of effective action on the part of the magistrate. See Miller, "Jonathan Edwards and the Great Awakening," in *Errand Into the Wilderness* (New York, paper edition, 1964), pp. 153–166.

14. Gilbert Tennent, *Remarks Upon a Protestation Presented to the Synod of Philadelphia* . . . (Philadelphia, 1741), pp. 19–20; *Unconverted Ministry,* p. 81.

15. Tennent, *Unconverted Ministry,* p. 80; Samuel Blair, *A Vindication of the Brethren who were unjustly and illegally cast out of the Synod of Philadelphia* . . . (Philadelphia, 1744), p. 57.

16. Tennent, *Unconverted Ministry,* pp. 24, 81, 95, 88.

17. *Ibid.,* p. 90.

18. *Ibid.,* pp. 97, 87, 89–90.

19. Tennent, *Remarks Upon a Protestation,* p. 20.

20. Blair, *Vindication of the Brethren,* p. 58.

21. Tennent, *Unconverted Ministry,* p. 87; *Remarks Upon a Protestation,* p. 29.

22. Tennent, *Unconverted Ministry,* pp. 87–89, 92, 95.

23. Jonathan Dickinson, *A Sermon Preached at the opening of the Synod of Philadelphia* . . . *1722* . . . (Boston, 1723), pp. 20–21.

24. Jonathan Dickinson, *Danger of Schisms and Contentions* . . . (New York, 1739), pp. 7, 10, 21, 24, 11.

25. *Ibid.,* pp. 11, 27, 14–15, 26.

26. *Ibid.,* p. 14.

27. *Ibid.,* p. 16.

28. John Thomson, *The Government of the Church of Christ, and the Authority of Church Judicatories established on a Scripture Foundation* . . . (Philadelphia, 1741), p. 19.

29. George Gillespie, *A Sermon Against Divisions in Christ's Churches* . . . (Philadelphia, 1740), pp. 23–24.

30. Synod of Philadelphia, *An Examination and Refutation of Mr. Gilbert Tennent's Remarks* . . . (Philadelphia, 1742), p. 10.

31. Gillespie, *Sermon Against Divisions,* pp. 25–30.

32. Syn. of Phil., *Examination and Refutation,* pp. 90, 106.

33. Gillespie, *Sermon Against Divisions,* pp. 3, 9–10, 14.

34. Thomson, *Government of the Church of Christ,* p. 1.

35. Gillespie, *Sermon Against Divisions,* pp. 10–12.

36. For a thorough study of the idea see Edmund S. Morgan, *Visible Saints: The History of a Puritan Idea* (New York, 1963). The most thorough explication and defense of the distinction between visible and invisible saints is

in one of the great neglected works of the seventeenth century, Thomas Hooker, *A Survey of the Summe of Church Discipline* (London, 1648).

37. Syn. of Phil., *Examination and Refutation,* pp. 14, 18, 85, 115; Thomson, *Government of the Church of Christ,* 22, 32, 48; [Robert Cross], *A Protestation Presented to the Synod of Philadelphia* . . . (Philadelphia, 1741), p. 11. A recent study has greatly sophisticated our understanding of the "affective" dimension of the Great Awakening by investigating "motifs" in the thought of selected German, English, and American evangelicals. Finley is one of the Americans investigated in the study, which deals creatively with language, aesthetics, and psychology in the thought of eighteenth-century evangelicals. See Clark Alva Thompson, "Motifs in Eighteenth Century Evangelical-Pietism," unpublished Ph.D. dissertation, Brown University, 1974.

38. Thomson, *Government of the Church of Christ,* p. 41.

39. Syn. of Phil., *Examination and Refutation,* p. 79.

40. Thomson, *Government of the Church of Christ,* pp. 34–35; November 5, 1740, Don. Pby. Min., 1: 198–201.

41. Finley, *Christ Triumphing,* pp. 20–21, 34.

42. September 24, 1734, *Records of the Presbyterian Church in the United States of America* . . . (Philadelphia, 1904), p. 111.

43. Tennent, *Remarks Upon a Protestation,* pp. 28–29.

44. Finley, *Christ Triumphing,* p. 19; Tennent, *Unconverted Ministry,* p. 98.

45. Tennent, *Unconverted Ministry,* p. 86.

46. See especially John Pierson, *The Faithful Minister* . . . (New York, 1748); and Caleb Smith, *Diligence in the Work of God, and Activity During Life* . . . (New York, 1758).

47. For the emphasis on public usefulness, see September 2, 1735, Don. Pby. Min., 1: 71, 78–79; August 10, 1737, Phil. Pby. Min., 2: 47; May 26, 1737, *Presbyterian Records,* p. 132.

48. Aaron Burr, *A Servant of God dismissed from Labour to Rest* . . . (New York, 1757), pp. 14–16.

Chapter III

1. Quoted in Michael Kraus, *The Atlantic Civilization: Eighteenth-Century Origins* (Ithaca, N.Y., paper edition, 1966), p. 52. Kraus's monograph provides an excellent starting place for the transatlantic Protestant community. But much more relevant is the always stimulating discussion in Clark Alva Thompson, "Motifs in Eighteenth Century Evangelical-Pietism," unpublished Ph.D. dissertation, Brown University, 1974.

2. Jonathan Edwards, *History of the Redemption of Mankind,* in *The Works of President Edwards* . . . (New York, 1856): 1, 423–507.

3. See the discussion in Alan Heimert, *Religion and the American Mind from the Great Awakening to the Revolution* (Cambridge, Mass., 1966), p. 66.

4. Jonathan Edwards, *Some Thoughts Concerning the Revival,* in C. C. Goen (ed.), *The Great Awakening,* Volume IV of *The Works of Jonathan Edwards* (New Haven, 1972), pp. 353–356.

5. Edmund S. Morgan, *The Puritan Dilemma: The Story of John Winthrop* (Boston, 1958), pp. 34–44, "A Shelter and a Hiding Place."

6. The apt phrase is Heimert's, *Religion and the American Mind,* p. 61.

7. For an excellent discussion of that chiliasm as it developed in the thought of Increase and Cotton Mather, see Robert Middlekauff, *The Mathers: Three Generations of Puritan Intellectuals, 1596–1728* (New York, 1971), Chapter 10. For a thoughtful introduction to Edwardsian millennialism, see Stephen J. Stein, "A Notebook on the Apocalypse by Jonathan Edwards," *William and Mary Quarterly,* Third Series, 29 (October, 1972): 623–634. Still useful is C. C. Goen, "Jonathan Edwards: A New Departure in Eschatology," *Church History,* 28 (1959): 25–40.

8. Quoted in Heimert, *Religion and the American Mind,* p. 62. Surely the material he himself uses contradicts Heimert's assertion that the revivalists saw the Awakening as a reversal of the course of history. Nothing seems more obvious than the extent to which it, rather, was welcomed as history's glorious culmination (p. 62).

9. Samuel Blair, *A Short and Faithful Narrative, Of the late Remarkable Revival of Religion In the Congregation of New-Londonderry, and other Parts of Pennsylvania* (1744), in Richard L. Bushman (ed.), *The Great Awakening: Documents on the Revival of Religion, 1740–1745* (New York, 1970), especially p. 72.

10. Aaron Burr, *The Watchman's Answer to the Question, What of the Night . . . ,* 2nd edition (New York, 1757), pp. 32–33.

11. Edwards, *History of the Work of Redemption,* in *Works,* 1: 482–483; Burr, *Watchman's Answer,* p. 41.

12. Blair, *Short and Faithful Narrative,* p. 71.

13. For the development of the "covenant theology" see Perry Miller, "The Marrow of Puritan Divinity," in *Errand Into the Wilderness* (New York, paper edition, 1964), pp. 48–98. For transformations in the idea of the covenant in New England see, especially, Robert G. Pope, *The Half-Way Covenant: Church Membership in Puritan New England* (Princeton, 1969); and E. Brooks Holifield, *The Covenant Sealed: The Development of Puritan Sacramental Theology in Old and New England, 1570–1720* (New Haven, 1974). As will be noted, both these useful books pull up short before the endlessly complex history of the covenant in the Awakening.

14. Jonathan Edwards, "Sinners in the Hands of an Angry God," in

Clarence H. Faust and Thomas H. Johnson (eds.), *Jonathan Edwards,* revised edition (New York, 1962), p. 170.

15. *Ibid.,* pp. 170–172.

16. The entire Thompson dissertation, "Motifs in Eighteenth Century Evangelical-Pietism," amplifies the developments here hinted at, but see, in particular, pp. 148–158, on the use of language.

17. Glenn T. Miller, "God's Light and Man's Enlightenment: Evangelical Theology of Colonial Presbyterianism," *Journal of Presbyterian History,* 51 (Summer, 1973): 98. Miller's is the best discussion available of the Presbyterian New Side theology. And it should be noted that his designation of "Evangelical Calvinist" will fit *only* the New Side.

18. See especially Thompson's Chapter X, "Evangelical Models: Christology and Self-Awareness and the Language of Appeal," in "Motifs in Eighteenth Century Evangelical-Pietism," pp. 228–250.

19. Quoted in Miller, "God's Light and Man's Enlightenment," p. 112.

20. Edwards, *History of the Work of Redemption,* in *Works,* 1: 493; Blair, *Short and Faithful Narrative,* p. 77; and Samuel Finley, *Christ Triumphing, and Satan Raging* (Philadelphia, 1741), pp. 26–29.

21. Edwards to William McCulloch, March 5, 1743/4, in Goen (ed.), *Great Awakening,* p. 560.

22. Gilbert Tennent, *The Necessity of Praising God for Mercies receiv'd* . . . (Philadelphia, [1745]), p. 39; Tennent, *The Necessity of Thankfulness for Wonders of divine Mercies* . . . (Philadelphia, 1744), p. 14; and Ebenezer Pemberton, *A Sermon Delivered at the Presbyterian Church in New-York, July 31, 1746* . . . (New York, 1746), p. 16. A major new interpretation of millennialism between the revival and the Revolution makes too much, perhaps, of the changes produced by the end of the revival. But the analysis is masterful. See Nathan O. Hatch, "The Origins of Civil Millennialism in America: New England Clergymen, War with France, and the Revolution," *William and Mary Quarterly,* Third Series, 31 (July, 1974): 407–430.

23. The definitive social history of the Great Awakening remains to be written. But see the following articles for some sense of the disordering power of the energy released by the revival: J. M. Bumstead, "A Caution to Erring Christians: Ecclesiastical Disorder on Cape Cod, 1717–1738," *William and Mary Quarterly,* Third Series, 28 (July, 1971): 413–438; Bumstead, "Religion, Finance, and Democracy in Massachusetts, The Town of Norton as a Case Study," *Journal of American History,* 57 (March, 1971): 817–831; Philip J. Greven, "Youth, Maturity, and Religious Conversion: A Note on the Ages of Converts in Andover, Massachusetts, 1711–1749," *Essex Institute Historical Collections,* 108 (1972): 119–134; Robert Sklar, "The Great Awakening and Colonial Politics: Connecticut's Revolution in the Minds of Men," *The Connecticut Historical Society Bulletin,* 28 (1963): 81–95; and,

most especially, the relevant sections of Richard L. Bushman, *From Puritan to Yankee: Character and the Social Order in Connecticut, 1690–1765* (Cambridge, Mass., 1967).

24. Bushman's treatment of the social consequences of religious separations is in Parts IV and XI of *From Puritan to Yankee.*

25. *Ibid.,* Parts X, XV, and XVI; Perry Miller, "Jonathan Edwards and the Great Awakening," *Errand Into the Wilderness,* pp. 153–166.

26. Richard L. Bushman, "Jonathan Edwards as Great Man: Identity, Conversion, and Leadership in the Great Awakening," *Soundings,* 52 (Spring, 1969): 40–41.

27. Ebenezer Prime, *The Importance of the Divine Presence with the Armies of God's People* . . . (New York, 1759), p. 45. For the distress among the Massachusetts clergy after the Awakening, see Kerry Arnold Trask, "In the Pursuit of Shadows: A Study of Collective Hope and Despair in Provincial Massachusetts in the Era of the Seven Years War, 1748–1764," (unpublished Ph.D. dissertation, University of Minnesota, 1971), Chapter II, "Amidst a Falling World."

28. Samuel Davies, "Religion and Patriotism the Constituents of a Good Soldier," *Sermons* (Boston, 1864), 3: 95, 112, 113; "The Crisis; or, the Uncertain Doom of Kingdoms at Particular Times," *ibid.,* 3: 143–44; *The Curse of Cowardice* . . . (Boston, 1759), pp. 13, 22.

29. The best general account of the Paxton raid remains Brooke Hindle, "The March of the Paxton Boys," *William and Mary Quarterly,* Third Series, 3 (October, 1946): 461–486. Less satisfactory though more directly relevant is Peter A. Butzin, "Politics, Presbyterians and the Paxton Riots, 1763–1764," *Journal of Presbyterian History,* 51 (Spring, 1973): 70–84.

30. "An Answer, To The Pamphlet Entituled the Conduct of the Paxton Men . . . ," in John R. Dunbar (ed.), *The Paxton Papers* (The Hague, 1957), pp. 325, 332. See the disappointing discussion in James E. Crowley, "The Paxton Disturbances and Ideas of Order in Pennsylvania Politics," *Pennsylvania History,* 37 (October, 1970): 317–339. Crowley does not produce what is promised in his intriguing title, and he makes too much of his contrast between an untutored Presbyterian frontier and a sophisticated Philadelphia.

31. [Hugh Williamson], *The Plain Dealer* . . . *Numb. I,* in Dunbar (ed.), *Paxton Papers,* pp. 341–342; *Numb. III,* pp. 374, 385; *A Declaration and Remonstrance, of the distressed and bleeding Frontier Inhabitants of the Province of Philadelphia* . . . ([Philadelphia], 1764), pp. 4, 6.

32. Davies, "Religion and Patriotism," *Sermons,* 3: 95.

33. William Balch, *A Public Spirit: Election Sermon* (Boston, 1749), p. 16; Jonathan Mayhew, *Seven Sermons* (Boston, 1749), p. 126.

34. Davies, "God is Love," *Sermons,* 1: 465–466, 476.

35. Burr, *The Watchman's Answer*, p. 30. See also Prime, *Importance of the Divine Presence*, p. 21; Samuel Davies, "Serious Reflections on War," *Sermons on Important Subjects* (New York, 1862), 3: 221; Gilbert Tennent, *The Happiness of Rewarding the Enemies of our Religion and Liberty* . . . (Philadelphia, 1756), p. 21.

36. Tennent, *Rewarding the Enemies*, pp. 21, 25–32; Davies, "On the Defeat of General Braddock," *Sermons on Important Subjects*, 3: 228.

37. Davies, "A Thanksgiving Sermon for National Blessings," *Sermons*, 3: 372, 370.

38. Quoted in David H. Fleming, *The Reformation in Scotland. Causes, Characteristics, Consequences* (London, 1910), pp. 518–519.

39. Osmund Aery (ed.), *Bishop Burnet's History of His Own Time* (London, 1897), 1: 524.

40. William Livingston, *et al., The Independent Reflector* . . . , ed. Milton M. Klein (Cambridge, 1963), L, November 8, 1753, 420–421.

41. For a suggestive discussion of professionalization see Daniel H. Calhoun, *Professional Lives in America: Structure and Aspiration, 1750–1850* (Cambridge, 1965).

42. September 22, 1735, September 18, 1736, *Records of the Presbyterian Church in the United States of America* . . . (Philadelphia, 1904), pp. 118–119, 128.

43. September 22, 1735, *ibid.*, p. 119; June 7, 1734, October 10, 1735, Minutes of the Presbytery of Donegal (microfilm in the Union Theological Seminary, Richmond, Va.), 1: 32, 96.

44. November 30, 1736, September 9, 13, 1737, July 12, 1739, Minutes of the Presbytery of Philadelphia (MSS in the Presbyterian Historical Society, Philadelphia, Pa.), 2: 20, 42–43, 74–75.

45. For extensive documentation of this process, see my "A Contracting Community: American Presbyterians, Social Conflict, and Higher Education, 1720–1820," (unpublished Ph.D. dissertation, University of Michigan, 1970), pp. 107–109.

46. For the "Log College," see Thomas C. Pears, Jr., and Guy S. Klett, compilers, "Documentary History of William Tennent and the Log College," *Journal of the Presbyterian Historical Society*, 28 (March, June, and September, 1950): 37–64, 105–128, 167–204; Archibald Alexander, *Biographical Sketches of the Founder, and Principal Alumni of the Log College* . . . (Princeton, 1845); Elijah R. Craven, "The Log College of Neshaminy and Princeton University," *Journal of the Presbyterian Historical Society*, 1 (March, 1902): 308–314; and Douglas Sloan, *The Scottish Enlightenment and the American College Ideal* (New York, 1971), pp. 36–72.

47. May 29, 1738, May 24–28, 1739, *Presbyterian Records*, pp. 141, 145–146.

48. May 29, 1739, *ibid.*, p. 149; April 5, 1739, Don. Pby. Min., 1: 177. For

the Old Side Academy see George H. Ryden, "The Newark Academy of Delaware in Colonial Days," *Pennsylvania History*, 2 (October, 1935): 205–224; Sloan, *Scottish Enlightenment*, pp. 73–102; and especially Elizabeth A. Ingersoll, "Francis Alison: American Philosophe, 1705–1799," (unpublished Ph.D. dissertation, University of Delaware, 1974), pp. 509–531. Ingersoll's treatment of the Old Side Academy is as flattering as her analysis of the New Side college at Princeton is damning. She is in fact at her least persuasive in this section.

49. Synod of Philadelphia to Thomas Clap, May 30, 1746, *Presbyterian Records*, p. 188.

50. Francis McHenry to Dutch Classis, June 4, 26, 1744, in James L. Good (ed.), "Early Attempted Union of Presbyterians with Dutch and German Reformed," *Journal of the Presbyterian Historical Society*, 3 (September, 1905): 124, 125, 127.

51. McHenry to Rev. Mr. Kennedy, June 26, 1744, *ibid.*, p. 128. For a similar expression of concern abut the vacant Old Side pulpits and a plea for the Old Side Academy see the broadside prepared for distribution in England and Ireland by the Reverend John Ewing and Hugh Williamson. *To the charitable and humane Friends of Learning, public Virtue, and Religion* . . . (broadside in the Presbyterian Historical Society), p. 2.

52. William Smith to S.P.G., December 13, 1753, in Horace W. Smith, *Life and Correspondence of the Rev. William Smith, D.D.* (Philadelphia, 1880), 1: 30–31; William Smith, *Discourses on Public Occasions in America,* 2nd edition (London, 1762), ix; Smith, "A General Idea of the College of Mirania," in *The Works of William Smith* . . . (Philadelphia, 1803), 1: 175.

53. Smith, "College of Mirania," *Works,* 1: 180.

54. Smith to S.P.G., December 13, 1753, Smith, *Life,* 1: 30; Smith, "A Letter . . . concerning the Duty of Protestant Ministers in Times of Public Danger," *Discourses on Public Occasions,* Appendix First, pp. 3–19; Smith, *A Brief State of the Province of Pennsylvania* . . . 2nd edition (London, 1755), p. 32.

55. Petition of Lancaster Germans to Trustees of the Charity School, 1754, in William F. Worner, "The Charity Schools Movement in 1755," *Historical Papers and Addresses of the Lancaster County Historical Society,* 42 (1938): 6.

56. Samuel E. Weber, *The Charity School Movement in Colonial Pennsylvania* (Philadelphia, [1905]), pp. 20–21, and Chapter IV, for the German counter-attack. For Smith's suggested disfranchisement, see *Brief State,* pp. 40–42.

57. The best secondary accounts of the Presbyterian-Anglican alliance remain Carl Bridenbaugh, *Mitre and Sceptre: Transatlantic Faiths, Ideas, Personalities, and Politics, 1689–1775* (New York, 1965), Chapter V; *Rebels and Gentlemen: Philadelphia in the Age of Franklin* (New York,

1965), Chapter II. For the records of the cooperation see June 2, 1755, May 27, 1756, and May 26, 1757, *Presbyterian Records,* pp. 219, 223, 226–228.

58. For a very different assessment of the academy, see Ingersoll, "Francis Alison."

59. For an extended discussion of the following, see my "Contracting Community," pp. 117–131; and my forthcoming essay, "Evangelical Religion and Colonial Princeton," in Lawrence Stone (ed.), *Schooling and Society* (Baltimore, 1976).

60. Gilbert Tennent, *Remarks Upon a Protestation Presented to the Synod of Philadelphia, June 1, 1741* (Philadelphia, 1741), p. 51; Samuel Finley, *Christ Triumphing,* p. 20.

61. Samuel Finley, *The Approved Minister of God . . .* (Philadelphia, 1749), pp. 6–7; John Pierson, *The Faithful Minister . . .* (New York, 1748), pp. 7–8.

62. December 7, 1749, May 18, 1750, and May 24, 1751, Minutes of the Presbytery of New Brunswick (MSS in the Presbyterian Historical Society), 2: 129, 138, 172.

63. October 21, 1761, *ibid.,* 2: 94.

64. Quoted in Francis L. Broderick, "Pulpit, Physics, and Politics: The Curriculum of the College of New Jersey, 1746–1796," *William and Mary Quarterly,* Third Series, 6 (January, 1949): 56.

65. Synod of New York to the Presbyterian General Assembly of Scotland, October 3, 1753, *Presbyterian Records,* p. 257n; *A General Account of the Rise and State of the College, Lately Established in the Province of New-Jersey, in America: And of the End and Design of its Institution* (New York, 1752), p. 4.

66. William Peartree Smith to John Witherspoon, November 19, 1766, in Lyman H. Butterfield (ed.), *John Witherspoon Comes to America: A Documentary Account Based Largely on New Materials* (Princeton, 1953), p. 8; John Rodgers to Witherspoon, December 24, 1766, in *ibid.,* pp. 21–22.

67. Beverly McAnear, "The Selection of an Alma Mater by Pre-Revolutionary Students," *The Pennsylvania Magazine of History and Biography,* 73 (October, 1949): 430–440. A recent statistical analysis of Princeton's student body between 1746 and 1800 finds that 75 percent of those students came from outside New Jersey and that 50 percent of them were born outside of New Jersey, Pennsylvania, and New York. See the excellent analysis in Phyllis V. Erenberg, "Change and Continuity: Values in American Higher Education, 1750–1800," (unpublished Ph.D. dissertation, University of Michigan, 1974), pp. 220–223.

68. "Aaron Burr," *The Presbyterian Magazine,* 3 (January, 1853): 35; "Samuel Finley, *ibid.,* 3 (March, 1853): 145.

69. College of New Jersey [Samuel Blair, Jr.,], *An Account of the College of New Jersey* . . . (Woodbridge, N.J., 1764), pp. 5, 6.

70. Margaret W. Masson, "The Premises and Purposes of Higher Education in American Society, 1745–1770," (unpublished Ph.D. dissertation, University of Washington, 1971), pp. 2–4, 208, 238, also sees college founding at the mid-century as response to a crisis of confidence in American society. Masson divides the colleges founded after the Awakening into "urban" (King's, College of Philadelphia) and "evangelical," the category which appropriately includes Princeton. Unfortunately, the categories raise more questions than they answer.

71. Livingston, *Independent Reflector,* XVII, March 22, 1753, 175; *ibid.,* L, November 8, 1753, 421.

72. *Ibid.,* XVII, March 22, 1753, 172.

73. Nor do all historians. See David C. Humphrey, "The Struggle for Sectarian Control of Princeton," *New Jersey History,* 91 (Summer, 1973): 79.

74. July 7, 1756, July 12, 1758, September 27, 1758, Minutes of the Hanover Presbytery (MSS in Union Theological Seminary, Richmond), 1: 3–5, 11.

75. Davies to the Bishop of London, January 10, 1752, in *The Biblical Repertory and Princeton Review,* 12 (April, 1840): 195; Davies to Benjamin Avery, n.d., in John Maclean, *The History of the College of New Jersey* . . . (Philadelphia, 1877), 1: 222–226.

76. For Davies's leadership in the struggle for complete toleration, see George W. Pilcher, "Samuel Davies and Religious Toleration in Virginia," *The Historian,* 28 (1965): 48–71; and Katherine L. Brown, "The Role of Presbyterian Dissent in Colonial and Revolutionary Virginia," (unpublished Ph.D. dissertation, The Johns Hopkins University, 1969), pp. 88–132.

77. Samuel Johnson to Cadwallader Colden, April 15, 1747, in Klein's introduction to the *Independent Reflector,* p. 34; "The Watch-Tower," #4, in New York *Mercury,* December 16, 1754; New York *Mercury,* January 27, 1755, March 3, 1755. The best introduction to the controversy is in David C. Humphrey, "King's College in the City of New York, 1754–1776," unpublished Ph.D. dissertation, Northwestern University, 1968. Humphrey traces the way in which the broad view of the Presbyterian lawyers is overtaken by the sectarian imperatives of New York's Anglicans. The dissertation is to be published in 1976 by Columbia University Press. Humphrey's history should now be read in conjunction with the sensitive and informed analysis in John M. Mulder, "William Livingston: Propagandist Against Episcopacy," *Journal of Presbyterian History,* 54 (Spring, 1976): 83–104.

78. "The Watch-Tower," ## V, XII, XX, XXIV, New York *Mercury,* December 23, 1754, February 10, April 7, and May 5, 1755.

79. Livingston, *Independent Reflector,* XVIII, March 29, 1753, 179–181;

XX, April 12, 1753, p. 195; "The Watch-Tower," ## II, IV, New York *Mercury*, December 2, 16, 1754.

80. Livingston, *Independent Reflector*, XVIII, March 29, 1753, 181.

81. *Ibid.*, XX, April 12, 1753, 191; "The Watch-Tower," # XVI, New York *Mercury*, March 10, 1755. Her failure to consider the religious or ideological context of the fight over King's charter reveals the endemic limits of the political emphasis in Patricia U. Bonomi, *A Factious People: Politics and Society in Colonial New York* (New York, 1971). In a book concerned with defining opposition theory and its colonial origins, the author misses one of the earliest defenses of conflict as a positive good. See especially pp. 176–177.

82. Livingston, *Independent Reflector*, XXII, April 26, 1753, 213.

83. (Philadelphia) *Pennsylvania Gazette*, August 13, 1747.

84. *Ibid.;* New York *Gazette*, August 20, 1747.

85. Synod of Philadelphia, *An Examination and Refutation of Mr. Gilbert Tennent's Remarks* . . . (Philadelphia, 1742), pp. 53–70.

86. May 25, 1744, *Presbyterian Records*, p. 176.

87. May 27, 1748, May 29, 1752, May 24, 1753, *ibid.*, pp. 194, 208, 210.

88. December 3, 1755, Han. Pby. Min., 1: 2; April 18, 1769, N. Bruns. Pby. Min., 2: 310–311; October 3, 1753, *Presbyterian Records*, p. 251; September 26, 1754, *ibid.*, p. 259.

89. May 22, 1761, *Presbyterian Records*, p. 309.

90. September 25, 1766, September 27, 1749, April 5, 1769, Minutes of the Board of Trustees of Princeton University (MSS in the Archives of Princeton University, Princeton, N.J.), 1: 112, 18, 160.

91. September 24, 1755, *ibid.* 1:41–42; [Blair], *College of New Jersey*, p. 16.

92. August 5, 1769, Pr. Bd. Min., 1: 161; October 12, 1769, Han. Pby. Min., 2: 2–3.

93. John Witherspoon to Benjamin Rush, October 8, 1768, in Butterfield (ed.), *Witherspoon Comes to America*, p. 80; December 10, 1767, Pr. Bd. Min., 1: 143–144; October, 1768, N. Bruns. Pby. Min., 2: 295; May 23, 24, 1769, *Presbyterian Records*, pp. 396, 398.

94. Belcher to Dickinson, October 8, 1747, in Maclean, *College of New Jersey*, 1: 82; May 23, 1753, Pr. Bd. Min., 1: 35–36.

95. Aaron Burr to the Governor, Deputy Governor, Assistants, and Deputies of Connecticut, May 8, 1754 (photostatic copy of MS in the Connecticut Archives in the Aaron Burr Collection, Princeton University Library); May 8, 1754, Pr. Bd. Min., 1: 37.

96. Belcher to Mr. Walley, October 2, 1747, in Maclean, *College of New Jersey*, 1: 148; Burr to Thomas Foxcroft, October 26, 1749 (Thomas Foxcroft Correspondence, Princeton University Library); September 7, 1749, Pr. Bd. Min., 1: 18.

97. October 6, 1753, *Presbyterian Records*, p. 256; *To the Worthy and*

Generous Friends of Religion and Learning. The Petition of Gilbert Tennent and Samuel Davies, in the Name of the Trustees of the Infant College of New Jersey . . . (London, 1754), pp. 2, 4.

98. George W. Pilcher (ed.), *The Reverend Samuel Davies Abroad* . . . (Urbana, Ill., 1967), May 7, 1754, p. 88.

Chapter IV

1. William Livingston, *A Funeral Elogium on the Reverend Mr. Aaron Burr* . . . (New York, 1757), p. 16; "A short account of the rise and state of the College in the province of New-Jersey in America," *The New American Magazine,* 27 (March, 1760): 104.

2. Quoted in "The Process of the Public Commencement in Nassau Hall, September, A.D. 1764 (MS in the Samuel Finley MSS, Princeton University Library, Princeton, N.J.).

3. Still useful as a survey of the history of the concept of virtue is J. H. Whitfield, "The Anatomy of Virtue," *The Modern Language Review,* 28 (July, 1943): 222–225. But I am grateful to Professor Jerrold E. Seigel of Princeton University, who kindly permitted me to see in manuscript his excellent article on "Virtù" that will be published in a forthcoming *Dictionary of the History of Ideas.*

4. Jonathan Edwards, "The Nature of True Virtue," *The Works of President Edwards* . . . (New York, 1856), 2: 262.

5. Quoted in Alan Heimert, *Religion and the American Mind from the Great Awakening to the Revolution* (Cambridge, Mass., 1966), p. 313.

6. Samuel Davies, *Religion and Public Spirit. A Valedictory Address to the Senior Class delivered in Nassau-Hall, September 21, 1760* (Portsmouth, N.H., 1762), pp. 4–7.

7. William Smith, "A General Idea of the College of Mirania," *The Works of William Smith, D.D.* . . . (Philadelphia, 1803), 1: 214; Thomas Clap, *The Religious Constitution of Colleges, Especially of Yale-College* . . . (New London, Conn., 1754), p. 13; William Livingston, *et al., The Independent Reflector* . . . , ed. Milton M. Klein (Cambridge, Mass., 1963), XXI, April 19, 1753, 199–206.

8. Livingston, *Independent Reflector,* XXI, April 19, 1753, 202.

9. Samuel Davies, "The Rejection of Gospel-Light the Condemnation of Men," *Sermons on Important Subjects* . . . , 6th edition (Philadelphia, 1794), 2: 463–465, 472, 466.

10. *Ibid.,* 2: 472, 464.

11. September 27, 1757, Minutes of the Board of Trustees of Princeton University (MSS in the Archives of Princeton University, Princeton, N.J.), 1: 63. For the trouble colonial Princeton's most illustrious graduate had making

do with his very generous allowance from his planter father, see James Madison, Jr. to James Madison, Sr., September 30, 1769, July 23, 1770, William T. Hutchinson and William M. E. Rachel (eds.), *The Papers of James Madison* (Chicago, 1962–), 1: 46, 50.

12. Samuel Davies, *Little Children Invited to Jesus Christ . . . With an Account of the late remarkable Religious Impressions Among the Students in the College of New Jersey,* 4th edition (Boston, 1762), pp. 21–23.

13. For other accounts of the state of religion at colonial Princeton, see "Samuel Finley," *The Presbyterian Magazine,* 3 (March, 1853): 145; John Maclean, *History of the College of New Jersey . . .* (Philadelphia, 1877), 1: 155, 273, 311; Edward Crawford to James Crawford, August 3, 29, 1774 (Papers of Reverend James Crawford, bound MSS in the Presbyterian Historical Society, Philadelphia, Pa.).

14. College of New Jersey [Samuel Blair, Jr.], *An Account of the College of New-Jersey . . .* (Woodbridge, N.J., 1764), pp. 11–12.

15. Aaron Burr to William Hogg, December 3, 1755 (Aaron Burr Collection, Princeton University Library).

16. John Eliot to Aaron Burr, n.d. (John Eliot MSS, Princeton University Library).

17. *To the charitable and humane Friends of Learning, public Virtue, and Religion . . .* (broadside in the Presbyterian Historical Society), p. 2.

18. William Smith, *Some Thoughts on Education . . .* (New York, 1752), pp. 9, 8, 11. Franklin also insisted that Philadelphia's college be established "if not in the Town, not many Miles from it . . . ." Benjamin Franklin, "Proposals Relating to the Education of Youth in Pensilvania," *Autobiography and Selected Writings,* ed. Larzar Ziff (New York, 1963), p. 208.

19. Quoted in David C. Humphrey, "King's College in the City of New York, 1754–1776," (unpublished Ph.D. dissertation, Northwestern University, 1968), p. 203. For the points on Smith and Franklin see the discussion in Margaret W. Masson, "The Premises and Purposes of Higher Education in American Society, 1745–1770," (unpublished Ph.D. dissertation, University of Washington, 1971), pp. 149–150.

20. John Witherspoon, *Address to the Inhabitants of Jamaica, and other West-India Islands, in Behalf of the College of New-Jersey* (Philadelphia, 1772), pp. 12, 24, 17. See also the discussion of the debate over the location of the Anglican college in New York City, in David C. Humphrey, "Urban Manners and Rural Morals: The Controversy Over the Location of King's College," *New York History,* 54 (January, 1973): 4–23.

21. For a masterful study of a colonial college curriculum, see Richard Warch, *School of the Prophets: Yale College, 1701–1740* (New Haven, 1973), pp. 186–249. For the influence of the dissenting academies on Princeton, see

Douglas Sloan, *The Scottish Enlightenment and the American College Ideal* (New York, 1971), pp. 64–72.

22. Smith, "College of Mirania," *Works*, 1: 181–182, 190–193.

23. Samuel Davies, "Religion and Patriotism, the Constituents of a Good Soldier," *Sermons* (Boston, 1864), 3: 100.

24. For the lecture method see Sloan, *Scottish Enlightenment*, pp. 25–27, 76–77, 113–114.

25. *A General Account of the Rise and State of the College, Lately Established in the Province of New-Jersey, in America* . . . (New York, 1752), p. 6; William Livingston, *Funeral Elogium*, p. 16.

26. *New American Magazine*, 27 (March, 1760): 104.

27. [Blair], *College of New-Jersey*, pp. 27–28.

28. Samuel Davies, *A Sermon delivered at Nassau-Hall, January 14, 1761 . . . To which is prefixed a brief Account of the Life, Character, and Death, of the Author. By David Bostwick* . . . (New York, 1761), p. ii.

29. Livingston, *Independent Reflector*, XXXVII, August 9, 1753, 315; *ibid.*, March 22, 1753, 173. See also Davies, *Little Children Invited to Jesus Christ*, p. 4.

30. For the first admissions requirements, see November 9, 1748, Pr. Bd. Min., 1: 14. For the curriculum in 1764, see [Blair], *College of New Jersey*, p. 24. For the emphasis on French, see John Witherspoon to Henry Lee, December 28, 1770 (The John Witherspoon Collection, Princeton University Library).

31. Livingston, *Independent Reflector*, L, November 8, 1753, 424–425.

32. Davies, *Religion and Public Spirit*, p. 3; Hugh H. Brackenridge, *Modern Chivalry*, ed. Claude M. Newlin (New York, 1962), p. 43. For a useful corrective to the overestimation of the classical impact on the colonial mind, see Bernard Bailyn, *The Ideological Origins of the American Revolution* (Cambridge, Mass., 1967), pp. 23–26.

33. Davies, *Religion and Public Spirit*, p. 3; Samuel Finley, *The Approved Minister of God* . . . (Philadelphia, 1749), p. 14n.

34. George W. Pilcher (ed.), *The Reverend Samuel Davies Abroad* . . . (Urbana, Ill., 1967), October 8, 1753, pp. 19–20.

35. [Blair], *College of New-Jersey*, pp. 26, 25, 46.

36. Joseph Shippen to Edward Shippen, May 12, 1750, September 14, 1751, May 23, 1752, December 2, 1751, in John Maclean, *History of the College of New Jersey* . . . (Philadelphia, 1877), 1: 141–143; September 29, 1769, Pr. Bd. Min., 1: 169; Francis L. Broderick, "Pulpit, Physics, and Politics: The Curriculum of the College of New Jersey, 1746–1796," *William and Mary Quarterly*, Third Series, 6 (January, 1949): 52.

37. Davies, "The Signs of the Times," *Sermons*, 3: 173–174; "The Religious Improvement of the Late Earthquakes," *ibid.*, 3: 264.

38. Davies, "Religious Improvement," *ibid.*, 3: 263–264; "Signs of the Times," *ibid.*, 3: 188.

39. Davies, "Signs of the Times," *ibid.*, 3: 181, 188, 175.

40. Quoted in Samuel Davies Alexander, *Princeton College During the Eighteenth Century* (New York, 1872), pp. 145–146.

41. [Blair], *College of New-Jersey*, p. 28.

42. Varnum Collins, *Princeton* (New York, 1914), p. 173.

43. Davies, *Sermons on Important Subjects*, 1: xxiv; Livingston, *Funeral Elogium*, p. 8.

44. See, for example, Rush's description of Samuel Finley in Rush to Mrs. Rush, July 31, 1791, Lyman H. Butterfield (ed.), *Letters of Benjamin Rush* (Princeton, 1951), 1: 601.

45. Joseph Shippen to Neddy Shippen, June 21, 1751 (Joseph Shippen, Jr. Letter Book, Princeton University Library).

46. Richard Hofstadter in *Academic Freedom in the Age of the College* (New York, 1955) treats only of *Lehrfreiheit*, the right of the teacher to teach free of coercion. Because of its clerical and denominational character, the Princeton faculty had no problem on this point.

47. Livingston, *Independent Reflector*, XVII, March 22, 1753, 174–175; "The Watch-Tower," XXV, New York *Mercury*, May 12, 1755.

48. Livingston, *Independent Reflector*, XXI, April 19, 1753, 203, 202; XVIII, March 29, 1753, 180; XXII, April 26, 1753, 209; XXVII, May 31, 1753, 242–249; New York *Mercury*, January 20, 1755.

49. Thomas Clap, *Religious Constitution of Colleges*, pp. 4, 7, 9–10, 15–16. The best discussion of the "Yale Controversy" is Chapter VIII of Louis L. Tucker, *Puritan Protagonist: President Thomas Clap of Yale College* (Chapel Hill, 1962).

50 Clap, pp. 12, 19.

51. [Blair], *College of New-Jersey*, pp. 23–24.

52. November 9, 1748, Pr. Bd. Min., 1: 14.

53. [Blair], *College of New-Jersey*, pp. 20, 19, 22, 21; John Witherspoon, *Inhabitants of Jamaica*, p. 18; Edward Crawford to James Crawford, November 25, 1773 (James Crawford Papers, Presbyterian Historical Society); Samuel Finley to Eleazer Wheelock (Samuel Finley MSS, Princeton University Library).

54. Livingston, *Funeral Elogium*, p. 17; Bostwick in Davies, *Sermon . . . January 14, 1761*, p. 10.

55. February 17, 1758, Pr. Bd. Min., 1: 68–69; November 23, 1758, April 20, 1774, *ibid.*, 1: 76, 203–204.

56. Franklin, "Education of Youth," p. 208; Davies, *Sermon . . . January 14, 1761*, p. 10.

57. June 26, 1766, Pr. Bd. Min., 1: 114; Smith, *Thoughts on Education,* pp. 6–7.

58. Charles Hodge, *The Constitutional History of the Presbyterian Church* . . . (Philadelphia, 1839–1840), Part II, 31–32.

59. See especially Elwyn A. Smith, *The Presbyterian Ministry in American Culture: A Study in Changing Concepts, 1700–1900* (Philadelphia, 1962), p. 45.

60. Hezekiah Davies, "History of the united congregations of Great Valley, Charleston, and West Chester," *Journal of the Presbyterian Historical Society,* 2 (September, 1904): 337.

61. Henry Ruffner, "Early History of Washington College, Now Washington and Lee University," Washington and Lee University, *Historical Papers* (Baltimore, 1890), p. 61.

62. William H. Whitsitt, *Life and Times of Judge Caleb Wallace* (Louisville, 1888), pp. 9–13.

63. William B. Sprague, *Annals of the American Pulpit* . . . (New York, 1860), 3: 371, 271, 208, 409, 216, 382; Joseph Smith, *History of Jefferson College* . . . (Pittsburgh, 1857), p. 414. As these citations show, other men, like the fathers of James Hall, Stephen Bloomer Balch, and John Ewing, were all eager for their sons to receive an education and even assisted them to the best of their abilities. Indeed, some men, like John McMillan, the founder of Jefferson College, were dedicated to the sacred service by their fathers.

64. Samuel Davies Alexander, *Princeton College,* p. 71; Robert Davidson, *History of the Presbyterian Church in the State of Kentucky* . . . (New York, 1837), pp. 65–66; Sprague, *Annals,* 3:263–264.

65. For an extensive list of these older, ministerial students, see my "A Contracting Community: American Presbyterians, Social Conflict, and Higher Education, 1720–1820," (unpublished Ph.D. dissertation, University of Michigan, 1970), pp. 194–195n. I treat this topic extensively in my forthcoming essay, "Evangelical Religion and Colonial Princeton," in Lawrence Stone (ed.), *Schooling and Society* (Baltimore, 1976).

Chapter V

1. George Duffield, *A Sermon Preached in the Third Presbyterian Church in Philadelphia, On Thursday, December 11, 1783* . . . (Philadelphia, 1784), pp. 3, 5; Israel Evans, *A Discourse in New York . . . On the 11th December, 1783* . . . (New York, 1784), p. 10.

2. Duffield, *Sermon, 1783,* pp. 5, 3, 24–25.

3. See especially Israel Evans, *A Discourse Delivered on the 18th Day of December, 1777* . . . (Lancaster, Pa., 1778), pp. 7, 8; Robert Davidson, *An*

Oration, on the Independence of the United States of America, Delivered on the 4th of July, 1787 (Carlisle, Pa., 1787), pp. 10–11.

4. John Witherspoon, *The Dominion of Providence over the Passions of Men* . . . (Philadelphia, 1776), pp. 34, 57.

5. For an extended, thoughtful discussion of the problem of relating human effort to divine providence, see Perry Miller, "From the Covenant to the Revival," in James Ward Smith and A. Leland Jamison (eds.), *The Shaping of American Religion* (Princeton, 1961), pp. 322–368.

6. Robert Smith, *The Obligations of the Confederate States of North America to Praise God* (Philadelphia, 1782), pp. 12–13. For a more eloquent expression of the same idea by a man not always in agreement with the American Presbyterians, see Thomas Jefferson, "A Declaration by the Representatives of the United Colonies of North America, setting forth the Causes and Necessity of their taking up Arms," in Julian P. Boyd (ed.), *The Papers of Thomas Jefferson* (Princeton, 1950–   ), 1: 217.

7. Witherspoon, *Dominion of Providence*, p. 34; Smith, *Obligations of the Confederate States*, pp. 16, 22–25; Evans, *Discourse, 1777*, pp. 12, 19; Evans, *Discourse, 1783*, p. 12; [John Murray], *Bath-Kol. A Voice From the Wilderness* . . . (Boston, 1783), pp. 71–73.

8. Evans, *Discourse, 1777*, p. 10; Hugh Williamson, *The Plea of the Colonies* . . . (Philadelphia, 1777), Preface and p. 30; John Murray, *Jerubbaal, or Tyranny's Grove Destroyed, and the Alter of Liberty Finished* . . . (Newburyport, 1784), pp. 68, 11. Significantly the Presbyterians refused to grant that British exertions might be rewarded by victory. Likewise, while Robert Smith noted that God frequently brought his people in America low before raising them to new heights, Williamson insisted that the British hope "against evidence" when they "take the frowns of heaven for certain proof you shall prosper in your iniquity." In short, the clergy's view of British effort was precisely the opposite of their attitude toward the efficacy of their own strivings. Smith, *Obligations of the Confederate States*, pp. 27–28; Williamson, *Plea of the Colonies*, pp. 29–30.

9. John Joachim Zubly, *The Law of Liberty* . . . (Philadelphia, 1776), p. xv; Witherspoon, *Dominion of Providence*, p. 18; Benjamin Rush to John Adams, August 8, 1777, Lyman H. Butterfield (ed.), *Letters of Benjamin Rush* (Princeton, 1951), 1: 152.

10. Willian Tennent, III, "To the Ladies of South Carolina," in Newton B. Jones (ed.), "Writings of the Reverend William Tennent, 1740–1777," *The South Carolina Historical Magazine*, 61 (July, 1960): 138. Edmund Morgan rightly points out the relation of the boycotts and nonimportation agreements to a "Puritan ethic," seeing in the renouncing of British goods and the reliance on American manufactures an effort to reaffirm habits of industry and frugality associated with seventeenth-century Puritans but not exemplified

by their eighteenth-century descendants. But he fails to relate the concern over luxury to the colonists' immediate past, that is, to the revival and war with France. See "The Puritan Ethic and the American Revolution," *William and Mary Quarterly,* Third Series, 24 (January, 1967): 3–43.

11. Davidson, *An Oration, 1787,* pp. 10, 8, 9, 14; Evans, *Discourse, 1777,* p. 15; Duffield, *Sermon, 1783,* p. 18; Witherspoon, *Dominion of Providence,* pp. 43, 45–46; "On the Controversy about Independence," *The Works of President Witherspoon* . . . (Edinburgh, 1815), 9: 78, 81; [Murray], *Bath-Kol,* p. 70.

12. Witherspoon, "Reflections on the Present State of Public Affairs," *Works,* 9:12; *Dominion of Providence,* pp. 45–56; Evans, *Discourse, 1783,* p. 10. Thad Tate has made the useful point that the colonists did not believe that they were breaking the *social* contract by declaring their independence of a king who, they insisted, was solely responsible for breaking the contract between ruler and ruled. See "The Social Contract in America, 1774–1787: Revolutionary Theory as a Conservative Instrument," *William and Mary Quarterly,* Third Series, 22 (July, 1965): 375–391.

13. See the very provocative ideas advanced in Nathan O. Hatch, "The Origins of Civil Millennialism in America: New England Clergymen, War with France, and the Revolution," *William and Mary Quarterly,* Third Series, 31 (July, 1974): 407–430; and Kerry Arnold Trask, "In the Pursuit of Shadows: A Study of Collective Hope and Despair in Provincial Massachusetts in the Era of the Seven Years War, 1748–1764," unpublished Ph.D. dissertation, University of Minnesota, 1971.

14. Thomas Paine, *Rights of Man,* in *"Common Sense" and Other Political Writings* (Garden City, N.Y., 1960), p. 112.

15. William Smith, *Some Thoughts on Education* . . . (New York, 1752), p. 23.

16. [Philip M. Freneau and Hugh H. Brackenridge], *A Poem on the Rising Glory of America* . . . (Philadelphia, 1772), pp. 24, 25. For another treatment of the theme, see Smith, *Obligations of the Confederate States,* pp. 26–27. My interpretation differs from that of Stow Persons insofar as it takes seriously the midcentury millennialism he dismisses as a "quaint excitement." See "The Cyclical Theory of History in Eighteenth Century America," *American Quarterly,* 6 (Summer, 1954): pp. 147–163.

17. Sermon by George Duffield, April, 1776, in Herbert Adams Gibbons, "Old Pine Street Church, Philadelphia, in the Revolutionary War," *Journal of the Presbyterian Historical Society,* 3 (June, 1905): 73; Zubly, *Law of Liberty,* p. xvii; Duffield, *Sermon, 1783,* p. 17; Evans, *Discourse, 1783,* p. 8; Witherspoon, *Dominion of Providence,* p. 40.

18. Witherspoon, "Reflections on the Present State of Public Affairs,"

Works, 9: 67, 70; "Speech . . . Upon the Confederation," *ibid.,* 9: 139–141; "On Conducting the American Controversy," *ibid.,* 9: 87.

19. W. Paul Adams, "Republicanism in Political Science Before 1776," *Political Science Quarterly,* 85 (September, 1970): 397–400.

20. Arthur O. Lovejoy, *Reflections on Human Nature* (Baltimore, 1961), pp. 36–65; Cecilia M. Kenyon, "Republicanism and Radicalism in the American Revolution: An Old-fashioned Interpretation," *William and Mary Quarterly,* Third Series, 9 (1962): 153–182.

21. Thomas Paine, "Common Sense," in *"Common Sense" and Other Political Writings,* pp. 43–49.

22. The most thoughtful analysis of the American response to republicanism is Chapter II of Gordon S. Wood's *Creation of the American Republic, 1776–1789* (Chapel Hill, 1969). For a sensitive review of the burgeoning literature on republicanism, see Robert E. Shalhope, "Toward a Republican Synthesis: The Emergence of an Understanding of Republicanism in American Historiography," *William and Mary Quarterly,* Third Series, 29 (January, 1972): 49–80.

23. Witherspoon, "The Druid, No. 1," *Works,* 9: 230; Rush to John Adams, July 2, 1788, Butterfield (ed.), *Letters,* 1: 468–469; *Carlisle* (Pennsylvania) *Gazette,* May 25, 1789.

24. Rush was particularly emphatic on this point. See "A Plan for the Establishment of Public Schools . . . to Which Are Added, Thoughts upon the Mode of Education, Proper in a Republic," in Frederick Rudolph (ed.), *Essays on Education in the Early Republic* (Cambridge, Mass., 1965), p. 15.

25. Rush, *ibid.* On that point, see also Witherspoon, "Speech in Congress Upon the Confederation," *Works,* 9: 139.

26. Charles Nisbet, Commencement oration, June 2, 1789 (MS in Charles Nisbet MSS, Dickinson College Library, Carlisle, Pa.), p. 20; Rush to Richard Price, April 22, 1786, Butterfield (ed.), *Letters,* 1: 386; Witherspoon, "The Druid, No. 1," *Works,* 9: 231; *Dominion of Providence,* p. 51; *Carlisle Gazette,* August 10, 1785; Rush, "To the Citizens of Philadelphia: A Plan for Free Schools," Butterfield (ed.), *Letters,* 1: 413.

27. Witherspoon, "The Druid, No. 1," *Works,* 9: 230–231; *Carlisle Gazette,* March 25, 1789; Rush to Richard Price, October 15, 1785, Butterfield (ed.), *Letters,* 1: 371; Rush, "Establishment of Public Schools," Rudolph (ed.), *Essays,* pp. 22–23.

28. Rush to Charles Nisbet, December 5, 1783, Butterfield (ed.), *Letters,* 1: 316.

29. Nisbet to the Earl of Buchan, November 12, 1782, in Samuel Miller, *Memoir of the Rev. Charles Nisbet* (New York, 1840), pp. 96–97.

30. Nisbet to the Earl of Buchan, December 15, 1785, in *ibid.,* p. 139.

31. Nisbet to Rev. James Paton, January 10, 1787, in *ibid.,* p. 167; Nisbet,

October Vacation oration, 1788 (Nisbet MSS, Dickinson College Library), pp. 20–21; Second Commencement Oration, May 7, 1788 (Nisbet MSS), pp. 9–10; Third Commencement Oration, June 2, 1789 (Nisbet MSS), p. 22. See James H. Smylie, "Charles Nisbet: Second Thoughts on a Revolutionary Generation," *Pennsylvania Magazine of History and Biography,* 98 (April, 1974): 189–205.

32. Nisbet to Ashbel Green, October 14, 1794 (Nisbet MSS, Dickinson College Library); Rush to the Earl of Buchan, June 25, 1795, Butterfield (ed.), *Letters,* 2: 761.

33. Rush to John Montgomery, October 18 and April 29, 1786 (Correspondence of Benjamin Rush relative to Dickinson College, microfilm in the Historical Society of Pennsylvania, Philadelphia), unpaginated; Nisbet to Rush, July 23, 1785 (Rush Correspondence).

34. For an elaborate statement of the equation of republicanism and presbyterianism—published during the nation's centennial—see William P. Breed, *Presbyterians and the Revolution* (Philadelphia, 1876), pp. 1–25. But see then the much more sophisticated discussion in Alice M. Baldwin, "Sowers of Sedition: The Political Theories of the New Light Presbyterian Clergy of Virginia and North Carolina," *William and Mary Quarterly,* Third Series, 5 (January, 1948): 52–76. In addition, the Department of History of the Presbyterian Church, U.S.A. and the Presbyterian Historical Society are sponsoring several publications in the years of the Bicentennial of the Revolution that provide an even more thoughtful analysis of the relationship between the republican revolution and American Presbyterianism. See especially the issues of the *Journal of Presbyterian History* that are devoted to the subject: Winter, 1974, and Spring, 1976.

35. Murray, *Jerubbaal,* p. 22.

36. The address is in *Extracts from the Minutes of the General Assembly . . . From A.D. 1789, to A.D. 1802 . . .* (Philadelphia, 1803), 1789: 5.

37. The implication of this emphasis for the study of the classics is discussed on pp. 170–171, below.

38. Rush to Jeremy Belknap, June 6, 1791, Butterfield (ed.), *Letters,* 1: 584; Rush to Adams, July 21, 1789, *ibid.,* p. 523.

39. Rush to E. Winchester, November 12, 1791, *ibid.,* p. 611; Rush to Thomas Jefferson, August 22, 1800, *ibid.,* 2: 821.

40. Thomas Reese, *An Essay on the Influence of Religion, in Civil Society* (Charleston, 1788), pp. 4–8, 10–14, 62–72. The essay is also an instructive example of one Presbyterian's confidence in an intricate but predictable mechanistic theory of cause-and-effect relationships. The effect of certain influences, in this case religion, upon society, was knowable, universal, and susceptible of codification and promulgation.

41. Rush to Adams, April 13, 1790, Butterfield (ed.), *Letters,* 1: 545; Rush, "Establishment of Public Schools," Rudolph (ed.), *Essays,* pp. 10–11.

42. May 21, 1779, *Records of the Presbyterian Church in the United States of America* (Philadelphia, 1904), p. 484; October 6, 1792, Minutes of the Transylvania Presbytery (microfilm of MSS in Louisville Theological Seminary, Louisville, Ky.), 1: 75; Rush, "Establishment of Public Schools," Rudolph (ed.), *Essays,* pp. 10–11.

43. Nisbet to Alexander Addison, October 21, 1786; January 26, 1786 (Letters of Charles Nisbet to Alexander Addison, 1786–1803, MSS in University of Pittsburgh Library, Pittsburgh, Pa.).

44. Same to same, May 26, January 26, October 21, 1786 (*ibid.*).

45. Rush to William Linn, May 4, 1784, Butterfield (ed.), *Letters,* 1: 333; Rush, "To American Farmers About to Settle in New Parts of the United States," *ibid.,* p. 503. Actually, there was apparently little difference between German and Scotch-Irish agricultural habits in late eighteenth-century Pennsylvania, and the accounts that emphasize the alleged differences tell us more about English stereotypes of the two immigrant nationalities than about reality of any sort. See James T. Lemon, "The Agricultural Practices of National Groups in eighteenth-century south-eastern Pennsylvania," *The Geography Review,* 56 (1966): 467–496.

46. Rush to Thomas Percival, October 26, 1786, Butterfield (ed.), *Letters,* 1: 401–404. See also Guy S. Klett, "The Presbyterian Church and the Scotch-Irish on the Pennsylvania Colonial Frontier," *Pennsylvania History,* 8 (April, 1941): 97–109.

Chapter VI

1. For a competent discussion of the Presbyterian educational empire, see especially Donald Robert Come, "The Influence of Princeton on Higher Education in the South Before 1825," *William and Mary Quarterly,* Third Series, 2 (October, 1945): 359–396.

2. The efforts of Smith were discovered by Katharine L. Brown and are discussed in "The Role of Presbyterian Dissent in Colonial and Revolutionary Virginia, 1740–1785," (unpublished Ph.D. dissertation, The Johns Hopkins University, 1969), pp. 255–260.

3. October 13, 1774, Minutes of the Hanover Presbytery (photostat in Union Theological Seminary, Richmond, Va.), 2: 55. For Graham, see William B. Sprague, *Annals of the American Pulpit* (New York, 1860), 3: 365–370; and "The Founders of Washington College: An Address by Hon. Hugh Blair Grigsby, L.L.D. Delivered June 22, 1870," in Washington and Lee University, *Historical Papers* (Baltimore, 1890), pp. 15–29.

4. John Brown to William Preston, August 24, 1775, quoted in Brown, "Presbyterian Dissent," p. 269.

5. The best study of Liberty Hall, Washington College, and finally Washington and Lee University is the genial if sometimes overly laudatory discussion in Ollinger Crenshaw, *General Lee's College: The Rise and Growth of Washington and Lee University* (New York, 1969).

6. October 14, 1774, Han. Pby. Min., 2: 57–58. For Smith, see Miles L. Bradbury, "Samuel Stanhope Smith: Princeton's Accommodation to Reason," *Journal of Presbyterian History*, 48 (Fall, 1970): 189–202; and Douglas Sloan, *The Scottish Enlightenment and the American College Ideal* (New York, 1971), pp. 146–184.

7. Dickinson College Board of Trustees to Charles Nisbet, September 29, 1784, Charter and Proceedings of the Trustees of Dickinson College (typescript in Dickinson College Library, Carlisle, Pa.), 1: 133; John Armstrong to Benjamin Rush, April 15, 1783, and John Montgomery to Rush, April 16, 1783 (Correspondence of Benjamin Rush relative to Dickinson College, microfilm in the Historical Society of Pennsylvania, Philadelphia), unpaginated. For a lively discussion of the founding of Dickinson, see Chapters One through Four of Charles Coleman Sellers, *Dickinson College: A History* (Middletown, Conn., 1973).

8. The standard work on the academies that became Washington and Jefferson College is Helen T. W. Coleman, *Banners in the Wilderness: Early Years of Washington and Jefferson College* (Pittsburgh, 1956), which should be read in conjunction with Dwight Raymond Guthrie, *John McMillan: The Apostle of Presbyterianism in the West, 1752–1833* (Pittsburgh, 1952). A competent treatment of Transylvania may be found in Walter Jennings, *Transylvania: Pioneer University of the West* (New York, 1955), a rather narrowly defined monograph. A more broadly conceived analysis of the culture that supported the college may be found in Niels Henry Sonne's excellent *Liberal Kentucky, 1780–1828* (New York, 1939). For the two Presbyterian founders of the Kentucky school see John Opie, "The Melancholy Career of 'Father' David Rice," *Journal of Presbyterian History*, 47 (December 1969): 295–319; and William W. Whitsitt, *Life and Times of Judge Caleb Wallace* (Louisville, 1888).

9. Benjamin Rush, "Thoughts upon Female Education," Frederick Rudolph (ed.), *Essays on Education in the Early Republic* (Cambridge, Mass., 1965), pp. 36, 27. See also Jean S. Straub, "Benjamin Rush's Views on Women's Education," *Pennsylvania History*, 34 (April, 1967): 147–157. Straub fails to note that the most significant reason for Rush's insistence on women's education was that women could then mitigate the dangerous passions of the men who ruled the fragile republic. For a more explicit treatment of Rush's educational ideas, see Hyman Kuritz, "Benjamin Rush: His Theory of Republican Education," *History of Education Quarterly*, 7 (Winter, 1967):

433–451; and David Freeman Hawke, *Benjamin Rush: Revolutionary Gadfly* (Indianapolis, 1971), pp. 295–298.

10. Rush to the Dickinson College Board, October 21, 1786, L. H. Butterfield (ed.), *Letters of Benjamin Rush* (Princeton, 1951), 1: 398; Rush, "A Plan for the Establishment of Public Schools," Rudolph (ed.), *Essays*, p. 9; Rush to Richard Price, May 25, 1786, Butterfield (ed.), *Letters*, 1: 388.

11. Rush, "Establishment of Public Schools," Rudolph (ed.), *Essays*, p. 17.

12. Samuel Stanhope Smith to Rush, August 27, 1787 (Samuel Stanhope Smith Collection, Princeton University Library).

13. Quoted in "Life and Times of the Rev. Joseph Smith," *Presbyterian Magazine*, 3 (October, 1853): 478.

14. Joseph Smith, *History of Jefferson College* . . . (Pittsburgh, 1857), pp. 416–417.

15. Quoted in *ibid.*, p. 26.

16. For the Presbyterian contribution to constitution-making before 1787, see my "The Grammar of Liberty: American Presbyterians and the First American Constitutions," *Journal of Presbyterian History*, 54 (Spring, 1976): 142–164.

17. The most detailed analysis of the religious dimensions of the imperial crisis in Pennsylvania may be found in Wayne L. Bockleman and Owen S. Ireland, "The Internal Revolution in Pennsylvania: An Ethnic-Religious Interpretation," *Pennsylvania History*, 41 (April, 1974): 125–159; and Owen S. Ireland, "The Ratification of the Federal Constitution in Pennsylvania," unpublished Ph.D. dissertation, University of Pittsburgh, 1966, which, despite its title, is a detailed study of the religious and ethnic dimensions of political life in Pennsylvania between 1776 and 1787.

18. The authoritative account of the document is J. Paul Selsam, *The Pennsylvania Constitution of 1776: A Study in Revolutionary Democracy* (Philadelphia, 1936). But see also Richard A. Ryerson's provocative "Leadership in Crisis: The Radical Committees of Philadelphia and the Coming of the Revolution in Pennsylvania, 1765–1776: A Study in the Revolutionary Process," unpublished Ph.D. dissertation, The Johns Hopkins University, 1973; and Gordon S. Wood's stimulating effort to relate the Pennsylvania revolution to the larger revolutionary movement in *The Creation of the American Republic, 1776–1787* (Chapel Hill, 1969), pp. 226–237.

19. Benjamin Franklin to William Strahan, August 19, 1784, in Selsam, *Pennsylvania Constitution*, p. 208.

20. (Philadelphia) *Pennsylvania Packet*, October 22, April 22, and May 20, 1776.

21. [William Graham], *An Essay on Government. By a Citizen of Frankland* (Philadelphia, 1786), pp. 21–22; *A Declaration of Rights, also the Constitution . . . of the State of Frankland* (Philadelphia, 1786), pp. 10, 13.

22. [Benjamin Rush], *Observations Upon the Present State of the Government of Pennsylvania* (Philadelphia, 1777), pp. 3, 4, 9, 10.

23. *Pa. Packet,* October 22, 1776.

24. [Rush], *Observations,* p. 10. See also the similar comments of Republican Samuel Howell in *Pa. Packet,* November 5, 1776.

25. [Rush], *Observations,* pp. 8, 12.

26. *Ibid.,* pp. 12, 10.

27. *Ibid.,* pp. 5, 8, 9; *Pa. Packet,* November 15, 1776.

28. George B. Wood, *Early History of the University of Philadelphia,* 3rd edition (Philadelphia, 1896), pp. 86–87. For a factually exhaustive but usually unimaginative study of the Pennsylvania school, see William L. Turner, "The College, Academy and Charitable School of Philadelphia: The Development of a Colonial Institution of Learning, 1740–1779," unpublished Ph.D. dissertation, University of Pennsylvania, 1952.

29. Minutes of the Council of Censors, August 27, 1784, in (Philadelphia) *Pennsylvania Gazette,* September 15, 1784; *The Freeman's Journal,* February 9, 1785; Joseph Reed, *Remarks on a Late Publication* . . . (Philadelphia, 1783), p. 50.

30. *Pa. Gaz.,* September 15, 1784; Wood, *Creation of the American Republic,* pp. 400–402.

31. (Baltimore) *Maryland Gazette,* June 17, 1785, quoted in Philip A. Crowl, *Maryland During and After the Revolution* (Baltimore, 1943), p. 86. For the Maryland colleges, see also *Commemoration of the One Hundredth Anniversary of St. John's College* (Baltimore, 1890), pp. 59–128; Bernard C. Steiner, "The History of University Education in Maryland," *Johns Hopkins University Studies in Historical and Political Science,* 9th series, 3 (1891): 145–181; and Steiner, *History of Education in Maryland* (Washington, D.C., 1894), pp. 69–117.

32. *Freeman's Journal,* March 2, 1785. For other Presbyterians supporting Ewing and the Presbyterian takeover of the College, see John Armstrong to Rush, January 6, 1789 (Rush Correspondence); Rush to John Montgomery, August 27, 1784, *ibid.;* John King to Montgomery, March 24, 1783, *ibid.;* William Linn to Rush, September 5, 1783, *ibid.;* Rush to Montgomery, November 15, 1783, Butterfield (ed.), *Letters,* 1: 314.

33. *Freeman's Journal,* January 19, 1785; Reed, *Remarks on a Late Publication,* p. 49.

34. *Pa. Gaz.,* September 15, 1784.

35. *Freeman's Journal,* January 19, 1785.

36. Charles Nisbet, *The Usefulness and Importance of Human Learning* . . . (Carlisle, Pa., 1786), p. 10. Nisbet and his colleague at Dickinson, the Reverend Robert Davidson, frequently described the goals of republican education in explicitly Newtonian terms, emphasizing that it would lead

students to appreciate the society in which "all are useful for the benefit of the Whole." See, Nisbet, Second Commencement Oration, May 7, 1788 (Nisbet MSS, Dickinson College Library); and Robert Davidson, *An Oration, on the Anniversary of the Independence of the United States* (Carlisle, Pa., 1787), p. 15.

37. *Freeman's Journal,* February 23, 1785; Rush to Armstrong, March 19, 1783, Butterfield (ed.), *Letters,* 1: 296; Rush to Nisbet, April, 1784, *ibid.,* 1: 322.

38. (Annapolis) *Maryland Gazette,* December 16, 1784, March 31, 1785; William Smith, *An Account of Washington College in the State of Maryland* (Philadelphia, 1784), p. 10; Patrick Allison to Rush, February 12, 1783 (Rush Correspondence).

39. Rush to Nisbet, August 27, 1784, Butterfield (ed.), *Letters,* 1: 337; Rush to Montgomery, April 15, 1784 (Rush Correspondence); Rush to Dickinson College Board, May 23, 1785, Butterfield (ed.), *Letters,* 1: 353. For Rush's comparison of the Germans and the Scotch-Irish, see Butterfield (ed.), "Dr. Benjamin Rush's Journal of a Trip to Carlisle in 1784," *The Pennsylvania Magazine of History and Biography,* 74 (October, 1950): 445–446. And for an intriguing discussion of the issue of ethnic stereotypes in Rush's Pennsylvania, see James T. Lemon, *The Best Poor Man's Country: A Geographical Study of Early Southeastern Pennsylvania* (Baltimore, 1972).

40. Rush to ?, July 30, 1785 (Rush Correspondence); Rush to King, April 2, 1783, Butterfield (ed.), *Letters,* 1: 298–299.

41. Rush, "To the Citizens of Pennsylvania," Butterfield (ed.), *Letters,* 1: 365–367 . See also Frederic Shriver Klein, "The Spiritual and Educational Background of Franklin College," *Pennsylvania History,* 5 (April, 1938): 65–76.

42. *Pa. Gaz.,* January 26, 1785; *Freeman's Journal,* January 26, 1785; *The* (Philadelphia) *Independent Gazetteer,* January 22, 1785.

43. *Freeman's Journal,* January 26, 1785; Rush, "To the Citizens of Phila-delphia," Butterfield (ed.), *Letters,* 1:414.

44. *Ind. Gaz.,* January 22, 1785; King to Rush, January 16, 1785 (Rush Correspondence); [Benjamin Rush], "An Address to the Citizens of Penn-sylvania of German Birth and Extraction," *Carlisle Gaz.,* September 21, 1785.

45. Rush to Armstrong, March 19, 1783, Butterfield (ed.), *Letters,* 1: 294; Rush, "To the Citizens of Pennsylvania," *ibid.,* 1: 367–368. For a discussion of Rush's views on diversity and unity in a republic, see Donald J. D'Elia, "The Republican Theology of Benjamin Rush," *Pennsylvania History,* 33 (April, 1966): 187–203.

46. *Freeman's Journal,* February 23, January 26, 1785.

47. *Ibid.,* January 26, 1785; *Ind. Gaz.,* January 22, 1785; Rush to Montgom-ery, February 17, 1787, Butterfield (ed.), *Letters,* 1: 412.

48. Quoted in Alvah Hovey, *Isaac Backus* (Boston, 1859), p. 210. See also the thoughtful discussion of the discomfited Whig leaders in William G. McLoughlin, "The Role of Religion in the Revolution: Liberty of Conscience and Cultural Cohesion in the New Nation," in Stephen G. Kurtz and James H. Hutson (eds.), *Essays on the American Revolution* (Chapel Hill, 1973), pp. 197–206.

49. The most sensitive analysis of the conflict between the Anglican gentry and the pietistic Baptists is in Rhys Isaac, "Evangelical Revolt: The Nature of the Baptists' Challenge to the Traditional Order in Virginia, 1765 to 1775," *William and Mary Quarterly,* Third Series, 31 (July, 1974): 345–368.

50. For the colonial conflict between the Virginia Presbyterians and the Anglicans, see *supra,* pp. 69–70.

51. Petition of Hanover Presbytery to Virginia legislature, November 11, 1774, in Charles Fenton James, *Documentary History of the Struggle of Religious Liberty in Virginia* (Lynchburg, Va., 1900), pp. 46–47.

52. Petition of dissenters in Albemarle, Amherst, and Buckingham counties, October 22, 1776, in *ibid.,* pp. 69–70. James is surely correct in identifying this as a Presbyterian petition (p. 75). The sentiments are identical to those expressed by the Hanover Presbytery to the legislature on October 24 (p. 71).

53. Quoted in *ibid.,* p. 72.

54. "Queries on the Subject of Religious Establishments" (Pinckney's Williamsburg) *Virginia Gazette,* October 18, 1776; Caleb Wallace, "Memorial of Hanover Presbytery," in Whitsitt, *Wallace,* p. 49.

55. "Petition of Sundry Inhabitants of Prince Edward County," September 24, 1776, quoted in Brown, "Presbyterian Dissent," p. 363.

56. Petitions of Hanover Presbytery, June 3, 1779, and April 15, 1777, in James, *Documentary History,* pp. 90, 226–227.

57. Quoted in *ibid.,* p. 81.

58. *Ibid.,* pp. 185–186.

59. See for example the provisions of the North Carolina Constitution of 1776. *The Colonial Records of North Carolina* (Raleigh, N.C., 1890), 10: 1011.

60. The best recent account of the move toward a general assessment in several colonies in the post-Revolutionary period is McLoughlin, "Role of Religion," pp. 209–228. In fact, McLoughlin's treatment is the only one of substance to deal with the phenomenon in more than one colony or state.

61. Petitions of Hanover Presbytery, May 26, 1784 and October, 1784, in James, *Documentary History,* pp. 227–228, 233–234.

62. James Madison to James Monroe, April 12, 1785, quoted in William C. Rives, *History of the Life and Times of James Madison* (Boston, 1859–1868), 1: 630.

63. Preamble to General Assessment Bill, December 3, 1784, in James, *Documentary History,* p. 129.

64. October 28, 1784, Han. Pby. Min., 2: 178; Petition of Hanover Presbytery, October, 1784, in James, *Documentary History,* pp. 234–236.

65. James, *Documentary History,* p. 238; May 19, 1785, Han. Pby. Min., 2: 186. By far the best detailed discussion of the Presbyterian involvement in the general assessment is in Brown's Chapter VIII, "Presbyterians in the Struggle for Religious Freedom in Virginia," in "Presbyterian Dissent," pp. 332–394.

66. For the idea of a congressionally appointed Christian censor, see William G. McLoughlin, *New England Dissent, 1630–1833: The Baptists and the Separation of Church and State* (Cambridge, Mass., 1971), 2: 711.

67. September 30, 1791, Minutes of the Synod of Virginia (microfilm of MSS in Union Theological Seminary), 1: 77; October 29, 1791, Han. Pby. Min., 3: 117.

68. The Presbyterians' reluctance to accept complete separation of church and state and their efforts to ensure informally that America was thoroughly and visibly Christian supports William McLoughlin's assertion that the evangelical, pietistic ideas of Isaac Backus on the separation of church and state—ideas which strongly parallel Presbyterian ideas on the subject—are closer to a traditional American stance than either the radical separatism of Roger Williams or the enlightened rationalism of Jefferson. See McLoughlin, "Isaac Backus and the Separation of Church and State in America," *American Historical Review,* 73 (June, 1968): 1392–1413.

69. [Graham], *Essay on Government,* pp. 11, 12, 17, 32.

70. Graham, *Declaration of Rights,* passim.

71. September 24 and 26, 1794, Va. Syn. Min., 1: 126, 140. For the Pennsylvania Presbyterians' reaction to the Rebellion, see Nisbet to William Young, July 29, 1794 (Nisbet MSS, Dickinson College Library); Guthrie, *McMillan,* p. 159, 162–163; and Ronald W. Long, "The Presbyterians and the Whiskey Rebellion," *Journal of Presbyterian History,* 43 (March, 1965): 28–36.

72. The bills outlining the proposed changes are in Julian P. Boyd (ed.), *The Papers of Thomas Jefferson* (Princeton, 1950–), 2: 526–534. There are no satisfactory monographic accounts of Jefferson's educational thought, but see Charles Flinn (ed.), *Thomas Jefferson and Education in a Republic* (New York, 1930), especially Chapters III and IV; John C. Henderson, *Thomas Jefferson's Views on Public Education* (New York, 1890), Chapter I; and, particularly, Robert Polk Thomson, "The Reform of the College of William and Mary, 1760–1860," *Proceedings of the American Philosophical Society,* 115 (June, 1971): 187–213.

73. Samuel Stanhope Smith to Jefferson, April 19, 1779, Boyd (ed.), *Jeffer-*

son Papers, 2: 254. See also the useful analysis of the interchange between Smith and Jefferson in Brown, "Presbyterian Dissent," pp. 292–294.

74. Smith to Jefferson, March, 1779, and April 19, 1779, Boyd (ed.), *Jefferson Papers,* 2: 247, 253.

75. *Ibid.,* pp. 248, 253, 254.

76. For the relationship between the Anglicans of Prince Edward County and the Presbyterian founders of Hampden-Sydney, see Brown, "Presbyterian Dissent," pp. 273–275, 282–283, and 288.

77. April 14, 1775, Han. Pby. Min., 2: 62; March 1 and 16, 1790, Alfred J. Morrison (ed.), *The College of Hampden-Sidney, Calendar of Board Minutes, 1776–1876* (Richmond, 1912), pp. 37, 38.

78. *The* (Lexington) *Kentucky Gazette,* September 1, 1787, November 10, 1787.

79. *Ibid.,* December 22, 1787, January 19, 1788. See also Alvin F. Lewis, *History of Higher Education in Kentucky* (Washington, D.C., 1899), pp. 36–38, 45.

80. October 24, 1782, Han. Pby. Min., 2: 158; January 30, 1783, Minutes of the Board of Trustees of Washington College (Virginia), (microfilm of MSS in the Washington and Lee University Library, Lexington, Va.), p. 17. At none of the more thoroughly Presbyterian schools was the denomination given any special privileges by charter right.

81. Brown, "Presbyterian Dissent," pp. 323–324.

82. September 30, 1791, Va. Syn. Min., 1: 74; Petition to the Synod of Virginia, 1972, Wash. Bd. Min. (Va.), p. 34; April 26, 1792, Minutes of the Presbytery of Lexington, Virginia (microfilm of MSS in the Union Theological Seminary, Richmond, Va.), 1: 127; April 24, 1793, *ibid.,* 2: 12.

83. October 21, 1791, *Minutes of the Presbytery of Redstone* (Cincinnati, 1878), p. 81; April 18, 1793, *ibid.,* p. 96. See also Coleman, *Banners in the Wilderness,* p. 45.

84. Patrick Allison to Rush, February 12, 1783 (Rush Correspondence). See also the letter of John Dickinson endeavoring to persuade Nisbet, still in Scotland, that all the acrimony in evidence in Pennsylvania in 1784 predated the Presbyterian effort to establish a college at Carlisle. Dickinson to Nisbet, September 29, 1784, quoted in Alfred O. Aldridge, "The 'Broad Bottom' of Early Education in Pennsylvania," in *Early Dickinsoniana: The Boyd Lee Spahr Lectures in Americana, 1957–1961* (Harrisburg, Pa., 1961), p. 100.

85. *Freeman's Journal,* February 23, 1785.

86. For stimulating discussions of denominationalism in American culture, see two articles by Sidney E. Mead, "From Coercion to Persuasion: Another Look at the Rise of Religious Liberty and the Emergence of Denominationalism," and "Denominationalism: The Shape of Protestantism in America," in *The Lively Experiment: The Shaping of Christianity in America* (New York,

1963), pp. 16–37 and 103–133; and Timothy L. Smith, "Congregation, State, and Denomination: The Forming of the American Religious Structure," *William and Mary Quarterly,* Third Series, 25 (April 1968): 155–176.

87. The best general discussion of the impact of the Revolution on denominational communities is in Sydney E. Ahlstrom, *A Religious History of the American People* (New Haven, 1972), pp. 360–384. For a magisterial discussion of one denomination's confrontation with the necessity for creating a community within the new pluralism, see William G. McLoughlin's analysis of the New England Baptists, Chapters IX, X, and XI of *New England Dissent.*

88. [John Witherspoon], *A Draught of a Plan of Government and Discipline for the Presbyterian Church in the United States of America* (Philadelphia, 1786), p. 18. The best treatment of the creation of the General Assembly remains Leonard J. Trinterud, *The Formation of an American Tradition: A Re-examination of Colonial Presbyterianism* (Philadelphia, 1949), Chapter 16.

89. *Extracts from the Minutes of the General Assembly* (Philadelphia, 1803), 1789, p. 7.

90. September 16, 1795, Minutes of the Presbytery of New Brunswick (microfilm of MSS in the Presbyterian Historical Society, Philadelphia, Pa), 4: 357–359; [Witherspoon], *Plan of Government,* pp. 26–31, 40–47.

91. October 22, 1783, Minutes of the Board of Trustees of Princeton University (MSS in Princeton University Library), 1: 240; September 15, 1783, Dick. Bd. Min., 1: 86; Dickinson Board to William Bingham, n.d. (Rush Correspondence); Rush to King, April 2, 1783, Butterfield (ed.), *Letters,* 1: 300.

92. Richard Price to Rush, January 1, 1783 (Rush Correspondence); Margaret W. Ross to Witherspoon, February 17, 1784 (Ashbel Green Collection, Princeton University Library); Benjamin Franklin to Witherspoon, April 5, 1784 (The John Witherspoon Collection in Photocopy and Typescript, copies of MSS in Princeton University Library); Bingham to Dickinson Board, December 29, 1783, in April 7, 1784, Dick. Bd. Min., 1: 112; September 30, 1784, Pr. Bd. Min., 1: 246.

93. October 1, 1784, Pr. Bd. Min., 1: 246–247.

94. October 1, 1791, Va. Syn. Min., 1: 81–82; August 14, 1793, Wash. Bd. Min. (Va.), pp. 39–40; November 9, 1793, Han. Pby. Min., 3: 167; April 24, 1794, N. Bruns. Pby. Min., 4: 278; February 29, 1792, Minutes of the Transylvania Presbytery (microfilm of MSS in Union Theological Seminary), 1: 52.

95. King to Rush, January 12, March 19, 1784, January 16, 1785 (Rush Correspondence); April 7, 1784, Dick. Bd. Min., 1: 110–111; April 24, 1794, Trans. Pby. Min., 1: 113.

96. September 27, 1791, Pr. Bd. Min., 1: 292; April 10, 1793, *ibid.*, 300–312; April 10, 1794, *ibid.*, 330–331.

97. April 18, 1787, *ibid.*, 1: 262; September 26, 1792, *ibid.*, 299; April 10, 1793, *ibid.*, 313–314; April 8, 1794, *ibid.*, 325.

98. October 1, 1790, Pr. Bd. Min., 1: 286; June 21, 1797, Dick. Bd. Min., 1: 236; Dickinson Board to Rush, December 23, 1789 (Rush Correspondence); Rush to Montgomery (?), May 10, 1788, *ibid.*

99. See two surviving petitions to Dr. James Sproat and to William Crawford in Samuel Stanhope Smith Collection (Princeton University Library).

100. *Pa. Gaz.*, October 27, 1784; Rush to Montgomery, June 27, 1785 (Rush Correspondence); Nisbet to Dickinson, July 13, 1785 (Nisbet MSS, Dickinson College Library).

101. September 25, 1783, Pr. Bd. Min., 1: 236.

102. For the correspondence relative to the Washington bequest see, January 5, 1796, Wash. Bd. Min. (Va.), p. 58; Liberty Hall Board to George Washington, December 7, 1796 (Liberty Hall MSS, Washington and Lee University Library); and Washington to Liberty Hall Board, June 17, 1798, John C. Fitzpatrick (ed.), *The Writings of George Washington* (Washington, D.C., 1931–1944), 36: 293.

103. Henry Ruffner, "Early History of Washington College, Now Washington and Lee University," Washington and Lee University, *Historical Papers* (Baltimore, 1890), pp. 68–69.

104. Morrison (ed.), *Calendar,* November 27, 1797, p. 48; January 31, April 20, 1797, Wash. Bd. Min. (Va.), pp. 66, 71. See also James M. Hutcheson, "Virginia's 'Dartmouth College Case'," *Virginia Magazine of History and Biography,* 51 (April, 1943): 134–140.

105. A major new interpretation of the relationship between college and state is John S. Whitehead, *The Separation of College and State: Columbia, Dartmouth, Harvard, and Yale, 1776–1876* (New Haven, 1973). While one is convinced by his central assertion that a clear distinction between public and private institutions of higher learning did not emerge in the United States until after the Civil War, Whitehead's stimulating analysis is fundamentally flawed by his failure to pay attention to the ideational foundation of the important changes he discusses. For an extended critique, see my review of the monograph in *Journal of Church and State,* 17 (Spring, 1975): 309–311.

106. Franklin B. Hough, *Historical and Statistical Record of the University of the State of New York* (Albany, 1885), pp. 43–44; John W. Pratt, *Religion, Politics, and Diversity: The Church-State Theme in New York History* (Ithaca, 1967), pp. 103–104; *Yale College Subject to the General Assembly* (New Haven, 1784), p. 22.

107. Daniel Walker Hollis, *South Carolina College* (Columbia, S.C., 1951),

pp. 21–22. See also the charter of the University of Georgia in Robert Preston Brooks, *The University of Georgia Under Six Administrations* (Athens, Ga., 1956), p. 6, for a representative pledge of nonsectarianism. Then see the useful discussion of all these first state universities in Merle Borrowman, "The False Dawn of the State University," *History of Education Quarterly*, 1 (June, 1961): 6–22.

108. For discussions of the proposed national university see Noah Webster, "On the Education of youth in America," Rudolph (ed.), *Essays*, pp. 52–57; Samuel Knox, "An Essay on the Best System of Liberal Education, Adapted to the Genius of the Government of the United States," *ibid.*, pp. 357–367; Washington to the Commissioners of the District of Columbia, January 28, 1795, Fitzpatrick (ed.), *Writings*, 34: 106–108; "Last Will and Testament," *ibid.*, 37: 278–281; Rush, "To Friends of the Federal Government: A Plan for a Federal University," [October 29, 1788], in Butterfield (ed.), *Letters*, 1: 491–495. See also the excellent discussion in David Tyack, "Forming the National Character: Paradox in the Educational Thought of the Revolutionary Generation," *Harvard Educational Review*, 36 (Winter, 1966): 29–41.

109. September 26, 1776, Morrison (ed.), *Calendar*, p. 20; February 19, 1778, Wash. Bd. Min. (Va.), p. 14; November 15, 1787, Minutes of the Board of Trustees, Washington College (MSS in the Washington and Jefferson College Library, Washington, Pennsylvania), p. 9; June 21, 1786, Records of the Proceedings of the Board of Trustees for the Transylvania Seminary (MSS in the Transylvania College Library, Lexington, Kentucky); hereafter cited as Trans. Sem. Bd. Min.

110. April 8, 1784, Dick. Bd. Min., 1: 116; June 16, 1785, *ibid.*, 144.

111. Copy of a form petition, n.d., in Rush Correspondence. See also Saul Sack, "The State and Higher Education," *Pennsylvania History*, 26 (July, 1959): 242–243.

112. January 7, 1795, Morrison (ed.), *Calendar*, p. 44; July 20, 1793, Wash. Bd. Min. (Va.), p. 18; April 10, 1797, *ibid.*, pp. 22–23. Bills passed by the Virginia legislature granting aid to Transylvania are appended to Trans. Sem. Bd. Min.

113. Memorial for the College of New Jersey, 1784 (Witherspoon Collection in photocopy and typescript, Princeton University Library).

114. January 13, April 13, September 26, 1796, Pr. Bd. Min., 1: 357, 365, 418; Smith to Ashbel Green, February 13, 1796 (Smith Collection, Princeton University Library).

115. College of New Jersey, *To the Honourable the Legislative-Council and General Assembly of the State of New Jersey* (Trenton, 1796).

116. John Maclean, *History of the College of New Jersey From Its Origin in 1746 to the Commencement of 1854* (Philadelphia, 1877), 2: 13–14.

Chapter VII

1. The best introduction to the Scottish school of common sense is S. A. Grave, *The Scottish Philosophy of Common Sense* (Oxford, 1960). The theological implications of its transition to America are treated in Sydney Ahlstrom, "Scottish Philosophy and American Theology," *Church History,* 24 (September, 1955): 257–272. A recent dissertation attempts to distinguish among the varieties of the American reception of the common sense philosophy. See Richard Petersen, "Scottish Common Sense in America, 1768–1850," unpublished Ph.D. dissertation, American University, 1963. But the most successful discussion of the common sense school in its American context is Daniel Walker Howe, *The Unitarian Conscience: Harvard Moral Philosophy, 1805–1861* (Cambridge, Mass., 1970).

2. Howe, *Unitarian Conscience,* pp. 27–44.

3. Petersen, "Scottish Common Sense," pp. 34–49.

4. John Witherspoon, "Lectures on Moral Philosophy," in *The Works of John Witherspoon* . . . (Edinburgh, 1815), 7: 22–23.

5. Quoted in Charles Coleman Sellers, *Dickinson College: A History* (Middletown, Conn., 1973), pp. 104–105.

6. William Graham, Lectures on Human Nature, notes taken by Joseph Glass in 1796 (microfilm in Union Theological Seminary, Richmond, Virginia), pp. 5, 11–13, 15, 17, 53–55, 65, 103; Witherspoon, "Lectures on Moral Philosophy," *Works,* 7: 47.

7. Graham, Lectures on Human Nature, pp. 9, 11, 13, 17, 73, 75; Samuel Stanhope Smith to James Madison, November, 1777–August, 1778, William T. Hutchinson and William M. C. Rachal (eds.), *The Papers of James Madison* (Chicago, 1962–), 1: 199.

8. Graham, Lectures on Human Nature, p. 39.

9. Smith to Madison, November, 1777–August, 1778, Hutchinson and Rachal (eds.), *Papers of Madison,* 1: 203–205, 208–209.

10. Samuel Stanhope Smith, "On the Utility and necessity of learning in a minister of the gospel" (Samuel Stanhope Smith Collection, MSS in Princeton University Library, Princeton, N.J.). See also Charles Nisbet, Questions and answers on Logic and Metaphysics, n.d. (MSS in Dickinson College Library, Carlisle, Pennsylvania), p. 41.

11. See the discussion in *supra,* pp. 88–89.

12. The most extended example of Rush's "associationism" is in Benjamin Rush, *An Inquiry into the Influence of Physical Causes upon the Moral Faculty* (Philadelphia, 1839). For discussions of Rush's peculiar kind of environmentalism, and its importance, see: Donald J. D'Elia, "Benjamin Rush, David Hartley, and the Revolutionary Use of Psychology," *Proceedings of the American Philosophical Society,* 114 (April 13, 1970): 109–118; Hyman

Kuritz, "Benjamin Rush: His Theory of Republican Education," *History of Education Quarterly,* 7 (Winter, 1967): 433–434; and Douglas Sloan, *The Scottish Enlightenment and the American College Ideal* (New York, 1971), pp. 213–221.

13. See, especially Gordon S. Wood, *The Creation of the American Republic, 1776–1787* (Chapel Hill, 1969), Chapter One.

14. Charles Nisbet, *The Usefulness and Importance of Human Learning* . . . (Carlisle, Pa., 1786), pp. 11–13. On the uses of history, see George H. Colcott, "History Enters the Schools," *American Quarterly,* 11 (Winter, 1959): 470–483. Colcott fails to see the ways in which eighteenth-century educators quite seriously used education, and especially the study of history, for very specific ends. The Presbyterian educators, at any rate, bear little resemblance to the dilettantes he discusses.

15. See, for example, April 30, 1792, and March 14, 1794, Hampden-Sydney College, Union Society Minutes (MSS in the Hampden-Sydney College Library Hampden-Sydney, Va.); and December 7, 1797, January 7, 1799, Washington College (Pa.), Philo Literary Society Minutes (MSS in the Washington and Jefferson College Library, Washington, Pa.), 1: 29, 113, for negative evaluations of the classical curriculum. For a general discussion of the classics in the secondary schools of New England, see Robert Middlekauff, *Ancients and Axioms: Secondary Education in Eighteenth-Century New England* (New Haven, 1963). Middlekauff is not adequately sensitive to the dynamics of the opposition to the classics in the Revolutionary period.

16. Charles Nisbet, Second Commencement Oration (MS in Charles Nisbet MSS, Dickinson College Library), pp. 2–3; Nisbet, October Vacation Oration, 1787 (MS in Charles Nisbet MSS, Dickinson College Library), p. 13.

17. Nisbet, October Vacation Oration, 1787, p. 2; Samuel Stanhope Smith to Benjamin Rush, November 10, 1794 (Samuel Stanhope Smith Collection, MSS in Princeton University Library).

18. Nisbet to Jonathan Ingham, January 14, 1793 (MS in Charles Nisbet MSS, Dickinson College Library).

19. Nisbet, October Vacation Oration, 1787, p. 13; Lectures on the Dead Languages, notes taken by David McConaughy, 1794 (MS in Washington and Jefferson College Library), pp. 47–48.

20. Benjamin Rush, "Observations upon the study of the Latin and Greek Languages . . . ," *Essays, Literary, Moral, and Philosophical,* 2nd edition (Philadelphia, 1806), pp. 22, 47–49; Rush to Rebecca Smith, July 1, 1791, Lyman H. Butterfield (ed.), *Letters of Benjamin Rush* (Princeton, 1951), 1: 586.

21. Rush, "Observations," *Essays,* pp. 24, 34; Rush to John Adams, June 15, 1789, July 2, 1789, February 24, 1790, Butterfield (ed.), *Letters,* 1: 516, 518, 535.

22. Rush to James Muir, August 24, 1791, Butterfield (ed.), *Letters*, 1: 606–607.

23. Rush, "Observations," *Essays*, pp. 21, 23–24.

24. *Ibid.*, pp. 27–28.

25. *Ibid.*, pp. 26–27, 31, 35, 39, 40–41; Rush, "To Friends of the Federal Government: A Plan for a Federal University," Butterfield (ed.), *Letters*, 1: 495. See also Rush to James Muir, August 24, 1791, *ibid.*, 1: 604.

26. Rush, "Observations," *Essays*, pp. 25, 36–37, 43–44; Rush to Adams, July 21, 1789, Butterfield (ed.), *Letters*, 1: 524. The standard work on the classics in colonial America suffers very much from its essay format. See Richard M. Gummere, *The American Colonial Mind and the Classical Tradition* (Cambridge, Mass., 1963). Gummere's *Seven Wise Men of Colonial America* (Cambridge, Mass., 1967) is no more satisfactory. His chapter on Rush (pp. 70–80) advances only the thesis that Rush was opposed to the pedantic presentation of the classics. A far more adequate approach may be found in Meyer Reinhold, "Opponents of Classical Learning During the Revolutionary Period," *Proceedings of the American Philosophical Society*, 112 (August 15, 1968): 221–234. See also Frank Klassen, "Persistence and Change in Eighteenth Century Colonial Education," *History of Education Quarterly*, 2 (June, 1962): 83–99.

27. The student debates of the late eighteenth-century literary societies remain one of the most promising untapped resources for the study of student life in the young republic, of the intellectual predilections of those young Americans who were able to attend an institution of higher learning, and, most important, of the essential relationship between the official curriculum and the unofficial extracurriculum offered by the student societies. One exciting exception to this general neglect, though, is James McLachlan, *"The Choice of Hercules:* American Student Societies in the Early 19th Century," in Lawrence Stone (ed.), *The University in Society* (Princeton, 1974), 2: 449–494.

28. September 7, 1785, and March 9, 1787, Alfred J. Morrison (ed.), *The College of Hampden-Sidney, Calendar of Board Minutes, 1776–1876* (Richmond, 1912), pp. 33, 35; September 26, 1799, Minutes of the Board of Trustees of Princeton University (MSS in the University Archives of Princeton University), 2: 33; September 23, 1800, *ibid.*, 2: 41.

29. For an enormously learned but never oppressive discussion, see Wilbur Samuel Howell's *Eighteenth-Century British Logic and Rhetoric* (Princeton, 1971), which treats colonial America as an important part of its subject and contains the best available discussion (pp. 671–691) of Witherspoon's contribution to the art.

30. Benjamin Rush, "A Plan for the Establishment of Public Schools and the Diffusion of Knowledge in Pennsylvania; To Which Are Added, Thoughts

upon the Mode of Education, Proper in a Republic," in Frederick Rudolph (ed.), *Essays on Education in the Early Republic* (Cambridge, Mass., 1965), p. 19.

31. Robert Davidson, Questions and Answers on Rhetoric, Student Notebook of G. D. Foulk, 1799 (typescript in Dickinson College Library), pp. 1, 4.

32. Morrison (ed.), *Calendar,* p. 28. The Reverend Manesseh Cutler, while on tour of the middle states in 1787, noted that a similar stage for oratorical exercises existed in Nassau Hall. John Maclean, *History of the College of New Jersey . . .* (Philadelphia, 1877), 1: 347.

33. John Witherspoon, *A Series of Letters on Education . . .* (New York, 1797), pp. 26, 76, 55, 53; "The Religious Education of Children," *Works of the Rev. John Witherspoon . . .* (Philadelphia, 1800–1803), 2: 254, 258, 253.

34. Witherspoon, *Letters on Education,* pp. 76, 68, 55, 33, 39, 34, 47–48.

35. Rush, "Thoughts upon the Amusements and Punishments Which are Proper for Schools," *Essays,* pp. 63, 64, 67–68; "Establishment of Public Schools," Rudolph (ed.), *Essays,* pp. 16, 33.

36. Quoted in "Ashbel Green," *Presbyterian Magazine,* 4 (October, 1854), 471–472.

37. See Edmund S. Morgan, *The Gentle Puritan: A Life of Ezra Stiles* (New Haven, 1962).

38. *Laws of the College of New-Jersey . . .* (Trenton, N.J., 1794), p. 31; June 11, 1794, March 15 and 16, 1793, Resolves and Minutes of the Faculty [of the College of New Jersey] (MSS in the Archives of Princeton University), unpaginated.

39. For examples of parents who physically attacked schoolmasters who had corporally punished their children, see James Axtell, *The School upon a Hill: Education and Society in Colonial New England* (New Haven, 1974), pp. 194–200.

40. Hampden-Sydney and Princeton were the exceptions.

41. Two representative actions are in January 8, 1794, Princeton Faculty Minutes; and September 28, 1791, and April 10, 1794, Pr. Bd. Min., 1: 213, 332.

42. Rush, "Establishment of Public Schools," Rudolph (ed.), *Essays,* p. 17; Rush to Walter Minto, March 24, April 30, and September 19, 1792, Butterfield (ed.), *Letters,* 1: 613, 615, 622; Rush, *An Inquiry,* p. 23; Samuel D. Alexander, *Princeton College During the Eighteenth Century* (New York, 1872), p. 233; Robert Davidson, A brief State of the College . . . , 1791 (MS in the Robert Davidson MSS, Dickinson College Library). For Nisbet's scathing critique of those same private houses, see Sellers, *Dickinson College,* pp. 99–100.

43. Rush to John Armstrong, March 19, 1783, and to John Montgomery, June 27, 1783, Butterfield (ed.), *Letters,* 1: 295, 302; October 1, 1790, Pr. Bd.

Min., 1: 278; June 21, 1797, Charter and Proceedings of the Trustees of Dickinson College (typescript in Dickinson College Library), 1: 206; January 30, 1783, Minutes of the Board of Trustees of Washington College (Va.) (microfilm of MSS in the Washington and Lee University Library, Lexington, Va.), p. 19.

44. See the discussion in *supra,* pp. 85–86.

45. Davidson, State of the College, 1791; (Lexington) *Kentucky Gazette,* January 19, 1788.

46. David W. Robson, "Higher Education in the Emerging American Republic, 1750–1800," (unpublished Ph.D. dissertation, Yale University, 1974), p. 118.

47. Rush, "Establishment of Public Schools," Rudolph (ed.), *Essays,* p. 20; Rush to Nisbet, April 19 (?), 1784, Butterfield (ed.), 1: 323–324.

48. *Carlisle Gazette,* August 10, 1785, March 29, 1797; June 25, 1798, Dick. Bd. Min., 1: 250–251.

49. Robert Davidson, Lectures on Universal Grammar, student notebook of George D. Foulk, 1799 (typescript in Dickinson College Library), pp. 46, 56, 84, 85.

50. Several recent dissertations deal to varying degrees with the revision of the college curriculum during the republican period. All merit consultation. In addition to the Robson dissertation mentioned in note 46, above, they are: Steven J. Novak, "The Rights of Youth: Student Unrest and American Higher Education, 1798–1815," unpublished Ph.D. dissertation, University of California, Berkeley, 1974; Phyllis V. Erenberg, "Change and Continuity: Values in American Higher Education, 1750–1800," unpublished Ph.D. dissertation, University of Michigan, 1974. See also Robert Polk Thomson, "The Reform of the College of William and Mary, 1763–1780," *Proceedings of the American Philosophical Society,* 115 (June 17, 1971): 187–213.

51. *Laws of the College of New-Jersey,* p. 37; Anonymous, Journal at Nassau Hall, February 24, 1786 (photostat of MS in Princeton University Library); for announcements concerning utilitarian curriculum innovations, see *Carlisle Gazette,* February 1 and March 22, 1786, and the *Pittsburgh Gazette* for September, 1792. See also Davidson to the Dickinson Board, May 10, 1786 (MS in the Robert Davidson MSS, Dickinson College Library); and especially Thaddeus Dod's synopsis of "Parallel" and "Middle Latitude" Sailing in Thaddeus Dod, Notes on Navigation (MS in Washington and Jefferson College Library.)

52. Rush, "Plan for a Federal University," Butterfield (ed.), *Letters,* 1: 493; "Observations on the Study of Latin and Greek," *Essays,* pp. 47–50; Rush to Montgomery, July 1, 1786 (Correspondence of Benjamin Rush Relative to Dickinson College, microfilm in the Historical Society of Pennsylvania, Philadelphia, Pa.).

53. September 27, 1787, Pr. Bd. Min., 1: 270–271; October 1, 1795, and September 23, 1800, *ibid.*, 1: 355, 2: 41; Rush to Montgomery, March 18, 1785 (Rush Correspondence); Archibald Alexander, "Address Before the Alumni Association of Washington College, June 29, 1843," Washington and Lee University, *Historical Papers,* No. 2 (Baltimore, 1890), p. 132.

54. See Brook Hindle, *The Pursuit of Science in Revolutionary America, 1735–1789* (Chapel Hill, 1956); Rush, "Establishment of Public Schools," Rudolph (ed.), *Essays,* pp. 19–20.

55. John Maclean, *Two Lectures on Combustion* . . . (Philadelphia, 1797), pp. 68, 71.

56. Walter Minto, An Inaugural Oration (MS in the Presbyterian Historical Society, Philadelphia, Pennsylvania), pp. 8, 13; Nisbet, Second Commencement Oration, p. 4.

57. Undoubtedly the single most significant aspect of eighteenth-century higher education still awaiting definitive treatment, moral philosophy will receive that investigation in the research currently pursued by Norman S. Fiering. Until those results are published, see Fiering's "Moral Philosophy in America, 1650–1750, and Its British Context," unpublished Ph.D. dissertation, Columbia University, 1969, and his "President Samuel Johnson and the Circle of Knowledge," *William and Mary Quarterly,* Third Series, 28 (April, 1971): 199–236.

58. Witherspoon, "Lectures on Moral Philosophy," *Works* (1815), 3: 10–11, 150.

59. Nisbet to Rush, January 30, 1786 (Rush Correspondence); Nisbet to Rush, July 18, 1785 (Nisbet MSS, Dickinson College Library); Nisbet to Alexander Addison, February 23, 1797 (Letters of Charles Nisbet to Alexander Addison, 1786–1803, photostats of MSS in the University of Pittsburgh Library, Pittsburgh, Pennsylvania); Nisbet to James Allison, 1791, as quoted in James Henry Morgan, *Dickinson College* . . . (Carlisle, 1933), p. 145.

60. Committee report, November 9, 1793 (MS in Transylvania University MSS, Archives of Transylvania University, Lexington, Ky.); "Laws and Ordinances," 1784, in Morrison (ed.), *Calendar,* pp. 29–30; September 24, 1788, Pr. Bd. Min., 1: 274.

61. Morrison (ed.), *Calendar,* April 28, 1786, p. 34; C. B. Swisher, "The Education of Roger B. Taney," *Bulwark of Liberty* . . . (New York, 1950), p. 154; April 17, 1794, Dick. Bd. Min., 1: 205.

62. Witherspoon to Nicholas Van Dyke, May 12, 1786 (John Witherspoon Collection, MSS in Princeton University Library); Smith to Rush, February 25, 1790 (Smith Collection, Princeton University Library); Nisbet to Rush, August 26, 1790 (Rush Correspondence).

63. Nisbet, State of Dickinson College, 1789 (Nisbet MSS, Dickinson College Library), p. 3; Nisbet to Addison, February 23, 1797 (Nisbet-Addison

Correspondence); Nisbet, State of Dickinson College, 1799 (Nisbet MSS, Dickinson College Library), pp. 1–3.

64. May 28, 1776, *Records of the Presbyterian Church* . . . (Philadelphia, 1904), p. 475; Smith, "Utility and Necessity of Learning," pp. 15, 16; May 21, 1785, *Presbyterian Records,* p. 511.

65. *Extracts from the Minutes of the General Assembly* . . . (Philadelphia, 1803), 1792, p. 12; 1793, p. 9; April 25, 1793, Minutes of the Presbytery of New Brunswick (MSS in the Presbyterian Historical Society), 4: 224–227; October 6, 1792, Minutes of the Transylvania Presbytery (microfilm in the Union Theological Seminary, Richmond), 1: 75; April 17, 1793, Minutes of the Presbytery of Philadelphia (microfilm in the Presbyterian Historical Society), 3: 191; April 19, 1793, *Minutes of the Presbytery of Redstone* (Cincinnati, 1878), p. 99; September 19, 1792, Minutes of the Presbytery of Lexington (microfilm in Union Theological Seminary, Richmond), 1: 153.

66. October 30, 1780, Minutes to the Hanover Presbytery (photostats of MSS in Union Theological Seminary, Richmond), 2: 99; April 25, 1780, April 30, 1787, *ibid.,* 2: 106, 3: 23.

67. The average length of time between admittance to candidacy and to licensure was thirteen months; the average from admittance to ordination was twenty-nine months. There was no significant differentiation from presbytery to presbytery.

68. *Minutes of the General Assembly,* 1800, p. 8.

69. For other examples of the sons of the upper class at Princeton, consult the careers of George Clarkson, Henry Kollack, John B. Wallace, who all graduated in the Revolutionary period at age sixteen; James A. Bayard, Joshua B. Wallace, and Abner and Aaron Woodruff, who all graduated at seventeen; Jacob Burnet, John H. Hobart, Robert Ogden, John C. Otto, George W. Reed, David Stone, Robert J. Taylor, and George W. Woodruff, who all graduated at eighteen; and Henry Clymer, William Branch Giles, Charles F. Mercer, and Richard N. Venable, who all graduated at nineteen. All became lawyers, merchants, or doctors, although Kollack and Hobart subsequently entered the ministry. All are discussed in Alexander, *Princeton College During the Eighteenth Century.*

70. For examples of the ministers' sons, consult the careers of Robert Finley, who graduated at fifteen; Aaron Burr, Jr., and John D. Blair, who graduated at sixteen; George S. Woodhull, who graduated at seventeen; Robert H. Chapman, Joseph Caldwell, and Thomas Craighead, who all graduated at eighteen; and Samuel Finley Snowden, who graduated at nineteen. All are discussed either in Alexander or in Volume III of William B. Sprague, *Annals of the American Pulpit* . . . (New York, 1860).

71. Consult also the careers of William Boyd and John Collins, who both graduated at twenty; Matthew Wallace, who graduated at twenty-one; James

Grier, who graduated at twenty-two; James F. Armstrong, Henry Axtell, Hugh H. Brackenridge, and James McKee, who all graduated at twenty-three; John Linn and Nathaniel W. Sample, who graduated at twenty-four; David Breck, who graduated at twenty-six; Stephen Bloomer Balch, and Andrew King, who both graduated at twenty-seven; and John Springer who graduated at thirty-one. All are discussed in Alexander and in Volumes III or IV of Sprague. It is clear that there already existed in the Presbyterian schools in the late eighteenth century the poorer, older students who, as David Allmendinger has demonstrated, transformed student life in the colleges and universities of antebellum New England. See *Paupers and Scholars: The Transformation of Student Life in Nineteenth-Century New England* (New York, 1975). Allmendinger's thoughtful and provocative work is the first book-length product of the current flurry of scholarship on student life in American colleges before the Civil War. For a review of that scholarship—and of Allmendinger's pioneering work in particular—see, David B. Potts, "Students and the Social History of American Higher Education," *History of Education Quarterly,* 15 (Fall, 1975): 317–327.

72. For Marquis and other examples of the young men at Canonsburg and Washington academies, see Sprague, Volumes III and IV. See especially the discussions of Joseph Patterson, who studied with McMillan at the age of thirty-two; Samuel Porter, who finished his theological studies at the age of thirty; Joseph Stockton, who finished his studies at the atypical age of twenty; James McGready, who was licensed at thirty; Elisha McCurdy, who graduated from the Canonsburg Academy in 1799 at thirty-six; George Hill, who completed his theological studies at twenty-seven; and John Brice, who studied with McMillan at the age of twenty-five.

73. Joseph B. Smith, "A Frontier Experiment with Higher Education: Dickinson College, 1783–1800," *Pennsylvania History,* 16 (January, 1949): 10.

74. See especially the sketches in Sprague, *Annals,* Volumes III and IV, of Samuel Rannals, age twenty-seven; Robert G. Wilson, age twenty-two; Henry R. Wilson, age eighteen; James Gilliand, age twenty-three; and Joshua Williams, age twenty-eight.

75. Lacy graduated from Hampden-Sydney at about twenty-eight, Blythe at twenty-four, Waddell at twenty-one. Consult also the careers of Richard Bibb, who graduated at about twenty-four; John Makemie Wilson, age twenty-two; Nash Legrand, age twenty; and David Smith and William Hill, both about age nineteen. All are discussed in Sprague and in Joseph P. Eggleston, "The Hampden-Sydney Boys of 1776–1783" (microfilm in Hampden-Sydney College Library, Hampden-Sydney, Va.), and in *General Catalogue of the Officers and Students of Hampden-Sydney College, Virginia, 1776–1906* (Richmond, Va., 1906).

76. Representative young ministers and the approximate ages at which

they graduated from Liberty Hall are: Daniel Blair, twenty-two; Samuel Carrick, twenty-five; Benjamin Grigsly, nineteen; Samuel Houston, twenty-five; Samuel Graham Ramsey, twenty-three; Adam Rankin, twenty-five; Samuel Brown, twenty-five; Moses Hoge, twenty-eight; and Andrew McClure, thirty. All are discussed in Sprague; William H. Ruffner, "The Lyle Chapter in the History of Washington and Lee University," *Historical Papers,* No. 3 (1892): 129–167; and William McLaughlin (ed.), "Sketches of Trustees," in *ibid.,* pp. 85–128. See also Thomas C. Wilson, Jr., *Washington and Lee University Alumni Directory, 1749–1949* (Lexington, Va., 1949).

77. Sprague, *Annals,* 4: 168–172.

78. Samuel Stanhope Smith, "On Industry," *Sermons* (Newark, N.J., 1799), pp. 160–163.

79. Samuel E. McCorkle, *A Sermon on the Comparative Happiness and Duty of the United States of America, Contrasted with other Nations, particularly the Israelites* . . . (Halifax, N.C. [?], 1795), p. 21.

Chapter VIII

1. David Rice, *A Sermon on the Present Revival of Religion in this Country* . . . (Washington, Ga., 1804), p. 3. For a Congregational analysis of the historical setting of the text, see Timothy Dwight, *A Discourse, in Two Parts, Delivered July 23, 1812, on the Public Fast, in the Chapel of Yale College* (Boston, 1813), pp. 3–4.

2. For a Presbyterian description of the change in deism, see Samuel E. McCorkle, *The Work of God for the French Republic, and Then Her Reformation or Ruin* . . . (Salisbury, N.C., 1798), p. 44. The best general account of the clergy's reaction to the French Revolution remains Gary Nash, "The American Clergy and the French Revolution," *William and Mary Quarterly,* Third Series, 22 (July, 1965): 392–412, although it neglects the crucial changes in the Americans' view of their own Revolution that paralleled the changes Nash does discuss.

3. Charles Nisbet to William Young, August 7, 1793 (Charles Nisbet MSS, Dickinson College Library, Carlisle, Pa.); Nisbet to William Marshall, February 16, 1799, in Guy S. Klett (ed.), "Letters of the Rev. Charles Nisbet to the Rev. William Marshall," *Journal of the Presbyterian Historical Society,* 39 (March, 1961): 57; Drury Lacy to William Williamson, July 24, 1799 (William Williamson MSS, Union Theological Seminary, Richmond, Va.); September 29, 1799, Minutes of the Synod of Virginia (MSS in Union Theological Seminary), 2: 30–31. For a representative sermon on the death of Washington, see Samuel Stanhope Smith, *An Oration, Upon the Death of General George Washington* . . . (Trenton, N.J., 1800).

4. Samuel Stanhope Smith, *The Lectures . . . on the Subjects of Moral and*

Political Philosophy (New York, 1812), 1: 325; Smith, *The Divine Goodness to the United States . . .* (Philadelphia, 1795), pp. 11–13; Rice, *Sermon on the Present Revival,* p. 39.

5. Alexander McDougall to Joseph Reed, March 25, 1779, in William B. Reed (ed.), *Life and Correspondence of Joseph Reed* (Philadelphia, 1847), 1: 159.

6. Noah Webster, *Sketches of American Policy* (Hartford, Conn., 1785), pp. 24–26.

7. The best discussion of the Americans' reassessment of the relationship between virtue and republican governments is in Gordon S. Wood, *The Creation of the American Republic, 1776–1787* (Chapel Hill, 1969), pp. 606–615. But for a useful corrective to Wood, see the emphasis on the Americans' abiding allegiance to organicism in Cecilia M. Kenyon, "Republicanism and Radicalism in the American Revolution: An Old-fashioned Interpretation," *William and Mary Quarterly,* Third Series, 19 (April, 1962): 153–182. For Madison's redefinition of the relationship between the size of a nation and the likelihood for republican success, see Douglass Adair, " 'That Politics May Be Reduced to a Science': David Hume, James Madison, and the Tenth *Federalist,*" *The Huntington Library Quarterly,* 20 (August, 1957): 343–360. For Adams, see Wood, *Creation of the American Republic,* pp. 567–592.

8. James Wilson, "Lectures on Law," in Bird Wilson (ed.), *The Works of . . . James Wilson* (Philadelphia, 1804), 1: 384.

9. Charles Nisbet was a grumpy, predictable exception. See Nisbet to Alexander Addison, November 5, 1790 (Nisbet-Addison Letters, MSS in the University of Pittsburgh Library, Pittsburgh, Pa.).

10. See, for example, the discussion in Samuel Miller, *Christianity the Grand Source, and the Surest Basis, of Political Liberty . . .* (New York, [1793]), p. 33n.

11. William Linn, *The Blessings of America . . .* (New York, 1791), p. 34; James Malcomson, *A Sermon, Preached on . . . the Anniversary of the French Revolution* (Charleston, S.C., 1795), pp. 30–32.

12. Miller, *Christianity the Grand Source,* p. 30. See also Linn, *Blessings of America,* p. 34; and John M'Knight, *God the Author of Promotion . . .* (New York, 1794), p. 15.

13. Linn, *Blessings of America,* p. 34; Malcomson, *Sermon,* p. 29.

14. Malcomson, *Sermon,* pp. 26, 42.

15. *Ibid.,* pp. 40–41; Miller, *Christianity the Grand Source,* pp. 33, 34n.

16. Malcomson, *Sermon,* p. 34.

17. McCorkle, *Work of God,* pp. 5–9, 12.

18. Nisbet to Addison, November 8, 1793, August 6, 1795 (Nisbet-Addison Letters); Nisbet to William Marshall, February 16, 1799, Klett (ed.), "Letters," p. 57. For a well-informed discussion of Nisbet during the post-Revolutionary

period, see James H. Smylie, "Charles Nisbet: Second Thoughts on a Revolutionary Generation," *Pennsylvania Magazine of History and Biography,* 98 (April, 1974): 189–205.

19. Samuel Stanhope Smith to Ashbel Green, March 20, 1796 (Samuel Stanhope Smith Collection, Princeton University Library); Smith, "On Industry," *Sermons* (Newark, N.J., 1799), p. 151. For a discussion of the political context in which Smith and other Presbyterians undertook this crucial reevaluation, see Marshall Smelser, "The Federalist Period as an Age of Passion," *American Quarterly,* 10 (Winter, 1958): 391–419.

20. That there is no full-scale monographic account of the Second Great Awakening remains one of the largest gaps in the study of nineteenth-century America. Some older works are still useful. The revival's western, and most colorful, phase is rather sketchily treated in a purely narrative work by Catharine C. Cleveland, *The Great Revival in the West* (Chicago, 1916), while its New England phase is treated somewhat more analytically in Charles R. Keller, *The Second Great Awakening in Connecticut* (New Haven, 1942). The relevant section of William W. Sweet, *Revivalism in America* (New York, 1944) is still a helpful introduction but is not as detailed or as analytical as the first two chapters of William G. McLoughlin, *Modern Revivalism: Charles Grandison Finney to Billy Graham* (New York, 1959), pp. 3–121. Perhaps more useful than Sweet's monograph are his volumes of collections of documents relating to the frontier experiences of the Baptist, Methodist, and the Presbyterian churches. Serious study of the Great Awakening now should begin with two articles: Donald G. Mathews, "The Second Great Awakening as an Organizing Process, 1780–1830: An Hypothesis," *American Quarterly,* 21 (Spring, 1969): 23–43; and Richard D. Birdsall, "The Second Great Awakening and the New England Social Order," *Church History,* 39 (September, 1970): 345–364. These provocative essays should be read in conjunction with Part One, "The Evangelical Basis," of Perry Miller, *The Life of the Mind in America From the Revolution to the Civil War* (New York, 1965) in an effort to understand that which was new in the frontier revival. That revival as an attempt to control social behavior on the frontier is the subject of T. Scott Miyakawa, *Protestants and Pioneers: Individualism and Conformity on the American Frontier* (Chicago, 1964). But any effort to understand the revival in terms of social control should be informed by the recent work of Lois W. Banner: "Religious Benevolence as Social Control: A Critique of an Interpretation," *The Journal of American History,* 60 (June, 1973): 23–41; and, more important, "The Protestant Crusade: Religious Missions, Benevolence, and Reform in the United States, 1790–1840," unpublished Ph.D. dissertation, Columbia University, 1970. Of late, the western revival has been treated in two monographs of differing emphasis and technique but uniform merit. John B. Boles, *The Great Revival, 1787–1805: The Origins of*

the Southern Evangelical Mind (Lexington, Ky., 1972) is more successful in analyzing the causes and course of the revival than in locating anything uniquely southern in it but is, nonetheless, a very welcome addition to works on the frontier camp meetings. By the same token, Dickson D. Bruce, *And They All Sang Hallelujah: Plain-Folk Camp-Meeting Religion, 1800–1845* (Knoxville, Tenn., 1974), fails in its effort to construct a "social anthropology" for the antebellum south but does break important new ground by attempting to use the techniques of the folklorist and the structuralist in studying the configurations of and participants in the frontier camp meeting. Finally, for a useful international context for the American revival, see the fascinating thesis elaborated by Bernard Semmel in *The Methodist Revolution* (New York, 1973).

21. For the triumph of evangelical orthodoxy and a discussion of its ramifications for the development of American culture in the early nineteenth century, see Martin E. Marty, *Righteous Empire: The Protestant Experience in America* (New York, 1970); Perry Miller, "From the Covenant to the Revival," in *Nature's Nation* (Cambridge, Mass., 1967), pp. 90–120; and "The Triumph of Fidelity" in G. Adolf Koch, *Republican Religion: The American Revolution and the Cult of Reason* (Gloucester, Mass., 1964), pp. 239–284.

22. For Dwight and the Yale revival, see Stephen E. Berk, *Calvinism versus Democracy: Timothy Dwight and the Origins of American Evangelical Orthodoxy* (Hamden, Conn., 1974).

23. To relate the western to the eastern phase of the revival remains the most pressing task of the students of the Awakening. One successful, if limited, effort in that direction is Bertram Wyatt-Brown's excellent "Prelude to Abolitionism: Sabbatarian Politics and the Rise of the Second Party System," *Journal of American History,* 58 (September, 1971): 316–341.

24. For representative initial reactions—invariably favorable—to the revival see: Presbyterian Church in the U.S.A., General Assembly, *Acts and Proceedings . . . 1801* (Philadelphia, 1801), pp. 9, 8; Presbytery of New Brunswick, *A Pastoral Letter . . .* (New Brunswick, N.J., 1807), p. 6; Synod of Kentucky, *A Serious Address . . . to the Churches Under their Care* (Lexington, Ky., 1804), p. 6; [Ashbel Green], *Glad Tidings . . .* (Philadelphia, 1804), pp. 3, 4; Synod of the Carolinas, *A Pastoral Letter . . .* (Salisbury, N.C., 1802), p. 6; *Extracts from the Minutes of the General Assembly . . . 1807* (Philadelphia, 1807), p. 154; October 9, 1801, Minutes of the Synod of the Carolinas (MSS in the Historical Foundation of the Presbyterian Church in the U.S., Montreat, N.C.), 2: 69; October 6, 1803, Records of the Synod of Albany (MSS in the Presbyterian Historical Society, Philadelphia, Pa.), 2: 17–18; October 22, 1801, Minutes of the Synod of New York and New Jersey (MSS in Presbyterian Historical Society), 1: 156.

25. John Montgomery to Benjamin Rush, September 15, 1801 (Correspon-

dence of Benjamin Rush Relative to Dickinson College, microfilm in Historical Society of Pennsylvania, Philadelphia, Pa.); Rush to Montgomery, January 9, 1802, in *ibid.*

26. Samuel Miller to Ashbel Green, March 8, 1802 (Samuel Miller Papers, Princeton University Library); Synod of Kentucky, *Circular Letter from the Synod of Kentucky to the Churches Under their Care* (Lexington, Ky., 1803), p. 3; *Extracts from the Minutes of the General Assembly . . . 1804* (Philadelphia, 1804), p. 66; November 8, 1804, Minutes of the Presbytery of Lexington, Virginia (microfilm in Union Theological Seminary, Richmond, Va.), 4: 151; *Extracts from the Minutes of the General Assembly . . . 1805* (Philadelphia, 1805), pp. 92–93.

27. September 29, 1821, Minutes of the Synod of North Carolina (MSS in Historical Foundation, Montreat), 1: 205.

28. Synod of the Carolinas to the Presbytery of Abingdon, November 6, 1799, in Synod of the Carolinas, Minutes, 1: 362–363.

29. Rice, *Sermon on the Present Revival,* pp. 8–9, 25; General Assembly, *Extracts, 1807,* pp. 155–160.

30. Charles F. Kilgore, *The James O'Kelly Schism in the Methodist Episcopal Church* (Mexico City, 1963); J. H. Spencer, *A History of the Kentucky Baptists from 1769 to 1885* (Cincinnati, 1886), 1: 175–184.

31. The best biography of Stone is William Garrett West, *Barton Warren Stone: Early American Advocate of Christian Unity* (Nashville, Tenn., 1954).

32. John P. MacLean, *A Sketch of the Life and Labors of Richard McNemar* (Franklin, Ohio, 1905).

33. Barton W. Stone, *et al., An Apology for Renouncing the Jurisdiction of the Synod of Kentucky . . .* (Lexington, Ky., 1802), p. 14.

34. The best account of these developments is in John Boles, Chapter Ten, on "Unity & Schism," in *The Great Revival,* pp. 141–164.

35. This coalescing is treated in depth in Winifred E. Garrison and Alfred T. DeGroot, *The Disciples of Christ: A History* (St. Louis, 1948), pp. 93–179. And the general movement to return to a pure primitive Christianity is the subject of James D. Murch, *Christians Only: A History of the Restoration Movement* (Cincinnati, 1962).

36. John Opie, Jr., in "James McGready: Theologian of Frontier Revivalism," *Church History,* 34 (December, 1965): 445–456, makes some extravagant claims for McGready as a creative theologian and tries too hard to dissociate him from his revivalist context. For the Cumberland schism, see Ernest Trice Thompson, *Presbyterians in the South, 1607–1861* (Richmond, 1963), pp. 144–165.

37. September 10, 1803, Minutes of the Synod of Kentucky (microfilm of MSS in the Historical Foundation, Montreat), 1: 27.

38. General Assembly, *Extracts, 1805,* pp. 85–86.

39. Synod of Kentucky, *Circular Letter*, p. 20.

40. General Assembly, *Extracts, 1804*, p. 54.

41. General Assembly to James W. Stephenson, May, 1811, included in a Pastoral Letter, April 7, 1812, Minutes of the Presbytery of West Tennessee (MSS in Historical Foundation, Montreat), 1: 47–48.

42. Synod of Kentucky, *Serious Address*, p. 5.

43. Pastoral Letter, April 7, 1812, Min. of Pby. of W. Tenn., 1: 48.

44. *Ibid.*, p. 49.

45. *Ibid.*, pp. 47–48.

46. Presbytery of West Tennessee to the Cumberland Presbytery, September 17, 1811, Min. of the Pby. of W. Tenn., 1: 14–15; Pastoral Letter, April 7, 1812, *ibid.*, p. 43.

47. October 19, 1820, Va. Syn. Min., 4: 290, 292.

48. Presbytery of West Tennessee to Cumberland Presbytery, September 17, 1811, Min. of the Pby. of W. Tenn., 1: 17; December 11, 1805, Min. of the Syn. of Kent., 1: 97–101.

49. Boles, *Great Revival*, pp. 143–164.

50. October 27, 1806, Min. of the Syn. of Kent., 1: 121.

51. September 7, 1803, October 15, 1808, *ibid.*, 1: 16, 162; Pastoral Letter, April 7, 1812, Min. of the Pby. of W. Tenn., 1: 32–35.

52. Synod of Kentucky, *Circular Letter*, pp. 22, 23, 26.

53. Presbytery of Springfield, *An Apology for Renouncing the Jurisdiction of the Synod of Kentucky* . . . (Carlisle, Pa., 1805), pp. 22, 37.

54. *Ibid.*, p. 38.

55. Richard McNemar, *The Kentucky Revival* . . . (Albany, N.Y., 1808), pp. 11, 29; Presbytery of Springfield, *An Apology*, p. 23.

56. Presbytery of Springfield, *An Apology*, p. 6.

57. September, 1803, Min. of Syn. of Kent., 1: 29.

58. General Assembly, *Extracts, 1805*, p. 84; Presbytery of Springfield, *Observations on Church Government* (Albany, N.Y., 1808), pp. 21–23.

59. McNemar, *Kentucky Revival*, p. 105.

60. Presbytery of Springfield, *An Apology*, pp. 30–31.

61. *Ibid.*, p. 44.

62. McNemar, *Kentucky Revival*, p. 30.

63. Presbytery of Springfield, *Observations*, pp. 15, 16.

64. Smith, *Divine Goodness*, pp. 32–33; Samuel Miller, *A Brief Retrospective of the Eighteenth Century* . . . (New York, 1803), 2: 254. For Mason's ideas see *The Christian's Magazine*, 3 (March, 1810): 170.

65. The classical formulation of the "jesuitical" charge is that made by a minister turned politician, Calvin Colton, in *Protestant Jesuitism* (New York, 1836). The most extensive discussions of the benevolent empire as attempted social control are in Charles Foster, *An Errand of Mercy: The Evangelical*

United Front, 1790–1837 (Chapel Hill, 1960); and Clifford Griffin, *Their Brothers' Keepers: Moral Stewardship in the United States, 1800–1865* (New Brunswick, N.J., 1960). These should now be read in conjunction with the criticisms advanced by Lois Banner that are mentioned in footnote 20 of this chapter. Banner's work is the best available on the "Christian republicanism" of the early nineteenth century, but see also the section dealing with "cultural cohesion" in the provocative essay by William G. McLoughlin, "The Role of Religion in the Revolution: Liberty of Conscience and Cultural Cohesion in the New Nation," in Stephen G. Kurtz and James H. Hutson (eds.), *Essays on the American Revolution* (Chapel Hill, 1973), especially pp. 247–255. Also very useful in marking the complexity of the "Christian republican" experience is the growing body of work produced by William Gribbin: *The Churches Militant: The War of 1812 and American Religion* (New Haven, 1973); "Republicanism and Religion in the Early National Period," *The Historian*, 35 (November, 1972): 61–74; and "Republicanism, Reform, and the Sense of Sin in Ante Bellum America," *Cithara: Essays in the Judaeo-Christian Tradition*, 14 (December, 1974): 25–41.

66. Smith, *Divine Goodness*, p. 32; Pby. of N. Bruns., *Pastoral Letter*, p. 14; October 29, 1814, Min. of the Syn. of Va., 3: 53. For additional comment on the proper relation of church and state, see [John Witherspoon], *A Draught of a Plan of Government and Discipline for the Presbyterian Church in North America* (Philadelphia, 1786), p. v; Linn, *Blessings of America*, p. 20; John M'Knight, *The Divine Goodness to the United States . . .* (New York, 1795), p. 16.

67. William G. McLoughlin, "Isaac Backus and the Separation of Church and State in America," *American Historical Review*, 73 (June, 1968): 1392–1413; James F. Maclear, " 'The True American Union' of Church and State: The Reconstruction of the Theocratic Tradition," *Church History*, 28 (March, 1959): 41–62.

68. Elizabeth Fleet (ed.), "Madison's 'Detached Memoranda'," *William and Mary Quarterly*, Third Series, 3 (October, 1946): 556–559.

69. Fred J. Hood, "Presbyterianism and the New American Nation, 1783–1826: A Case Study of Religion and National Life," (unpublished Ph.D. dissertation, Princeton University, 1968), pp. 81–82.

70. Thomas Jefferson to Samuel Miller, January 23, 1808, in Paul L. Ford (ed.), *The Writings of Thomas Jefferson* (New York, 1892–1899), 9: 174–175.

71. Fleet, "Madison's 'Detached Memorandum'," pp. 560–561.

72. October 14, 1814, Records of the Synod of Geneva (MSS in Presbyterian Historical Society), 1: 59–61.

73. It is one of the most important contributions of the first part of Lois Banner's work, "The Protestant Crusade," to relate the early nineteenth-century reform movement to an interrupted eighteenth-century development. For

another view of the relation of the nineteenth- to eighteenth-century reform, see David J. Rothman, *The Discovery of the Asylum: Social Order and Disorder in the New Republic* (Boston, 1971), pp. 3–78.

74. For these and other ideas, see the stimulating discussions in Hood, "Presbyterianism and the New American Nation," pp. 218–235; and Banner, "The Protestant Crusade,", pp. 97–106.

75. *Extracts from the Minutes of the General Assembly . . . 1815* (Philadelphia, 1815), pp. 236–238.

76. For representative calls, see October 4, 1806, Min. of the Syn. of the Carolinas, 2: 182; October 9, 1813, Min. of the Syn. of North Carolina, 1: 11; October 17, 1806, Minutes of the First Presbytery of South Carolina (MSS in Historical Foundation, Montreat), 1: 86–88.

77. October 31, 1823, Min. of Syn. of New York and New Jersey, 2: 116.

78. For the Society see the intriguing speculations in Douglass Adair and Marvin Harvey, "Was Alexander Hamilton a Christian Statesman?" in Jacob E. Cooke (ed.), *Alexander Hamilton: A Profile* (New York, 1967), pp. 230–255.

79. The best discussion of Ely's "Christian Party" is in Wyatt-Brown, "Prelude to Abolitionism," pp. 323–327.

80. September 20, 1816, Minutes of the Synod of Philadelphia (MSS in Presbyterian Historical Society), 1: 497.

81. October 9, 1809, Min. of the Syn. of New York and New Jersey, 1: 255. Hood, "Presbyterianism and the New American Nation," advances the intriguing thesis that before 1800 the Presbyterians emphasized the need for Christian rulers in America and after that date, the necessity for producing Christian voters (pp. 84–89).

82. October 14, 1811, Min. of the Syn. of Kent., 2: 14.

83. General Assembly, *Extracts, 1815,* pp. 256–258; October 14, 1811, Min. of the Syn. of Kent., 2: 14–15; October 2, 1823, Rec. of the Syn. of Albany, 2: 227; April 2, 1816, Min. of the Pby. of W. Tenn., 1: 104–105.

84. Again, the best discussion of the subject is Wyatt-Brown "Prelude to Abolitionism." But also see the less imaginative study in John R. Bodo, *The Protestant Clergy and Public Issues, 1812–1848* (Princeton, 1954).

85. For representative recommendations, see: October 18, 1811, Min. of the Syn. of New York and New Jersey, 1: 292; October 15, 1818, Minutes of the Presbytery of Abingdon (transcript of MSS in Historical Foundation, Montreat), 1: 89; September 13, 1821, Min. of the Syn. of Albany, 2: 168–169; October 9, 1824, October 8, 1828, *ibid.,* 2: 243–245, 346; April 2, 1811, Minutes of the [Second] Presbytery of South Carolina (MSS in Historical Foundation, Montreat), 1: 160; October 7, 1824, Records of the Synod of Geneva (MSS in Presbyterian Historical Society), 1: 411–412; September 1, 1818, Minutes of

the Presbytery of Concord (MSS in Historical Foundation, Montreat), 1: 365.

86. May 20, 1807, Min. of the Syn. of Philadelphia, 1: 346–347.

87. For an interesting discussion of the impact of the "printing revolution," and especially the penny press, on one reform movement see, Leonard L. Richards, *"Gentlemen of Property and Standing:" Anti-Abolition Mobs in Jacksonian America* (New York, 1971), pp. 71–81. The importance of that revolution for the creation of American religious denominations has not yet been considered.

88. Banner, "The Protestant Crusade," p. 338.

89. October 20, 1827, Records of the Synod of Ohio (MSS in Presbyterian Historical Society), 1: 263; May 18, 1815, Min. of the Syn. of Philadelphia, 1: 484.

90. Robert Richardson (ed.), *Memoirs of Alexander Campbell* (Cincinnati, 1913), 1: 502–503. See also Hood, "Presbyterianism and the New American Nation," pp. 99–106.

91. Gen. Ass., *Extracts, 1807,* p. 154; October 4, 1807, Min. of the Syn. of the Carolinas, 2: 205.

92. Rice, *Sermon on the Present Revival,* pp. 19–20; Syn. of the Carolinas, *Pastoral Letter,* p. 6. See also Frederick Kuhns, "Religious Rivalries in the Old Northwest," *Journal of the Presbyterian Historical Society,* 36 (March, 1958): 21.

93. September 5, 1816, Minutes of the Transylvania Presbytery (MSS in Louisville Theological Seminary, Louisville, Ky.), 4: 98–99; April 21, 1818, *ibid.,* 4: 122. See especially the discussion in Ben M. Vorpahl, "Presbyterianism and the Frontier Thesis: Tradition and Modification in the American Garden," *Journal of the Presbyterian Historical Society,* 45 (September, 1967): 180–192.

94. April 12, 1787, Minutes of the Presbytery of Philadelphia (microfilm of MSS in Presbyterian Historical Society), 4: 58; September 27, 1798, September 26, 1799, October 19, 1809, Min. of the Syn. of Virginia, 2: 8, 25, 3: 62–63. A particularly good discussion of the session as court and a lengthy transcript of a case are in Miyakawa, *Protestants and Pioneers,* pp. 21–32. A broader study that is more exciting in conception than execution is Cortland V. Smith, "Church Organization as an Agency of Social Control: Church Discipline in North Carolina, 1800–1860," unpublished Ph.D. dissertation, University of North Carolina, 1967. It is not clear why Smith decided to ignore the North Carolina Presbyterians, for whom extensive materials are available.

95. September 26, 1799, Min. of the Syn. of Virginia, 2: 24. See also the Syn. of the Carolinas, *Pastoral Letter,* p. 16.

96. October 16, 1787, Minutes of the New Brunswick Presbytery (MSS in Presbyterian Historical Society), 4: 83; August 13, 1788, *Minutes of the Presbytery of Redstone . . .* (Cincinnati, 1878), p. 41.

97. October 1, 1790, Min. of the Syn. of Virginia, 1: 59–60; October 28, 1790, Lexington Pby. Min., 1: 68.

98. McNemar, *Kentucky Revival,* pp. 24, 26, 31; Rice, *Sermon on the Present Revival.* For the revival as community see the provocative discussion in Bruce, *And They All Sang Hallelujah.*

99. September 30, 1791, October 19, 1820, Min. of the Syn. of Virginia, 1: 76, 4: 287–291; October 5, 1820, *Records of the Synod of Pittsburgh* . . . (Pittsburgh, 1852), p. 163; September 30, 1803, Min. of the First Pby. of South Carolina, 1: 57; November 14, 1818, Min. of the Syn. of South Carolina and Georgia (MSS in Historical Foundation, Montreat), 1: 51; October 6, 1804, Min. of the Syn. of the Carolinas, 2: 117.

100. *Extracts from the Minutes of the General Assembly* . . . *1817* (Philadelphia, 1817), p. 27; *Extracts from the Minutes of the General Assembly* . . . *1818* (Philadelphia, 1818), p. 11. In 1801 the Presbyterian General Assembly and the Congregational General Association of Connecticut entered into a plan of union providing for cooperation between the two denominations in settling the west. In effect, the "Plan of Union" stipulated that a church would be organized in a frontier town along congregational or presbyterial lines depending upon which group arrived first. The Plan—and other interdenominational activities in which the Presbyterians cooperated in no way invalidate the thesis advanced in this chapter. The Plan of Union had literally no effect south of the Ohio and only a limited impact in the old northwest, where it was most effective. The Plan was effective only until real differences arose between the Congregationalists and Presbyterians. And the Presbyterians cooperated in interdenominational activities only so long as they did not feel their denominational interests were affected. In general, the interdenominational activities of the early nineteenth century have been overemphasized at the expense of emerging denominational patterns. This is one reason why, as in Perry Miller's *Life of the Mind,* a strident denominationalism frequently emerges full-blown from nowhere around 1825. For the Plan, see: Robert Hastings Nichols, "The Plan of Union in New York," *Church History,* 5 (March, 1936): 29–51; and Charles L. Zorbaugh, "The Plan of Union in Ohio," *ibid.,* 6 (June, 1937): 145–164.

101. Hood's dissertation advances a very different thesis concerning the power of the General Assembly. But that thesis illustrates the dangers in relying upon the printed material produced by the central organization at the expense of the wealth of manuscript materials produced by the lower levels of the hierarchy.

102. Gen. Ass., *Extracts, 1805,* p. 90.

103. October 5, 1805, Min. of the Syn. of the Carolinas, 2: 148.

104. Gen. Ass., *Extracts, 1818,* p. 9; October 7, 1820, Min. of the Syn. of North Carolina, 1: 127, 129; September 29, 1803, Min. of the First Pby. of

South Carolina, 1: 54; October 17, 1804, Min. of the Syn. of New York and New Jersey, 1: 195.

105. Gen. Ass., *Extracts, 1818,* pp. 11–14; September 6, 1804, Min. of the Concord Pby., 1: 141; December 23, 1811, Minutes of the Presbytery of Harmony (MSS in Historical Foundation, Montreat), 1: 151.

106. October 2, 1802, *Records of the Synod of Pittsburgh,* p. 13; October 14, 1803, Min. of the Syn. of Virginia, 2: 124; Gen. Ass., *Extracts, 1804,* p. 53; Samuel Miller to Ashbel Green, March 12, 1805 (Samuel Miller Papers, Princeton University Library).

107. Gen. Ass., *Extracts, 1804,* pp. 45–46.

108. Representative actions may be found in: September 17, 1794, Min. of the New Brunswick Pby., 4: 302–303; September 27, 1800, Min. of the Syn. of Virginia, 2: 51–53; April 11, 1801, Minutes of the Hanover Presbytery (MSS in Union Theological Seminary), 4: 74; December 15, 1808, Min. of the Transylvania Pby, 3: 70; Gen. Ass., *Extracts, 1804,* pp. 51–52.

109. *Education Papers by the Board of Education of the General Assembly of the Presbyterian Church, No. 1* (Philadelphia, 1832), pp. 8, 19; *Extracts from the Minutes of the General Assembly . . . 1819* (Philadelphia, 1819), pp. 165–167.

110. The sixth volume of the minutes of the Lexington Presbytery (1811–1814) illustrates this process especially well.

111. September 27, 1793, Min. of the Syn. of Virginia, 1: 109; October 29, 1791, Min. of the Hanover Pby., 3: 119.

112. April 7, 1803, Min. of the Hanover Pby., 4: 104; October 18, 1786, Min. of the New Brunswick Pby., 4: 64; September 30, 1802, *Records of the Synod of Pittsburgh,* p. 9.

113. July 30, 1792, Min. or the Hanover Pby., 3: 135; December 11, 1798, *Minutes of the Redstone Presbytery,* p. 145.

114. December 21, 1791, *Minutes of the Redstone Presbytery,* pp. 82–83; September 27, 1792, Min. of the Syn. of Virginia, 1: 91.

115. September 26, 1794, Min. of the Syn. of Virginia, 1: 133; April 28, 1795, Min. of the New Brunswick Pby., 4: 332; April 20, 1796, *Minutes of the Redstone Presbytery,* p. 121.

116. May 17, 1782, May 23, 1783, *Presbyterian Records,* pp. 495, 499.

117. Quoted in John Opie, "The Melancholy Career of 'Father' David Rice," *Journal of the Presbyterian Historical Society,* 47 (December, 1969): 296. See April 19, 1817, Min. of the Lexington Pby., 6: 131; April 5, 1823, Min. of the Transylvania Pby., 4: 194; April 30, 1825, *Records of the Synod of Pittsburgh,* p. 132.

118. April 21, 1813, *Minutes of the Redstone Presbytery,* p. 259; October 7, 1813, *Records of the Synod of Pittsburgh,* p. 99; Rice, *Sermon on the Present Revival,* pp. 14–15.

119. October 7, 1803, *Records of the Synod of Pittsburgh*, p. 20; April 22, 1783, Min. of the New Brunswick Pby., 4: 10.

120. McNemar, *Kentucky Revival*, p. 12.

121. Pby. of Springfield, *An Apology*, p. 39.

122. Gen. Ass., *Extracts, 1805*, p. 87; *Extracts, 1804*, pp. 47–48; Synod of Kentucky, *Circular Letter*.

123. Gen. Ass., *Extracts, 1804*, pp. 47–49.

Chapter IX

1. Thomas Jefferson to Thomas Cooper, November 2, 1822, Paul Leicester Ford (ed.), *The Writings of Thomas Jefferson* (New York, 1892–1899), 10: 242–243. For a thorough discussion of the conflict between Jefferson and the Virginia Presbyterians over the nature of the University of Virginia, see especially Robert O. Woodburn, "An Historical Investigation of the Opposition to Jefferson's Educational Proposals in the Commonwealth of Virginia," unpublished Ph.D. dissertation, American University, 1974. And for the stormy relationship between Cooper and the Presbyterians at Dickinson College, where the free-thinker, incredibly, taught chemistry between 1811 and 1815, see Charles Coleman Sellers, *Dickinson College: A History* (Middletown, Conn., 1973), pp. 137–161.

2. The following discussion of the struggle for control of Transylvania relies heavily on Niels H. Sonne's excellent *Liberal Kentucky, 1780–1828* Lexington, 1968).

3. April 24, 1794, Minutes of the Transylvania Presbytery (microfilm in the Union Theological Seminary, Richmond, Va.), 2: 112, 116–117; February 17, 1795, *ibid.*, 2: 166–168; Act for establishing the Kentucky Academy . . . . Also minutes of meetings of trustees . . . (bound MSS in the Presbyterian Historical Society, Philadelphia, Pa.; hereafter cited as Ky. Acad. Bd. Min.), pp. 3, 5; [John McFarland] (ed.), *The Literary Pamphleteer* . . . (Paris, Ky., 1823), 1: 10.

4. October, 1798, Ky. Acad. Bd. Min., p. 85; October 1, 1798, Records of the proceedings of the Board of Trustees for the Transylvania Seminary (MSS in the Transylvania College Library, Lexington, Ky.; hereafter cited as Trans. Sem. Bd. Min.), p. 168.

5. All quotes are from Sonne, *Liberal Kentucky*, pp. 119–123.

6. Quoted in *ibid.*, pp. 125–127.

7. *Ibid.*, p. 199n.

8. *Literary Pamphleteer*, 1: 3–4.

9. *The* (Lexington, Ky.) *Evangelical Record and Western Review*, 2: 10.

10. *Literary Pamphleteer*, 1: 13; 2: 5.

11. *Ibid.*, 3: 3–5.

12. *Ibid.*, 1: 6–7; 2: 2; 3: 9; 5: 16.

13. Sonne, *Liberal Kentucky*, p. 199n.

14. *Literary Pamphleteer*, 3: 9–10.

15. *Ibid.*, 3: 5, 8.

16. All quotations are from Norman L. Snider, "Centre College and the Presbyterians: Cooperation and Partnership," *The Register of the Kentucky Historical Society*, 67 (April, 1969): 106–108.

17. *Ibid.*

18. Philip Lindsley, "Baccalaureate Address, 1829," L. J. Halsey (ed.), *The Works of Philip Lindsley* (Philadelphia, 1859–1866), 1: 202–206. The best discussion of Lindsley is in John Edwin Pomfret, "Philip Lindsley, Pioneer Educator of the Old Southwest," in Willard Thorp (ed.), *The Lives of Eighteen From Princeton* (Princeton, 1946), pp. 158–177.

19. Lindsley, "Inaugural Address," *ibid.*, 1: 14; "Baccalaureate Address, 1829," *ibid.*, 1: 203.

20. Lindsley, "Baccalaureate Address, 1829," *ibid.*, 1: 204, 203, 205. For an earlier use of the same idea by Rush, see *supra*, pp. 136–137.

21. *Ibid.*, 1: 205–206.

22. See the rather sketchy analysis in Edgar W. Knight, "North Carolina's 'Dartmouth College Case'," *Journal of Higher Education*, 19 (March, 1948): 116–122.

23. Quoted in *ibid.*, p. 122. See also Luther L. Gobbel, *Church-State Relationships in Education in North Carolina Since 1776* (Durham, N.C., 1938), pp. 13–26; and Merle Borrowman, "The False Dawn of the State University," *History of Education Quarterly*, 1 (July, 1961): 6–22.

24. *Remarks on Washington College, and on the "Considerations" Suggested by Its Establishment* (Hartford, 1825), pp. 21–23.

25. [Chauncey Allen Goodrich], *Considerations Suggested by the Establishment of a Second College in Connecticut* (Hartford, 1824), pp. 17, 18; [Nathaniel S. Wheaton], *An Examination of the "Remarks" on Considerations Suggested by the Establishment of a Second College in Connecticut* (Hartford, 1825), pp. 21, 24.

26. *Remarks on Washington College*, pp. 9, 10, 19–21, 40, 48. The Episcopalians were no less open in their simultaneous effort, eventually successful, to charter Geneva College, later Hobart College, in western New York. Indeed, by 1822 Bishop John Henry Hobart was arguing that a charter ought to be granted to the Episcopalians for Geneva College simply because they had raised the funds necessary to support the college—in light of eighteenth-century organic views of corporations, an astonishing view. See *Hobart: The Story of a Hundred Years, 1822–1922* (Geneva, N.Y., 1922), pp. 89–90.

27. September 30, December 8, 1803, Minutes of the Board of Trustees of

Princeton University (MSS in the Archives of Princeton University, Princeton, N.J.), 2: 111–112, 117–118.

28. Samuel Stanhope Smith, *Announcement of the Restoration of Nassau Hall* (broadside in Princeton University Library); September 27, 1804, April 3–4, 1805, April 7, 1808, April 10, 1811, Pr. Bd. Min., 2: 147–148, 154, 230, 313.

29. Miller to Green, as quoted in Thomas Jefferson Wertenbaker, "The College of New Jersey and the Presbyterians," *Journal of the Presbyterian Historical Society,* 36 (December, 1958): 215; Miller to Green, March 12, 1805 (Samuel Miller Collection, Princeton Theological Seminary, Princeton, N.J.).

30. Benjamin Rush to Green, May 22, 1807, Lyman H. Butterfield (ed.), *Letters of Benjamin Rush* (Princeton, 1951), 2: 946.

31. Miller, quoted in Wertenbaker, "College of New Jersey," p. 215; Rush to John Montgomery, July 5, 1808, Butterfield (ed.), *Letters,* 2: 970; Jeremiah Atwater to Rush, July 4, 1810 (Correspondence of Benjamin Rush relative to Dickinson College, microfilm in Historical Society of Pennsylvania, Philadelphia, Pa.).

32. Samuel Miller, *A Brief Account of the Rise . . . of the Theological Seminary . . . At Princeton . . .* (Philadelphia, 1822), pp. 4, 16–17.

33. October 26, 1820, Minutes of the Synod of New York and New Jersey (MSS in the Presbyterian Historical Society), 2: 51–52.

34. The Reverend Drury Lacy explicitly contrasted the lack of ministerial correspondence to the interchanges between members of the legal and even the mercantile professions in a letter to William Williamson, July 24, 1799 (William Williamson MSS, Presbyterian Historical Society); and Smith made his urgings to a very receptive leader of New England Congregationalism, the Reverend Jedidiah Morse, February 24, 1799 (Samuel Stanhope Smith Collection, Princeton University Library.)

35. Miller, *Brief Account,* p. 17; Miller to Green, January 23, 1810 (Miller Collection, Princeton Theological Seminary).

36. Miller to Green, January 23, 1810 (Miller Collection, Princeton Theological Seminary); Miller, *Brief Account,* p. 9n. For examples of the opposition to a single seminary, see: October 8, 1808, Minutes of the Synod of the Carolinas (MSS in the Historical Foundation, Montreat, North Carolina), 2: 250; October 14, 1820, Minutes of the Synod of Kentucky (MSS in the Historical Foundation, Montreat), 3: 20; October 25, 1819, Minutes of the Synod of Ohio (MSS in the Presbyterian Historical Society), 1: 110–111; April 1, 1824, Minutes of the [Second] Presbytery of South Carolina (MSS in the Historical Foundation, Montreat), 2: 112–113; November 22, 1824, Minutes of the Synod of South Carolina and Georgia (MSS in the Historical Foundation, Montreat), pp. 113–114; October 6, 1820, Minutes of the Synod

of North Carolina (MSS in the Historical Foundation, Montreat), pp. 111–112, 117–119.

37. Miller, *Brief Account,* pp. 19, 20, 23–24.

38. Miller to Green, May 13, 1805 (Samuel Miller Papers, Princeton University Library); Miller, *Brief Account,* pp. 4–6.

39. Jeremiah Atwater to Rush, April 22, 1810 (Rush Correspondence); Jeremiah Atwater, *An Inaugural Address . . . September 27, 1809 . . .* (Carlisle, Pa., 1809), p. 12.

40. September 25, October, 1801, Minutes of the Synod of Virginia (microfilm of MSS in the Union Theological Seminary, Richmond), 2: 46, 63, 79; October 2, 1802, *ibid.,* 2: 105–106; April 15, 17, 1795, Minutes of the Presbytery of Lexington (microfilm of MSS in the Union Theological Seminary, Richmond), 3: 17; September 24, 1796, November 10, 1805, *ibid.,* 3: 52–53, 4: 116.

41. Board's quotation is from Joseph Smith, *History of Jefferson College . . .* (Pittsburgh, 1857), p. 135. For the close relationship between the Presbyterian hierarchy and the Jefferson College Board, see April 26, 1814, Minutes of the Transactions of the Board of Trustees of Canonsburgh Academy [and Jefferson College], (MSS in Washington and Jefferson College Library, Washington, Pa.), p. 84; October 4, 1822, *Records of the Synod of Pittsburgh . . .* (Pittsburgh, 1852), pp. 197–198.

42. September 25, 1806, June 20, 1808, Alfred J. Morrison (ed.), *The College of Hampden-Sidney, Calendar of Board Minutes, 1776–1876* (Richmond, 1912), pp. 61, 63; Joseph D. Eggleston, "The Department of Theology at Hampden-Sydney . . . ," (microfilm of unpublished essay in Union Theological Seminary, Richmond), pp. 4, 6–7.

43. October 25, 1819, Min. of the Syn. of Virginia, 4: 268; October 24, 1822, October 23, 1823, *ibid.,* 5: 15–17, 45–47; March 17, 1823, Minutes of the Board of Directors of Union Theological Seminary (microfilm in the Union Theological Seminary, Richmond), p. 1.

44. Miller, *Brief Account,* pp. 11–12, 3; Miller to Green, January 23, 1810 (Miller Collection, Princeton Theological Seminary Library); Thaddeus Dod, Introductory Lectures to Divinity Students, n.d. (MSS in the Washington and Jefferson College Library), pp. 13, 22; Samuel Stanhope Smith, "On the Utility and necessity of learning in a minister of the gospel" (Smith Collection, Princeton University Library), pp. 17–18.

45. April 11, 1805, Min. of the Transylvania Pby., 3: 110; October 16, 1805, April 8, 9, 1806, *ibid.,* 3: 120, 126.

46. October 2, 1805, December 26, 1809, April 5, 7, 1810, *ibid.,* 3: 118, 245, 251, 255–267.

47. *Ibid.,* Vol. IV, 1811–1824, especially the years between 1816 and 1822, reflects the impact of the increased severity of trials. That the Transylvania

Presbytery was not atypical is demonstrated by the candidacy of one Thomas Davis, an elder in the Second Presbyterian Church of Pittsburgh. He was encouraged to enter the ministry by several members of the Redstone Presbytery in 1820. Because he was older than usual, he was licensed and ordained within two years. Experiences like his had been frequent during and immediately following the Revolution, but in the early nineteenth century a significant part of the presbytery wished to reconsider his admission to candidacy, believing it was "not strictly constitutional." The presbytery finally decided that his lack of education and his abbreviated candidacy should be considered an extraordinary case because his hopes had been raised by some overly eager members and because he had in fact worked so diligently. The presbytery sternly noted, though, that the case was not to set a precedent, and, in the context of the presbytery's usual procedures, it was a highly unusual one. October 8, 1820, *Minutes of the Presbytery of Redstone* . . . (Cincinnati, 1878), pp. 312, 316; January 18, 1821, April 17–18, 1821, November 6, 7, 13, 1822, *ibid.,* pp. 318, 320–323, 330.

48. October 29, 1816, Min. of the Syn. of Virginia, 3: 132–137; October 25, 1819, *ibid.,* 4: 272.

49. April 25, September 12, 13, 1823, April 22, 1824, Min. of the Lexington Pby., 8: 38, 58–62, 64–65, 73; April 3, October 2, 11, 1824, Min. of the Transylvania Pby., 4: 205, 210; October 28, 1816, Min. of the Syn. of Virginia, 3: 101.

50. Presbytery of New York, *An Address from the Presbytery of New-York to the Churches Under Their Care* . . . (New York, 1805), pp. 3–4, 6.

51. See, for example, the constitution drafted by the Synod of North Carolina to be emulated by the presbyteries and sessions under its care. October 4, 1822, Min. of the Syn. of North Carolina, pp. 230–236.

52. Quoted in the Minutes of the Board of Education of the General Assembly of the Presbyterian Church in the United States of America (MSS in the Presbyterian Historical Society), 1: 1.

53. *Ibid.,* p. 8. For a presbyterial committee, see the Minutes of the proceedings of the Standing Committee of the Presbytery of Philadelphia for the education of pious youth for the Gospel ministry (MSS in the Presbyterian Historical Society). For an excellent discussion of the issue of a learned ministry in the early nineteenth century, see Natalie Ann Naylor, "Raising a Learned Ministry: The American Education Society, 1815–1860," unpublished D.Ed. dissertation, Columbia Teachers College, 1971.

54. October 1, 1801, October 16, 1804, Min. of the Syn. of Virginia, 2: 63, 145–146. See also Henry Richard Mahler, "A History of Union Theological Seminary in Virginia, 1807–1865," unpublished Th.D. dissertation, Union Theological Seminary (Va.), 1951.

55. October 21, 23, 1813, Min. of the Syn. of Virginia, 3: 13–15, 23–24;

October 29, 1814, October 13, 1815, October 17, 1818, October 25, 1819, *ibid.,* 3: 65, 76–77, 4: 220, 258.

56. October 5, 1808, *Records of the Syn. of Pittsburgh,* p. 49; October 5, 1815, *ibid.,* p. 103; September 23, 1819, Min. of the Lexington Pby., 7: 77–79; April 5, 1820, Min. of the Trans. Pby., 4: 149.

57. May 19, 1802, Pr. Bd. Min., 2: 67–68; *Extracts from the Minutes of the General Assembly . . . 1789 to 1802 . . .* (Philadelphia, 1803), 1802, p. 5.

58. September 28, 1809, September 26, 1810, Pr. Bd. Min., 2: 278, 302.

59. September 29, 1813, September 28, 1815, October 1, 1818, *ibid.,* 2: 387, 438, 483–486.

60. April 25, 1805, Minutes of the Board of Trustees of Hampden-Sydney College (microfilm in Union Theological Seminary, Richmond), p. 238; March 19, 1810, *ibid.,* p. 279. For a representative bequest see October 17, 1818, Min. of the Syn. of Virginia, 4: 217.

61. November 24, 1818, Pr. Bd. Min., 2: 491; September 29, 1820, Hampden-Sydney Bd. Min., 2: 8–9; Miller, *Brief Account,* p. 37; October 16, 1824, Min. of the Syn. of Kentucky, 3: 101; *Extracts from the Minutes of the General Assembly . . . 1818* (Philadelphia, 1818), p. 21.

62. Smith to Rush, March 20, 1802 (Smith Collection, Princeton University Library).

63. October 29, 1819, Min. of the Syn. of New York and New Jersey, 2: 44–45.

64. Atwater, *Inaugural Address,* p. 13.

65. Quoted in Smith, *Jefferson College,* p. 47.

66. October 9, 1800, Records and Proceedings in the Board of Trustees of the Transylvania University (MSS in the Archives of Transylvania College), p. 63; January 8, 1811, Minutes of the Washington College Board of Trustees (MSS in the Washington and Jefferson College Library), p. 66; July 20, 1803, Hampden-Sydney Bd. Min., p. 228; November 24, 1818, Pr. Bd. Min., 2: 492; March 13, 1806, Charter and Proceedings of the Trustees of Dickinson College (typescript in Dickinson College Library), 1: 329; September 14, 1797, Act for establishing the Kentucky Academy . . . also minutes of meetings of trustees (MSS in the Presbyterian Historical Society), p. 57.

67. Atwater to Rush, April 22, 1810 (Rush Correspondence).

68. October 4, 1811, *Records of the Syn. of Pittsburgh,* p. 83.

69. October 28, 1816, October 8, 1817, October 24, 1822, Min. of the Syn. of Virginia, 3: 124, 164; 5: 14.

Chapter X

1. Charles Nisbet to Alexander Addison, March 16, 1802 (Charles Nisbet MSS, in the Dickinson College Library, Carlisle, Pa.).

2. For an excellent introduction to these, and other, instances of student rebellions between 1798 and 1815, see Steven J. Novak, "The Rights of Youth: Student Unrest and American Higher Education, 1798–1815," (unpublished Ph.D. dissertation, University of California, Berkeley, 1974), pp. 20–35. Novak's study is by all accounts the best available on this neglected topic, and I am much indebted to it.

3. Richard Hofstadter, *Academic Freedom in the Age of the College* (New York, paper edition, 1964), pp. 216, 218; Evarts B. Greene, "A Puritan Counter-Reformation," *Proceedings of the American Antiquarian Society,* New Series, 43 (1932): 17–46.

4. March 16–19, 1802, Minutes of the Board of Trustees of Princeton University (MSS in the Archives of Princeton University, Princeton, N.J.), 2: 60–69.

5. Samuel Stanhope Smith to Jedidiah Morse, March 10, 1802 (Samuel Stanhope Smith Collection, Princeton University Library).

6. [Ashbel Green], *An Address to the Students and Faculty of the College of New Jersey. Delivered May 6th 1802* (Trenton, N.J., 1802), p. 5.

7. *Ibid.,* pp. 3–5; March 19, 1802, Pr. Bd. Min., 2: 68.

8. August 29, 1803, Resolves and Minutes of the Faculty [of the College of New Jersey], 1787–1810 (MSS in the Archives of Princeton University), n.p.

9. [Green], *An Address,* pp. 3–4; *Laws of the College of New Jersey . . . 1802* (Philadelphia, 1802), p. 17. For the more rigorous regulations at the other institutions, see Novak, "Rights of Students," p. 28.

10. Kemp P. Battle, *History of the University of North Carolina, 1789–1868* (Raleigh, N.C., 1907), 1: 204.

11. *Laws of the College of New Jersey,* pp. 25–26; March 19, September 30, 1802, Pr. Bd. Min., 2: 69–70, 85; May 7, 1807, *ibid.,* 2: 206; Ashbel Green, Report to the Princeton Trustees, April, 1813 (Green Family Papers, Princeton University Library), pp. 15, 16. For similar developments, see: December 21, 1819, Minutes of the Board of Trustees of Hampden-Sydney College (microfilm in the Union Theological Seminary, Richmond, Va.), p. 349; and May 3, 1803, Records of the Proceedings in the Board of Trustees of Transylvania University (MSS in the Archives of Transylvania College, Lexington, Ky.), pp. 249–250.

12. April 4, 1801, Trans. Bd. Min., p. 75; May 1, 1804, Minutes of the Board of Trustees of Washington College (Va.), (microfilm of MSS in the Washington and Lee University Library, Lexington, Va.), p. 109; January 4, 1804, Alfred J. Morrison (ed.), *The College of Hampden-Sidney, Calendar of Board Minutes, 1776–1876* (Richmond, Va., 1912), p. 57; April 25, 1805, Hampden-Sydney Board Minutes, p. 240.

13. [Green], *An Address,* pp. 7–9. For complaints about the regimen at North Carolina, see John L. Connor to his unnamed brother, September 23,

1805, in Battle, *University of North Carolina*, 1: 210. For an expression of parental concern about discipline at Princeton, see September 26, 1805, Pr. Bd. Min., 2: 163.

14. [Green], *An Address*, pp. 5–6.

15. *Ibid.*, p. 5.

16. Battle, *University of North Carolina*, 1: 206.

17. Joseph Caldwell to Richard Henderson, quoted in *ibid.*, 1: 205.

18. For discussions of the relationship between the faculty and the student societies, see Novak, "Rights of Youth," pp. 35–53, and, especially, James McLachlan, *"The Choice of Hercules:* American Student Societies in the Early 19th Century," in Lawrence Stone (ed.), *The University in Society* (Princeton, 1974), 2: 449–494.

19. January 2, 1802, Pr. Fac. Min.; Princeton Board of Trustees, *To the Public,* 1807 (broadside in Princeton University Library).

20. Jan. 2, 1802, Pr. Fac. Min.; John L. Connor to his brother, September 23, 1805, in Battle, *University of North Carolina*, 1: 209.

21. Quoted in Novak, "Rights of Youth," p. 78.

22. Quoted in *ibid.*, p. 79.

23. The point is most effectively made in Pauline Maier, "Popular Uprisings and Civil Authority in Eighteenth-Century America," *William and Mary Quarterly,* Third Series, 27 (January, 1970): 3–35.

24. Princeton Board, *To the Public* (1807).

25. William R. Davie to John Haywood, September 22, 1805, in Kemp P. Battle (ed.), "Letters of William R. Davie," *James Sprout Historical Monograph* (Chapel Hill, 1907), p. 60.

26. July 25, 1805, Morrison (ed.), *Calendar,* p. 59; September 26, 27, 1810, Pr. Bd. Min., 2: 298, 306.

27. April 28, 1804, Wash. Bd. Min. (Va.), p. 119. For a similar effort at Princeton to get the villagers to inform on the students, see August 10, 1807, Pr. Bd. Min., 2: 199.

28. September 23, 1807, Wash. Bd. Min. (Va.), p. 131; December 21, 1807, Morrison (ed.), *Calendar,* pp. 62, 63.

29. May 3, 1803, Trans. Bd. Min., pp. 254–255.

30. June 6, 1810, Pr. Bd. Min., 2: 292–293.

31. Nisbet to the Dickinson College Board, October 18, 1802 (Nisbet MSS, Dickinson College Library); August 26, 1806, Morrison (ed.), *Calendar,* p. 61.

32. Princeton Board, *To the Public* (1807); Benjamin Rush to Ashbel Green, December 31, 1812, Lyman H. Butterfield (ed.), *Letters of Benjamin Rush* (Princeton, 1951), 2: 1174.

33. Henry Chambers to John Steele, n.d., in Battle, *University of North Carolina*, p. 208. One suspects that college students in the early nineteenth century resisted official inquiries at least partly because those investigations

challenged the remarkable solidarity produced by the literary societies being established at the time.

34. Davie to Haywood, September 22, 1805, Battle (ed.), "Letters," pp. 58–59, 62, 60.

35. September 24, 25, 1806, Pr. Bd. Min., 2: 180–181, 191.

36. June 16, 1801, October 29, 1804, Wash. Bd. Min., (Va.), pp. 89, 120; March 22, 1804, May 13, 1813, Hampden-Sydney Bd. Min., pp. 234, 303.

37. April 13, 1803, Pr. Bd. Min., 2: 100–101; September 25, 1805, Morrison (ed.), *Calendar*, p. 60.

38. *The* (Richmond, Va.) *Examiner*, April 10, 1802, as quoted in Novak, "Rights of Youth," p. 32.

39. April 11, 1807, Pr. Bd. Min., 2: 201; October 21, 1807, Wash. Bd. Min. (Va.), p. 134; Battle, *University of North Carolina*, p. 215. For similar provisions see December 21, 1819, Hampden-Sydney Bd. Min., p. 347; October 10, 1805, Trans. Bd. Min. p. 294.

40. February 28, 1804, Pr. Fac. Min.; May 8, 1807, Pr. Bd. Min., 2: 206–207, 211; April 8, 1808, *ibid.*, 2: 233; December 21, 1819, Hampden-Sydney Bd. Min., p. 359.

41. December 2, 1816, Minutes of the Board of Trustees of Washington College (Pa.), (MSS in the Washington and Jefferson College Library, Washington, Pennylvania), p. 87; October 28, 1802, Minutes of the Transactions of the Board of Trustees of Canonsburgh Academy [and Jefferson College], (microfilm in Washington and Jefferson College Library), p. 40.

42. For the board's war with the taverns, see: April 11, October 1, 1807, April 6, 1808, April 5, September 27, 1815, October 1, 1818, and April 14, 1819, Pr. Bd. Min., 2: 203, 215, 228, 424–425, 487, 500. For their participation in the incorporation campaign, see: March 19, September 30, 1802, September 28, 1820, *ibid.*, 2: 73, 87, 529.

43. March 19, 1802, *ibid.*, 70–72. For the circular letters, see the one dated November, 1804, and addressed to one Nathaniel Ellmaker in the Samuel Stanhope Smith Collection at Princeton. In that same collection and on that subject, see Smith to John Irwin, November 5, 1804.

44. Princeton Board, *To the Public* (1807); April 13, 1819, Pr. Bd. Min., 2: 494, 496. For similar expressions of concern, see October 10, 1805, Trans. Bd. Min., p. 299; December 21, 1819, Hampden-Sydney Bd. Min., p. 360. Even a relatively strict father like Benjamin Rush never failed to respond generously to his son James's frequent requests for money while at Princeton. Rush to James Rush, January 25, 1802, March 29, 1803, and March 27, 1804, Butterfield (ed.), *Letters*, 2: 842, 860, 879.

45. Joseph Caldwell, *A Discourse Delivered . . . July, 1802* (Raleigh, N.C., 1802); Jeremiah Atwater, *An Inaugural Address delivered . . . September 27th, 1809 . . .* (Carlisle, Pa., 1809), pp. 9–10.

46. Samuel Stanhope Smith, *The Lectures . . . Which have been delivered . . . in the College of New Jersey . . .* (New York, 1812), 1: 100.

47. Samuel Miller, *A Brief Retrospect of the Eighteenth Century . . .* (New York, 1803), 2: 29, 295, 297–298, 300.

48. Battle, *University of North Carolina,* 1: 7; August 4, September 29, 1809, March 12, 1812, November 19, 1813, Hampden-Sydney Bd. Min., pp. 275, 276, 278, 287, 299. Students at Harvard and at North Carolina were forbidden to attend elections, the crucial republican rite, in 1805 and 1804 respectively. Novak, "Rights of Youth," p. 82.

49. Rush to John Montgomery, July 3, 1807 (Correspondence of Benjamin Rush Relative to Dickinson College, microfilm in the Historical Society of Pennsylvania, Philadelphia, Pa.); Rush to James Hamilton, June 27, 1810, Butterfield (ed.), *Letters,* 2: 1053.

50. John Henry Hobart to Caldwell, November 30, 1796, quoted in Luther L. Gobbel, *Church-State Relationships in Education in North Carolina since 1776* (Durham, N.C., 1938), p. 20; "Essay on Education #III," *The Literary Pamphleteer . . . ,* ed., John McFarland (Paris, Ky., 1823), 4: 16.

51. Smith, *Lectures,* 1: 124, 126; Atwater, *Inaugural Address,* p. 6; Miller, *Brief Retrospect,* 1: 110. See also Caldwell, *Discourse, 1802,* p. 6.

52. September 24, 1800, September 29, 1801, April 7, 1808, Pr. Bd. Min., 2: 44, 53, 229–230.

53. Alexander is quoted in John Maclean, *History of the College of New Jersey . . .* (Philadelphia, 1877), 2: 131. For the board's actions in relation to the scientific diploma, see September 27, 1809, Pr. Bd. Min., 2: 273–274. Similar diplomas were given at Virginia's Washington Academy and at Transylvania. See October 21, 1807, October 17, 1809, Wash. Bd. Min. (Va.), pp. 133, 135; and October 10, 1805, Trans. Bd. Min., p. 298.

54. Smith, *Lectures,* 1: 10, 11, 14, 15, 122. For two rather laudatory discussions of Smith, see Winthrop Jordon's introduction to Smith's *An Essay on the Causes of the Variety of Complexion and Figure in the Human Species* (Cambridge, Mass., 1965); and William H. Hudnot, "Samuel Stanhope Smith: Enlightened Conservative," *Journal of the History of Ideas,* 17 (October, 1956): 540–552. More balanced and useful are Miles L. Bradbury, "Samuel Stanhope Smith: Princeton's Accommodation to Reason," *Journal of Presbyterian History,* 48 (Fall, 1970): 189–202; and Douglas Sloan's chapter on Smith in *The Scottish Enlightenment and the American College Ideal* (New York, 1971), pp. 146–184.

55. Quoted in the Introduction to Smith, *An Essay on the Causes . . . ,* p. xxvi.

56. Smith, *Lectures,* 1: 104–105n.

57. *Ibid.,* 1: 20, 127–128, 137–139.

58. See especially Green's 1813 report to the board (Green Family Papers, Princeton University Library).

59. Archibald Alexander, "Review of Dr. Chalmer's *Mental and Moral Philosophy," Princeton Review,* 20 (1848): 529–530; and *Outlines of Moral Science* (New York, 1852), p. 247; quoted in Richard J. Petersen, "Scottish Common Sense in America, 1768–1850: An Evaluation of Its Influence" (unpublished Ph.D. dissertation, American University, 1963), pp. 99, 101.

60. Miller, *Brief Retrospect,* 1: 12, 62.

61. Atwater, *Inaugural Address,* p. 6.

62. Miller, *Brief Retrospect,* 1: 184, 186–188, 248.

63. "Remarks on the Study of Natural Philosophy," *Virginia Evangelical and Literary Magazine,* 1 (June, 1818): 263.

64. [Green], *An Address,* p. 9.

65. *The* (Lexington) *Kentucky Gazette,* May 15, 1800; [Green], *An Address,* p. 11. The Princeton American Whig Society is quoted in Novak, "Rights of Youth," p. 132.

66. September 29, 1801, April 5, 1810, Pr. Bd. Min., 2: 53, 285–286; Kemp P. Battle, *Sketches of the History of the University of North Carolina . . .* (Chapel Hill, 1889), pp. 42–43.

67. *Kentucky Gazette,* April 3, 1802.

68. *Ibid.,* April 16, May 7, May 14, June 1, 1802.

69. *Ibid.,* April 16, May 7, 1802.

70. *Ibid.,* May 7, May 14, June 1, 1802.

71. *Ibid.,* June 5, 1800.

72. *Ibid.,* June 5, June 19, June 26, 1800.

73. *Ibid.,* June 5, 1800.

74. Novak makes the interesting suggestion that the classics were most attractive to educators interested above all else in maintaining discipline simply because they were difficult, rigorous. "Rights of Youth," pp. 230–232.

75. Quoted in Thomas Jefferson Wertenbaker, "The College of New Jersey and the Presbyterians," *Journal of the Presbyterian Historical Society,* 36 (December, 1958): 214.

76. Novak ingeniously relates Green's relations with the college to tragedies in his personal life. The discussion is excellent. "Rights of Youth," pp. 215–224.

77. Quoted in Charles Coleman Sellers, *Dickinson College: A History* (Middletown, Conn., 1973), p. 151.

78. The best discussions of this period in Dickinson's history are in Sellers, *ibid.,* pp. 137–162; and Novak, "Rights of Youth," pp. 207–214.

Epilogue

1. See especially Earl M. Pope, "New England Calvinism and the Disruption of the Presbyterian Church," unpublished Ph.D. dissertation, Brown University, 1962; Chapter 3 of George M. Marsden, *The Evangelical Mind and the New School Presbyterian Experience: A Case Study of Thought and Theology in Nineteenth-Century America* (New Haven, 1970); Earl R. MacCormac, "Missions and the Presbyterian Schism of 1837," *Church History,* 32 (March, 1963): 32–45; and Elwyn A. Smith, "The Forming of a Modern American Denomination," *Church History,* 31 (March, 1962): 74–99.

2. Quoted in Robert E. Thompson, *A History of the Presbyterian Churches in the United States* (New York, 1895), p. 109n.

3. A concise summary of the historiographical debate over the schism's causes is in Marsden, *The Evangelical Mind,* pp. 250–251.

4. See the Old Side "Memorial" to the 1834 General Assembly in Isaac V. Brown, *A Historical Vindication of the Abrogation of the Plan of Union . . .* (Philadelphia, 1855), pp. 88–90.

5. See the *Minutes of the Proceedings of the Pittsburgh Convention . . .* (Pittsburgh, 1835).

6. Brown, *Vindication,* pp. 240–244.

7. *Ibid.,* pp. 244–254.

8. Chapter I of [Absalom Peters], *A Plea for Voluntary Societies . . .* (New York, 1837).

9. Smith, "Modern American Denomination," pp. 92–93.

10. Quoted in *Minutes of . . . the Pittsburgh Convention,* p. 11–13.

11. Samuel Miller, *Letters to Presbyterians . . .* (New York, 1833).

12. N. S. J. Beman's "Review and Vindication" appended to Ashbel Green, *An Appeal to the Presbyterian Church . . .* (New York, 1831), p. 19.

13. William Ellery Channing, *Remarks on the Disposition which Now Prevails to form Associations . . .* (London, 1830), pp. 3–4.

14. Quoted in Robert T. Handy, "The Voluntary Principle in Religion and Religious Freedom in America," in D. B. Robertson (ed.), *Voluntary Associations . . .* (Richmond, 1966), p. 133.

15. Green, *An Appeal,* p. 9.

16. See the discussion of Van Buren in Richard Hofstadter, *The Idea of a Party System* (Berkeley, 1969).

17. John C. Calhoun, "Speech On the Slavery Question, delivered in the Senate, March 4th, 1850," in Richard K. Cralle (ed.), *Speeches of John C. Calhoun, Delivered in the House of Representatives, and in the Senate of the United States* (New-York, 1856), 4: 556–558.

A Note on The Sources

The secondary literature on the history of education and religion in early America is voluminous. Where that work seemed relevant to the issues raised in the present study, it was discussed in the notes in the text.* Those discussions, of course, are not intended to be exhaustive. By and large, this work is based on extensive research in manuscript sources that have seldom been used by historians. A few words about those sources are perhaps in order.

Those parts of the work that deal with the development of Presbyterianism in early America are based on manuscripts in three archives: The Presbyterian Historical Society of the United Presbyterian Church in the United States of America, located in Philadelphia; The Historical Foundation of the Presbyterian and Reformed Churches, in Montreat, North Carolina; and the library of Union Theological Seminary in Richmond, Virginia. The Presbyterian Historical Society and the Department of History of the General Assembly that supports it are effectively collecting all the extant sessional, presbyterial and synodical records of eighteenth century Presbyterianism above the Mason-Dixon line. By gathering these documents into a central location, the Society is creating one of the richest archives for the study of American ecclesiastical history in the nation today. Less extensive but equally useful for this study was the collection of denominational records at Montreat in the Historical Foundation of the southern Presbyterian church. The Foundation's collection is particularly rich in material on the Presbyterian role in the second Great Awakening and on the development of Presbyterianism in the South. That southern experience is also the focus of the special collection of Presbyterian material in the library of Richmond's Union Theological Seminary. Much of Union's Presbyterian material is the product of a massive program by the Synod of Virginia to locate and microfilm the extant records of all the synod's constituent parts and its institutions.

---

* Since the text was written, two major works have appeared that greatly sophisticate our understanding of the relationship between religion and the American Enlightenment. See the essays in Joseph Ellis (ed.), "An American Enlightenment," a special edition of *American Quarterly,* 28 (Summer, 1976); and, especially, the discussion of *four* American Enlightenments in Henry F. May, *The Enlightenment in America* (New York, 1976).

At first these records appear unpromising. The musty pages of ecclesiastical records seem only to record attendance at inconsequential meetings, unsuccessful efforts to raise money for godly enterprises, and endless exhortations to the faithful. It is only when the student patiently reads through decades of the records of many ecclesiastical bodies that the contours of important institutional developments and changes begin slowly to take shape. Those developments should interest the political, the social, and the intellectual historian, as well as the student of religious history strictly defined. At their most obvious level, the Presbyterian records document for the political historian the Presbyterian reaction to and attitudes toward significant events like the American Revolution. And, as has been indicated in the present study, debates over the nature of religious unions and leadership often paralleled or even anticipated similar debates in secular society in America.

The manuscript records of early American Presbyterianism would also reward the investigations of those historians interested in significant American social institutions, such as the professions and the family. They illuminate the development within the Presbyterian clergy of the first instance in America of a self-conscious professional awareness. And they illustrate, sometimes dramatically, the ways in which that ministerial community began to usurp some of the important functions of the family in American society. Perhaps most significantly, the Presbyterian records reveal the Presbyterian congregation as the formative, sometimes the definitive, social force in hundreds of communities in early America outside of New England.

The records of the Presbyterian hierarchy should also prove helpful to the student of American intellectual history. For instance, the theological debates at the presbyterial and synodical meetings were often more pointed and revealing than were the polemics published after those debates. Also, theological discussions at presbyterial and synodical meetings usually were couched in an institutional frame of reference; consequently, those debates often appear weightier than those that appeared in print, arguing issues in abstractions. The intellectual historian also might look with profit at Presbyterian ministerial education as its development is charted in the denomination's manuscript records. Obviously, the entire debate over a learned versus a pious clergy is an important one for any student of the American mind. But during the eighteenth century the Presbyterian sessions, presbyteries and synods were in a very real sense institutions of higher learning, charged with the professional education of society's ecclesiastical leaders. The way in which they discharged that task is an important chapter in the story of American education, and it is told only in the manuscript records of the Presbyterian hierarchy.

The manuscript records of the Presbyterian colleges were of crucial importance to the present study. Each of those colleges today maintains an archive, usually in conjunction with the college library. Most of those collections—the ones at Washington and Jefferson, Washington and Lee, Hampden-Sydney, and Transylvania—are modest affairs. They contain, at the very least, the minutes of the institutions' boards of trustees. Those minutes, in turn, invariably contain the names, usually the home states, and sometimes the ages of those students who graduated in any given year. They often contain, in addition, the same information for the entire student body. These smaller collections frequently hold the minutes of student literary societies, the correspondence and notebooks of a few eighteenth century students, and, occasionally, manuscripts of lectures given in the eighteenth century.

Much more extensive are the collections at Dickinson and at Princeton. Dickinson has just celebrated its bicentennial, and as part of that celebration the college at Carlisle has assembled one of the best collegiate archives in the nation. It contains extensive information about early Dickinsonians and its materials on Charles Nisbet could support a substantial biography of that neglected early American educator. Even more impressive and useful is the collection of material at Princeton. The University Archives and the Rare Books Collection contain the papers of Princeton's eighteenth century presidents and house the only collection that includes the minutes of faculty as well as trustee meetings. Those three sources in combination enable the historian to view from several vantage points the development of the Presbyterians' premier institution of higher learning. Finally, the Princeton Archives contain a particularly valuable and, as yet, largely unused source, the extensive manuscript records and membership lists of the college's quite active student literary societies, the Cliosophic and the American Whig.

Like the records of the Presbyterian hierarchy, these collegiate records often appear inconsequential. Boards of trustees seem to deal with the same issues year in and year out, and faculties seem to react defensively to the same problems of discipline and finance that apparently are endemic to all institutions of higher learning. But, again, the historian must read the records over an extended period of time—for decades, that is—before he can begin to spot significant changes. Board members come and go, as do professors and presidents; student bodies change and force the colleges to deal with significant shifts in the culture the educational institutions wish to serve and mold. Instead, gradually the colleges themselves change, following those cultural shifts. The historian who would understand that interaction between college and culture in early America can no longer be content merely to read the published treatises of selected American educators. He or she must now delve into the manuscript records of those colleges and of the religious denominations that created them. In the instance of the American Presbyterians, at any rate, that task can be a rewarding one.

Index